# African American Psychology
## Theory, Research, and Practice

editors

**A. Kathleen Hoard Burlew**
**W. Curtis Banks**
**Harriette Pipes McAdoo**
**Daudi Ajani ya Azibo**

**SAGE Publications**
*International Educational and Professional Publisher*
Newbury Park  London  New Delhi

*For information address*:

 SAGE Publications, Inc.
2455 Teller Road
Newbury Park, California 91320

SAGE Publications Ltd.
6 Bonhill Street
London EC2A 4PU
United Kingdom

SAGE Publications India Pvt. Ltd.
M-32 Market
Greater Kailash I
New Delhi 110 048 India

Printed in the United States of America

**Library of Congress Cataloging-in-Publication Data**

Main entry under title:

African American psychology: theory, research, and practice / edited
by A. Kathleen Hoard Burlew . . . [et al.].
p.    cm.
Includes bibliographical references and indexes.
ISBN 0-8039-4765-8 (hard).—ISBN 0-8039-4766-6 (pbk.)
1. Afro-Americans—Psychology.   I. Burlew, A. Kathleen Hoard.
E185.625.A38   1992
973′.0496073′019—dc20                          92-20394
                                                CIP


92  93  94  95  10  9  8  7  6  5  4  3  2  1

Sage Production Editor:  Judith L. Hunter

# African American Psychology

Dedicated to the members of
the Association of Black Psychologists:
past, present, and future

# Contents

## COGNITIVE STYLE

### PERSONALITY AND CLINICAL

### SOCIAL AND HEALTH

# Preface

There is increasing evidence that behavior and personality must be understood within the cultural context. Simultaneously, there is a growing awareness that existing theories and research in psychology do not sufficiently consider the uniqueness of the experience of African Americans. One explanation for this phenomenon is the faulty assumption that Eurocentric psychological theories and research can be blindly applied across a variety of cultural groups.

One of the goals of the Association of Black Psychologists is "to develop an approach to psychology that is consistent with the experience of Black people." To that end, the Association has played an important role since its establishment in 1968 in stimulating and contributing to the body of literature that is available on the psychology of African Americans.

One of the Association's accomplishments related to that goal is the ongoing publication of *The Journal of Black Psychology*. That journal has been publishing scholarly papers since 1974 on a wide range of topics including, but not limited to, personality, social behavior, physiological functioning, cognition, child development, education, and clinical application.

Over the years, *The Journal of Black Psychology* has accumulated an outstanding collection of classical papers on the experiences of African Americans. Yet, many classroom instructors find it difficult to use this body of literature fully because the papers are distributed among so many issues. This volume is a collection of a select group of those papers that are often requested by scholars.

The papers have been organized into five major sections. Each section begins with a brief introduction. These introductions were designed to introduce some key concepts to individuals unfamiliar with these topic areas.

The examination of the experience of African Americans requires the development of alternative theories that conceptualize behavior and personality in a manner consistent with the cultural context of African Americans. However, a Eurocentric point of view is inherent not only in most psychological theory but also in the research methods developed to test psychological theories; therefore, those who would add to the understanding of the experiences of African Americans must not limit themselves to traditional conceptualizations or research methods. Part I provides both alternative theoretical perspectives and new approaches to conducting research. Several papers in that section also discuss the use of psychology in practice to improve the quality of life for African Americans.

African American families are known to be diverse in structure. Consequently, theoretical perspectives that assume a nuclear family structure have limited utility for understanding African American families. The chapters in Part II consider this diversity in describing the forces that strengthen, threaten, and remold the African American family.

Part III focuses on African American children. Two recurrent issues are how African American children perceive themselves and their racial group. Several of the chapters in Part III address this issue. The other chapters examine how African American children interact with and conceptualize the social world in which they live.

Part IV includes two controversial, albeit critical, areas of study—intelligence and cognition. The core of the controversy on IQ, as we are reminded in this section introduction, centers on the role of race. The chapters addressing that issue review the active role of the Association of Black Psychologists in that controversy, as well as describe some of the controversial issues in that debate. In recent times, a number of African American psychologists have raised the question of whether the African American cognitive style is different from the Euro-American style. However, this discussion of group differences is markedly different from the tradition associated with Arthur Jensen in that it poses questions about whether different cultural groups utilize different cognitive strategies for processing information. That is a substantially different question from whether one group is innately more intellectually talented than another.

The final section reminds us that the process of developing a psychology of African people requires us to use information from various divisions within the division of psychology. Some of the major divisions—personality, clinical, social, and health—are represented in this section. These chapters examine whether theoretical perspectives germane to these divisions can be useful for understanding African Americans and also propose alternative perspectives.

This publication is different from previously published books on African American psychology in several ways. First, aspects of the field are highlighted in this volume that received limited, if any, attention in any of the other books. Also, since these papers first appeared as journal articles, they are the primary sources in contrast to the secondary reporting of findings common in most of the previously published books on the topic. Third, the chapters have been written by leading professionals in their respective areas.

The substance of this volume comes from the cumulative work of a collection of scholars who have contributed to the field over the past 17 years. The publication of this volume, likewise, reflects the contributions of several editors and associate editors, along with a legion of reviewers and editorial board members. The coeditors of this volume (Daudi Azibo, W. Curtis Banks, A. Kathleen Burlew, and Harriette McAdoo) have all contributed substantially to the development and fruition of the compilation of work that comprises this book. The order of their presentation here simply reflects the leading role Kathleen Burlew has taken in the conception of the project, and the relative contributions made by each historically in the editing and refinement of the works included here.

We are grateful to the large number of individuals who contributed to this effort either directly or indirectly. Obviously, this book would not be possible without these contributors. We applaud their commitment to the study of African American psychology. We also are indebted to the many reviewers of *The Journal of Black Psychology* whose comments made a significant difference in the final versions of these chapters. We owe a special thanks to the current and former staff of *The Journal of Black Psychology,* especially Dr. Lori Smith and Ms. Mickey Godshalk, for their commitment to excellence in the preparation of these manuscripts. Special praises are in order for the late Dr. William David Smith who served as the first editor of *The Journal of Black Psychology.*

Of course, we wish to express our gratitude to the editorial board of *The Journal of Black Psychology,* the Board of Directors and the membership of the Association of Black Psychologists. We are grateful for the encouragement, support, and assistance that these sectors of the Association of Black Psychologists gave to us. The collective spirit of the Association is a valuable network of support that motivates our members as we strive to integrate our training as psychologists, the wisdom passed down from our ancestors, and the power that flows from our spiritual nature to promote the interests of the people of African descent throughout the world.

Finally, we appreciate the support of our spouses, Sheryl Banks, Muthy Fatama, John Burlew, and John McAdoo, during this project. As always, our children—Randi and Robin Burlew; David, Michael, John, and Julie McAdoo; and Marcus, Robert, and Ellen Banks—had to sacrifice some precious time with their parents to make this project possible. We only hope that our efforts will contribute, in some small way, to making the world that we pass on to all of you a better place to live.

# Theory, Research, and Practice

Theory, research, and practice (TRP) are the three areas of professional psychology. All psychological work is based on some theory of the nature of human nature, turns on knowledge generated in research, and is applied in professional practice. Two important concerns here are the implications of psychological work for social policy and "science." Mental health laws, directives, and policies at federal, state, and local levels are shaped profoundly by psychological TRP that has become established. Likewise, what is required as "scientific" psychological knowledge is also inextricably bound to psychological TRP.

When the prevailing TRP is non-Africentric, discounting of Africentric conceptualization, or anti-African, the consequences in social policy and "science" for Africans are dire. The history of Eurocentric psychology as revealed, for example, by Guthrie's *Even the Rat Was White* or Thomas and Sillens' *Racism in Psychiatry,* is proof positive of this. Amid this Eurocentric psychology, African psychologists, mostly but not solely from the United States, have articulated a TRP base that emanates from the African worldview conceptual universe and the authentic cultural and social realities of continental and diasporic Africans. Much of nascent African (Black) psychology is underpinned and sustained by this work, which has had its greatest impact on "science" and much too little impact on social policy.

Myers's chapter clarifies the concept of transpersonal psychology, which has proven problematic for Eurocentric psychological conceptualization, as originating in and part and parcel to African Worldview based psychology. Consequently, the nature, meaning, and knowledge base requisite for understanding of the transpersonal concept is elucidated. Complementary to the underpinning Africentric theoretical base revealed in the first chapter, research approaches in African (Black) psychology have been reconsidered as well. The chapter by Azibo deconstructs (*deconstruction* refers to the refutation, falsification, and otherwise voiding of theses and research findings that are anti-African) the prevalent, albeit scientifically untenable, comparative research framework for cross-race comparisons. The "scientific" inferiorization of African people has been accomplished in large measure with this research approach. The pursuit of differences by race as revealed through statistical significance testing is a methodological mainstay in Eurocentric psychology. Shamefully, though, the prerequisites for its epistemological integrity or its validity as knowledge are violated with regularity. Axioms that spell out the conditions for proper and improper use of the comparative approach and illustrative examples are provided.

In Word's chapter, the prevailing methods for survey research used on urban African American samples are critiqued. They are found wanting because of a reliance on a Euro-American cultural framework that is presumed to be valid for others. This leads to faulty measurement technology, concept formulation, and interpretation of results. What could be a more critical concern given the importance of opinion and attitude polling and social science surveys of the African American community for social policy and generating "scientific" knowledge? Fortunately, corrective methodology is discussed and demonstrated.

The chapter by T. Hilliard, Dent, Hayes, Pierce, and Poussaint is a quintessential example of African psychologists applying their professional skills in the interests of African survival. Five psychologists from the San Francisco Bay Area chapter of the Association of Black Psychologists served as consultants for the defense in the historically important Angela Davis trial. Using their psychological expertise, they evaluated attitudinal, personal, and personality characteristics of prospective jurors and advised regarding jury selection. Regrettably, using psychology to thwart institutionalized white supremacy like the hailing and trial of our heroine Angela Davis is a rare event in African psychologists' activities. Hilliard et al.'s work on the Angela Davis trial should be instructive and inspirational.

At present, the main control that African Americans, nay, all African psychological workers, have over psychological TRP is their own praxis in the areas of theory building, research, clinical-applied and professional development activities. The chapter by Baldwin is thought provoking. It is a hard hitting but fair reproof of African American psychologists' performance in these areas. Thus it provides a jolting and sobering self-assessment. The medicine here is strong, but the patient, frankly, may be critical and in need of role redefinition. This is provided within the context of African survival thrust.

# 1 Transpersonal Psychology: The Role of the Afrocentric Paradigm

## LINDA J. MYERS
*The Ohio State University*

Conspicuously absent in the literature of transpersonal psychology in its search for a paradigm is an exploration of traditional African culture and world view. Such a legacy of omission from philosophical and psychological endeavors is common. This is due to the fact that until recently African culture has been so badly misunderstood because of the imposition of alien world view in its analysis. The unity and integration of knowledge that we seek in a transpersonal paradigm has its framework already existent in the African world view and is identified in Afrocentric psychological theory.

Transpersonal psychology seeks to expand the field of psychological inquiry to include the study of optimal psychological health and well-being. The potential for experiencing a broad range of states of consciousness is recognized, allowing identity to extend beyond the usual limits of ego and personality (Walsh & Vaughn, 1980). Within this frame it is understood that the reality one perceives is shaped by an underlying system of beliefs often implicit, assumed, or unquestioned, that serve as self-fulfilling, self-prophetic organizers of experience. From this basis all psychologies have evolved as implicit or explicit models of human nature. The pervasive dynamic interplay between cultural beliefs and psychological models is now being recognized. The models posed by psychologists are a part of their own beliefs and experience and reflect both the culture and individual that produce them.

Transpersonal psychology represents a paradigm shift in Western psychology, benefiting from exposure to cross-cultural beliefs about the nature of consciousness and reality. Changing the prevailing limiting cultural beliefs about our basic nature and our relationship to the world may be one of the most important tasks confronting psychology

Linda J. Myers, Department of Black Studies, The Ohio State University, 486 University Hall, 230 North Oval Mall, Columbus, OH 43210-1319.

today. Recognition of the upper reaches of psychological development supports the investigation of maximal positive well-being and higher states of consciousness. This awareness has always been characteristic of non-Western psychologies. The failure of materialistic external strivings to provide the satisfaction, peace, and well-being has led some people to look for a more adequate source. One of the principal aims of transpersonal psychology must be to help us overcome the perceptual distortions identified by the many consciousness disciplines, yielding a view of reality more consistent with that which modern physics has shown to be the true nature of the material universe.

The purpose of this article will be to present a paradigm that unifies the insights of modern physics and Eastern mysticism under the philosophical structure of traditional African philosophy. This endeavor will be pursued in four phases. First, African philosophical-cultural tradition as a missing link in human history will be briefly discussed. Second, the resultant Afrocentric paradigm of psychological functioning will be delineated, based on the philosophical legacy of ancient Africans exemplified through the Egyptian Mystery Systems. Third, an example of the unfoldment of Afrocentric psychology will be reported. The last stage will outline some future research directions for adherents to the paradigm.

## The Missing Link

A cursory review of the literature in the *Journal of Transpersonal Psychology* over the past ten years reveals that, for the most part, search for a paradigm has been focused toward Oriental philosophy and modern physics. But as Capra (1975) notes neither of these approaches have been fruitful in terms of offering clear applicability and implications for day-to-day existence. This limitation appears to be a function of the world views of the cultures from which these fields of study come. The modern physicist experiences the world through an extreme specialization of the rational mind; the mystic through an extreme specialization of the intuitive mind (Capra, 1975).

According to Capra (1975; 1982) the mystical experience is necessary to understand the deepest nature of things, and science is essential for modern life. What we need, therefore, is not a synthesis, but a dynamic interplay between mystical intuition and scientific analysis. The world view implied by modern physics is inconsistent with the dominant view of our present society. The prevailing Western world view does not reflect the harmonious interrelatedness we observe in nature. In order to achieve such a state of dynamic balance, a radically different philosophical, social, and economic structure will be needed: a cultural revolution in the true sense of the word. The survival of our whole civilization may depend on whether or not we can bring about such a change.

Looking at contemporary cultures, Cook and Kono (1977) state that each of the three primary races exhibits an overdevelopment of one aspect of being, producing three cultural extremes: a materially advanced but spiritually bankrupt culture in the West; a spiritually developed and socially stagnant culture in the East; and a developed social consciousness and fluid social structure, but relatively undeveloped material culture in Africa. They concede that significant exceptions tend to indicate the oneness of humanity and the possibility for a universal psychology. In the West there are genuine religious and spiritual traditions that are pervasive. In the East there originated the concept of advancement in government service through merit alone in the Chinese examination system. And in precolonial Africa there was metal technology, commerce, medical science, and architecture far surpassing that of Europe and Asia at the time. Yet, they perceive that the general priorities of these races, then and now, pushed each culture toward a particular extreme.

Although I do not agree with all of their conclusions, their underlying premise is consistent with the point being made here regarding the outcome of a particular world view or cultural orientation. Each world view will yield its own particular consequences and what is needed now is the unity that contains and transcends all opposites. The Western materialistic construction of reality culminates in the modern physicist's examination of materiality and conclusion that the material world constitutes the world of appearance and that the "stuff of the world is mind stuff" (Eddington, 1931). However, despite the fact that science points toward this view, a fragmented, mechanistic world view is adhered to on a daily basis. Eastern religion philosophies, so long concerned with timeless mystical knowledge, see it lying beyond reasoning and inexpressible in words, therefore unknowable in the general realm and inapplicable in the state of non-transcendence. Africa offers the middle ground, a centering. The fullest potential of what Africa can provide may be identified in contemporary times by her displaced children, African Americans. For it is they that are the inquiring offspring of the strongest 100,000,000 ancestors (some estimates range upwards to 200,000,000) torn from the motherland during over three hundred years of European slave trade. African Americans represent the union of opposites, culturally and racially.

Conspicuously absent in the literature of transpersonal psychology in its search for a paradigm is an exploration of traditional African culture and world view. Such a legacy of omission from philosophical and psychological endeavors is common. Until recently, African culture has been badly misunderstood because of the imposition of alien world views in its analysis. The unity and integration of knowledge that we seek in a transpersonal paradigm has its framework already existent in the African world view. This is discussed in detail, as it relates to Afrocentric psychology.

## The Afrocentric Paradigm

Within the past several years a number of psychologists have independently converged on an approach to the science of mind and behavior that is rooted in the traditional African world view (Akbar, 1976, 1981; Baldwin, 1981; Frye, 1980; Khatib & Nobles, 1978; Myers, 1981a, 1981b; Nobles, 1972, 1974; X Clark, McGee, Nobles, & X Weems, 1975). The Afrocentric paradigm of psychological functioning that has been developed is consistent with and reinforces the paradigmatic shift currently taking place in the sciences in Western culture (Bateson, 1979; Capra 1975, 1982; Gelwick, 1977; Jantsch, 1980; Polyani, 1967) and the "new philosophy of science" (Bhaskar, 1975; Harre, 1972; Manicas & Secord, 1983). In addition, being psychological theory, it adds the dimension of practical applicability to everyday life.

According to Glaser and Strauss (1967), in discovering theory, one generates conceptual categories or their properties from evidence. The evidence, then, from which the category emerged is used to illustrate the concept. In terms of African American psychological theory an entire set of conceptual categories and properties has been generated from the evidence presented by traditional African culture, and its correspondent world view. Many scholars have detailed the existence of such a generalized world view and certain cultural ethos continually predominate (Asante, 1980; Diop, 1978; Forde, 1954; Gerhart, 1978; Levine, 1977; Mbiti, 1970; Nobles, 1972; Sowande, 1973; Thompson, 1974; Williams, 1976; Zahan, 1979). Dixon (1971) and Nichols (1976) have been particularly clear in delineating and articulating the philosophical aspects of the world view.

A brief discussion follows of some of the conceptual categories and properties of the paradigm/theory. Each category represents one of the philosophical assumptions that comprises the conceptual system, which is the basis of the paradigm/theory (Myers, 1984). The Afrocentric conceptual system of the paradigm is truly holistic, because ontologically it assumes reality to be both spiritual and material at once. In this regard everything becomes one thing, spirit manifesting. Spirit refers to that permeating essence that is known in an extrasensory fashion (e.g., energy, consciousness, God). For our purposes, consciousness manifesting will be assumed; and, if the properties of the conceptual system are followed in a highly structured fashion starting with ontology, all is God manifest.

Drawing from the teachings of ancient Africans (i.e., Egyptians over 5,000 years ago), the aim of the conceptual system is to structure reality such that man/woman can achieve everlasting peace and happiness (James, 1954). This deification process seeks to transform the finite, limited conception of human consciousness into an infinite consciousness that is supremely good or divine. In order to accomplish this task, one must begin to know that everything, including self, is the manifestation of one permeating essence that is the source of all things good. When the spiritual/material ontology is adhered to completely, one loses the sense of individualized ego/mind and experiences infinite mind or consciousness manifesting as oneself. Remember that any other ontological assumption (e.g., material, or material and spiritual) falls within the realm of nonreality or illusion to one adopting the Afrocentric conceptual system.

Before discussing other conceptual categories and properties of the paradigm/theory, an example of this conceptual system functioning in African culture might be appropriate. However, the purpose of identifying such a paradigm/theory is not to replicate the surface structure (i.e., rituals, specific practices or beliefs) of African culture. What is being articulated is a conceptual system in pure form, which will be reflected in the way one views the world and can be adopted by anyone across cultures and time. It is also important to note in this regard that what is being advocated is at this point not exclusively African, nor could or should it be, if the paradigm/theory is valid. The point is that the conceptual system seems to have originated in Africa (Diop, 1974; James, 1954; ben-Jochannon, 1970) and among Black people who would in modern context likely be labeled of African descent. Equally important, however, it is in the process of people of African descent

(African Americans) rediscovering their heritage that this way of viewing life in total is recaptured, and is consequently termed *Afrocentric*.

Nobles (1972, 1980) and Zahan (1979) discuss the African concept of extended self, which is particularly illustrative of the Afrocentric spiritual/material ontology at work. *Self* in this instance includes all of the ancestors, the yet unborn, all of nature, and the entire community. In addition, consubstantiation was assumed. In other words they believed "I am because we are; we are, therefore, I am." Holonomy, the whole being somehow contained in each of its parts, may be a universal property of nature and is characteristic here.

It is critical to note, however, that one's "being" did not automatically make one a part of the community nor admit one to the position of ancestor at a later date. Both positions held requisite the adoption of a "proper" belief structure (conceptual system). This adherence is evidenced through behavior and attitude (Zahan, 1979). The role and importance of consciousness in African thought is further evidenced in concepts such as *Nommo* (the power of the word) and the belief that one had not "died" until the last person who knew him/her by name "died." Then the person was believed to enter the realm of ancestral spirits (universal consciousness).

The second conceptual category to be discussed is epistemology. In order to be internally consistent with the ontology, self knowledge would have to be viewed as the basis of all knowledge, and it is. One knows through symbolic imagery and rhythm (Nichols, 1976). In order to make this idea more easily comprehensible to those of us more familiar with the dominant epistemology of Western culture, which is that external knowledge is the basis of all knowledge, Polyani's notion of tacit knowledge will be introduced. Michael Polyani is one of the foremost Western scientist/philosophers being identified as fostering the general paradigm shift in science (Gelwick, 1977; Manicas & Secord, 1983). Polyani (1966) believed that all knowing has a tacit dimension, and this "hidden" dimension is the greater part of knowledge. Within knowledge there are two awarenesses: the subsidiary, those unspoken assumptions we rely on which are very close to us or proximal; and the focal, that to which we attend to as though far from us, or distal. We use our body to attend from it things outside of it. We interiorize and dwell on "clues" as the proximal terms of our existence. The idea that all knowing is a form of indwelling, overthrows centuries of the Western dichotomy that separates mind and body, reason and experience, theory and practice, subject and object, the knower and the known. Whenever we form an integration (perception) or recognition, the subsidiary particulars (assumptions being relied on, i.e., aspects of conceptual system) appear in the phenomenon of the pattern they produce. Focal awareness or distal terms are dependent on subsidiary awareness or proximal terms to determine what we mean. Tacit knowing guides us to the comprehension of something real.

In many ways Polyani's notion of tacit knowledge is analogous to the Afrocentric epistemology of the paradigm/theory. Within the Afrocentric conceptual system all knowledge is assumed to be self knowledge or tacit knowledge from the beginning. In other words, the Afrocentric epistemology starts out assuming the interrelatedness of all things and that whatever you believe is, is for you, given your conceptual system (interplay of subsidiary and focal awareness). Power in this world view is the ability to define reality. Symbolic imagery and rhythm as a way of knowing is in itself an open acknowledgment that focal awareness (symbolic imagery) is merely a reflection of the nature of subsidiary awareness (indwelling rhythm). Both are inextricable parts of how one knows. One can structure reality in order to experience infinite divine consciousness or whatever else one chooses. The power of God is within us. Polyani noted the use of the body in experience, and the false inside/outside dichotomy. In the Afrocentric conceptual system an additional role of the body/mind as an important affective/cognitive barometer must be mentioned. As symbolized in the architecture of the pyramids, ancient Africans believed that the heart, symbolic of how one is feeling about things or processing them, must be dealt with before the ascension to higher consciousness (infinite consciousness) could be achieved.

The logic, process, and axiology of the paradigm will be examined together because of the way their interrelatedness follows so closely from the two major categories of ontology and epistemology and for the sake of brevity of this article. That the nature of reality is perceived to be both spiritual and material at once, speaks to a type of logic that emphasizes the union of opposites, diunital logic. In line with the schema of general systems theory, the process is ntuology, all sets are interrelated through human and spiritual networks and through them all goals will be achieved. The highest goal in this framework is to achieve everlasting peace and happiness. The highest value lies in the interpersonal relationship between man/woman. Such an axiological position rests on the realization of the interrelatedness of all things and the role of consciousness as that permeating essence. These ideas place humankind in a highly responsible position in terms of perpetuating the natural

order. Self-knowledge being the basis of all knowledge, the uncondi-
tional positive regard for the natural order must begin within and be
generated outwardly, manifesting at a critical point in terms of interpersonal relations among people. Self-love as the basis of all love, starts
within and moves outward in phases of the most similar to most
dissimilar. Taken together the philosophical assumptions of this paradigm form a conceptual system that structures consciousness such that
everlasting peace and happiness will be achieved.

## An Example of the Unfoldment

In December, 1981, I attended a meeting of the Southern Regional
Education Board Black Psychology Task Force in Atlanta, Georgia. At
that meeting Wade Nobles, a leading theorist in development the African perspective in psychology, outlined the requisite characteristics of
a theory worthy of the name Black Psychology. Among other important
characteristics, he stressed that it must come from the deep structure of
African culture (i.e., philosophy, cosmology, axiology). Na'im Akbar,
another noted figure in the field, discussed our destiny as the authors
of scientific revolution. He noted expected differences in the application of psychological models from African versus European world
views. Of particular interest here is the difference in normative standards. Nature provides the standard in the African world view, the
Western world view utilizes an ethnocentric (e.g., White, Anglo-Saxon,
Protestant, property-owning male) or relative standard (Akbar, 1981).
Joseph Baldwin, an Afrocentric theorist of personality, defined Black
personality structure in terms of an African self-extension orientation
or spiritual core. Edwin Nichols elaborated on the philosophical aspects
of cultural difference. Other papers included the reconceptualization of
the African American woman, interpersonal relationships between Black
men and women, and the strengths of the Black community. My paper
described the Afrocentric paradigm of psychological functioning discussed here. I reference this experience to make a point of the independent convergence of thought among scholars of the Afrocentric persuasion
at that meeting.

The consistency between what Nobles called for, what Akbar proph-
esied, and the subsequent theory I presented was uncanny. If I had seen
their particular papers I could not have matched their ideas any better
point for point. Baldwin's paper on the African personality, especially
his ideas of the spiritual core, also mirrored my thoughts. I was familiar

with Nichol's work, but I did learn more about the differences between the African and Asian philosophy/culture/world view, which needed greater clarification in my work at that time. The topics and issues covered in other papers were readily and effectively addressed when the Afrocentric paradigm was applied in their solution.

To a degree, psychological theory is shaped by autobiography, and the personal history of the theoreticians directly influencing their articulation of and emphasis in theory (Walsh & Vaughn, 1980). I believe this to be true in my case and that of Afrocentric psychology. Afrocentric psychological theory has evolved in such a manner that it has reinforced the relationships I see between personal experience, culture, and psychological paradigms. The experienced I cited is but one small example of how consciousness has unfolded and continues to unfold vis-à-vis Afrocentric psychology.

## Future Research Directions

The Afrocentric paradigm being proposed offers a method for structuring consciousness, which unless you already adhere to it, would yield an altered state of consciousness (ASC). This particular ASC seeks to unify finite human consciousness with infinite consciousness or God consciousness. Although this conceptual system characterizes most of the consciousness disciplines philosophically, what differs is the assumed methodology and process. Despite having been identified in African culture first, the world view is by no means exclusionary. Utilizing the conceptual system and assuming a single gene pool, if we accept the most current archeological/anthropological evidence and what biogenetics tell us about dominant versus recessive genes for color, all people are African people if they go back far enough into their ancestry. From this view it is not surprising that the same basic ancient wisdom has been found throughout the world. According to Homer and Herodutus, in early times Black people were the inhabitants of what we now refer to as the Sudan, Egypt, Arabia, Palestine, Western Asia, and India (James, 1954). The English word *Egyptian* comes from the Greek word *Aiguptos,* which means Black.

One direction that research from the Afrocentric perspective might take is in the area of semantics and hermeneutics. The meaning and interpretation of words and concepts mark the state of consciousness of their speakers. As we observe the meanings of words and concepts changing over time and across cultures, we can note the unfolding of the consciousness of a people. For example, the term *Jew* is reputed to have originally referred to "people who follow God," and *Israel,* "the land of the people who follow God." When and how did these meanings change, for whom, and why? The same questions should be asked of the word *Egyptian* and other concepts. The answers will tell us something of the nature of the functioning of consciousness itself.

Having delineated the specifics of the deep structure of ancient traditional African culture in terms of its philosophical underpinnings, the resultant paradigm, if used to structure reality, fulfills all purposes of other consciousness disciplines and adheres to the same basic assumptions. Walsh (1983) identified six characteristics of the consciousness disciplines that can be summarized with reference to the Afrocentric paradigm as follows: (1) Consciousness is primary, the source of all pleasure and suffering is in the mind. (2) A mind untrained in the Afrocentric conceptual system is vastly less under our control than we imagine, but when trained, provides optimal means for enhancing well-being and enabling us to contribute to the well-being of others. (3) The trained mind is aware of itself as a manifestation of God (its true nature and identity), and as such, uses this knowledge to avoid destruction and suffering.

When interpreted from the Afrocentric world view, Christ's teachings articulate these same premises. Both Christ and Moses were Initiates of the Egyptian Mysteries. Moses is said to have been a Hierogrammat: and Christ, to have taken final initiation at the Great Pyramid of Cheops in Egypt after attending the Mysteries lodge at Mt. Carmel (James, 1954; Levi, 1972). Another research direction for the Afrocentric paradigm is the Afrocentric interpretation of Biblical Scripture. The following is an Afrocentric interpretation of the Lord's Prayer:

AFROCENTRIC INTERPRETATION OF LORD'S PRAYER

Our being that is in Oneness inviolatible is your Truth/Law. Our realization of Oneness be with us. Thy will be done, so that we no longer believe in our separation.

Give us day by day our highest good, and grant us relief from payment for our seeing ourselves as separate, for we also grant relief to everyone that might owe gratitude and recognition to us.

And do not let us be aroused by false hope for false desires of pleasure or gain, but protect us from things that bring suffering.

For thine is the kingdom and the power and the glory forever. Amen

With regard to the concept of Christ and his teachings, the Afrocentric paradigm acknowledges Christ as humankind realizing itself as God manifest. According to Graves (1875) there were sixteen crucified saviors before Christ, starting with Horus, the Christ figure of ancient Egypt, to Buddha, Krishna, and Mohammed, and so on. Each manifestation and teaching is worthy of study and must be studied. The author begins with the Christ of Biblical Scripture because of her own personal experience and cultural background.

The last research direction to be mentioned here will be the psychohistorical (history of the spirit/mind) analysis of individuals through autobiography and biography, and racial groups, the sexes, cultural groups, nations, and so on through ethnography, folklore, and ethnomethodology. The premise of these analyses will be that because everything is God manifesting, it is important to see how he/she manifests through the behaviors of specified beings. What do specific individuals do, what have they done, and what of groups of individuals? In this regard it is important to note that the purpose of these analyses serves self-knowledge. All that is real is God, the good, all else is illusory, nonreality. In this process the researcher must be committed to the clear articulation and reexamination of his/her own belief system. Testable predictions must be the consequence of these investigations. The clear delineation of the deep structure of the Afrocentric conceptual system makes state-specific science more probable in this case (Tart, 1983).

## Conclusion

In sum, the paradigm that is being articulated is far too global and comprehensive to be covered in any but a cursory fashion here. Yet to be addressed is the specific therapeutic approach of the Afrocentric paradigm called Belief Systems Analysis. Also the detailed application of the paradigm to specific social problems and issues is omitted. In addition, questions arising about the implication of the paradigm and its relationship to other consciousness disciplines and traditional Western psychology must be addressed in another forum.

Eagerness to fill these gaps immediately is related to two principles, that of *adequatio* (adequateness) and grades of significance. That is, the understanding of the knower must be adequate to the thing to be known, and the same phenomenon may hold entirely different grades of meaning and significance to different observers with different degrees of adequatio (Schumacher, 1977). Learning and practice seem to be the compensatory factors ameliorating this historic problem of knowing and understanding (Walsh, Elgin, Vaughn, & Wilber, 1980). Therefore, the sense is that the more information given, the more learning and practice and resultant enlightenment. Because of the ontological and epistemological assumptions of the paradigm, what emerges is a metapsychology, which makes the task enormous. Suffice it to say that being true to the paradigm, the unfoldment will be accomplished in perfect time. Being truth, this is inescapable.

## References

Akbar, N. (1976). *Natural psychology and human transformation.* Chicago: World Community of Islam in the West.

Akbar, N. (1981). Mental disorder among African Americans. *Black Books Bulletin, 7*(2), 18-25.

Asante, M. (1980). *Afrocentricity: Theory of social change.* Buffalo, NY: Amulefi Publishing.

Baldwin, J. (1981). Notes on an Africentric history of Black personality. *The Western Journal of Black Studies, 5*(3), 172-179.

Bateson, G. (1979). *Mind and nature: A necessary unity.* New York: E. P. Dutton.

ben-Jochannon, Y. (1970). *African origins of major western religions.* New York: Alkebulan Books.

Bhaskar, R. (1975). *A realist theory of science.* Leeds, England: Leeds Books.

Capra, F. (1975). *The tao of physics.* New York: Bantam Books.

Capra, F. (1982). *The turning point: Science, society and the rising culture.* New York: Simon & Schuster.

Cook, N., & Kono, S. (1977). Black psychology: The third great tradition. *The Journal of Black Psychology, 3,* 18-28.

Diop, C. A. (1974). *The African origin of civilization: Myth or reality.* New York: Lawrence Hill.

Dixon, V. (1971). *Beyond Black or White: An alternative America.* Boston: Little, Brown.

Eddington, A. (1931). *The nature of the physical world.* New York: Macmillan.

Forde, D. (1954). *African worlds: Studies in the cosmological ideas and social values of African peoples.* London: Oxford University Press.

Frye, C. (1980). *Level three: A Black philosophy reader.* Lanham, MD: University Press of America.

Gelwick, R. (1977). *The way of discovery.* New York: Oxford University Press.

Gerhart, G. M. (1978). *Black power in South Africa: The evolution of an ideology.* Berkeley: University of California Press.

Glaser, B., & Strauss, A. (1967). *The discovery of grounded theory: Strategies for qualitative research.* Chicago: Aldine.

Graves, K. (1875). *The world's sixteen crucified saviors: Christianity before Christ.* New York: Free Thought Books.

Harre, R. (1972). *Philosophies of science.* Oxford: Oxford University Press.

James, G. (1954). *Stolen legacy.* New York: Philosophical Library.

Jantsch, E. (1980). *The self-organizing universe: Scientific and human implications of the emerging paradigm of evolution.* Elmsford, NY: Pergamon.

Khatib, S. M., & Nobles, W. (1978). Historical foundations of African psychology and their philosophical consequences. *The Journal of Black Psychology, 4*(1 & 2), 91-102.

Levi. (1972). *The aquarian gospel of Jesus Christ.* Marina Del Rey, CA: DeVorss.

Levine, L. W. (1977). *Black culture and Black consciousness.* New York: Oxford University Press.

Manicas, P., & Secord, P. (1983). Implications for psychology of the new philosophy of science. *American Psychologist, 38*(4), 399-413.

Mbiti, J. S. (1970). *African religions and philosophy.* Garden City, NY: Doubleday.

Myers, L. (1981a, August). *African American psychology: Another way.* Paper presented at the Fourteenth Annual National Convention of Black Psychologists, Denver, CO.

Myers, L. (1981b). The nature of pluralism and the African American case. *Theory into Practice, 20*(1), 3-6.

Myers, L. (1984). The psychology of knowledge: The importance of world view. *New England Journal of Black Studies, 4,* 1-12.

Nichols, E. (1976, November). *The philosophical aspects of cultural differences.* Paper presented at the meeting of the World Psychiatric Association, Ibadan, Nigeria.

Nobles, W. (1972). African philosophy: Foundations for Black psychology. In R. Jones (Ed.), *Black psychology.* New York: Harper & Row.

Nobles, W. (1974). Africanity: Its role in Black families. *The Black Scholar, 5,* 10-17.

Nobles, W. (1980). Extended self: Re-thinking the so-called Negro self concept. In R. Jones (Ed.), *Black psychology* (2nd ed.). New York: Harper & Row.

Polyani, M. (1966). *The tacit dimension.* Garden City, NY: Doubleday.

Schumacher, E. (1968). *A guide for the perplexed.* New York: Harper & Row.

Sowande, R. (1972). The quest of an African world view: The utilization of African discourse. In J. Daniel (Ed.), *Black communication dimensions of research and instruction.* Washington, DC: National Endowment for the Humanities.

Tart, C. (1980). States of consciousness and state specific science. In R. Walsh & F. Vaughn (Eds.), *Beyond ego: Transpersonal dimensions in psychology.* Los Angeles: J. P. Tarcher.

Thompson, R. (1974). *African art in motion.* Los Angeles: University of California Press.

Walsh, R. (1983). The consciousness disciplines. *Journal of Humanistic Psychology, 23*(2), 28-30.

Walsh, R., Elgin, D., Vaughn, F., & Wilber, K. (1980). Paradigms in collision. In R. Walsh & F. Vaughn (Eds.), *Beyond ego: Transpersonal dimensions in psychology.* Los Angeles: J. P. Tarcher.

Walsh, R., & Vaughn, F. (1980). *Beyond ego: Transpersonal dimensions in psychology.* Los Angeles: J. P. Tarcher.

Williams, C. (1976). *The destruction of Black civilization.* Chicago: Third World Press.

X (Clark), C., McGee, P., Nobles, W., & X (Weem), L. (1975). Voodoo or I.Q. An introduction to African psychology. *The Journal of Black Psychology, 1*(2), 9-30.

Zahan, D. (1979). *The religion, spirituality, and thought of traditional Africa.* Chicago: University of Chicago Press.

# 2 Understanding the Proper and Improper Usage of the Comparative Research Framework

**DAUDI AJANI YA AZIBO**
*Temple University*

> Whites or Europeans are no longer the standard by which the psychology of people is judged.
>
> (Khatib & Nobles, 1977, pp. 97–98)

The comparative research framework, contrasting distinct groups by statistical significance tests, is examined for major epistemological and practical problems inherent in its usage with African-European (Black-White) groups. Three axioms are given regarding the proper and improper usage of this approach in the context of epistemological soundness. Published examples of proper and improper usage are presented. Three kinds of proper usage are identified. And, the intricacy in determining whether a given implementation of this research framework is proper or improper is discussed.

This commentary presents a viewpoint of the proper and improper usage of the comparative research framework by focusing on the practical and epistemological problems inherent in it.

## The Practical Problem of Hegemony

Perhaps because of their fundamental and profound xenophobia, identified by Dr. Cheik Diop (Diop, 1978; Wobogo, 1976), a characteristic behavior of Europeans[1] is to judgmentally compare different people

This article is dedicated to Dr. Robert "Big Bob" Williams, a mentor of mine. He, and others, almost 20 years ago raised the challenge to the validity and scientific appropriateness of the comparative research framework to a serious epistemological debate. My observations on this matter are founded in large part on his critical, deconstructive groundwork. Correspondence concerning this commentary should be addressed to Daudi Ajani ya Azibo, Department of African American Studies, Temple University, Philadelphia, PA 19122.

to themselves, using themselves as a standard. This ethnocentric bias presents a practical problem for African social scientists who are studying Africans, but who are subject to Eurocentric hegemony: It is expected and often required that African data be compared to European data, which it is further expected will be used as the standard data or reference point data. Frequently African psychologists can be heard complaining that they were not permitted to publish in prestigious Eurostream (as opposed to mainstream) journals because they only had data on Africans, and none on Europeans for comparison, even though the constructs and variables under study, like "African consciousness" and "Negro-to-Black" metamorphosis, usually had meaning only for Africans.

To close the point, I shall relate my experiences in two colloquia. Interviewing for a psychology post during April 1987, I presented three empirical studies on African Self-Consciousness (Black personality). The instruments, Williams' *Black Personality Questionnaire* (Wright & Isenstein, 1978) and Baldwin's *African Self-Consciousness Scale* (Baldwin & Bell, 1985), were circulated. The first question of the Q & A period from a European was "*Why* didn't you use a White *control* group?" I underscore "why" as it illustrates the expectation, and "control" because it illustrates the further expectation (assumption) that the European is the standard reference point. My reply:

1. "What is it that I would be controlling for?" Response: well, um, ah . . .
2. "You've seen the instruments. For a non-Black to answer those questions would be meaningless in terms of the construct. Right? So what would we be comparing?" Response: red-faced, mouth-open stare, and marked discomfort evident in the rest of the all-European faculty.
3. "Whites or Europeans are no longer the standard by which the psychology of people is judged." [2]

Thus having forced the White psychologists to recognize the intellectual truth that the comparative framework in this case would be barren, their general consensus, I surmise, was that the work was of little value. Just how little value can be gleaned from the question of one Euro-American psychologist, who quite soberly queried during my graduate student colloquia on African personality research the following: "This is interesting, but when are you going to do some *human* research?"! Can you imagine the mind-set that would generate a question premised with the denial of integrity and humanity for Africans, unless somehow Europeans figure in?

This, then, is the basis of the practical problem of hegemony: "Without sensitivity to the intellectual and cultural elements of others, the white social scientist has often proceeded as if what is correct for Whites is correct for everybody" (Asante, 1987, p. 172). Thus, if you study Africans, you usually cannot get the grant, the job, the publication, the serious appreciation of your work, without comparing to Europeans, as long as the unenlightened Europeans, he and she, sit in judgment (or the ignoble African who only parrots the European mind-set).

## The Epistemological-Scientific Problem

From the purely intellectual angle, the epistemological debate over the worth of the comparative framework is most fundamental.[3] Understanding the epistemological issue will end this debate and clarify the proper and improper usage of the comparative framework.

The comparative research framework requires a statistical significance test between any two groups, like race, sex, or treatment groups. Its epistemological base as science rests on John Stuart Mills' method of difference canon. Fundamentally, this canon "requires that the two groups be equated, that is, equal in all respects . . . on *relevant* variables . . . known or believed to [have] influence" (Plutchik, 1974, p. 179). If the comparison groups are not equated as specified in the canon, then the observed difference can only be described; any attempt to interpret or otherwise address the meaning of the difference, especially in terms of a presumed underlying construct, is epistemologically baseless. There can be no meaning or interpretation given to the difference, nor can causality be inferred.

Regarding African-European, perhaps all, racial comparisons, the most important "relevant" variable for equating purposes is culture. Culture (Nobles, 1982) is defined as patterns for interpreting reality that give people a general design for living, and consists of surface (e.g., folkways, language, behavior, beliefs, values) and deep structures (ethos, worldview, ideology, cosmology, axiology, ontology). Culture is important because it determines the meaning attached to the observed facts. Surface structure differences between Africans and Europeans would appear self-evident. Moreover, deep structure differences contrasted so clearly by Africentric scholars like Diop (Wobogo, 1976) and others (Baldwin, 1985; Dixon, 1976; Nobles, 1976a, 1982) are profound.

Racial comparisons still are prominent in Eurocentric psychology and many African researchers continue to readily employ this methodology, lack of cultural equating notwithstanding (the hegemony problem again: see Semmes, 1982). These researchers apparently are either unaware of the inherent epistemological problem or disregard it assuming *cultural monism* between Africans and Europeans. The assumption may be convenient and indispensable for the comparative frame; nevertheless it is incorrect. Consequently the epistemological base of much race comparison research is absent, giving rise to serious question regarding the meaning of any observed difference (Banks, McQuater, & Ross, 1979).

PROPER AND IMPROPER USAGE

Understanding the epistemological problem permits the following general axioms:

1. It is proper to make racial comparisons using the comparative research framework when the racial groups are equated on all relevant variables, especially that of culture (there is a caveat here which will be introduced below);

2. It is improper if the racial groups are not equated on any relevant variable to do more than describe or report the difference; and

3. Whenever constructs are employed in the research, culture will be relevant.

The scientific potential of the comparative research framework for racial comparisons is drastically diminished by these axioms. The axioms in turn rest squarely on the importance of culture in determining the meaning of observed "facts." The emic (within-cultural) and etic (cross-cultural) research frameworks are viable alternatives that respect culture (Azibo, 1985, 1988; Triandis, 1972, ch. 3).

It must be pointed out that the proper and improper usage of the comparative research framework is a more intricate matter than the neat axioms might suggest. Consideration of some research examples will, hopefully, nail down the understanding of the epistemological issue in all of its intricacy. Three kinds of proper usage can be identified based on the reason that compels the comparison: deconstructive compulsion, research question compulsion, and construct compulsion.

*Example of Proper Usage: Deconstructive Compulsion.* The deconstructive approach[4] used in African psychology refutes or falsifies, and thereby renders void, "facts" about Africans that prevail in Eurocentric psychology (Banks, 1982; Nobles, 1986). Grubb's (1987) comparative analysis of African- and Euro-American mentally retarded populations yielded no significant differences that would uphold the genetic inferiority in IQ view of Africans. Grubb's refutation of this hereditary viewpoint is a major contribution to the deconstruction of this Eurocentric thesis, which is an embarrassment to many European psychologists, but which is a bench mark for many others, influential like the Eysencks, Jensens, Harlows, and the rank in file. Grubb's refutation could not have been accomplished directly without using the comparative framework. (Racial comparisons on intelligence may also be compelled by the research question.)

*Examples of Proper Usage: Research Question Compulsion.* Often the research question simply is one of race differences on some variable. The question thus innocently compels the comparison. Differences in societal indexes like sex ratio, income, and health status usually are straightforward. For example, Singleton, Harrell, and Kelly (1986) compared fetal development and mortality statistics of African- and Euro-Americans.

However, comparisons compelled by the research question can be problematic epistemologically if the researcher is not cautious. Hare and Castenell (1985) were interested in the status of African boys relative to African girls and to European boys to hopefully yield insight into their future prospects. The variables included locus of control, achievement orientation, achievement test scores, and others. Observed racial differences were presented, and the authors discussed the "reasons for the [observed] contemporary comparative status" (p. 208). This is proper.

Had they attempted discourse on the meaning of the research constructs relative to the observed race differences, they would have had an epistemological problem. Because the two groups of boys are not equated culturally (no cultural monism), the meaning of the Eurocentrically defined constructs and operationalized variables is likely *not* to be uniform for both groups. For example, Ogletree (1976) has shown why locus of control may not be an appropriate construct for African Americans. Her argument mainly deals with cultural surface structure differences that render the control ideology thesis void.[5] The cultural deep structure level might pose problems for the achievement orientation construct which, in the Eurocentric way, may include aspects of individualism and Machiavellianism; as opposed to the collectivism and Maat (Carruthers, 1984; Hilliard, Williams, & Damali, 1987;

Karenga, 1984) characteristic of the Africentric way. With these cultural differences any discussion of meaning in terms of the constructs would perforce be committing a transubstantive error, taking the cultural and psychological norms of one group and applying them in establishing the meaning of the cultural and psychological functioning of another group (*African Psychology Training Module Handbook,* 1982). Caution must be exercised to avoid the transubstantive error when conducting comparative analyses.

*Examples of Proper Usage: Construct Compulsion.* The expectation of racial differences is inherent in the content of some constructs. The construct of worldview or cosmology (representing the entire deep structure of culture) is a prime example. Scholars Linda James-Myers (1988, ch. 2) and Joseph Baldwin (personal communication, January, 1988) are interested in the Africentric worldview construct. Baldwin developed an instrument and compared African- and Euro-American responses to it, hypothesizing that Africans would score higher in the Africentric direction. It is the construct itself that compels that comparison here. Note that in studying the African worldview construct a researcher need not have an interest in racial differences per se, but the comparative question is inherent.[6]

This is the caveat mentioned earlier in axiom 1 where the importance of equating on culture was pointed out. It is actually the deep structure cultural differences (Africentric vs. Eurocentric worldviews) between the comparison groups that warrant the comparative analysis of the African worldview construct. (The cross-cultural framework could be used here as well.) This caveat demonstrates part of the intricacy involved in assessing the proper usage of the comparative research framework, which may be obscured by the neat axioms given earlier.

*Examples of Improper Usage.* Many comparative studies, perhaps most, that manifest improper usage simply violate axiom 1 and/or axiom 2. Furthermore, the only discernable compulsion for employing the comparative framework is often a blind acceptance of this methodological approach (and attendant conceptual parameters) as practiced in Euro-American psychology (hegemony issue again). Jones (1978), for example, compared Africans and Europeans on various personality tests developed in Eurocentric psychology. His purpose was to generate "better understanding of the *meaning* of Black-White personality differences" (p. 245, italics original).

The manifest impropriety is not always as obvious as in Jones' study. For example, Barbara Shade's (1986) study on African American cognitive style will reveal intricacy in establishing the impropriety of some comparative studies. Her article is nicely and concisely done, and there is both construct compulsion (Is there a unique African cognitive style?) and research question compulsion (Do Africans and Europeans differ in cognitive style?). Transubstantiation, however, is inherent in her methodology.

Her *operationalization* of the cognitive style construct was strictly Eurocentric, employing the Group Embedded Figures Test, the Myers-Briggs Type Indicator, and the Clayton-Jackson Object Sorting Task. If these variables were etically or pan-culturally operationalized, transubstantiation would not be inherent (the Myers-Briggs variable is most problematic of the three). But, the Myers-Briggs variable, if not the others, is emically or within-culturally (Eurocentric) derived. It may be erroneous to presume that emic variables have a uniform meaning across cultures. Triandis (1972) called this the *pseudoetic error*.

The solution here would be to translate the emic variables to a pan-cultural abstraction. Then either a comparative or cross-cultural approach could be undertaken. In either case, the undertaking of an emic analysis would be missed. Emic analyses can be rich because they draw on the conceptual framework of the subject population's culture. For example, African cognitive style might be formulated using African personality traits (Baldwin, 1981) and intuitive synthesis (Mayers, 1976) notions. African cognitive structure or conceptual schema could be formulated using Robert Williams' Afrocentric space construct (Azibo, 1983; Williams, 1981). Emic analysis can be functional to the subject population and build theory in its own cultural terms (Azibo, 1988). The greater the breadth and depth of emic research, the greater the conceptual pool for developing etic abstractions, which under Eurocentric hegemony are frequently pseudoetic.

## Conclusion

The proper and improper usage of the comparative research framework can be either an intricate or simplistic matter. There is much to understand: it cannot be used blindly or used as a matter-of-course; nor should it be dismissed outright. Its proper usage may be of diminished utility in African psychology; however, it likely will continue to be a mainstay in Euro-American social science where its improper usage is ingrained and inherent for White supremacy purposes (e.g., Guthrie, 1976; Thomas & Sillen, 1972). This is an important point because of the practical problem of hegemony with which this article began. Thence arises the "Black researcher's paradox," theorizing the same theory and implementing the same methodology that in large measure is designed to maintain African inferiority (see Nobles, 1976b). However, the elucidation of the proper usage of the comparative research framework can scale back its indiscriminate and oppressive usage. Thus African psychologists and social scientists are a step closer to accomplishing the paradigm shift in the social sciences, towards cultural science (Semaj, 1981), which is "Our Destiny" (Akbar, 1985).

## Notes

1. The term *European* is used to designate all Whites of European descent. The term *African* is similarly used for all Blacks of African descent. Ethnic and geographical distinctions will be made if necessary.

2. This was a bitter pill for the Europeans. It threw them more than I had calculated. I tried to sweeten it by appealing to their intellect, explaining the difference between a comparative and cross-cultural approach (Azibo, 1985, 1988) and pointing out the internationalization occurring in their psychology. No offer was tendered.

3. However, because intellect serves White supremacy in European culture, it would be a gross mistake to ignore the practical problems of hegemony while pursuing a purely intellectual angle.

4. The distinction between approaches and Schools is important. Deconstruction, reconstruction (revising Eurocentric psychological views of Africans to better fit or jibe with the African cultural reality), and construction (developing psychological knowledge of Africans from Africentric cultural concepts) are *approaches* to psychological inquiry. *Schools* of African psychology take positions on the nature, definition, content, and purpose of what is currently called psychology. Jackson (1979) and Karenga (1982, ch. 8) have identified the Traditional-Reactive, Reform-Inventive, and Radical-Innovative Schools.

5. Those who do locus of control research of Africans rarely reference her article.

6. The conversation with Dr. Baldwin was instrumental in clarifying my thoughts on construct compulsion of the comparative research framework.

## References

*African Psychology Institute Training Module Handbook.* (1982). Atlanta, GA: African Psychology Institute.

Akbar, N. (1985). Our destiny: Authors of a scientific revolution. In H. McAdoo & J. McAdoo (Eds.), *Black children: Social psychological and educational environments.* Beverly Hills, CA: Sage.

Asante, M. (1987). *The Africentric idea.* Philadelphia: Temple University Press.

Azibo, D. (1983). Perceived attractiveness and the Black personality: Black is beautiful when the psyche is Black. *The Western Journal of Black Studies, 7*(4), 229-238.

Azibo, D. (1985). *Appropriate and inappropriate research frameworks for Blacks* [Videotape]. Washington, DC: The Association of Black Psychologists.

Azibo, D. (1988). *Personality, clinical, and social psychological research on Blacks: Appropriate and inappropriate research frameworks.* Manuscript submitted for publication.

Baldwin, J. A. (1981). Notes on an Africentric theory of Black personality. *The Western Journal of Black Studies, 5*(3), 172-179.

Baldwin, J. A. (1985). Psychological aspects of European cosmology in American society: African and European cultures. *The Western Journal of Black Studies, 9*(4), 216-223.

Baldwin, J. A., & Bell, Y. (1985). The African self-consciousness scale: An Africentric personality questionnaire. *The Western Journal of Black Studies, 9*(2), 61-68.

Banks, W. C. (1982). Deconstructive falsification: Foundations of a critical method in Black psychology. In E. E. Jones & S. J. Korchin (Eds.), *Minority mental health* (pp. 59-74). New York: Praeger.

Banks, W. C., McQuater, G., & Ross, J. (1979). On the importance of White preference and the comparative difference of Blacks and others: Reply to Williams and Morland. *Psychological Bulletin, 86,* 33-36.

Carruthers, J. (1984). *Essays in ancient Egyptian studies.* Los Angeles: University of Sankore Press.

Diop, C. A. (1978). *The cultural unity of Black Africa.* Chicago: Third World Press.

Dixon, V. J. (1976). World views and research methodology. In L. King, V. Dixon, & W. Nobles (Eds.), *African philosophy: Assumptions and paradigms for research on Black persons.* Los Angeles: Fanon Research & Development Center.

Grubb, H. (1987). Intelligence at the low end of the curve: Where are the racial differences? *The Journal of Black Psychology, 14,* 25-34.

Guthrie, R. (1976). *Even the rat was white: A historical view of psychology.* New York: Harper & Row.

Hare, B., & Castenell, L. (1985). No place to run, no place to hide: Comparative status and future prospects of Black boys. In M. Spencer, G. Brookins, & W. Allen (Eds.), *Beginnings: The social and affective development of Black children.* Hillsdale, NJ: Lawrence Erlbaum.

Hilliard, A., Williams, L., & Damali, N. (1987). *The teachings of Ptahhotep: The oldest book in the world.* Atlanta, GA: Blackwood Press.

Jones, E. (1978). Black-White personality differences: Another look. *Journal of Personality Assessment, 42,* 244-252.

Karenga, M. (1984). *Selections from the Husia.* Los Angeles: Kawaida Publications.

Khatib, S., & Nobles, W. (1977). Historical foundations of African psychology and their philosophical consequences. *The Journal of Black Psychology, 4,* 91-101.

Mayers, S. (1976). Intuitive synthesis in Ebonics: Implications for a developing African science. In L. King, V. Dixon, & W. Nobles (Eds.), *African philosophy: Assumptions and paradigms for research on Black persons.* Los Angeles: Fanon Research & Development Center.

Myers, L. (1988). *Understanding an Afrocentric world view: Introduction to an optimal psychology.* Dubuque, IA: Kendall/Hunt.

Nobles, W. (1976a). Extended self: Rethinking the so-called Negro self-concept. *The Journal of Black Psychology, 2*(2), 15-24.

Nobles, W. (1976b). African science: The consciousness of self. In L. King, V. Dixon, & W. Nobles (Eds.), *African philosophy: Assumptions and paradigms for research on Black persons.* Los Angeles: Fanon Research & Development Center.

Nobles, W. (1982). The reclamation of culture and the right to reconciliation: An Afro-centric perspective on developing and implementing programs for the mentally retarded offender. In A. Harvey & T. Carr (Eds.), *The Black mentally retarded offender: A wholistic approach to prevention and habilitation.* New York: United Church of Christ Commission for Racial Justice.

Nobles, W. (1986). *African psychology: Toward its reclamation, reascension and revitalization.* Oakland, CA: Institute for the Advanced Study of Black Family Life and Culture.

Ogletree, K. (1976). Internal-external control in Black and White. *Black Books Bulletin, 4,* 26-31.

Plutchik, R. (1974). *Foundations of experimental research.* New York: Harper & Row.

Semaj, L. T. (1981). The Black self, identity, and models for a psychology of Black liberation. *The Western Journal of Black Studies, 5,* 158-171.

Semmes, C. (1982). Black studies and the symbolic structure of domination. *The Western Journal of Black Studies, 6,* 116-122.

Shade, B. J. (1986). Is there an Afro-American cognitive style? *The Journal of Black Psychology, 13,* 13-16.

Singleton, E., Harrell, J., & Kelly, L. (1986). Racial differentials in the impact of maternal cigarette smoking during pregnancy on fetal development and mortality. *The Journal of Black Psychology, 12,* 71-83.

Thomas, A., & Sillen, S. (1972). *Racism and psychiatry.* Secaucus, NJ: Citadel.

Triandis, H. (1972). *The analysis of subjective culture.* Belmont, CA: Brooks/Cole.

Williams, R. L. (1981). *The collective Black mind: An Afrocentric theory of Black personality.* St. Louis, MO: Williams & Associates.

Wobogo, V. (1976). Diop's two cradle theory and the origin of white racism. *Black Books Bulletin, 4*(4), 20-29, 72.

Wright, B. J., & Isenstein, V. (1978). *Psychological tests and minorities* (DHEW Publication No. ADM. 78-482). Washington, DC: Government Printing Office.

# 3 Cross-Cultural Methods for Survey Research in Black Urban Areas[1]

## CARL O. WORD
*Cable Communications Resource Center/West,
San Francisco*

Kenneth Clark (1965) is credited with first focusing attention on problems associated with survey research conducted on Black respondents. So little attention is typically paid to pre-testing questions for use with Black populations that the results of such surveys are scientifically unsound and probably misleading. Questions are seldom derived from cognitive categories utilized by and meaningful to respondents, but instead represent university and research center concepts. Further, as Cedric X (Clark) points out, the very act of conceptualizing a problem being investigated introduces a systematic error to the questions being asked when the researchers are not themselves immersed in the culture under investigation (Clark, 1972).

When some 80% of a national Black sample express doubts about the results of national polls of Black opinion (e.g., NBMC Summary, 1975) the social scientist would do well to question procedures utilized by survey research organizations. A careful examination of those procedures raises serious doubts about the ability of standard survey research methods to obtain valid samples of Black attitudes. We will here concern ourselves with an examination of those methods; their shortcomings in respect to polling urbanized Black populations, with the development of alternative strategies, and implications for survey data from a variety of settings.

## Shortcomings of Survey Research Models

We are here concerned with assumptions about attitude models and their utility in describing the thought processes of a wide variety of persons in the world, i.e., the universality of majority (White) culture models of attitude structure and the utility of majority culture concepts to understanding Black attitudes.

Attitude measurement technology originated with the desire to quantify on a physical continuum the affect or feeling associated with some psychological object (Thurstone, 1946). Considering the wide diversity of opinion about the nature and structure of conscious thought, the assumption that feelings may be assigned a place on a linear yardstick seems reasonable, the metaphor useful, particularly when such a process allows the scientist to utilize statistical manipulations appropriate for ordinal measurement. However, metaphors have a way of illuminating and obscuring at the same time. Metaphorical concepts quickly become reified, taken as a fact, so that when taken out of context in which they were originally created, variations are seen as errors, not as challengers to the original conception. McGuire describes such a process as stages in the life of an artifact (McGuire, 1969).

The model of attitudes as quantities of feeling carries with it several assumptions about processes of thought. First, attitudes, like pencils, are already available to respondents; all that need be done is to turn them over to the interviewer. Second, attitudes are individual constructs, formed by the individual as no other person may articulate for him. Third, there is an implicit model of consciousness, consisting of feelings that may be separated from a network of modifiers, associations, transitory impulses, salient values, without doing violence to their depiction.

It is easy to see how researchers in major White institutions might make such assumptions, given the American core values of independence and individualism (Hsu, 1972), and the tendency towards atomistic as opposed to wholistic thinking (Nobles, 1974).

However, these assumptions are called into question when respondents are unlike the persons for whom attitude technology has been developed, when contexts are changed. In a country where self-reliance is emphasized, where individual achievement is idealized, it is easy to see how attitude researchers assume individuals form an opinion for themselves, that no one can speak for another. But what happens in cultures where it is unknown to have individual opinions, where a village headman is spokesman for the village? Individuals in such cultures as Drake (1973) reports, do not feel they need to form an opinion about policy or national politics because that is an appointed leader's function. What does the concept "opinion" mean to individuals in cultures where private ownership is unknown, where collective achievement is stressed? Surely a model of individual opinion is not useful across cultures.

Even if we accept the implicit model of individual opinion, attitude polling runs up against formidable problems in the design of questions. Not only are there differences in the languages different cultures speak, but also there are large differences in the use of language, paralanguage, pauses, and silences to communicate meaning. Further, fundamental differences exist in the ways different cultures perceive reality. Underlying philosophical orientations may render meaningless questions based on other systems of belief. Translating words into other languages, for instance, must sometimes involve interpretation as well as finding words for things (Young, 1972).

We can appreciate the magnitude of this problem by recalling the attention directed to children's understanding of concepts. Where adults take conservation for granted, children do not do so, and questions concerning the conservation of quantities elicit peculiar replies. Just so, when there are fundamental differences between the researchers' notion of what they are asking, and the subject's thinking, there is bound to be a great deal of error in replies.

For example, there are several words for snow in some Eskimo languages, reflecting these cultures' attention to, and consciousness of variations in the types of snow. What does the Eskimo make of a question involving a hypothetical sequence involving snow? In some American Indian cultures, cooperation rather than individual competition is stressed. What meaning is given questions about achievement?

Some cultures do not see time through Western assumptions, namely, that time is linear, unchanging, and constantly moving into the future, independent of human existence. What does the West African tribesman make of questions about planning for future events when his concept of time is

a composition of events which have occurred, those that are taking place now, and those which are immediately to occur. What has not taken place or what has no likelihood of an immediate occurrence falls into the category of "No-time." What is certain to occur, or what falls within the rhythm of natural phenomenon, is in the category of inevitable or potential time (Mbiti, 1970, p. 21).

What value are scales devised to measure a psychological object such as personal achievement in cultures emphasizing cooperative effort?

Differences such as these recall the tale of the White researcher in an African village. He administered some difficult problems to one man and was puzzled when the man refused to do the task. When questioned, the man replied *it was not intelligent* to try to complete the task alone, when his friends and relatives were available to help him. In situations where concepts related to the variables of interest are likely to vary, as in attitude measurement in mutlicultural settings, the researcher must not only exercise exceptional care in insuring the scalability, reliability, and validity of attitude items, but also conduct sufficient ethnographic research to understand the cognitive frameworks meaningful to respondents before scales are constructed (Brislin, Lonner, & Thorndike, 19730; Frey, 1970).

Anthropologists have criticized attempting to measure things in other cultures without an understanding of the culturally defined system of concepts, categories, classifications, and contextual variables which are meaningful to the native speaker:

> Even with reference to quite obvious kinds of material objects, it has long been noted that many people do not "see things" quite the way we do. . . . Classification means that individual bird specimens must be matched against the defining attributes of conceptual categories and thereby judged to be equivalent for certain purposes to some other specimens but different from still others. Since no two birds are alike in every discernable feature, any grouping into sets implies a selection of only a limited number of features as significant for contrasting kinds of birds. A person learns which features are significant from his fellows as part of his cultural equipment. He does not receive this information from the birds. Knowing how the Indian himself groups these objectives and which attributes he selects as dimensions (will) generate a taxonomy of avifauna. With the latter knowledge we learn what these people regard as significant about birds. (Frake, 1962)

Even within Anglo-American culture, the use of research designs capable of uncovering the respondents' own understanding of the concepts under scrutiny has been urged:

> An underlying cause of many methodological problems may be that sociologists often assume that they know a great deal about what people think before they have collected any data. They implicitly assume that cognitive content does not vary greatly across subcultures or social positions, therefore little effort is devoted to discovering the meaning of the questions and

responses to the people who are being studied. And no effort is directed to
the more difficult task of examining how the subjects structure the relevant
cognitive domain, i.e., what categories they use and what components or
critical attributes determine categorization. For example, a typical sociological study of the political attitudes of students would not investigate
what kinds of opinions were treated as "political" by students or what
components of an opinion were relevant in categorizing it as "left" or "right."
Yet this type of information probably would be very useful for understanding radical student political activity. The substitution of preconceptions for
evidence about meanings and categories will obviously result in inaccurate
descriptions of what people think. (Cancian, 1973)

Considering the paucity of research on Black cognitive functioning,
it is easy to see how researchers have obtained questionable data from
responses to questions like "how would you punish misbehavior?"
Blacks may regard misbehavior as not coming to dinner at all, while
Whites may interpret the questions as ten minutes late for dinner.
Responses of "a slap in the face," and "a scolding" may then be wholly
misinterpreted because researchers neglected to uncover the meanings
of the questions to respondents.

Such regard for the cultural distinctiveness of populations under
study is seldom observed in cross-cultural investigations (O'Brien,
Spain, & Tessler, 1973). Within the United States, ethnographic procedures are practically unknown in survey research.

## Black Language, Black Sociolinguistics

The second major source of error in survey research conducted on Black
population lies in the assumption of homogeneity with respect to linguistic
and sociolinguistic aspects of speech. Such errors probably operate most
at the question creation and data collection stage of survey research.

Anthropologists and linguists, perhaps because of their training, have
of late begun investigations of the language spoken by Black Americans, their speaking styles and the contextual variables affecting speech
production. Cross-cultural ethnographic investigations have long established the tremendous variability, not only in the languages spoken but
in the ways cultures influence speakers' willingness to verbalize.

Ignorance of Black sociolinguistic styles has led some White researchers (e.g., Dale, 1972, p. 249) to conclude Black children have no
speech at all when Black children decline to speak to White researchers
in unfamiliar situations. Such myopic errors are, in part, the result of a

deficit ideological approach (Baratz & Baratz, 1970) and also the result of simplistic research designs that allow for only one comparison, typically Blacks versus Whites, on a variable of interest.

Studies by Labov (1969), Stewart (1967, 1968) and Dillard (1967) have demonstrated the survival of the pigdin language the African captives learned in order to survive on slave plantations. An amalgam of standard English and African grammatical rules has survived, such that Dillard (1972) estimates 80% of American Blacks speak some mix of Black English, though all understand standard English.

The implications of language differences between White interviewers and Black respondents are particularly acute when it is observed that Black Americans, for the most part, accept the deficit assumption White Americans hold for their "deviant" speech. Many are ashamed of their "bad English." Studies of interviewer errors note a great many interviewers fail to probe following a partial response. (i.e., Willcock, 1956). White interviewers probably unintentionally influence Black responses by subtly "correcting" Black English, by rephrasing it, a process sure to curtail responses, particularly in open-end interviews.

Ethnographic studies of the sociolinguistics of Black speech have observed Black styles of speaking as distinctive as Navaho or Apache or Mexican-Americans. All three groups have been classified as sullen or uncommunicative by White researchers ignorant of the cultural influences affecting speech production. Philips (1972) investigated the conditions for speech usage among children of the Warm Springs Indian reservation in Oregon. In contrast to the speech situations encountered in the White reservation school, children were exposed to speech situations that emphasize leaderless discussions where everyone participates in the discussion. The childrens' silence in school cannot be understood without references to the sociolinguistic patterns in evidence in their home and community, patterns which are never followed in the school.

Naturalistic observation (i.e., ethnographic investigations) of Black speech behavior are beginning to sketch out patterns of speech usage in Black homes and communities. In contrast to the rigid question and answer routine that is standard procedure for opinion pollsters, Abrahams and Gay (1972) speculate that

> the Black model of discussion is not our first-you-speak-and-I'll-be-quiet, then-I'll-speak-and-you-be-quiet sort. Rather, the voice is used as an expression of the self and if one wants to be listened to he will not hestitate (at least among one's peers) to speak on top of other voices and to repeat

the same sentiments either until he is responded to by someone in the group or until someone else catches his attention. Corollary to this, when someone speaks he expects the overlap of other voices because that generally means that the others are listening and reacting to what he is saying. (Abrahams & Gay, 1972)

Amen. I hear you. Uh-huh. Yes Sir. Right on.

The Black call-and-response communication pattern survives in Black urban communities. What happens when White interviewers, or Black ones for that matter, try to impose the former model on a different communication style? Are the "don't knows," silences, and failures to probe partly a function of the Black respondents' desires to disengage himself from unfamiliar speaking styles?

Another potential source of error lies with the inability of standard English speakers to understand the subtleties and nuances of paralanguage cues, intonation, pauses, and nonverbal gestural clues (e.g., hands on hips, rolling of eyes) which accompany messages. Such interviewers may repeat questions, ask "what," or score some responses as "no opinions" or "don't know," or fail to probe where opinions are ambivalent because they are not able to understand the respondent.

The most comprehensive investigation of response effects in interviews concludes "response effects occur when the respondent has not arrived at a firm position on the issue and when the subject of the study is highly related to the respondent or interviewer's racial characteristics" (Sudman & Bradburn, 1974, p. 137).

The large response effects associated with interviewer respondent race differences (e.g., Schuman & Hatchett, 1974) might be mediated by either a failure to understand the concepts Black respondents use to think about topics, or sociolinguistic variations, or the White interviewer's reluctance to interview in Black neighborhoods (Wheeler, 1976). That reluctance may be communicated in subtle, nonverbal ways without the interviewer's awareness (Word, Zanna, & Cooper, 1974). The potential for serious error in the questioning and recording of responses is very high. Cannell, Lawson, and Hausser (1975) report tape recordings of interviewers at work showed interviewers frequently misclassify the responses given them when there are no race differences. Thirty-six percent of the questions were not asked as they were written, 20% altered enough to destroy comparability. When there are differences between the researcher's constructs and respondents' categories, the slippage might thereby be easily manifested in higher rates of interviewer misclassification. Having interviewers rate the responses of interviewees is even more apt to show errors, as such procedures are notoriously unreliable (Selltiz, Jahoda, Deutsch, & Cook, 1959, p. 355).

## Refusal Rates

Even when Black interviewers are used, and ethnographic procedures are employed to develop categories meaningful to respondents, there remains the problem of obtaining unbiased estimates of population parameters when large proportions of Black residents refuse to be interviewed. Greenberg and Dervin (1970) for instance report 33% of those contacted refused to participate. Jackson (1975) reports studies conducted by Michigan's Institute for Social Research obtained refusal rates of 40% in Black communities. We know of no investigations that describe the reasons why so many Blacks refuse to be polled, but speculate that Black sociolinguistic styles, fear of welfare and police investigators masquerading as interviewers, and alienation from dominant institutions are behind the extraordinarily high rates. Commercial pollsters, in contrast, typically report that 20-22% of the population cannot be reached after three call-backs, or refuse to be polled.

Since significant proportions of the Black population are not polled, systematic biases are built into summaries of Black opinions. People who refuse to be sampled are probably more alienated from dominant institutions, and thereby more critical of society in general.

The aggregate of the studies we have reviewed make it clear traditional survey research techniques leave much to be desired in ascertaining the attitudes of Black populations. The popularity of the technique, and its ubiquitiousness on American political and social science make it imperative that Black social scientists develop alternative techniques.

## Cross-Cultural Methods for Survey Research

Social scientists assume they know the universe of content extant in the minds of populations under study, and then create attitude questions from the presumed universe. A careful reading of the literature on minority attitudes and behavior cannot but lend to a healthy skepticism of such armchair procedures. What is needed is an explicit ethnographic investigation to discover the cognitive categories subject populations actually use in thinking about the topic under study. An effort must be directed at getting as broad a spectrum of feelings about the topic so that questions are not arbitrarily narrowed down.

In short, even minority scientists have to recognize that they may not know how minority persons evaluate a topic, or the universe of possible attitudes associated with it. A group of techniques developed by anthropologists for cross-cultural investigations of cognitive functioning provide the starting point for creating new attitude assessment procedures. Two recent studies have approached the task in ways that guide our thinking. In an attempt to understand a social subculture in the United States, Spradley (1972) utilized an ethnographic approach to the study of urban nomads, i.e., hobos. Starting with participant observation, Spradley identified elements of the culture that he felt were operationally significant within the domain of "places to sleep," for example. Then, structured statements about these elements of the culture were created, and presented to subjects to define domains, question frames, and "substitution frames." Without imposing his own categories on the population of nomads, Spradley was able to generate domains of attitudes and life functions relevant and meaningful to his subjects. Coincidentally, he found the cultural definitions of the general population were at considerable variance with the categories utilized by such nomads to describe or structure their value orientations.

For instance, while the majority culture describes hobos in terms of their deviant life-styles, i.e., drinking, unemployment, public drunkenness, the nomads think most about a place to sleep safe from police harassment. The predominant evaluative dimension in rating themselves and each other was found to be cleverness at garnering "a place to flop."

In the area of attitude measurement, Knapper, Cropley, and Moore (1973) utilized a procedure similar to ethnoscientific methods to study Canadian attitudes toward the use of seat belts. A series of interviews was first conducted with "experts" such as police, civic safety council, state transportation companies, etc. Interviews were taken with members of the general public. A variety of techniques were employed to get at underlying feelings and attitudes. After these, a series of open-ended, nondirected interviews were conducted with another sample drawn at random from the Canadian population. From the analysis of responses, categories relevant to the population under study were identified, and a questionnaire constructed. The actual wording of responses elicited from open-ended interviews was used in questionnaire items. Again, the questions can be said to have come from the cognitive domains of respondents, rather than being imposed on the population from investigators' viewpoints alone.

When persons are approached in public settings, while they are waiting in line at the store, waiting in the laundromat, at the barber shop, etc., refusals have been almost nonexistent. A recent study of Black theater patron's attitudes toward Black movies conducted in a public setting obtained very few refusals (Lovelace & Fairchild, 1975). However, in subsequent waves of interviews, when interviewers abandoned the random intercept and approached respondents in driveways, porches, and front yards of their homes, respondents began findings excuses why they could not be polled "right now." This trend increased as interviewers began ringing doorbells asking admission into the home. Clearly there are factors that generate anxiety about being polled in or near one's home that do not operate in public settings. Further, ethnographic research is needed along the lines suggested by Bauman (1972) for sociolinguistic research to understand the reluctance Blacks exhibit when approached at home.

## Implications for Future Research

The procedures described to create categories meaningful to respondents are not new, but well known to cross-cultural researchers. The utility of this decentering process is enormous in countries with heterogenous populations whose concepts of reality may vary along unknown dimensions. Certainly the experiences of the 26 million men and women of color in the United States are sufficient to expect major differences. In a related paper (Word, 1975), this author advanced the thesis that a large body of African habits of thought and speech have in fact survived slavery and second-class citizenship, and may be operating at unconscious levels of awareness.

The implications for researchers in such areas as personality measurement are clear. Just as cross-cultural investigations utilizing U.S. standardized instruments have had to not only translate, but interpret test items to make sure they tap the same things in other countries (e.g., Brislin, Lonner, & Thorndike, 1973), anytime questions designed to measure psychological dispositions are created with one population in mind, their utility for other populations must be demonstrated before results can be accepted. The question and answer sequence typically employed by dominant institutions, social service agencies, schools, counseling centers must be seen as an alien sociolinguistic mode for the large majority of Black respondents. Results of such interviews must be tempered with an understanding of the contributions of the mode to opinions expressed, especially as respondents decline to verbalize or elaborate.

| *Source* | *Control* |
|---|---|
| Incorrect Cognitive Categories | Ethnographic Elicitation of Concepts and Categories |
| Questions Misunderstood by Respondents | Questions Created From Responses to Open-Ended Questions |
| Responses Inhibited by Rigid Question-and-Answer Model | Flowing Conversational Style, Respondent Speaks His/Her Mind, Use of Tape Recorder |
| Paralanguage Cues Lost in Coding | Responses Recorded for Later Scoring |
| Errors in Coding Responses | Tapes Available for Reliability and Error Checks |
| Interviewer Uncomfortable in Black Neighborhood | Interviewers Recruited From Same or Nearby Neighborhood |
| High Refusal Rates | a) Interviewer Identifies Herself as Employee of Black Nonprofit Organization, Offers to Return at a More Convenient Time |
| | b) Respondents Approached in Public Places. |

**Figure 3.1.**  Sources of Error and Control Procedures

Finally, further research is needed, especially on sociolinguistic patterns in everyday communication, in contacts between pastoral counselors and persons seeking help, and on the cognitive styles utilized by Black Americans to describe themselves, their surroundings, and the universe of ideas meaningful to them.

## Method

Two phases were proposed. The funding organization was interested in garnering more valid samples of audience viewing indices than commercial rating services could provide. It was proposed to first utilize ethnographic techniques to elicit the concepts and categories Blacks use in thinking about television offerings. Then efforts were directed at trying to eliminate the other major sources of error.

Figure 3.1 illustrates the procedures utilized to control for sources of error.

### RANDOM INTERCEPT IN PUBLIC AND PRIVATE SETTINGS

In order to generate the categories Blacks use in evaluating the television fare they watch, a wide variety of persons had to be approached, and induced to talk about television in such a way as to reveal the categories. Getting Black people to talk to interviewers at all, as we have seen, is a serious problem. It was decided to adopt a random intercept procedure. Interviewers were dispatched to a variety of settings in San Jose, East Palo Alto, San Francisco, and Oakland, California. Settings included barber shops, beauty parlors, laundromats, stores, and on the street. No attempt was made to obtain a statistically valid sample, per se, since the task was generating concepts and evaluative dimensions, and garnering as wide a universe of attitudes as exist in the Black community. Samples did not represent the proportion of persons holding a particular view; we sought to insure the net was sufficiently broad to get the whole range. Interviewers sought interviews at a variety of times of day. Males and females of all ages were approached, roughly in proportion to their numbers as enumerated in the most recent census.

At the same time attempts were begun to control for some of the other sources of potential error. The break in the flowing conversational style necessitated by interviewers writing down responses was eliminated by having interviewers carry a small tape recorder, asking respondents to speak toward the microphone. To insure a more conversational flow, interviewers were instructed not to stand mute while respondents spoke, but to respond with "un-huh" "um-hum" "all-right" "I hear you" where appropriate such that the intercepts took on the style of a flowing exchange rather than I-speak-then-you-speak. Interviewers were trained to refrain from expressing opinions; their comments were to reinforce whatever respondents said.

The tape recorder was invaluable in correcting interviewer errors. After trial interviews, interviewers listened to their own and others' tapes. In this manner, errors in asking questions, or responding to interviewees were spotted and eliminated. Intercoder reliabilities could be obtained as well.

Interviewers were trained not to rephrase respondents' replies in any manner, since such a process might inhibit speakers ashamed of their "bad English."

In order to generate the evaluative dimensions Blacks use in thinking about television, the first 100 persons approached were asked to "talk about television. Anything you want to say about it." From the responses obtained in this first wave, some slightly more structured questions were asked, using the themes and categories that emerged from the first. By the third or fourth wave, more structured questions were created, using the actual words used as replies to the less structured questions. In one sense the waves were a pretest, pretesting the questions for their meaningfulness to respondents. But not merely a pretest, for the initial waves generated the evaluative dimensions from which questions were created. For instance, in the unstructured first few waves, the most frequently mentioned attribute used to evaluate statements about television is the concept "realness." Good-bad dimensions are almost always related to the degree to which respondents see dramatic or comedy shows approach their concepts of reality.

A recent study of attitudes toward the media in Boston found reality was a salient evaluative dimension (Jones, 1975). Such a finding, substantially replicated results obtained in California lends credence to the elicitation process.

The random intercept method allows comparisons of different question wordings, open versus closed question wordings, aided versus unaided recall, etc. At the same time, our interviewers have generated a body of anecdoctal data on factors that tend to enhance or delimit rapport in the survey situation.

Interviewers have noted:

Sometimes "don't know" responses are a way of saying, "Give me a minute to think about it." Interviewers have rephrased questions and politely asked again with surprisingly good results.

While "Um-hum" seems to reinforce respondents and encourages them to continue, "OK" seems to imply, "That's enough, stop!"

Sunglasses are very inhibiting to respondents.

Interviews proceed much better when interviewers concentrate on the respondent and less the task, or the answers. Respondents are quite sensitive to whether or not interviewers appear concerned with them as individuals.

Respondents open up better when interviewers do not immediately rush into the questions but begin a conversation after announcing their request for an interview, then proceed with the questions.

Timing is crucial in interviews. Respondents sense a lack of concern when interviewers seem to be rushing through the questions.

## Notes

1. This research was supported by NSF Grant No. AFR75-01757 to William D. Wright, principal investigator.

2. Some of the procedures described are the contributions of Sunny Bradford, Steve Millner, Abena Richardson, Richard Allen, and Douglas Fuchs. Their assistance is gratefully acknowledged.

## References

Abrahams, R. D., & Gay, G. (1972). Black culture in the classroom. In R. D. Abrahams & R. C. Troike (Eds.), *Language and cultural diversity in American education.* Englewood Cliffs, NJ: Prentice-Hall.

Baratz, J., & Baratz, S. (1970). Early childhood intervention: The social science base of institutional racism. *Harvard Educational Review, 40,* 30-49.

Bauman, R. (1972). An ethnographic framework for the investigation of communicative behaviors. In R. D. Abrahams & R. C. Troike (Eds.), *Language and cultural diversity in American education.* Englewood Cliffs, NJ: Prentice-Hall.

Brislin, R. W., Lonner, W. J., & Thorndike, R. M. (1973). *Cross cultural research methods.* New York: John Wiley.

Campbell, D. T. (1961). The mutual methodological relevance of anthropology and psychology. In F. L. K. Hsu (Ed.), *Psychological anthropology.* Homewood, IL: Dorsey Press.

Cancian, F. M. (1973). New methods for describing what people think. *Sociological Inquiry, 41,* 85-93.

Cannell, C. F., Lawson, S. A., & Hausser, D. L. (1975). *A technique for evaluating interviewer performance* (p. 4). Ann Arbor, MI: Survey Research Center of the Institute for Social Research.

Clark, Cedric X. (1972). Black studies or the study of Black people? In R. Jones (Ed.), *Black psychology.* New York: Harper & Row.

Clark, K. B. (1965). *Dark ghetto: Dilemmas of power.* New York: Harper & Row.

Dale, P. S. (1972). *Language development: Structure and function.* Hinsdale, IL: Dryden.

Dillard, J. L. (1967). Negro children's dialect in the inner city. *Florida FL Reporter, 5*(3).

Dillard, J. L. (1972). *Black English.* New York: Vintage.

Drake, H. M. (1973). Research method or culture bound technique? In W. M. O'Brien, D. Spain, & M. Tessler (Eds.), *Survey research in Africa: Its application and limits.* Evanston, IL: Northwestern University Press.

Frake, C. O. (1969). The ethnographic study of cognitive systems. In S. A. Tyler (Ed.), *Cognitive anthropology.* New York: Holt, Rinehart & Winston.

Frey, F. W. (1970). Cross cultural survey research in political science. In R. Holt & J. Turner (Eds.), *The methodology of comparative research.* New York: Free Press.

Greenberg, B. S., & Dervin, B. (1970). *Use of the mass media by the urban poor.* New York: Praeger.

Hsu, F. L. K. (1972). American core value. In F. L. K. Hsu (Ed.), *Psychological anthropology.* Cambridge, MA: Schenkman.

Jackson, J. (1975, August). Personal communication.

Jones, J. (1975, June). Personal communication.

Knapper, C. K., Crowley, A. J., & Moore, R. J. (1973). A quasi-clinical strategy for safety research: A case study of attitudes to seat belts in the city of Regina Saskatchewan. Regina, Saskatchewan: University of Regina.

Labov, W. (1969). The logic of nonstandard English. *Monograph Series of Language and Linguistics, No. 22.* (J. E. Alatis, Ed.) Washington, DC: Georgetown University Press.

Lovelace, V., & Fairchild, H. (1975, August). *Attitudinal effects of Black movies.* Paper presented at the Eighth Annual Convention of the Association of Black Psychologists, Boston, MA.

Mbiti, J. S. (1970). *African religions and philosophy.* Garden City, NY: Anchor.

McGuire, W. J. (1969). Suspiciousness of experimenter's intent. In R. Rosenthal & R. Rosnow (Eds.), *Artifact in behavioral research.* New York: Academic Press.

Nobles, W. (1974). *Extended self: Rethinking the so-called Negro self-concept issue.* Paper presented at Association of Black Psychologists Convention, Nashville, TN.

O'Brien, W. M., Spain, D., & Tessler, M. (Eds.). (1973). *Survey research in Africa: Its application and limits.* Evanston, IL: Northwestern University Press.

Philips, S. (1972). Acquisition of roles for appropriate speech usage. In R. C. Abrahams & R. C. Troike (Eds.), *Language and cultural diversity in American education.* Englewood Cliffs, NJ: Prentice-Hall.

Schuman, H., & Hatchett, S. (1974). *Black racial attitudes: Trends and complexities.* Ann Arbor: University of Michigan, Survey Research Center.

Selltiz, C., Jahoda, M., Deutsch, M., & Cook, S. W. (1959). *Research methods in social relations.* New York: Holt.

Spradley, J. P. (1972). Adaptive strategies of urban nomads. In J. Spradley (Ed.), *Culture and cognition: Rules, maps and plans.* San Francisco: Chandler.

Staff. (1975, June). National Black Omnibus, Inc., New York, N.Y. Poll. *National Black Media Coalition,* p. 5.

Stewart, W. (1967). Urban Negro speech: Sociolinguistic factors affecting English teaching. In R. Shuy (Ed.), *Social dialects and language learning.* Champaign, IL: National Council of Teachers of English.

Stewart, W. (1968). Continuity and change in American Negro dialects. *Florida Foreign Language Reporter, I.*

Sudman, S., & Bradburn, N. (1974). *Response effects in surveys.* Chicago: Aldine.

Thurstone, L. L. (1946). Comment. *American Journal of Sociology, 52,* 39-50.

Wheeler, M. (1976, April). Political polling, the German shephard factor. *Washington Monthly, 8,*(2) 42-50.

Willcock, H. E. (1956). Field observation: A progress report. In M. Harris (Ed.), *Selected papers on interviewers and interviewing* (pp. 125-131). London: The Social Survey and J.M.S.D.

Word, C. O. (1975). *An iceberg model of Black American behavior.* Unpublished monograph.

Word, C. O., Zanna, M. P., & Cooper, J. (1974). The nonverbal mediation of self-fulfilling prophecies in interracial interaction. *Journal of Experimental Social Psychology, 10,* 109-120.

Young, R. W. (1972). Language in culture. In R. D. Abrahams & R. C. Troike (Eds.), *Language and cultural diversity in American education* (pp. 101-104). Englewood Cliffs, NJ: Prentice-Hall.

# The Angela Davis Trial: Role of Black Psychologists in Jury Selection and Court Consultations[1]

THOMAS O. HILLIARD*
*Chairman, The Association of Black Psychologists*
HAROLD DENT,** WILLIAM HAYES, WILLIAM PIERCE
*All of Westside Community Mental Health Center*
ANN ASHMORE POUSSAINT

The process of jury selection represents a critical though relatively neglected area of scientific investigation. The monotonous regularity with which Blacks are seriously underrepresented point out the severity of this situation. Clearly this situation indicates a violation of a fundamental constitutional right provided by the Sixth Amendment: The right of every citizen to an impartial jury trial in criminal cases. Obviously, the present jury system represents a critical factor in the disproportionately large numbers of Blacks in prisons and correctional institutions. Unfortunately, the Black Panther Party has often been alone as a most vocal and consistent critic of the present jury system with its persistent demands that Blacks in court be allowed a jury of their peers.

This paper is designed to describe the role of Black Psychologists in the trial of Angela Davis and its implications for the future. Essentially, five Black psychologists from the Bay Area Association of Black Psychologists participated in the selection of jurors and served as psychological consultants to attorneys Howard Moore and Leo Branton, during the trial. More specifically, we were requested to provide psychological expertise in the assessment of sociopolitical attitudes and personality characteristics of the prospective jurors. The selection of the jury was viewed as a particularly key area in a political trial such as that of Angela Davis', especially since the trial was changed to Santa

© 1992 The Association of Black Psychologists
EDITORS' NOTES: *Deceased, ** Currently at the National Center for Minority Special Education Research and Outreach.

Clara County, which is reputed to be one of the most conservative counties in Northern California. Further, the fact that only one Black was on the jury list eliminated any possibility that Angela Davis would realistically be afforded a trial by her peers. The early removal of Janie Hemphill by the prosecuting attorney with a peremptory challenge demonstrated the reality of those fears.

After several conferences between the Black psychologists involved and attorney Howard Moore, it was decided that the idea of using our psychologists in the selection of jury, given a number of inherent limitations was a viable approach. We decided that our approach would be to first interview Miss Davis, who at the time was lodged in the County Jail in Palo Alto. The purpose of this interview was to get a "feel" for Angela, the type of image that she projects and to predict her courtroom behavior. Her courtroom behavior was deemed crucial as the jurors' actual perceptions of Miss Davis would be largely derived from her behavior in court. We conducted the interviews in jail, and went in pairs and on different occasions. This method was utilized so that we would have independent assessments and interviews of her on different days which would control for a transient mood that she may have on a particular day.

During the jury selection process, we quietly and inconspicuously sat in the courtroom and made observations of the behavior of each potential juror during the examination of *Voir Dire* conducted by the defense attorneys. The assessment of attitudes ranged from the prospective jurors' feelings and attitudes toward Blacks, Black militancy, Communism, women, and Miss Davis since certain feelings and attitudes toward her may have already developed due to the pretrial publicity and the considerable publicity she had received during her controversy at UCLA.

In addition to the assessment of attitudes, personal and personality characteristics of potential jurors were also evaluated. The assessment of the personal and personality characteristics of potential jurors presented a new angle in jury selection. While the relevance and significance of the social attitudes are well acknowledged, the role of personal and personality variables in the decision-making process of juries has been comparatively overlooked. The rationale underlying the personality assessment was based on the conjecture that the actual voting of a juror would be determined not only by their interpretation of the court evidence and their sociopolitical attitudes, but also by the interaction between their personality characteristics and the subsequent group dynamics in the jury room. Certainly the voluminous body of psychological literature on group norms and group pressure by social psychologists such as Asch and Sheriff support this direction. In the jury room when the peer pressures have been known to be considerable, personality variables may be the critical determinant in the decision-making process. A juror with positive attitudes toward Miss Davis may, on a personal level be a weak, dependent, and indecisive person, and, thus may be swayed by the group or a strong individual.

Since the actual *Voir Dire* or examination of the jurors was conducted by the defense attorneys, the observations and recommendations by the psychologists were communicated to Miss Davis and her attorneys during recesses and at the end of the day's sessions. During these conferences, we presented our perceptions of the jurors and would then compare perceptions with Miss Davis and her attorneys. Our observations would, then, be evaluated along with other data collected on the jurors. If a juror was seen to be inappropriate either in terms of attitudes or personality characteristics, it was suggested that the defense use a peremptory challenge to remove the prospective juror. In those cases, in which the defense attorneys and the psychologists were undecided about the juror, the psychologists suggested approaches and questions that could be used by the defense attorneys in order to obtain the data needed to arrive at a decision. It is important to note that as psychologists we offered our professional opinion to the defense lawyers; however, the final decisions were made by attorneys Howard Moore and Leo Branton.

In summary, the utilization of Black psychologists in the Angela Davis case represents a beginning model for functioning of psychologists in similar cases of Blacks in the courts. However, I must warn against any premature and overly optimistic and "magical" notion that once Black psychologists are involved in jury selection that suddenly all Blacks will be tried before a jury that is representative of the community. However, we do feel safe in saying that a genuine collaborative relationship between Black psychologists and Black lawyers will facilitate the selection of fair and impartial juries.

Additionally, a related area of investigation that presently is unexplored, virgin territory for behavioral scientists is the racism and cultural biases inherent in instruments and selection procedures for juries. For instance, Charles and Rita Boags (1971), a Black lawyer and a Black psychologist, in an article titled "The Misuse of a So-Called Psychological Examination of Jurors" indicated how culturally biased and inappropriate quasi-intelligence tests, have selectively excluded Blacks from jury service in California. They report that in Oakland, "The Clear Thinking Test," a jury qualification examination resulted in 81.5% of Blacks failing in comparison to 14.5% of Whites failing the examination. Further, despite the expert testimony of a number of psychologists in the pretrial proceedings indicating the lack of validity and the violation of acceptable standards of test construction by the jury qualifying exam, the test continues to be used in Los Angeles. They also reported, consistent with other studies of the jury system, that the use of registered voter lists and the number excused for economic hardships severely limit the number of Blacks on jury lists. Similar inequities in the selection of juries led the court in *Carmical v. Craven* to rule that when qualification tests for jury service lead to a disproportionately low number of Blacks on juries, the burden shifts to the state to explain why passing such a test is a necessary prerequisite to being an effective juror.

Finally, a small but suggestive body of social-psychological studies show certain definite biases in selection procedure in capital punishment cases. That is, in capital punishment cases, in which jurors must believe in the death penalty are to be removed from jury service, certain attitudinal biases are evident. For instance, one study found that "death qualified juries" were significantly more conservative in their political views, as measured by the Rokeach Conservatism-Liberalism scale than were members excluded for scruples against the death penalty. Other studies show respondents favoring capital punishment to demonstrate a significantly greater tendency to convict than respondents that do not believe in the death penalty. Their studies have considerable racial implications for there is evidence that Blacks in comparison to Whites are less likely to vote the death penalty.

Overall, the role of psychologists in the area of jury selection would appear to be a robust and vital one. Since the court system is a critical factor, the disproportionately large number of Blacks in prisons and correctional institutions, the role of Black psychologists in the area of jury selection offers a real possibility for *prevention,* in addition to the present *rehabilitative* efforts directed at reforms of prisons and penal institutions.

In closing, the words of Brother James Baldwin are a timely statement of the significance of the plight of Black Political Prisoners to the entire Black community:

The enormous revolution in Black consciousness which has occurred in your generation, my dear sister, means the beginning or the end of America. Some of us White and Black know how great a price has already been paid to bring into existence a new consciousness, a new people, an unprecedented nation. If we know, and do nothing, we are worse than the murderers hired in our name.

I know, then we must fight for your life as though it were our own—which it is—and render impassable with our bodies the corridor to the gas chamber. For, if they take you in the morning, they will be coming for us that night.

Therefore: peace.

## Notes

1. Paper presented at the National Association of Black Psychologists Convention on the Community Mental Health Symposium, "Black Psychologists and the Law," August 29, 1972.

2. Excerpts of "A Letter from James Baldwin to Angela Davis."

# 5  The Role of Black Psychologists in Black Liberation

## JOSEPH A. BALDWIN
*Florida A & M University*

To begin, let me state that most of us Black psychologists, I believe, have failed to fully understand the fundamental political meaning of our discipline, and of our role as Black psychologists within the discipline of psychology. Because we are an oppressed people who are engaged in struggle for our liberation (for our very survival—whether we realize it or not), then this fundamental failure or misperception on our part of the role of psychology and psychologists in the world order has crucial implications for the *survival* and *proactive development* of our people here in America, in Africa, and throughout the world.

Succinctly stated, my thesis is that up to this point in time, *we Black psychologists,* by and large, *have functioned in the service of the continued oppression and/or enslavement of Black people rather than in the service of our liberation from Western oppression and positive Black mental health* (unconscious on our part, no doubt, but the consequences are still the same). Thus, if Black people are to survive the 1990s and beyond without totally self-destructing (as our present course clearly seems designed to take us), then this "unconscious co-optation" in the psychological genocide of Black people by Black psychologists must cease. We Black psychologists must therefore cease to operate as unwitting coconspirators in the oppression of our own people through our active contribution to the psychological destruction of Black people.

This is a very strong indictment; so I am sure that many of us will think that it is totally unfounded and unjustified, and will try to write it

Correspondence regarding this article should be addressed to Dr. Joseph A. Baldwin, Florida A & M University, Tallahassee, FL 32307. Dr. Baldwin is a past president of ABPsi and presently serves as Professor of Psychology and Department Chair at Florida A & M.

This article was originally published in *Psych Discourse,* the Newsletter of the Association of Black Psychologists, Volume 17, Number 1, 1985, pp. 16–20, and with minor revisions is reprinted here with Dr. Baldwin's permission.

off as a mere personal ideological problem on my part. Notwithstanding the fact that some will undoubtedly find my thesis objectionable, let me try to demonstrate briefly some of the basic ways in which we Black psychologists have and continue in most instances to facilitate the continued oppression of Black people in our work as psychologists.

## Theory Building Activities

For example, in much of our work in developing or building theories (mostly designed to explain Black people's psychological functioning and behavior), rather than operating as intellectually independent scholars/scientists employing our true creative genius in conceptualizing and explaining the psychological universe from the framework of the true historical, philosophical, and cultural reality of African people, we instead follow the obscure and misrepresenting intellectual leadership of our "European mentors," our oppressors (the enemies of our people) by relying upon their historical, philosophical, and cultural reality to direct and inspire our theoretical developments. (Indeed, this is what they have in fact "trained" us to do, i.e., to be intellectual parasites). Therefore, in our so-called development of basic theoretical models of Black psychological functioning and behavior, as well as other psychological phenomena, we Black psychologists have *distorted* and *misrepresented* the true nature of the psychological universe relative to the true survival needs of Black people. This has occurred by our either employing directly some existing European models to explain Black people's psychological reality, or by attempting to "Blackenize" these same models in some obscure way to give them the false appearance of being relevant to the true survival needs of our people. In either case, however, we commit the fundamental "self-destructive" error of failing to look to our own "African" historical, philosophical, and cultural reality to give intellectual direction and inspiration to our theoretical developments. Thus, most of our so-called Black theories have in reality turned out to be reactive and obscure rather than being proactive and genuinely reflective of our African cultural/psychological reality, and therefore have little or nothing to do with the real survival needs of Black people on this planet. We definitely then must change this self-destructive tradition in the 1990s.

## Research Activities

In our so-called Black psychological research activities, we Black psychologists have similarly been unable to pose intelligent and "culturally relevant" questions or employ relevant methodologies in our attempts to examine and explain so-called Black psychological phenomena. In fact, up to this point in time, we Black psychologists have acted as if we are intellectually helpless when it comes to developing a science of psychology that is truly relevant to the real survival needs and proactive development of Black people. As seems to be true of our people generally, we have waited for White people—our oppressors— to do this for us (and I hope we all recognize just how ludicrous and dysfunctional this sounds). We allow Europeans to dictate to us what sources and kinds of data are valid for Black people, and what methods are legitimate in our research endeavors. All of this has usually resulted in our arriving at some of the most obscure, anti-Black and misrepresenting results imaginable in our so-called Black psychological research. I would even argue that up to this point most of our Black psychological research has reflected the backward situation of "drawing the cart before the horse," since we have generally been conducting so-called psychological research (and many of us continue to do so in an oppression-induced intellectual arrogance) in the absence of any basic and culturally relevant theoretical models to direct our efforts. Some of us have even become so caught up in the rhetoric of our European mentors (those who trained us and/or the White authorities and sources to whom we intellectually defer) that we tend to "devalue" the highly relevant theoretical work of some of our most brilliant Black colleagues because such work is not preceded by or concomitant to some Eurocentric-oriented empirical exercise. These kinds of reactionary/imitative attitudes and activities on our part then are also self-destructive to our developing a viable science of psychology that is truly Africentric and thereby relevant to the real survival needs of Black people. This anti-self orientation must also be changed in the 1990s.

## Clinical-Applied Activities

Similarly, in our clinical practice and applied activities, we Black psychologists—up to this point in time—have also been operating without any clearly definable models of positive Black mental health based on the African American cultural reality. As a result of our fundamental flaws in theory building and research (that I have already noted), we have been operating in our practical applications without really knowing just what we are doing when we attempt to deliver mental health and/or psychological services to our Black community.

In applied situations, we are naturally expected (by the public and ourselves) to be able to do something for our people (since we are "professionally trained" psychologists and our people come in contact with us usually at a time when they need something "done," i.e., they need some immediate "help" from us). Yet, we must recognize at the same time that "our Eurocentric-oriented training" has virtually rendered us incapable of providing any type of truly culturally relevant services to Black people. Thus, we have often ended up treating Black people as if they were "White people in Black skin," with only their experience of European racism being viewed as their distinguishing psychological characteristic. Since we really don't know what we are doing in the clinical service arena (without any clearly relevant Africentric base of knowledge to direct our approach to Black psychological functioning and behavior), and our people don't know what to do either, we Black psychologists—up to this point in time—have perpetuated a vivid illustration of "The blind leading the blind" in the critical area of mental health service delivery to the Black community. This situation also obviously represents self-destructive activity on our part, and it must be changed if we African Americans are to survive the 1990s and into the 21st century.

## Professional Development Activities

Finally, we can observe similar problems in the area of our professional growth and development as "Black psychologists," i.e., through relevant collaborative efforts with other Black psychologists and with Black social scientists generally to benefit the Black community, as in The Association of Black Psychologists (ABPsi). Instead of joining and being active in Black professional organizations like ABPsi, many— and probably most—of us Black psychologists join White professional organizations like the American Psychological Association (APA) supporting and participating in their professional efforts to maintain and further their oppression of African people. (Notwithstanding the fact that we usually commit those "self-destructive" acts unconsciously, and are largely ignorant of their true political consequences for the Black community, this does not alter the fact that we do it just the same.)

Let us take the United States as an illustrative case. Would you believe that most of the Black psychologists (the overwhelming majority, in fact) in this country—master's level and above—(as well as other Blacks who could benefit from membership in APBsi) are not members of our organization? At the same time, however, I would wager rather confidently that most of these very same individuals hold membership in APA (the White psychologists' group) and/or some other White-controlled professional organizations. Unfortunately, from my observations, I have found that we Black psychologists and social scientists (as a result of our educationally conditioned disrespect for Black life and Black institutions) tend to work harder in and for White-controlled organizations than in and for our own, and in so doing we participate in and contribute to our own racial-cultural oppression here in American society.

Now I am also aware of the fact that many of us have an extensive repertoire of rationales and justifications for our continuing to participate in various White-controlled organizations. However, after all of this defensive rhetoric has been expounded (and I believe that I have heard just about all of it), the bottom line remains that by diverting our intellectual and creative energies away from our own organizations through our participation in the various White professional groups (for whatever reasons), *the undeniable consequence is that we ultimately contribute to making their groups stronger and our own groups weaker.* And some of us have the audacity to criticize our Black professional groups' failures and shortcomings while at the same time perpetuating these self-fulfilling anti-Black prophecies. This is definitely "self-destructive" behavior that must be changed in the 1990s if our community is to survive into the 21st century.

Europeans have indeed twisted Black people's reality to the point where we actually believe that we have a vested interest in the further development of Western society, when—at the same time—history and the present show us consistently that *the vested interest of Western society itself is to oppress Black people.* This issue, as well as most of the observations that I have been discussing throughout this presentation, reminds me of the frequent indictment by our esteemed colleague the late Dr. Bobby Wright of Chicago, that "the only contradiction among Black people in America is that there are no contradictions." This statement (as I interpret it) means that because Europeans have turned Black people's reality upside down, we African Americans consequently engage in some of the most illogical, nonsensical and contradictory behaviors imaginable without recognizing or experiencing any contradiction (or nonsense) in them whatsoever. In other words, we regard ourselves as sane while constantly engaging in "insane" behaviors. Clearly then, where our professional growth and development as Black psychologists is concerned, we cannot serve two masters,

Brothers and Sisters, and we certainly can't serve other people's interests before we first serve our own, and still regard ourselves as sane and self-determining people. Thus, we must also change this self-destructive course that we have been on in our professional growth and development as Black psychologists during the 1990s and beyond.

### Redefining the Role of Black Psychologists

Now that I have indicted us for our intellectual meandering as Black psychologists, what then are we to do to change this embarrassing, self-destructive course that we have been on up to this point in time? Given this generally shameful state of affairs among us Black psychologists today, certainly it is imperative that during the 1990s and beyond, we must drastically *redefine* and *redirect* our role as Black psychological scientists and practitioners in relation to the psychological survival and proactive development of the African (Black) world. And for those of us who persist in claiming—despite the analysis advanced thus far—that we Black psychologists haven't really failed in assuming our true responsibility to our people to the blatant extent that I am proposing herein, then I suggest the following: Take a serious, honest, sober, and intelligent look at the predicament of our people generally, and then, please explain "intelligently" how our plight as a race of people has become so dismal if we Black psychologists have been doing our job in providing relevant-meaningful psychological leadership and direction for our people, up to this point in time. Unless you are blind as well as insane, then you will have to admit that, if we Black psychologists had been providing the Black community with the kind of progressive (Africentric) psychological leadership that our situation ultimately requires, surely we as a race of people would not be as close today to the brinks of self-destruction (and indeed we are) than ever before in our history here in Western society. For example, our homicides and suicides are increasing daily (especially among our young male population) as well as drug addictions, Black-on-Black homicide, and self-directed violence and crimes. In addition, we are still totally dependent on the Euro-American community in almost every important respect (as in slavery); we even presently acquire more college degrees and make more money as a group than ever before. Beyond this, most of us African Americans still don't know "who we are" (racially-culturally, philosophically, and historically speaking), despite the consciousness-raising 1960s, and "what our true interests are" relative to American society and the world order; and so on and so forth.

How can there be anything so meritorious in our past efforts as Black psychologists if our people are in such a self-destructive state, and it seems to be increasing every minute of every passing day. This suggests to me ( and I believe to any "sane" African person) that we Black psychologists haven't yet gotten our role together relative to what it could and must ultimately become, if our people are to survive the destructive psychological thrust of European oppression. While I do recognize and understand the powerful forces that have been working against our development as Black psychologists here in America, I still do not believe that the celebration of false, hollow, premature, and even irrelevant victories is appropriate or progressive if our ultimate goals of liberation and self-determination have not been substantively approached. For self-criticism is healthy and functional so long as it points in the direction that we must ultimately go.

In order to accomplish this redefinition and redirection of our role, I believe that Black psychologists in the 1990s must first of all recognize the true nature of the "European Worldview" (the reality structure of framework which dominates this society and Black people within it) upon which Western Psychology itself is based, and out-rightly "reject it." We must recognize that the basic nature of the European Worldview is diametrically opposed to the psychological development, survival, and liberation of Black people. In its basic nature, the European Worldview is "anti-Black/anti-African," and world history clearly suggests that we Blacks can continue to plead, pray, protest, and plot until we exhaust ourselves, but we will not be able to change this basic fact of the European Worldview to reality. It is "anti-Us," and we must therefore reject it once and for all since we are not and cannot become European people (although some of us seem to try our very best to defy nature in this regard). And in our recognition and rejection of this alien cosmology, we Black psychologists must then (and I believe naturally will) adopt or reinstitute our own "African" Worldview orientation and Africentric ideological posture in the totality of our professional activities.

## Black Psychologists and African Self-Consciousness

To clarify the full meaning of what I am proposing as the new (correct) role and posture of Black psychologists, let me briefly elaborate upon three key concepts in African Psychology: These are, *Cosmology, Social Theory,* and *African Self-Consciousness.* The concept of "cosmology," as earlier indicated, refers to the system for describing or organizing the reality structure/framework of a racial-cultural group. It comprises their particular ontology, philosophy, epistemology, axiology, system of logic, etc., all of which collectively defines their "Worldview," i.e., their collective orientation to reality, to nature, the cosmos. Furthermore, a people's Worldview also represents their "Social Theory." Their social theory defines for them who they are and what they represent, who is not them and what their relationships to other peoples, to nature and the world are, and ultimately their distinct *survival thrust*.

The European Worldview, as I have noted, is anti-African. If defines European people (i.e., European-Americans) as the center of the universe at the exclusion of all other peoples. Whatever is good and necessary for European people's survival, it projects and superimposes as good and necessary for everybody else on the planet. The central tenet of the Eurocentric social theory is "White or European supremacy and domination." *This is their survival thrust.* The African Worldview, our (African American's) true cosmology, on the other hand, while not excluding the significance of other racial-cultural groups, it similarly projects Black or African people (in essence, the core of "humanity") as the center of the social universe. In African Cosmology, we are "one with nature." Our African social theory similarly defines for us the true nature of our Africanity, what being African means biologically, psychologically, culturally, historically, politically, etc., as well as who is not African, what our relationship to non-African peoples should be, and ultimately what our survival thrust must be as African people.

At the individual level, all of this is operationalized for Black people in terms of what we call "African self-consciousness." African self-consciousness represents (relevant to our purpose here) the "conscious" expression of the social theory of African people (i.e., the practice by Black people of our Africentric social theory). Under normal and natural conditions, it reflects: (a) the recognition of oneself as "African" (biologically, psychologically, culturally, etc.) and of what being African means as defined by African Worldview; (b) the recognition of African survival as one's first priority value; (c) respect for and active perpetuation of all things African, African life and institutions; (d) a standard of conduct toward all things and peoples non-African, and toward all things and peoples, etc., that are "anti-African" (e.g., active opposition against all things that are anti-African). Collectively, these standards and activities represent the "survival thrust" of African people as dictated by our Africentric social reality.

Many of us who are presently engaged in the development of Afri-centric psychology firmly believe, in fact, that the highest level of positive Black mental health is this vital psychological orientation that we refer to as African self-consciousness. And given the obvious criticalness of the role of Black psychologists in the survival and liberation struggle of our people today, we definitely must get our own African self-consciousness together first, before we can truly help our people. This is what I believe is the correct philosophical, ideological, and operational posture that the Black psychologist must assume if our work is to be truly relevant to the real survival needs of Black people in the 1990s and beyond.

In the 1990s and beyond, then, we Black psychologists must be about developing basic models of the human psychological condition that are consistent with African Worldview and our contemporary condition. We must develop an intellectual orientation toward theory development and epistemology (or the methods through which we validate our Africentric reality) that is consistent with our liberation and self-deter-mination. And from these very fundamental developments, we will then be able to develop a relevant system of application in the vital areas of mental health service delivery and preventive-intervention strategies for our community. Again, in order for us to accomplish these extremely crucial developments, *we Black psychologists must first remove the alien Eurocentric self-consciousness from our own psyches* that has so distorted our perception of our true role in the Black survival and liberation struggle of today. Presently, we Black psychologists—I be-lieve—are as much "distorted" in our African self-consciousness as are our people generally. And given the critical nature of the need for psychological leadership and direction in the Black community today, the fact that we (Black psychologists) are also severely distorted in our African self-consciousness obviously places the Black/African world in a highly precarious predicament, stating it mildly. I believe that we (Black people) have totally misread and misunderstood our oppressors, and we have consequently misread and misunderstood the true nature of our conditions of oppression, and ultimately our true nature as African people. In the 1990s and beyond, then, let us as Black psychol-ogists work diligently toward discovering, extracting, and articulating those unassailable truths representing the fundamental realities of our African experience, and thereby serve the interest of the true survival needs of our people.

Many of us who are engaged in developing the science of Black/ African psychology also firmly believe that based on all of the evidence known to mankind, the one unassailable truth is that we Black people are the legitimate heirs of the *human essence* on this planet, and we Black psychologists must ultimately validate and articulate this legitimacy for our people. In our theory developments, our research, and our practical applications, we must begin to project a science of psychology that truly addresses the psychological needs of African people here in the diaspora and in Africa, and in so doing, we will assume our true role in forming the ideological nucleus of the African survival and liberation struggle today. For this I believe is our true responsibility as Black psychologists. Indeed it is our mandate based on our great ancient heritage, and on the historical suffering and constant struggle of our people.

Given then the *centrality* of our role in the survival and liberation struggle of African people we must not continue to exercise our role in the self-destructive fashion that has clearly characterized our past tradition. The countless numbers of Black men and women, boys and girls, and our Black babies whose rich African blood has stained the soil of this "nightmare" called America (or Southern African, or the whole European dominated world) demands that we Black psychologists must wait no longer in defining and articulating the correct philosophical/ideological basis for our people's struggle. Thus, just as our struggle must surely continue, we Black psychologists must intelligently, sophisticatedly, and religiously commit ourselves, our work, and our science to ultimate victory for our people.

# African American Families

One of the most important considerations that must be understood about African American families is that they are diverse, complex, and have multilevel complexity. This is despite centuries of writers who have attempted to make these families unidimensional and simplistic in role variations. The study of families has continually placed authors in the position of correcting stereotypes and misunderstandings that abound in the media, in policy discussions, and in everyday perceptions. One of the goals of this section of the book is the presentation of chapters that discuss the major variations that exist in families: in three-generation families, in middle-class families, and in the perception of two-parent stepfamilies and biological families.

One of the most common stereotypes that exists about African American families is that most are poor, probably on welfare, female-as-head, disorganized, and generally down-and-out. Contrary to this media presentation of families and the public policy debates that are held each year, the largest proportion of families are economically self-sufficient. The majority of African Americans are solid working class and about a third are middle class. The one common thread that runs throughout is that members of these families are of an economical level that is vulnerable to the external forces that exist in the outside society. These family members are more vulnerable to economic changes, as has been the experience in the latter part of the decade, with no hope for an economic turnaround. Changes in family structure occur with increased economic stress and show the importance for the study of stereotypes that are related to structural changes.

McAdoo examined the mobility patterns over three generations of families who were of middle-class status. Status depended on both spouses working or for the single parent to have higher status education and thus be eligible for higher paying jobs. Education was the one criterion that insured a greater degree of stability, for there were only limited means of passing on the gains of one generation to another. The extended family was very active; educational achievement was often made on the backs of hardworking poor parents. There are parenting concerns that were found to transcend social class. Parents were particularly concerned with preparing their children to live in a society that does not value the diversity that they represent in the wider society.

A cultural pattern that has continued in African American families is that of the strong extended family interactions and the kin help network. This is an African pattern that has continued to the present time. It has been found to exist at all economic levels and becomes an economic necessity when greater stresses are placed upon families. Wilson's chapter analyzes perceptions of grandmothers' parenting behavior that is dependent upon the family structure and whether or not the grandmother lives in the home with other family members. The complexity of family interactions is again emphasized in this chapter, for no one single description is possible for these 60 families. Grandmothers were more active with parenting in families with only the mother and children present, a family composition that must actively draw upon the wider extended family support networks. Although extended families may represent different domestic residences, they are pulled together through the cultural patterns of interlocking mutual helping networks.

Both the chapters by Miller and by Taylor remind us that race-related attitudes are a critical component of the socialization that occurs within the African American family. African American families, although they may share many commonalities in cultural orientation, are still quite heterogeneous in how they socialize their offspring, even about race. The Miller chapter demonstrates how family background variables influence the attitudes of African American families about racial discrimination along with interpersonal trust and self-esteem.

The marital bond is clearly the centerpiece of the family system. Much has been written about how social structural, personality, and background factors are associated with the success of the marital relationship. However, the chapter by Taylor adds that attitudes about one's own race may influence how one responds to one's own mate as another member of that race.

African American families have a tradition of mobilizing resources within the family and the community to ensure the survival and health of individual family members. The chapter by Bowman illustrates the efficacy of such resources among adult males experiencing role strain due to the difficulties they encounter in fulfilling the traditional roles of husband and father.

# 6 Upward Mobility and Parenting in Middle-Income Black Families

**HARRIETTE PIPES MCADOO**
*Michigan State University*

A review of the various cycles in research on non-poor Black families is related to various movements within the Black community. The relevance of various SES classifications and characteristics of economically mobile families are explored. The roles of dual-parent employment, high mobility aspirations, and discrimination on parenting are covered. In a sample of 178 families with 305 parents, the extended family help network was found to be still an important source of support, from kin and fictive kin, for newly mobile and those one or two generations of middle-income status, yet the reciprocal obligations for help received were not felt to be excessive.

The study of the Black family has gone through many stages: initially the family was denied an existence, then viewed as pathological and disorganized, defended as a more or less reactive structure, viewed as a culturally different phenomenon, and lately it has had race ignored as a variable in preference to class and individual initiative. For the past twenty years we have clearly been going through a revisionist phase of the study of Black family life and socialization. Several reviews (Aschenbrenner, 1975; English, 1974; Nobles, 1974; Scanzoni, 1977), and empirical or historical studies (Chase, 1977; Gutman, 1976; Heiss, 1975; Jones, 1965; Nobles, 1976; & Hill, Note 1) have been conducted to examine critically some of the various concepts of the Black family. The weight of information on Black families is only now having a faint impact on how Blacks are viewed in the traditional social science literature. Throughout all of these stages only one segment has usually been studied: those who are under the greatest economic stress.

Every few years one will find articles that try to find out "if the Black middle-class families are still as bad as they used to be." The assumption that is accepted without challenge, often apparently by both Black and White writers, is of the same negative image. Recently several

This research was supported by a grant from the Department of Health, Education and Welfare, Office of Child Development 90-C-631(1). Harriette Pipes McAdoo, 101 Morrill Hall, Michigan State University, East Lansing, MI 48824.

writers for lay audiences have attempted to compare Frazier's work with the study being reported here to find out if Frazier's views were supported by contemporary data. It must be remembered that Frazier's (1939) early focus on social class and family life evolved from his doctoral research at a leading White institution, where he had to meet the criteria of a White faculty and later of White colleagues, all of whom had their prevailing images. In addition, he had to meet the needs of the publishers. Those familiar with the problems now associated with getting a publisher for Black-oriented research can only imagine the situation in the 1930s. It would have been impossible to get anything published that contained any other view of the Black family. Frazier was presenting the Black family through the filters of the acceptable negative conceptual framework of his time. When Frazier's works are viewed within their proper context, that of the situation of the Black community and of White values systems, it is impossible to make a simplistic summary of his work. Unfortunately, too many writers read only certain parts and focus only on these parts. There is a great richness of data to be found when his total works are examined.

In his study, Frazier (1939) outlined two distinct segments of the Black middle class: the traditional Black middle class and the Black bourgeoisie. The traditionalists were those Blacks who, through frugality, abstention, and industry, were able to receive the education that allowed them to become teachers, preachers, or doctors early in the 1900s. They lived with great attention to morality and the maintenance of conservative appearances. Some were descendants of free men, freed men, or house slaves. Others were the newly mobile who sought and gained entry into the upper crust of Black society. Family contacts and education were often just as important as money, or more so. These traditional middle-class Blacks, according to Frazier, attempted to conform to the tradition of gentleness and manners. There was often a strong identification with the poorer Black masses, for rigid educational and residential segregation prevented the physical or emotional removal from the Black community that may be possible today. Some of these two- or three-generation middle-class families still exist today. These families produced many of the leaders in civil rights, education, and community leadership in later generations. There was a strong pride in Black achievement. These families do not seek publicity; in fact, they may shun it, and thus media coverage is rare. Their very invisibility has contributed to the view that the middle-class stratum has just come into existence.

The second wave of middle-class Blacks, according to Frazier, arrived during the early 1940s and 1950s. This group was mobile into middle class on the basis of the acquisition of money alone. This caused a break from the more traditional old-line family values. A class- and value-conflict often was found between the two groups. The gradual loosening of the rigid housing segregation was seen as resulting in a breaking down of the strong identification with the larger Black underclass. This second group comprised Frazier's notorious "Black bourgeoisie." These families were often more flamboyant with their possessions, and were frequently viewed by the wider society as ostentatious. Blacks were seen as having "made it" when they had a high level of consumption, or when they became as assimilated as possible into White society. Some middle-class Blacks were often out-group oriented, and felt embarrassed by their blackness. The mode selected to obtain mobility often was assimilation. This move was supported by the wider White environment that saw no value in Black culture or achievement. Many Blacks felt that if they acted, dressed, and went to school with Whites, they would eventually be accepted and treated fairly by them. This group has received much wider media coverage and, therefore, has become projected as the only middle-class Blacks in existence. The failure of their dream led to the next movement within the Black community.

A third wave of movement in the Black community occurred in the 1960s and 1970s during the Civil Rights and the Black Consciousness movements. The Civil Rights thrust was to open legal barriers so that Blacks could have the right to wider opportunities. Because of the double-bind of discrimination and limited opportunities, often those who benefited most from the movement, in spite of wide community support of these efforts, were those who were upwardly mobile. Adults who knew that it was too late for them still marched with the hope that life would be better for their children. The leaders, who were the children of both the traditionalists and the Black bourgeoisie, came from community churches and Black colleges.

The Black Consciousness movement grew out of the frustration of the interracial experiences during the Civil Rights attempts and resulted in a reevaluation of pervasive current out-group orientation. The awakened Black consciousness was not new; rather it grew from the values of earlier Black movements and their strong community identification and racial pride. Surprisingly, many of these activists were college and graduate students who were children of the older traditional classes. Changes began at first on an emotional level of group pride and identification, and then continued to the reassertion of African American continuities and to a growing own-group orientation. The process that almost all Black intellectuals experienced during that period has been called a "convergence experience" by Cross (1978). A period of intense activity ensued that broke out in many forms. One such thrust was the growing number of Black researchers who attempted to destroy some of the current myths by conceptualizing the strengths found in the Black community (Billingsley, 1968; Hill, 1971; Staples, 1978). Other researchers (Nobles, 1974; Sudarkasa, 1981) went on to look for African carryovers to attack the myth that Black families were void of all culture, whereas cultured remnants of other ethnic groups were widely accepted. Some writers were focusing on the family myths, and others were addressing myths about the Black child. One important area was that of personal race identity and the "self-hatred" hypothesis in which Black children were seen as hating themselves and their racial group, and as having low self-concepts. This myth was tested repeatedly and found lacking (Baldwin, 1979; Banks, 1976; H. McAdoo, 1970, 1977a; J. McAdoo, 1979).

## Class Status and Upward Mobility

The traditional models of status attainment are of limited relevance to Blacks in general because of their nearly exclusive focus on SES (Allen, 1976). Class status in the wider community is usually based upon education, occupation, and financial achievements and/or upon birth into a family with an established status. According to Scanzoni (1977) the traditional interaction between race and social class has resulted in a Black ethnic subsociety or "ethclass." Ogbu (1978) further stated that the inferior status of Blacks fits all of the criteria of caste stratification, rather than class stratification. A caste system exists when an individual's lifetime position within a status/class group is permanently determined at birth by skin color and/or racial group membership. Being Black has become synonymous with lower caste status. Blacks with equal educational status receive fewer rewards because of the discrimination against their ethnic group. In other words, because of the institutional and economic racism, achievement of all the trappings of middle-class society (education, occupation, money) will not bring comparable "pay-offs."

The same status criteria are also found in the Black community, with additions that are the result of the history of this ethnic group. Lack of access to the status-giving institutions in the past resulted in a Black caste-like status system superimposed upon the larger status pyramid. For Blacks, the line between social classes was flexibly drawn. Statuses that would have been middle class in White communities were regarded as upper class in the Black communities because jobs that allowed a feeling of power, mobility, and freedom from hard physical work were considered higher in status. Gradually, with the increase of wider opportunities, the caste system expanded until it became similar to the White status groupings.

In the present study, the standard SES classification data were collected and then modified. The standard Hollingshead-Redlich rating procedure, which places greater emphasis on occupation than on education, was seen as unsatisfactory. This was considered an unrealistic scoring scheme for the subjects' SES because job discrimination against Blacks truncates job attainment commensurate with education. This meant that five different calculations were used to determine SES: (a) the standard one; (b) a modification of Hollingshead-Redlich in which education was weighted greater than occupation; (c) self-ratings over three generations; (d) standard occupation status ratings, and (e) standard education status ratings. The modified scaling was used predominantly.

In addition to the standard SES determinants, the legacy of slavery left an additional layer of unique status criteria. Skin color and hair type in the past have been major intragroup divisive factors. These factors have had an impact on status in the community and choice of marriage partners. Preferences for White-oriented physical attributes have been strong in the past and are reportedly decreasing, although no studies to date have adequately addressed this issue.

Although historically influential, the proportion of Black middle class remains small. According to the most recent reports from the Bureau of the Census (U.S. Department of Commerce, 1979), the proportion of Black middle-class families earning $25,000 or more has increased from 1% in 1969 to 9% in 1976. But the proportion of middle-class families declined by 1981 because of the impact of inflation and changes in governmental fiscal policies. There has been a related decline in Black total family income earned in relation to that of Whites from 61% in 1970 to 51% in 1979.

Blau and Duncan (1969) have maintained that the more education the Black male receives, the more disadvantaged he becomes when compared with Whites of similar education. Therefore, there is less incentive for Blacks to make the sacrifices that are greater. Blacks have advanced, but Whites have moved even farther. This is in direct contrast with Wilson's (1978) statement that race has become increasingly less important than class in determining one's eventual status.

Surprisingly enough, wider media coverage is now being given just at a point in our history when the actual proportion of middle-class Blacks is decreasing in relation to Whites. An unusual interest has been shown in the Black middle class in the press (Roberts, *New York Times,* lead article of 12/3/78; Caldwell, 1978; Coombs, 1978; West, 1979). The reason for such coverage has been questioned by many observers. One explanation that has been given is that it is being done to mold public opinion. With the economic slowdown now occurring, in which social services may have to be drastically cut, the emphasis is now being placed on the Black middle class, even though they represent only 7% to 10% of Blacks. If the general population feels that Blacks have "made it" and are living middle-income life-styles or have cushion supports for the "truly needy," then it will be easier to justify reducing services, affirmative actions, and supportive educational programs without public censure. The majority Black under-class would then be allowed to drift out of the public's consciousness. One feature that these writers, almost all of whom are non-Black, have emphasized is the frictions that are growing between the "haves" and "have-nots." To date, no empirical studies have addressed this topic, but articles repeatedly emphasize this point.

## Maternal Employment and Mobility

One characteristic of Black family mobility that differs from White families is that stability and upward mobility have required that both parents work. The two-parent units had higher comparable earnings than other units, for they earned 81% of White income ($16,726 : $20,680). But the higher Black income represented both parents working, while only half of White families had both parents working outside of the home. The model of working mothers has resulted in a minimum of mother versus worker conflict. This involvement in economic support had led to a greater egalitarian husband-wife relationship, a strength often mistaken for dominance by outsiders.

Status attainment is less clear and certain for women than for men regardless of race (Scanzoni, 1977). In spite of the increased numbers of workers outside of the home, women still tend to gain their status from their spouses. There are problems that are unique to Black women. The Black female has less control over "status destiny," for her status is linked to the pool of eligible Black men who are constantly bombarded by occupational discrimination. For a wide variety of factors (low birth/ sex ratio, high incarceration rate, early death, homosexuality), fewer Black males of comparable or higher status are available for these women. For this reason Black middle-class females, and those with mobility goals, are under greater stress. They more often must select mates from a variety of lower-status levels than do the comparable White females.

Scanzoni (1977) found that a Black male from a middle-class family had a greater chance of maintaining that status via marriage than a Black female from a middle-class family. Only 28% of the middle-class women in his sample were able to marry middle-class men. Seventy-two percent had married working-class men. In contrast, Black males had a choice of a wider variety from those of his own status and females of lower status. Their wives took on their middle-class status. But the status of the middle-class women often fell or caused class strains. Such strains may have an impact on male-female relations and on the socialization of their children.

## Socialization of Children for Achievement

The basic assumption about socialization is that it occurs as the result of the behavior of parents that reflects their basic values and life-style. Black parents must prepare their children to function in both a Black and a White arena. Parents, through their overt and covert behaviors, attempt to help their children become prepared for their positions in the duality of Black existence (H. McAdoo, 1974). This is no easy task, for the very values that permeate the wider society are, for the most part, detrimental to the development of their positive self-esteem, ethnic identity, and achievement in school. Earlier empirical studies have shown that these Black children have been able to maintain positive feelings of self-worth, while they have tended at an earlier age to be out-group (White) oriented but became markedly own-group oriented (Black) by late childhood (H. McAdoo, 1977a).

A Black family that is able to be upwardly mobile has to ensure that these gains will not be lost in the next generation. The traditional route to the maintaining of parental achievement has been education that can be turned into economic gains. Excess wealth to flow into the next generation has not existed. The emphasis upon education exists because education is seen as the most viable route by which their status can be maintained and the *only* route open in the past.

The emphasis on education during socialization is usually made without clear knowledge of those parental behaviors that are supportive of this desired achievement. A review of the literature indicated a cluster of characteristics that would help. Billingsley (1968) stated that achievers tended to come from strong families. Blau and Duncan (1967) found that the optimum family conditions that help mobility were economic and social support, social support including molding thought patterns, language, encouragement to study and achieve, and role modeling. Maternal employment has a definite impact on the socialization of the family's children. Kohn (1977) found that when a mother works, greater stress is placed by both parents on the child's developing autonomy, rather than on obedience. The higher the mother's status, the greater the emphasis on autonomy. Autonomy is another of the characteristics associated with educational achievement. Other clusters of behavior that are found to be related to achievement are warmth, goal orientation, positive self-esteem, closeness within families, and the development of independence in the child's thinking.

Greene (1976) found that Black parents' educational wishes for the child influenced to some degree the academic performance of children at the high school level. But these wishes had a negligible influence in elementary school. Blau and Duncan (1967) also found that interpersonal stress on education is the strongest Black aid. They, along with Scanzoni (1977), found that the father's occupation was the strongest predictor of the child's education and occupation. In contrast, Allen (1976) did find that for Whites the father represented the pivotal factor, but for Black male adolescents the mother constitutes the pivotal factor in the family social system. Her aspirations, her level of attainment, her education, and her role modeling determined her son's level of aspirations. One important factor of Allen's sample, though, was that the mothers were better employed than the fathers, consistent with Scanzoni's (1977) findings. In other words, the education of the higher-status parent, regardless of sex, was the mediating factor.

Allen (1976) found that Black achievements were high if the parent-son relationship was close and if parent aspirations were high. But for White teens, parental approval, not aspirations, was more important than for Blacks. Role modeling of both parents and in male reference groups had a great influence on job mobility (Scanzoni, 1977). In working Black middle- and underclass families Scanzoni found a "strong father-figure," a father or male-reference person, and not the stereotyped matriarch.

The presence of one or two parents was not found by Scanzoni (1977) to be prerequisite to family stability in spite of the financial vulnerability of single-parent homes. He found no difference in occupational achievement between one-parent and two-parent homes because these Black families were able to overcome many hurdles with the help of their extended family support network.

Another characteristic commonly cited about middle-class Black families is the tendency to protect their children. Many tended to fear the negative influence of children who were not achievers, and attempted to isolate the child from the stings of racism. One of the results of the parents' protectiveness could be a lack of preparation for the stresses that will be encountered later. An example is the quote of a minister's son, enrolled in college, who was studied by Coles (1968):

> They brought us up to work and study, and get along nice and easy with people—the way they do. So it's a shock, leaving home to find people swearing at you, and not even being able to talk to them, to ask them why they're saying what they are. (p. 139)

Both Blacks and Whites are hurt by overprotectiveness. Wayne (1978) found that suburban families who move because of the schools have children who are so sheltered as to be unprepared to function in the wider world. Therefore, the overprotectiveness may avoid pain for the children now, but may leave them unprepared for the real pain that is guaranteed them as adults.

## Kin Help Network

The extended family network has long been cited (Billingsley, 1968; Hill, 1971; Staples, 1978) as one of the supportive structures that have enabled Black families to transcend a multitude of circumstances across the generations. This network, combined with the church and a close community network, has played an important role in the socialization of adults into parents, and of children into their roles in the wider society.

The "extended family" no longer is composed of the three-generation domestic arrangement, but refers instead to the close relations within and across generations (H. McAdoo, 1978; Sussman & Burchinal, 1962). The typical urban family is composed of a neo-nuclear or modified extended structure (Litwak, 1960). The family lives in separate nuclear domestic units that function independently, but are linked in an intense arrangement of shared help. This system of relating in a bilateral or generational manner is the basis of the kin help network patterns. Billingsley (1968) stated that Black families go beyond the blood kin to interact and to develop mutual aid within the wide community. These friends and neighbors are intimately incorporated, and become like kin, or "fictive kin."

The kin network was found by Stack (1975) to be an extended cluster of kin related through children, marriage, and friendship who rally to provide basic domestic functions of feeding, clothing, and child care. These ties were often formed between the women. The residents of a house may have changed, but they were part of a single network that had a strong continuity over time.

Operational definitions were then made of the theory components of the extended family and upward mobility. *Extended family* was defined as a measure of the extent and intensity of involvement with kin and the reciprocal exchange of goods, services, and ongoing emotional support. Inherent in any exchange is a degree of reciprocity. The reciprocal obligations that result from the support were hypothesized to be clearly understood by all family members. Yet this generalized reciprocity was not expected to be perceived as being excessive. Upward mobility was defined as the educational and occupational status changes that occurred over three adult generations, in both the maternal and paternal lines. It is assumed that if an African American cultural pattern existed, it would be present in families that were newly mobile and also in families that had been of middle-class status for two or three generations. Therefore it was predicted that families of all mobility patterns would be equally involved in the kin help exchange.

## Basic Assumptions and Hypotheses

Socialization of Black children is not an easy task, even in middle-class homes. In addition to the normal joys and strains of child rearing, the Black parents face a multitude of additional tasks that they must perform as they prepare their children for adulthood. Traditionally the extended family and the closed Black community have formed a protective shield around the family members. As families become geographically mobile, and some of them become economically mobile, the domestic unit's sources and forms of support may change. In order to empirically examine the role that the extended family help networks play in the maintenance of stability in the socialization of upwardly mobile families, this research project was designed. The theoretical orientation of the project was twofold: (a) that the socialization of children in Black families differs from that of other families because of their nonsupportive wider environment, and (b) that the extended kin network facilitates upward mobility.

The conceptual framework for the study was provided by the necessarily defensive reflection of the positive cultural aspects of Black life (Billingsley, 1968; Hill, 1971; and others). We were at the point in our theoretical development where it was felt that we should empirically examine the identified supportive components of Black life, such as the roles of the extended family and of the Black church. The study began with the theoretical hypothesis that the support provided by the extended kin network patterns, found so often in Black families, would facilitate the upward mobility of their younger members. The assumption was made that if extended family patterns were functional and supportive, they would be found at all economic class levels and over different stages of upward mobility over generations. Another assumption was that the kin help patterns were not simply coping mechanisms that are used in poverty and discarded when families are no longer poor, but were cultural patterns that were supportive regardless of mobility pattern of status. This study was designed because no empirical studies of the Black middle-class have been found in the literature. The result has been that gaps are left in our knowledge of this segment of Black families—gaps that have been closed by a writer's own personal experiences or biases. There are various reasons why the Black middle class has been ignored. Many Black researchers have felt that poverty-related problems are so pervasive that their energies should be concentrated where the need is greatest. On the other hand, non-Blacks have tended to distort or ignore *all* Black families, in a perpetuation of stereotypes that have matched the wider societal view of Black families.

One of the most difficult concepts for writers about Black families to grasp is that of the diversity that exists among the Black families. For whatever reason, repeated attempts are made to describe Blacks as fitting into only one mode. This lack of the awareness of diversity is probably the most insidious form of discrimination that is imposed upon all minority-group members. This element was confronted continuously over the last five years as concentration has been placed upon one element within the range of Black families: those who are upwardly mobile. Because of the concentration of research effort on poor Black families, our studies are the only ongoing empirical examination of economically secure Black families (H. McAdoo, 1977b).

## Method

To test these hypotheses, a study was conducted with the following controls:

1. Demography
   (a) Half urban
   (b) Half suburban
2. Family type (to reflect the U.S. Census)
   (a) Two-thirds with two parents
   (b) One-third with one parent
3. Mobility pattern
   (a) Born working class, two generations
   (b) Born middle class, two or three generations
   (c) Born working class of parents who were born in poverty

Background data on three generations were collected.

### SAMPLE SELECTION

To test the impact of these family factors during mobility, parents who were already in the middle-income range were selected as that target group. They were chosen from a mid-Atlantic metropolitan center to fit into the independent variables of demography and family type. One half were in the District of Columbia, and the other half were in the nearby suburban town of Columbia.

Columbia is a ten-year-old planned new town located in Maryland, between Washington and Baltimore. Although unique in the convenience of its urban planning, it is typical of pleasant suburban sites across the country. A nearly complete list of all Black families was constructed from membership lists of every Black organization, from church rolls and lists gathered from public and private preschools, and from elementary school rosters. These lists were then assembled into one master list from which the names and their replacements were randomly selected. The suburban sample was selected first, and then Census tracts matching the suburban sample on income and education were selected in the urban center. All of the families had to meet the following criteria: (a) They were Black; (b) they were at that time in the middle-income status, according to the Department of Labor current level; (c) they had school-age children under the age of 18 years living in the home; and (d) one parent was over the age of 25 years. The parental age cut-off was used because the period before age 25 is the time during which the prerequisites of socioeconomic status are developed: education, occupation, and income level. By age 25 the SES level begins to become apparent.

DATA COLLECTION PROCEDURE

In light of the differing views of the impact of mobility on the extended family relationships, a questionnaire was developed to explore this variable. The original interview questions were field-tested twice before the protocols were considered to be in final form. The McAdoo Family Profile Scale was used to gather data on:

1. Basic background information
2. Extended familialism and kin help scale
3. Educational and occupational mobility over four generations
4. Family structure and parental decision making
5. Schedule of recent life experiences
6. Family size change
7. Comfort with child care
8. Satisfaction with life
9. Preference for and utilization of family support systems.

In each family, the father was interviewed for two hours by a Black male interviewer. The mother was then interviewed separately for two-and-a-half hours by a Black female interviewer. Each parent was then asked to fill in personal data sheets, at their leisure, for 45 minutes, that provided background demographic information and three separate scales.

In one-parent homes, the head of the household, regardless of sex, was asked to fill out a background data sheet on the other parent. Although there was some missing information on the nonresident or deceased parent, we were thus able to get some mobility data on both sides of all of our families. Comparisons of both the paternal and maternal line were made to allow a more accurate analysis of the family's mobility over three generations (only 17% had different patterns between the lines). Data were obtained from, or about, both parents in the home, but the family as a whole was the unit of analysis. In cases of conflicting information between the parents on mobility patterns and certain background variables, the father's data were consistently selected in two-parent homes. When conflicts occurred on child-rearing and on kin help and interaction variables, the mother's responses were selected.

## SAMPLE

All of the 305 parents, representing 178 domestic units in mid-Atlantic areas, were Black, and were minimally of middle income ($10,000 for single parents, $14,000 for two parents). They all had school-age children in the home, and at least one parent was over 25 years of age. The average age of the mothers was 37 and of the fathers was 40. Half (51%) of the children were boys, with 2.37 children on the average in each family, and were of similar age range in both sites. Parents were born in the mid-Atlantic states, and the grandparents were born in the South and migrated to the East and North.

Seventy-two percent were two-parent families, and 28% had one parent in the home. Of the single mothers, 89% had been married previously (see Table 6.1). Contrary to prevailing images, the majority (67%) of the families of orientation in which the present subjects grew up were working class with both parents present. Thirty-three percent were raised in one-parent homes. No significant family-type difference was found in the structure of families of orientation between mothers who now reside in one- or two-parent homes. Seventy-eight percent of the now-single mothers and 82% of the married mothers were raised in two-parent homes (see Table 6.2). It must be reiterated that the majority (85%) of their families as children were working class and not middle class.

Forty-one percent of the parents had graduate or advanced professional degrees, and 53% had some college training (see Table 6.3). The fathers were significantly better educated than the mothers. Mothers earned an average of $12,000, and fathers earned an average of $22,000. Fathers tended to be managers or executives, while mothers were managers, teachers, or administrators. The mothers tended to contribute only one-third of the total income and were less well educated than the fathers. Therefore, the family's status was determined greatly by the education and occupation of the father. The mother's income was used as an extra stabilizer that allowed continuation of their middle-class status.

After their education and occupation had been combined using the Hollingshead-Redlich scale, their social economic status was then calcu-

**TABLE 6.1** Frequency Distribution of Sample by Demography, Family Type, Sex and Marital Status of Head of Household, and Family Structure

| | Urban | | Suburban | | Total | |
|---|---|---|---|---|---|---|
| Group | f | % | f | % | f | % |
| Demography Total | 88 | 49 | 90 | 51 | 178 | 100 |
| Parents interviewed | | | | | | |
| Mothers | 87 | 56 | 87 | 58 | 174 | 57 |
| Fathers | 68 | 44 | 63 | 42 | 131 | 43 |
| Total | 155 | 100 | 150 | 100 | 305 | 100 |
| Sample | | | | | | |
| Two-parent units | 68 | 77 | 60 | 67 | 128 | 72 |
| One-parent units | 20 | 23 | 30 | 33 | 50 | 28 |
| Total | 88 | 100 | 90 | 100 | 178 | 100 |
| One-parent units | | | | | | |
| Mother as head | 19 | 95 | 27 | 90 | 46 | 93 |
| Father as head | 1 | 5 | 3 | 10 | 4 | 7 |
| Total | 20 | 100 | 30 | 100 | 50 | 100 |

| *Marital Status* | Mothers | | Fathers | | Total | |
|---|---|---|---|---|---|---|
| *One-Parent Head* | f | % | f | % | f | % |
| Divorced | 21 | 46 | 3 | 75 | 24 | 48 |
| Separated | 17 | 37 | 1 | 25 | 18 | 36 |
| Single | 5 | 11 | — | — | 5 | 10 |
| Widowed | 3 | 6 | — | — | 3 | 6 |
| Total | 46 | 100 | 4 | 100 | 50 | 100 |

lated. Using the modified procedure, (a) 42% were in Class I, or upper-middle-class status, (b) 31% were in solid middle class, and (c) 9% were at the lower-middle-class level. The Modified SES ratings developed for the study rated more families higher than did the Standard procedure, indicating that occupational discrimination against the Black male *had* truncated his family's occupational mobility. Subjects rated themselves significantly lower on SES than they actually were.

Eighty-five percent were born working class, and 15% were middle class. Four different mobility patterns over three generations were found: (a) 62% were born working class and became middle class; (b) 23% had grandparents in poverty and had working-class parents; (c) 9% were middle class over three generations; and (d) 6% had parents who had moved up to middle class. No one in this generation went from under-class directly to middle-class status, but 6% of the grandparents had made such a jump. It would appear that such a sharp upwardly

**TABLE 6.2** Frequency Distribution of Structure of Present Family by Demography, and Structure of Family of Orientation by Family Type and Sex of Head of Household

| Family Type | Structure | Defined | Urban f | Urban % | Suburban f | Suburban % | Total f | Total % |
|---|---|---|---|---|---|---|---|---|
| | | *Structure of Present Family* | | | | | | |
| 2-parent | Simple nuclear | Parents, children | 66 | 97 | 55 | 92 | 121 | 95 |
| | Simple extended | Parents, children, relatives | 2 | 3 | 3 | 5 | 5 | 4 |
| | Augmented nuclear | Parents, children, non-relatives | — | — | 2 | 3 | 2 | 2 |
| | | Total | 68 | 100 | 60 | 100 | 128 | 101 |
| 1-parent | Attenuated nuclear | Parent, children | 16 | 80 | 28 | 93 | 44 | 88 |
| | Attenuated extended | Parent, children, relatives | 3 | 15 | 2 | 7 | 5 | 10 |
| | Augmented attenuated nuclear | Parent, children, non-relatives | 1 | 5 | — | — | 1 | 2 |
| | | Total | 20 | 100 | 30 | 100 | 50 | 100 |
| | | Total nuclear units | 82 | 93 | 83 | 92 | 165 | 93 |
| | | Total extended units | 5 | 6 | 5 | 6 | 10 | 6 |
| | | Total augmented | 1 | 1 | 2 | 2 | 3 | 2 |
| | | Total | 88 | 100 | 90 | 100 | 178 | 101 |

| Structure | *Present Family by Sex of Head* | | | | | | | | | |
|---|---|---|---|---|---|---|---|---|---|---|
| | 2-Parent Mother f | 2-Parent Mother % | 2-Parent Father f | 2-Parent Father % | 1-Parent Mother f | 1-Parent Mother % | 1-Parent Father f | 1-Parent Father % | Total f | Total % |
| Simple nuclear | 121 | 95 | [Same | | — | — | — | — | 121 | 68 |
| Simple extended | 5 | 4 | as | | — | — | — | — | 5 | 3 |
| Augmented nuclear | 1 | 1 | Mothers] | | — | — | — | — | 1 | 1 |
| Augmented extended | 1 | 1 | | | — | — | — | — | 1 | 1 |
| Attenuated nuclear | — | — | | | 40 | 87 | 4 | 100 | 44 | 24 |
| Augmented attenuated nuclear | — | — | | | 1[a] | 2 | — | — | 1 | 1 |
| Attenuated extended | — | — | | | 5 | 11 | — | — | 5 | 3 |
| Total | 128 | 101 | | | 46 | 100 | 4 | 100 | 178 | 101 |

*continued*

mobile move would be too great to manage with contemporary economic pressures. These adults, then, generally were born into solid working-class families and were upwardly mobile as a result of their own educational and occupational achievements.

**TABLE 6.2** Continued

| | Family of Orientation by Sex of Present Head | | | | | | | |
| | 2-Parent Mother | | 2-Parent Father | | 1-Parent Mother | | 1-Parent Father | |
| Structure | f | % | f | % | f | % | f | % |
|---|---|---|---|---|---|---|---|---|
| Simple nuclear | 74 | 55 | 69 | 53 | 29 | 71 | 2 | 50 |
| Simple extended | 39 | 29 | 28 | 22 | 7 | 17 | — | — |
| Augmented nuclear | 2 | 1 | 1 | 1 | — | — | — | — |
| Augmented extended | 2 | 1 | 4 | 3 | — | — | — | — |
| Attenuated nuclear | 10 | 7 | 17 | 13 | 4 | 10 | — | — |
| Augmented attenuated nuclear | — | — | 1 | 1 | — | — | — | — |
| Attenuated extended | 5 | 4 | 7 | 5 | 1 | 2 | 2 | 50 |
| Incipient extended | 1 | 1 | 1 | 1 | — | — | — | — |
| Missing data | 1 | 1 | 2 | 2 | | | | |
| Total | 134 | 99 | 130 | 101 | 41 | 100 | 4 | 100 |

a. Woman; 4 long-term foster care children.

## Results

### EXTENDED KIN AND RECIPROCAL OBLIGATIONS

The major hypotheses were supported. The extended family patterns were very much in evidence. Sixty-six percent reported receiving a great deal of help and only 10% received none. The family support had performed an important function in their upward mobility. They had not been forced to cut themselves off from their families to be upwardly mobile, nor had they emotionally separated themselves from the wider Black community and culture once they had higher status. The kin involvement was found equally in the newly mobile and in cases where the family had been middle class for two or more generations ($\chi^2(2) = 1.80$, ns). Assistance was being given and received by families of all mobility patterns. Similar kinds of help were exchanged by all groups. The most frequently exchanged kinds of help were child care, financial assistance, and emotional support (see Table 6.4). Newly mobile adults gave more different types of help than those born middle class ($\chi^2(6) = 13.33$, $p < .04$). No urban-suburban differences were found.

The reciprocal obligations of the kin help exchange were present, but were balanced and not perceived as excessive. Families in all groups reported that only "moderate" levels of reciprocity were expected.

**TABLE 6.3** Summary of Educational Achievement for Subjects, Degrees of Paternal and Maternal Lines and Educational Level by SES Self-Rating for Two-Parent Homes

| Educational Level of Household | % | Degrees Earned by Subjects | Father's | | Mother's | |
|---|---|---|---|---|---|---|
| | | | f | % | f | % |
| Graduate/Professional Training | 41 | | | | | |
| College | 53 | | | | | |
| High School | 6 | Ph.D., Ed.D. | 17 | 12 | 8 | 5 |
| | | Med., Law | 12 | 8 | 2 | 1 |
| | 100 | Master's | 29 | 20 | 37 | 24 |
| | | Bachelor's | 51 | 36 | 52 | 34 |
| | | AA, AS, RN, Business | 7 | 5 | 12 | 8 |
| | | High School + | 27 | 19 | 44 | 29 |
| | | Total | 143 | 100 | 155 | 101 |

| | Degrees Earned by Paternal Ancestors | | | | | | | | | | | |
| | Father | | Mother | | Paternal Grandpa | | Paternal Grandma | | Maternal Grandpa | | Maternal Grandma | |
| Degree | f | % | f | % | f | % | f | % | f | % | f | % |
|---|---|---|---|---|---|---|---|---|---|---|---|---|
| Ph.D., Ed.D. | 1 | 1 | — | — | — | — | — | — | — | — | — | — |
| Med., Law | 1 | 1 | — | — | — | — | — | — | 1 | 1 | — | — |
| Master's | 5 | 4 | 7 | 5 | 1 | 1 | — | — | — | — | — | — |
| Bachelor's | 9 | 7 | 14 | 10 | 2 | 3 | 1 | 1 | 1 | 1 | 2 | 3 |
| AA, AS, RN, Business | 5 | 4 | 4 | 3 | 3 | 4 | 1 | 1 | 2 | 3 | 2 | 3 |
| High School + | 59 | 45 | 71 | 53 | 16 | 23 | 18 | 26 | 20 | 28 | 24 | 31 |
| None | 50 | 39 | 39 | 29 | 47 | 68 | 49 | 71 | 48 | 67 | 50 | 64 |
| Total | 130 | 101 | 135 | 100 | 69 | 99 | 69 | 99 | 72 | 100 | 78 | 101 |

| Two-Parent Unit | Born Working Class | | | | | | Born Middle Class | | | | | |
| | Mother's | | | Father's | | | Mother's | | | Father's | | |
| Education | Moth. % | Pa % | Ma % | Fath. % | Pa % | Ma % | Moth. % | Pa % | Ma % | Fath. % | Pa % | Ma % |
|---|---|---|---|---|---|---|---|---|---|---|---|---|
| Grad/Professional Training | 38 | 12 | 5 | 43 | 5 | 4 | 4 | 14 | 4 | 35 | 15 | 19 |
| College | 27 | 6 | 14 | 41 | 7 | 8 | 30 | — | 9 | 35 | 15 | 19 |
| Some College | 24 | 15 | 20 | 11 | 12 | 19 | 61 | 14 | 17 | 26 | 15 | 24 |
| High School | 11 | 37 | 41 | 6 | 34 | 37 | 4 | 36 | 26 | 4 | 35 | 29 |
| Some High School | 1 | 1 | 1 | — | — | 1 | — | — | — | — | — | — |
| Junior High | — | 13 | 17 | — | 22 | 18 | — | 18 | 13 | — | 10 | — |
| Less Than 7 years | — | 16 | 2 | — | 21 | 14 | — | 18 | 30 | — | 10 | 10 |
| | 101 | 100 | 100 | 101 | 101 | 101 | 99 | 100 | 99 | 100 | 100 | 101 |
| N | 84 | 80 | 86 | 86 | 80 | 84 | 23 | 22 | 23 | 23 | 17 | 19 |

There was significantly more pressure on the newly mobile to maintain the help patterns ($\chi^2(9) = 19.72$, $p < .02$). When a person "makes it" or "moves up," sharing is expected from the newly mobile, but not from those born middle class. This was expected because their kin would possibly be in weaker financial straits than the other kin who themselves were middle class. The kin-insurance policies were very much in effect.

The same patterns of exchanging help existed with friends, indicating a continuation of the fictive kin patterns. Seventy-one percent grew up in homes in which nonrelatives were considered as kin. When found, these relatives filled the role of aunt or uncle (56%), siblings (27%), or cousins (11%). This flexibility of family boundaries was more common in working class (77%) than in middle-class (53%) families ($\chi^2(1) = 4.70$, $p < .02$). The same patterns had been brought into the present generation, regardless of the SES of family of orientation. The role of such "kin" had changed to become siblings (59%), aunts (17%), and cousins (12%). In other words, the subjects had developed emotionally close friendships with peers who were as aunts and uncles for their own children, perpetuating the same pattern of the extended family.

Another facet of the extended family has often been the Black church. It appeared to be less important with this sample. Religion played an important role in the lives of only half of the families. One-fourth felt the church was of no significance at all. More suburban families (31%) than urban families (22%) were out of contact with a church. Over the three generations, a strong shift was made from Baptist and fundamentalist churches to so-called "high" churches. This would indicate that the emotional support typically found in the traditional church was not available to these parents and their children.

## EDUCATIONAL ASPIRATIONS

The values of the parents reflected a wide variety of life-styles. One prevailing emphasis reported by the parents was the value of education. Many mentioned great sacrifices that relatives had made on their hands and knees, scrubbing floors, to help them get their education. Their educational mobility was not seen as an individualistic achievement, but rather a process shared by the wider kin group and nonrelatives who had become as kin. These middle-class parents tended not to have an accumulation of wealth to pass on to their children, for almost all were in salaried positions. All indicated a belief that each generation of Blacks must make the upwardly mobile cycle again. They also felt on

**TABLE 6.4** Types of Help Exchanged by Mobility Patterns as Reported by Mothers

| Mobility Patterns[a] | Family | | | Friends | | |
|---|---|---|---|---|---|---|
| | *1* | *2* | *3* | *1* | *2* | *3* |
| | % | % | % | % | % | % |
| Help Received From | | | | | | |
| Child care | 38 | 32 | 35 | 24 | 32 | 36 |
| Financial | 27 | 2 | 24 | 14 | 13 | 25 |
| Emotional | 22 | 24 | 29 | 48 | 52 | 31 |
| Repairs, chores | 11 | 9 | 6 | 9 | 3 | 6 |
| Clothes, furniture | 2 | 6 | 6 | 5 | — | 3 |
| Total | 100 | 100 | 100 | 100 | 100 | 101 |
| *N* | 55 | 34 | 34 | 58 | 31 | 36 |
| Help Given to | | | | | | |
| Child care | 24 | 34 | 44 | 25 | 17 | 36 |
| Financial | 37 | 25 | 23 | 18 | 25 | 33 |
| Emotional | 28 | 22 | 26 | 46 | 53 | 31 |
| Repairs, chores | 8 | — | — | 7 | 6 | — |
| Clothes, furniture | 13 | 19 | 8 | 5 | — | — |
| Total | 100 | 100 | 101 | 101 | 101 | 100 |
| *N* | 62 | 32 | 39 | 61 | 36 | 36 |

a. Mobility Patterns
 1 — Upward in present generation
 2 — Upward in each generation
 3 — Born middle class
 Upward in parent's generation
 Middle class over three generations

guard because they could easily slip back to working-class status or lower. Therefore, the education of their children became a major concern of and expense in their lives. Consistent with the literature, the parents were attempting to protect the children from the pressures of racism in order to promote their feelings of self-worth and to protect their achievement potential.

## Discussion

The continuation of the extended family helping systems could be accounted for by two interacting factors. The first was that the family patterns of the cultural memories, carried over from Africa and continued through the slavery experience, were still valued and functional. The other factor could be that because the wider social agencies are still not perceived by Blacks as sensitive to their normal developmental and unique needs, the family members have worked to maintain the shared kin help network, knowing that this was their only sure source of help in times of trouble. The heavy emphasis on education is a reflection of this same belief in self-reliance. In other words, their children must be as highly educated as possible so that they can take care of themselves, since no one else will.

How were these families different from other families of their economic status? On a superficial level, these Black middle-class families may appear similar to middle-class families everywhere: Those in suburbia lived in contemporary homes on integrated curving streets near every possible convenience; those in the city dwelt in stately older homes in an all-Black area, dense with mature trees. However similar these Black life-styles were to dominant ones from the outside, there were internal differences that became apparent when the parents' attitudes and behaviors were observed more closely. They felt that they were unique—different from all other ethnic groups. This uniqueness existed in the forms of music, hairstyles, and the extended family. Many references were made to the joys of their youth within the security of a close Black community. Whether these differences are a result of a carryover of cultural attributes of African cultures, or whether they evolved because of generations of coping with racism and poverty, is a continuing argument among scholars of Black and American families. Both factors were clearly interacting with these families. Many cultural traits were evident in the extensive involvement in kin help patterns, while external discrimination was clearly having an impact upon their lives.

One distinct difference of these families from comparable White families was the awareness of racial oppression. They selected different means to offset it. In attempting to cope with discrimination, many families were enjoying the pleasant life-style that their incomes afforded, but were articulate in their belief that racial oppression was to be their continuing destiny regardless of social status. These findings are consistent with a recent national survey that found that the upwardly mobile Blacks felt a high level of mistrust for Whites. They felt that they were discriminated against in top managerial jobs in spite of their training (Denton & Sussman, 1981).

Some families were clearly opting for the assimilation route to maintain stability. Others were continuing their strong involvement in the Black church, with the professed belief that things may be hard now, but that there would be salvation in heaven after death, while others clearly rejected a church that was seen as a form of accommodation to the wider society. Some had opted for the route of accumulating wealth, with the mistaken hope that enough trappings would protect them from the outside world. Some lived well beyond their income and some were fiscally conservative. Only a very few were espousing pan-African beliefs or a strong identification with Africa. Other families showed a mixture of these elements. There were remnants of Frazier's bourgeoisie excesses present in some families and not in others.

The one factor that reiterated itself was that of diversity in attitudes and life-styles within this sample. One would be amiss to attempt to lump them as having any one characteristic orientation. Whereas they were different in many ways, they coalesced in their awareness of the need to protect their children from the press of the majority and the feelings of inevitability of change in the attitude of the wider culture.

From a theoretical view, the author agrees with Staples' (1978) presentation of the current conceptual models of viewing the Black family. It is impossible to explain the life-styles of these families totally by using just one model. The colonial model, with its emphasis on racism in the provision of economic resources to cultural groups, provides explanations for many factors of Black life. However, to use only this model one would have to focus only on the families that are deviations from majority norms to provide illustrations of inequity. This could only imply that the strengths of Black families are only coping mechanisms that allow the family to survive. The colonial model would not allow one to investigate stable families or the Afro-American cultural continuities that are found in a more pan-African model (Nobles, 1974). The incorporation of the second pan-African model with the first would provide for a fuller examination of the characteristics of Black families (extended family, role of the Black church, etc.) that allow them to *transcend,* not just cope with, factors that are produced under a racially inequitable system. Wilson (1978) posited that class is more important than race, but these families are constantly experiencing an interaction between race and class. The data from these families indicate that although they have obtained all of the economic life-style trappings of their class, they are continually placed under the tension of transcending race as they attempt to maintain stability in their families.

effects of racial discrimination on the personality development of college females, Miller (1979) exposed 108 Black and White college females to discrimination tasks. The tasks were administered by either a Black or White female examiner. It was found that the identity aspect of the self-esteem of the Black females who received high discrimination from the Black examiner was significantly lower than the identity/self-esteem of the Black females who received high discrimination from a White examiner. This finding suggests that in-group perceptions of self may be more important than those of out-group members. That is, an individual internalizes aspects of her social environment in order to develop a sense of self. More specifically, aspects of the females' background may have provided the network supports necessary to positively influence Black women's perception of self. Mead's (1934) research on the looking glass self supports this interpretation. This internalization of a culturally based self-identity may buffer the negative effects that racial discrimination might have on the self-esteem of Black women. Since neither Black or White males were used in the study, the possible effects of sexual discrimination on the self-esteem of the Black females remain an open question.

It has been proposed that exposure to sexual discrimination affects the self-esteem of women (Bardwick, 1980; Dion, 1975). Although exposure to sexual or racial discrimination may result in lowered levels of self-esteem, this explanation does not account for the relatively high levels of self-esteem for some Blacks and women (especially those who report exposure to racial and/or sexual discrimination). It may be that exposure to stressful life events is not the critical variable in the development of the self; rather, variables within one's social environment may be the critical determinant (Banks et al. 1977; Barnes, 1980). Presently, research on sex roles and self-esteem has not addressed the relationship between self-esteem and social environmental variables. More importantly, these variables have not been examined in relation to Black women. Since it has been proposed that network structure is significantly related to the social development of females, it seems to follow that Black females' attitudes toward self are products of their network structure and, more generally, their social environment.

## Trust

The effects of the social environment on one's trust level has received only moderate attention. Erikson (1963) proposed that trust is dependent on the type of early socialization a child encounters in his or her social environment. Similarly, Rotter (1967) suggested that the type of social interaction one receives will affect attitudes of trust toward others. As a result of the type of interaction experienced in a given situation, the expectancies held in that situation will generalize to similar situations. The development of a mistrustful attitude has been proposed as maladaptive (Erikson, 1963). Mistrust, however, may be a necessary mechanism for many people. That is, mistrust may be essential for providing barriers against the physical and mental pain that often accompanies exposure to race or sex-related discrimination.

Although there are not many studies addressing the trust/mistrust issue, some empirical evidence exists suggesting that Blacks are mistrustful of others (Terrell & Barrett, 1979; Terrell & Miller, 1979). Schuman and Hatchett (1974), in a comparative study of the trust level of younger and older Blacks in which Black family members were surveyed over several periods of time, found that younger Blacks were more mistrustful of the intentions of others than older Blacks. It may be that older Blacks vicariously transmit their experiences to younger Blacks, who in turn respond to a combination of a particular incident and the emotion surrounding the Civil Rights Movement. That is, the younger Blacks may be relying on their network structure to determine perceptions of and interaction with others. Consequently, the network structure may foster negative feelings and suspicions toward Whites. Older Blacks, on the other hand, may have been responding in a culturally adaptive manner. That is, years of experience with racial discrimination may result in older Blacks evaluating the merits of people on an individual basis, thereby allowing their experiences in a given situation to dictate the more appropriate behavior or mode of response. Or, the older Blacks may have been more accommodating toward Whites. Although this study focuses on the trust level of Blacks, it does not specifically address the relationship between one's social environment and the development of a cultural or general trust level. However, since women have been found to be less trusting of others than men (Terrell & Barrett, 1979), it would seem that the structure of the family (which would include the experiences of the family) might be more readily internalized by the females. Grier and Cobbs (1968) have also spoken of the effects that exposure to racial discrimination has on the trust level of Blacks. They have reported that the seemingly low level of trust among Blacks is a realistic and adaptive mechanism for dealing with the multitudes of negative life situations to which Blacks are often exposed. It would, therefore, seem that understanding the trust level of Black women is critical for an understanding of their psychosocial development. Thus, in addition to an assessment of the way in which attitudes of trust are developed in young college-aged Black families, the present study examined both their general and cultural mistrust.

## Summary

In summary, one purpose of this study was to examine the role of such stressful life events as racial and sexual discrimination on the trust and self-esteem level of Black women. A second purpose was to determine whether a relationship exists between the type and nature of Black women's familial background and their self-esteem or trust levels. In this study, *network structure support* was broadly defined to include the various types of support to which one can be exposed and the nature of support within their environments. *Nature* of support, in this study, refers to the network structure of the family, which includes the occupational and educational status of parents and grandparents and the general make-up of the family (i.e., presence or absence of parents during the child's school years and the role of the grandparents throughout that time period).

## Method

### SUBJECTS

A total of 159 Black females enrolled at two predominantly Black southwestern colleges and one predominantly White southwestern college volunteered to participate in the study. Since the students were from three different colleges, demographic data concerning age, college grade level, and estimated grade point average were collected. The group mean age of the students was 20.14 (range of 19.8 to 20.57), the mean grade level was 2.29 (range 2.2 to 2.4), and the mean grade point average was 2.85 (range of 2.7 to 2.88).

### MATERIALS

Six objective questionnaires were presented to the subjects.[1] Two of the questionnaires were trust scales. The Rotter (1967) Interpersonal Trust Scale, a 40-item Likert-type scale, was used to assess the subjects' general trust level. The Cultural Mistrust Inventory (Terrell & Terrell, 1981) was used to assess the trust/mistrust level of Blacks toward

Whites in social, business, and political settings. The mistrust inventory, a 48-item questionnaire, was selected because it differentiates between a pathological and adaptive attitude of mistrust for Blacks. The M. Rosenberg (1965) Self-Esteem Scale was used to determine the subjects' attitudes toward self. The self-esteem scale consists of ten items. Two different discrimination scales were used. The Miller-Timm Sexism Scale, a 30-item scale, was used to measure the subjects' frequency of exposure to sexual discrimination and feelings toward situations that have been described as sexist in nature.[2] Reliability of the sexism scale has been estimated as .96 by Cronbach's coefficient alpha method (Miller, 1980). The Terrell-Miller (1979) Racial Discrimination Index, a 24-item scale, was used to measure frequency of exposure to racial discrimination and feelings toward situations that have been described as having racial overtones.[3] The test-retest reliability of the racial discrimination scale is .78.

The final questionnaire, the background questionnaire, included 32 demographic information items. In addition to standard demographic information such as age, family status, parents' marital status and education level, information about grandparents' status (i.e., educational and occupational), emotional support, and financial support was requested. The status, education, and support variables served as the network structure support variables.

PROCEDURE

Since multiple measures were used in the study, subjects were arranged in small groups ranging from two to eight persons per session. Subjects were informed that the purpose of the study was to identify components of social interaction.

Next, the subjects were given a folder containing the background, racial discrimination, sexual discrimination, self-esteem, trust, and cultural mistrust scales previously mentioned. The order of the scales was counterbalanced. Attached to the front of the folder was a letter from the experimenter that described the study, assured subjects of confidentiality and anonymity of their responses, and informed subjects that their decision to complete the questionnaires or not would be entirely voluntary.

PREDICTOR VARIABLES

One of the questions addressed by the present research was what predictor variables may be associated with personality and social development of Black women. Social environment variables were categorized as predictor variables. The variables were measured by the Frequency of Exposure to Racial Discrimination subscale, the Frequency of Exposure to Sexism subscale, and the network structure items on the background information questionnaire.

Since the background questionnaire was developed specifically for this study, it was necessary to examine the psychometric properties before attempting to use it in statistical analyses. The results of the item analysis revealed relatively high item-total intercorrelations for the items on parents' status, grandparents' status, emotional support, and financial support. Items concerning education level of parents, religion, and occupation of parents received negative or low item-total intercorrelations.

## CRITERION VARIABLES

Another question addressed by this study was what personality variables are related to differential treatment/stressful life events. The personality or attitude variables were measured by a self-esteem, interpersonal trust, and cultural mistrust scale. These variables were selected based on the findings of previous research (Grier & Cobbs, 1968; Miller, 1979, 1980; O'Malley & Bachman, 1979; Terrell & Barrett, 1979) examining the relationship between exposure to racial or sexual discrimination and self-esteem or trust. In addition to the personality question, it was thought that direct or vicarious exposure to race or sex discrimination leads to emotional reactions to the exposure. The subjects were therefore asked to complete the Feelings Toward Racial Discrimination and Feelings Toward Sexism subscales.

## Results

### PRELIMINARY DATA ANALYSES

Raw scores were obtained for the subjects on each of the scales. Since the subjects were from three different schools, it was necessary to inspect the data for possible differences among schools. Table 8.1 contains the means of the subjects on the scales.

Inspection of the data in Table 8.1 revealed fluctuations among mean scores of the groups on the scales, which suggests that the subjects' responses might not be homogenous. To examine these fluctuations,

**TABLE 8.1**  Mean Responses of Subjects on the Social Environment and Personality
Scales

| | | Colleges | |
|---|---|---|---|
| *Scales* | *A* | *B* | *C* |
| Racial Discrimination | | | |
| Frequency Subscale | 18.13 | 28.75 | 19.11 |
| Feelings Subscale | 128.31 | 150.58 | 168.58 |
| Sexual Discrimination | | | |
| Frequency Subscale | 19.44 | 30.49 | 23.40 |
| Feelings Subscale | 156.70 | 202.32 | 195.69 |
| Interpersonal Trust | 67.41 | 66.21 | 63.18 |
| Cultural Mistrust | 192.72 | 215.83 | 188.02 |
| Self-Esteem | 2.33 | 2.60 | 2.49 |
| | $N = 60$ | $N = 53$ | $N = 46$ |

Note: A & B are predominantly Black colleges, and C is a predominantly White college.

three different analytical techniques were used. An intercorrelation
analysis of the scores of each participant at each school was averaged
across schools. This technique resulted in the identification of the
average participant at each school. The average participants were then
intercorrelated, yielding a consistent $r = .99$. This correlation coefficient suggests that the subjects' responses are homogeneous. A multiple
discriminant analysis also was computed, testing for discriminability
among schools. The purpose of the test was to determine whether the
three groups differ in their mean responses to items on the questionnaires. Neither of the discriminant functions, however, reached statistical significance, which suggests no statistical difference among the
three schools. Finally, the subjects' responses to items on the racial and
sexual discrimination scales seem to suggest that differences among the
three schools might exist; therefore *t* tests were computed that took into
account unequal *n*'s (an unweighted means approach was used to address
the problems that arise when comparisons are made between groups that
have different numbers of subjects). No significant differences were
found in the racial and sexual discrimination scores of the subjects
enrolled at the predominantly Black colleges or the scores of these
subjects with those of the subjects enrolled at the predominantly White
college. Based on the findings of these three analyses, the data from the
three schools were collapsed for further analyses.

**TABLE 8.2** Coefficient Alphas of the Social Environment and Personality Scales

| Scales | Coefficient Alpha (Cronbach) |
|---|---|
| Background | .70 |
| Racial Discrimination | .88 |
| Sexual Discrimination | .89 |
| Interpersonal Trust | .62 |
| Cultural Mistrust | .85 |
| Self-Esteem | .40 |

$N = 159$

## MEASUREMENT REFINEMENT

A principal components analysis was used to identify possible subscales within the background questionnaire and to identify items with low factor loadings. The analysis yielded four factors with eigenvalues greater than 1.2 that accounted for 62% of the total variance. The items that loaded heavily on Factor 1 appeared to reflect a network structure support dimension and included items on occupation of parents from the subjects' grade school to college years, family cohesiveness and structure, and family support. The items that loaded heavily on Factor 2 appeared to reflect an education dimension and included items on the level of education attained by parents, grandparents, and other family members. The items that loaded heavily on Factor 3 appeared to reflect a grandparents' status dimension and included items on occupation status of grandparents from the subjects' grade school to high school years. Factor 4 had salient loadings on the item associated with mother's employment status during the subjects' junior and senior high school years, and mother's present occupation; these items reflected a mother's status dimension. The four factors were retained for further analyses.

## RELIABILITY AND CORRELATION OF THE SCALES

Coefficient alphas were computed for each of the scales used in the study (see Table 8.2). The reliabilities of the scales were evaluated as to both their coefficients and their conceptual value. Coefficient alphas of the scales ranged from .40 to .89. The self-esteem scale, which has only ten items in the scoring, obtained a coefficient alpha of .40. Such a small coefficient alpha may suggest limited predictive validity or

**TABLE 8.3** Canonical Correlation Analysis of the Predictor and Criterion Variables for the First Canonical Variate

| Variables | Canonical Correlation (CI) .47* Canonical Coefficients | $R$** |
|---|---|---|
| Criterion Variables | | |
| Feelings Toward Racism | .48 | .50 |
| Feelings Toward Sexism | −.24 | .29 |
| Interpersonal Trust | .25 | .14 |
| Cultural Mistrust | .49 | .22 |
| Self-Esteem | .39 | .58 |
| Predictor Variables | | |
| Father/Parents F1 | −.02 | .01 |
| Education Level F2 | .65 | .60 |
| Grandparents F3 | .08 | .04 |
| Mother's Status F4 | .78 | .74 |
| Exposure to Racism | .30 | .13 |
| Exposure to Sexism | −.12 | .19 |

*Wilk's Lambda = .22, $p < .01$, df = 157; $N = 159$
**$R$ = Canonical Variable Loadings
F1, F2, F3, and F4 are the factors retained from the principal components analysis.

predictability. However, because small numbers of items lower the coefficient alpha, all the scales were retained for further analyses.

The correlation coefficients between the scales ranged from .26 to .69. The exposure to sex discrimination and the exposure to race discrimination subscales were highly correlated ($r = .69$, $p < .001$), as were the race and sex feeling subscales ($r = .62$, $p < .001$). Father/parents education level was correlated with interpersonal trust ($r = .26$, $p < .01$), and grandparents' status and self-esteem were correlated ($r = .27$, $p < .01$).

## SOCIAL ENVIRONMENTAL AND PERSONALITY/AFFECT VARIABLES

To determine which of the variables best predicts the personality and social development of Black women, the data were analyzed by a canonical correlation analysis. Table 8.3 presents the results of the canonical correlation. The first canonical variate reflected a significant relationship, $F$ (157) = 9.20, $p < .01$, between education level of parents/grandparents, mother's status (the predictor variables) and feelings toward race discrimination, self esteem, and cultural mistrust (the criterion variables). None of the other canonical variates were statistically significant and, therefore, are not reported.

Also, as indicated in Table 8.3, feelings toward racial discrimination accounted for significantly more variance than feelings toward sexual discrimination ($p < .01$). There was no significant difference, however, in the amount of variance accounted for by exposure to race and sex discrimination. Since frequency of exposure to racial or sexual discrimination was so low, examination of the role of these two stressors on the trust or self-esteem levels of the Black females in this study was infeasible. Feelings toward the stressors seemed to be a more distinguishing characteristic in assessing the psychosocial development of the females than exposure to the stressors.

Interpretation of canonical correlations must be done with caution (Darlington, Weinberg, & Walberg, 1973; Kerlinger & Pedhazur, 1973). It seems fair to conclude, however, that the education level of parents and grandparents, coupled with the mother's status, best predicts how Black females feel about race discrimination, self, and others. It can also be concluded that Black females tend to have stronger feelings toward racial discrimination than toward sexual discrimination.

To further assess the possible influence of social environment variables on the personality of Black women and to substantiate the findings of the canonical correlation, six stepwise multiple regression analyses were computed. The regression weights for normalized variables and the multiple correlation of the criterion variables are given in Table 8.4. Each criterion variable represents the results of a multiple regression analysis. Statistical tests of significance with the alpha level adjusted for the number of tests (Hays, 1973) revealed a significant relationship between education level of parents/grandparents and trust, $F(1, 152) = 10.89$, $p < .01$, education level of parents/grandparents and feelings toward racial discrimination, $F(2, 151) = 7.90$, $p < .05$, and education level of parents/grandparents and self-esteem, $F(3, 150) = 5.34$, $p < .05$. A significant relationship was also found between mother's status and self-esteem, $F(1, 152) = 0.99$, $p < .01$.

## ADDITIONAL DATA ANALYSES

Sixty-eight percent (108 subjects) of the subjects' parents had completed high school, whereas only 30% (48) of the subjects' grandparents had completed high school. All of the subjects (100%) had a parent

**TABLE 8.4** Predicting Personal Characteristics From Social Environment Variables

| Variables | Beta | F | R |
|---|---|---|---|
| Feelings Toward Racism | | | |
| Father/Parents | .02 | .09 | |
| Education Level | .22 | 7.90* | |
| Grandparents | −.05 | .37 | .33 |
| Mother's Status | .12 | 2.28 | |
| Exposure to Racism | .08 | .50 | |
| Exposure to Sexism | −.03 | .06 | |
| Feelings Toward Sexism | | | |
| Father/Parents | .01 | .02 | |
| Education Level | .13 | 2.50 | |
| Grandparents | −.07 | .77 | .21 |
| Mother's Status | .08 | 1.02 | |
| Exposure to Racism | −.15 | 1.88 | |
| Exposure to Sexism | .14 | 1.54 | |
| Interpersonal Trust | | | |
| Father/Parents | .00 | .00 | |
| Education Level | .32 | 10.89** | |
| Grandparents | .05 | .18 | .37 |
| Mother's Status | −.03 | 2.37 | |
| Exposure to Racism | −.01 | .12 | |
| Exposure to Sexism | .01 | .05 | |
| Cultural Mistrust | | | |
| Father/Parents | .15 | 3.35 | |
| Education Level | −.02 | .08 | |
| Grandparents | −.10 | 1.42 | .25 |
| Mother's Status | .13 | 2.53 | |
| Exposure to Racism | .16 | 1.96 | |
| Exposure to Sexism | −.01 | .01 | |
| Self-Esteem | | | |
| Father/Parents | .00 | .00 | |
| Education Level | .18 | 5.34* | |
| Grandparents | .12 | 2.34 | |
| Mother's Status | .24 | 9.00** | .33 |
| Exposure to Racism | −.08 | .52 | |
| Exposure to Sexism | −.01 | .01 | |

Note: The alpha level is an adjusted alpha for number of analyses. $R$ stands for multiple correlation.
*$p < .05$
**$p < .01$
df = 6, 152; N = 159
See Table 8.3 for further explanation of the variables.

and/or an older sibling who had completed high school. Subjects' whose parents had either a graduate or professional degree (only 15% or 24 subjects) reported that at least one of their grandparents had either a graduate or professional degree, some college, or a college diploma. The majority of the students, 117 or 74%, listed themselves as their major emotional and financial supporter. Parents were listed as the second major emotional supporter. Financial support was viewed as money the student obtained from grants, scholarships, and/or loans. Only the Black students at the predominantly White school listed parents as their major financial supporter (27 out of 46 or 59%).

In addition, 83% of 132 subjects were raised in homes where both the parents were present during the grade school years. Absent parents during this time were mainly reported as dead. In those families where both parents were not present, the subjects indicated that they were raised in extended families (i.e., mother and grandparents or mother and grandmother).

Ninety-five percent (151) of the subjects reported that their mothers worked either part-time or full-time during their grade school and junior/senior high school years. Seventy-five percent (119) of the grandmothers also working during those years. The grandmothers who did not work throughout the subjects' school years were either retired, disabled, or deceased.

## Discussion

This study examined the relative influence of social environment variables on the social and personality development of Black women. Specific aspects of the environment, such as level of education attained by parents/grandparents and mother's status, tend to affect Black females' feelings toward racial discrimination, self-esteem, and general trust level. Perceived frequency of exposure to racial or sexual discrimination was too low to allow for examination of the relationship between exposure to discrimination and social or network structure support.

The results of the present study attest to the utility of social environmental variables as predictors of attitudinal and affective expressions toward self and others. Network structure support (e.g., education of parents/grandparents, mother's status) appears to be a critical component in the formation and maintenance of attitudes. Although no previous research could be found that addressed network structure in relation to personality and attitudes, some support for this approach may be found in Fishbein and Ajzen's (1975) work on the influence of normative group members (e.g., parents, peers) on one's attitudes and intentions. The educational level of family members across generations tends to influence future generations' attitudes and behaviors toward education, as well as their intent toward graduate or professional education. This finding suggests that educational attainment is an incremental family phenomenon and, as such, serves in a network structure support capacity. In other words, the level of education attained by older family members is related to the level of education other family members of future generations will attain. The trend in the data suggests a trickle-up effect. That is, educational values may be transmitted from one generation to another. An economic deprivation analysis can also be used to explain the finding of a trickle-up education effect. According to an economic deprivation analysis, the lower the educational status of parents and grandparents, the more likely the parents and grandparents are to hold low status or low paying jobs and, consequently, the lower the capacity to assist with the child's educational expenses. In this instance, both the transmission of values and the economic status of the family are important for the attainment of a trickle-up effect within families.[4]

As indicated in Table 8.1, perceived exposure to race or sex discrimination was low, but feelings toward discriminatory situations were relatively high in comparison. The results indicate that the subjects may have been raised in environments that were both preventive and cathartic. That is, the subjects may have been sheltered from potential situations involving discrimination, but told of instances of other's experiences that were discriminatory in nature. The cathartic experience would arouse the emotions when told of similar discrimination situations, thereby, accounting for the subjects' expressed emotions in view of their limited direct exposure.

The way in which emotions are resolved may be related to self-evaluations. Previous researchers (Lott & Lott, 1963; Riessman, 1962) have proposed that education is related to self-esteem. That is, education leads to a higher social class status, which often results in an enhanced sense of social and personal worth. The position taken by Clark and Clark (1947) is that self-esteem is a function of perceived societal position. Cooley (1922) and Mead (1934), on the other hand, have proposed that one's self-esteem is a product of the type of interactions and evaluations received from significant others. The educational level of parents and grandparents may serve as an evaluator of one's own self-worth. In this study, education may serve not only as an evaluator but also as a status symbol. The greater the degree of education the less perceived the societal rejection and the greater the sense of self-esteem. It could be argued that the females in this study internalized the educational status and values of their parents/grandparents, which in turn provided them with the perception of a viable and available network structure support system.

The results of this study also indicated that educational level of parents/grandparents influences the general trust level of Black females. It may be that a positive network structure leads to positive internalizations about the intentions and personality of others. This internalization might then affect one's perceptual evaluation of others. The cultural mistrust level of the subjects in this study was viewed as adaptive. None of the subjects' mean responses were either extremely trusting or extremely mistrusting. Extreme responses are indicative of a possible maladaptive view of others (Terrell & Terrell, 1981).

Parents' and grandparents' educational level seems to be important for personality development; however, support (either emotional or financial) variables had no significant relationship to personality or social development. It may be that parental support is important during childhood development but not as important during adult development. Theoretical and empirical investigations of the concept and evaluation of the self (Freud, 1921/1959; Hartup, 1970; Maccoby & Masters, 1970; McGuire, 1981; McGuire & McGuire, 1982) have proposed that significant others are invariably important during our dependency stages (infancy and early childhood), but as we become more autonomous, our self-definition derives little from our relationships with our parents. In other words, such things as parental status, education, and values are important to a child's development, but must at some point be viewed as separate by the child before he or she is able to internalize the nature of the family. This internalization would allow for the development of a self that is both independently and dependently determined.

Although supportive content variables did not relate to personality or social development, there was a significant relationship between mother's status and self-esteem. The mother's achievements and sense of independence may have been regarded by the subjects as an indication of the mother's feelings of self-worth. When the mother feels good about herself, it is likely to affect her interaction with her children and their self-esteem. It seems that the mother's accomplishments outside the home are important to the development of Black females. Research (Hoffman, 1974; Kandel & Lesser, 1969; Siegfried, MacFarlane, Graham,

Moore, & Young, 1981) on the daughters of working mothers supports this finding. Thus, it seems that network structure support is not the only critical variable for the social/personality development of Black families; the accomplishments of the mother are also important. The results of this study indicated no significant relationship between race or sex discrimination and the subjects' attitudes toward self or others. It must be pointed out, however, that the lack of a relationship between social problems and attitudes does not necessarily undermine the validity of such a relationship. Certainly, race- or sex-related discriminatory situations may be so stressful that components of one's mental and/or physical health can become adversely affected (Rabkin & Struening, 1976; Whitlock, 1978). Clearly, more research examining the relationship between social problems and possible indicants of attitudinal strength or definition, as well as research exploring possible physiological consequences, is necessary before the validity of the relationship can be fully understood. On the other hand, the present research does address the need to examine factors within one's social environment as both a predictor and a mediating variable. For example, the educational level of parents and grandparents may not only predict the trust level of Black females but also serve to mediate any possible negative effects from exposure to stressful life events. In this study, however, exposure to racial or sexual discrimination was too low to determine whether or not the possible negative effects of such exposure can be mediated by the presence of a supportive network structure.[5]

In summary, it has been found that network structure support (i.e., historical family structure), specifically the educational background of parents and grandparents, influences the way in which Black females feel about situations that suggest racial discrimination, their self-esteem, and trust of others. This study addressed the interactive, and in some instances additive, nature of one's social environment and attitudes about self and others. Exploration of network structure variables as related to personality and social development is empirically manageable and promising. Future research in this area will address the question of whether network structure variables do indeed serve as mediators for the possible negative effects of exposure to racial or sexual discrimination.

## Notes

1. A prejudice scale was also administered. The purpose of collecting the prejudice data was to determine the degree of prejudice toward Whites and to determine whether

the social setting (Black vs. predominantly White) played a role in race desensitization. The subjects had low scores on the prejudice scale which suggested a nonprejudicial attitude toward Whites. Also there was no difference in the prejudice scores because of social setting.

2. Items on the sexism scale were specific to the school environment, work, and society in general. An example of items on the scale is: A female student and a male student were considered the top students in their major. Their work was of the same quality and was usually very good. The male student, however, was recommended for an achievement award. The award carried a scholarship and would increase the male's chances for entering graduate or medical school. The woman was not recommended.

3. One item on the racism scale was: A Black put in an application for a job. The Black's qualifications for that particular position were exceptional, the interview was perfect, but the Black did not get the job. When the Black visited that place of employment a short time later, the Black was surprised to see that one of the White applicants who had been ranked lower than he had gotten the job. A Black person called to ask if an apartment which had been advertised as being for rent was still available. The person answering the phone said "yes." The Black person, therefore, went to look at the apartment. When the Black arrived, the manager told the Black that the apartment had been rented. A week later the Black called the apartment manager again and asked if the same apartment had been rented. The Black was told "no" the apartment had not been rented.

4. I thank one of the reviewers of my paper for suggesting the economic deprivation explanation.

5. Only a small number of the subjects indicated a high frequency of exposure to racial or sexual discrimination. Most of the subjects reported a moderate to low (with low being the most frequent response) exposure to racial or sexual discrimination. The majority of the subjects at the Black colleges who reported a high exposure to racial discrimination also reported a supportive network structure and a high level of self-esteem. In contrast, students at the predominantly White college, who reported a supportive network structure, had a high self-esteem or trust level.

## References

Ball, R., Warheit, G., Vandizer, J., & Holzer, C. (1979). Kin ties of low-income Blacks and Whites. *Ethnicity, 6,* 184-196.

Ball, R., Warheit, G., Vandizer, J., & Holzer, C. (1980). Friendship networks: More supportive of low-income Black women? *Ethnicity, 7,* 70-77.

Banks, E. J., Stitt, K. R., Curtis, H. A., & McQuater, C. V. (1977). Perceived objectivity and the effect of evaluative reinforcement upon compliance and self-evaluation of Blacks. *Journal of Experimental Social Psychology, 13,* 452-463.

Bardwick, J. M. (1980). *Psychology of women.* New York: Harper & Row.

Barnes, E. J. (1980). The Black community as the source of positive self-concept for Black children: A theoretical perspective. In R. L. Jones (Ed.), *Black psychology.* New York: Harper & Row.

Caplan, G., & Killilea, M. (1976). *Support systems and mutual help.* New York: Grune & Stratton.

Cauce, A. M., Felner, R. D., & Primavera, J. (1982). Social support in high-risk adolescents: Structural components and adaptive impact. *American Journal of Community Psychology, 10,* 417-428.

Clark, K. B. (1963). *Prejudice and your child.* Boston: Beacon.

Clark, K. B. (1965). *Dark ghetto: Dilemmas of social power.* New York: Harper & Row.

Clark, K. B., & Clark, M. P. (1939). The development of consciousness of self in the emergence of racial identification in Negro pre-school children. *Journal of Social Psychology, 10,* 591-597.

Clark, K. B., & Clark, M. P. (1947). Racial identification and preferences in Negro children. In T. M. Newcomb & E. L. Hartley (Eds.), *Readings in social psychology.* New York: Holt, Rinehart & Winston.

Cohen, S., & McKay, G. (1984). Social support, stress, and the buffering hypothesis. In A. Baum, J. E. Singer, & S. E. Taylor (Eds.), *Handbook of psychology and health: A theoretical analysis* (Vol. 4). Hillsdale, NJ: Lawrence Erlbaum.

Cooley, C. H. (1922). *Human nature and the social order.* New York: Scribner.

Darlington, R. B., Weinberg, S. L., & Walberg, H. J. (1973). Canonical variate analysis and related techniques. *Review of Educational Research, 43,* 433-454.

Dion, K. L. (1975). Women's reactions to discrimination from members of the same or opposite sex. *Journal of Personality and Social Psychology, 9,* 292-306.

Erickson, E. H. (1963). *Childhood and society.* New York: Norton.

Fanon, F. (1967). *Black skin, white masks.* New York: Grove.

Fishbein, M., & Ajzen, I. (1975). *Belief, attitude, intention, and behavior.* Reading, MA: Addison-Wesley.

Freud, S. (1959). *Group psychology and the analysis of the ego.* New York: Norton. (Original work published 1921)

Grier, W. H., & Cobbs, P. M. (1968). *Black rage.* New York: Basic Books.

Hacker, H. M. (1975). Women as a minority group twenty years later. In R. K. Unger & F. L. Denmark (Eds.), *Woman: Dependent or independent variable?* New York: Psychological Dimensions.

Hartup, W. (1970). Peer interaction and social organization. In P. H. Mussen (Ed.), *Carmichael's manual of child psychology* (Vol. 2). New York: John Wiley.

Hays, W. L. (1973). *Statistics for the social sciences.* New York: Holt, Rinehart & Winston.

Heider, F. (1958). *The psychology of interpersonal relations.* New York: John Wiley.

Hoffman, L. (1974). Effects of maternal employment on the child: A review of the research. *Developmental Psychology, 10,* 204-228.

House, J. S. (1981). *Work, stress and social support.* Reading, MA: Addison-Wesley.

House, J. S., & Kahn, R. L. (1985). Measures and concepts of social support. In S. Cohen & L. Syme (Eds.), *Social support and health.* New York: Academic Press.

James, W. (1890). *Principles of psychology.* New York: Holt.

Kandel, D., & Lesser, G. (1969). Parental and peer influences on educational plans of adolescents. *American Sociological Review, 34,* 213-223.

Kardiner, A., & Ovesey, L. (1951). *The mark of oppression: A psychological study of the American Negro.* New York: Norton.

Kerlinger, F. N., & Pedhazur, E. J. (1973). *Multiple regression in behavioral research.* New York: Holt, Rinehart & Winston.

Lott, A. J., & Lott, B. E. (1963). *Negro and White youth: A psychological study in a border-state community.* New York: Holt, Rinehart & Winston.

Maccoby, E. E., & Masters, J. (1970). Attachment and dependency. In P. H. Mussen (Ed.), *Carmichael's manual of child psychology* (Vol. 1). New York: John Wiley.

McGuire, W. J. (1968). Personality and susceptibility to social influence. In E. F. Borgotta & W. E. Lambert (Eds.), *Handbook of personality theory and research.* Chicago: Rand-McNally.

McGuire, W. J. (1981). The spontaneous self-concept as affected by personal distinctiveness. In A. A. Norem-Hebelson & M. Lynch (Eds.), *Self-concept.* Cambridge, MA: Ballinger.

McGuire, W. J., & McGuire, C. V. (1982). Significant others in self-space: Sex differences and developmental trends in the social self. In J. Suls (Eds.), *Social psychological perspectives on the self.* Hillsdale, NJ: Lawrence Erlbaum.

Mead, G. H. (1934). *Mind, self, and society.* Chicago: University of Chicago Press.

Miller, F. S. (1979). *The effects of racial discrimination upon the self concept and interpersonal trust level of Black and White college females.* Unpublished master's thesis, Texas Christian University.

Miller, F. S. (1980, September). *Self-esteem, locus of control, and attitudes toward women among college females as a function of sexism.* Paper presented at the American Psychological Association meeting, Montreal, Canada.

O'Malley, P., & Bachman, J. (1979). Self-esteem and education: Sex and cohort comparisons among high school seniors. *Journal of Personality and Social Psychology, 37*(7), 1153-1159.

Pettigrew, T. F. (1964). *A profile of the Negro American.* Princeton, NJ: Princeton University Press.

Proshansky, H., & Newton, P. (1972). The nature and meaning of Negro self-identity. In M. Deutsch, I. Katz, & A. Jensen (Eds.), *Social class, race, and psychological development.* New York: Harper & Row.

Rabkin, J. G., & Struening, E. L. (1976). Life events, stress, and illness. *Science, 194,* 1013-1020.

Raymond, J., Rhoads, D., & Raymond, R. (1980). The relative impact of family and social involvement on Chicano mental health. *American Journal of Community Psychology, 5,* 557-569.

Riessman, F. (1982). *The culturally deprived child.* New York: Harper & Row.

Rosenberg, F., & Simmons, R. G. (1975). Sex differences in the self-concept in adolescence. *Sex Roles, 1,* 147-159.

Rosenberg, M. (1965). *Society and the adolescent self-image.* Princeton, NJ: Princeton University Press.

Rotter, J. B. (1967). A new scale for the measurement of interpersonal trust. *Journal of Personality, 35,* 651-665.

Samuel, N., & Laird, D. (1974). The self concepts of two groups of Black female college students. *The Journal of Negro Education, 43,* 104-110.

Schuman, H., & Hatchett, S. (1974). *Black racial attitudes: Trends and complexities.* Ann Arbor: University of Michigan, Survey Research Center.

Shumaker, S. A., & Brownell, A. (1983, August). *A taxonomy of social support: Disentangling a conceptual morass.* Paper presented at the American Psychological Association meeting, Anaheim, CA.

Siegfried, W. D., MacFarlane, I., Graham, D. B., Moore, N. A., & Young, P. L. (1981). A reexamination of sex differences in job preferences. *Journal of Vocational Behavior, 18,* 30-42.

Smedley, J. W., & Bayton, J. A. (1978). Evaluative race-class stereotypes by race and perceived class of subjects. *Journal of Personality and Social Psychology, 36,* 530-535.

Terrell, F., & Barrett, R. K. (1979). Interpersonal trust among college students as a function of race, sex, and socioeconomic class. *Perceptual and Motor Skills, 48,* 1194.

Terrell, F., & Miller, F. S. (1979, April). *Effects of racial discrimination upon the interpersonal trust level of Black college students.* Paper presented at the Southwestern Psychological Association meeting, San Antonio, TX.

Terrell, F., & Terrell, S. (1981). An inventory to measure cultural mistrust among Blacks. *The Western Journal of Black Studies, 5,* 180-185.

Turner, R. J. (1983). Direct, indirect, and moderating effects of social support upon psychological distress and associated conditions. In H. B. Kaplan (Ed.), *Psychological stress: Trends in theory and research.* New York: Academic Press.

Whitlock, G. E. (1978). *Understanding and coping with real-life crisis.* Monterey, CA: Brooks/Cole.

# 9 Relationship Between Internalized Racism and Marital Satisfaction

JEROME TAYLOR
*University of Pittsburgh*

This investigation evaluates the extent to which level of marital satisfaction is affected by level of internalized racism in a sample of 96 Black inner-city couples. The hypothesis that internalized racism is inversely related to marital satisfaction is marginally to acceptably supported. Husbands reporting more internalized racism tended to report less marital satisfaction just as wives reporting more internalized racism tended to report less marital satisfaction. Marital satisfaction of wives was not affected directly by internalized racism of husbands, nor was marital satisfaction of husbands directly affected by internalized racism of wives. However, since marital satisfaction of husbands and wives was moderately correlated, it is possible that the effect of internalized racism of one spouse on marital satisfaction of the other is mediated through explanatory links identified in this paper. The role of socioeconomic status in mediating relationships between internalized racism and marital status is examined along with implications.

In evaluating the legacy of slavery in the United States, Grier and Cobbs (1968) argued that "the culture of slavery was never undone for either master or slave" and that "the minds of our citizens have never been freed" (p. 26). This condition of cultural alienation has been referred to variously as Negromacy (Thomas, 1971), pre-encounter (Cross, 1971, 1980; Cross, Parham, & Helms, in press), preconsciousness (Milliones, 1973), and ethnic captivity (Banks, 1981).

Taylor and Grundy (in press) suggested that the legacy of slavery is preserved to the extent Blacks internalized White racist conceptions of

---

This study was made possible by an award from the Office of the Provost, University of Pittsburgh. The writer expresses sincere thanks to Carolyn Grundy, without whose assistance this study would not have been possible.

Correspondence concerning this article should be sent to Dr. Jerome Taylor, Institute for the Black Family, Department of Black Community Education Research and Development, 3S09 Forbes Quad, University of Pittsburgh, Pittsburgh, PA 15260.

Blacks. On the one hand, the risk of internalization derives from the ubiquity of racism implied by Taylor and Grundy's revised taxonomy of 362 forms of racial oppression. On the other hand, the risk of internalization is greater to the extent that Blacks feel estranged from their culture of origin (Taylor, in press). It follows that cultural estrangement in face of endemic racism heightens vulnerability to internalization. To the extent that Blacks set adrift from their culture of origin think of themselves as White racists do, the whip of oppression has dominion over personal, social, and educational outcomes.

In the personal domain Blacks who internalize relatively high levels of racism are at greater risk of depression (Tomes & Brown, 1986), have lower self-esteem (Denton, 1985), are more aggressive and less nurturing (Denton, 1985), have less mature ego identity (Brown, 1979; Denton, 1985), and are likely to consume more alcohol (Taylor & Jackson, in press a, in press b) than Blacks who internalize relatively low levels of racism. In the social domain high internalizers relative to low internalizers are perceptibly less affiliative in relating to other Blacks who in turn are less affiliative in relating to them (Brown, 1979; Denton, 1985). Furthermore, high relative to low internalizers are more likely to commit serious crimes against the persons of other Blacks (Terrell, Taylor, & Terrell, 1980).

In the educational domain Asbury, Adderly-Kelly, and Knuckle (1987) found that middle school Black children with relatively high scores on select scales of a measure of Black cultural identity had significantly higher scores on subscales of the WISC-R than did Black children with relatively low scores on these scales. Relatedly, Spencer (1986) found Black children with Afrocentric orientation outperformed Black children with Eurocentric orientation on a cognitive task.

Although studies reviewed are consistent in implicating negative consequences of internalized racism in personal, social, and educational domains, the writer was unable to locate any studies that examined effects of internalized racism on the most intimate of relationships, marriage. However, since internalized racism is inversely related to variables theoretically related to marital satisfaction—nurturing disposition, relational warmth, positive self-esteem, mature ego identity—it is argued that internalized racism is inversely related to marital satisfaction, the basic hypothesis of this investigation. Evaluation of factors influencing marital quality seems all the more important since marital quality in general affects parenting attitudes (Goldberg & Easterbrooks, 1984) and child outcomes (Bond & McMahon, 1984; Ellison, 1983).

# Methods

## PARTICIPANTS

This investigation was part of a larger field study of factors affecting marital quality in Black inner-city families. Of the 100 Black married couples participating, approximately one-third came from each of three predominantly Black areas of a large Northeastern city. Within these neighborhoods, the percentage of Black residents ranged from 83% to 93%, with overall marriage percentage ranging from 46% to 49%. Student teams, dispatched to these neighborhoods, knocked on doors or randomly preselected addresses to determine household eligibility and interest.

More than 85% of Black households meeting the marriage eligibility criterion agreed to participate under the terms of this investigation that also included a small payment of $10.00 per couple. Median income for the sample ranged from $13,318 to $14,443 across the three neighborhoods and the percentage completing high school ranged from 61% to 64%. For the year these data were collected (1986), median income and educational attainment levels of the sample reached or exceeded those reported for the city as a whole.

Since data necessary for this study were missing on 4 couples, only 96 of the 100 couples were used in the analyses reported.

## INSTRUMENTS

The Marital Adjustment Test (MAT) designed by Locke and Wallace (1959) was used to estimate global marital satisfaction. On this 15-item self-report measure, respondents indicated overall satisfaction with the marriage and interspousal agreement or disagreement on a variety of marital issues. Responses were weighted as per instruction, and weighted scores were summed to obtain a total adjustment score. The MAT differentiates maritally distressed and nondistressed spouses (Koren, Carlton, & Shaw, 1980; Floyd & Markman, 1985).

The internalized racism scale of the Nadanolitization Inventory (NAD) developed by Taylor, Wilson, and Dobbins (1972) contains 24 items, each rated on a 0 to 8 scale. Items such as "Blacks are born with greater sexual lust than Whites" or "Blacks are just not as smart as Whites" were designed to estimate the extent to which Blacks internalize White racist stereotypes about Blacks. Blacks with higher NAD scores reported more depressive symptoms, lower self-esteem, and impaired relationships with other Blacks (Taylor, 1980; Taylor & Grundy, in press). Internal reliabilities have uniformly exceeded .80.

Finally, socioeconomic status was estimated from Hollingshead's (1975) four-factor index status, which is based on educational level and occupational attainment of husband and wife.

## PROCEDURES

Eight Black male and female undergraduate students were selected to conduct interviews with respondents in their homes. Interviewers received instructions on the mechanics of administration, were alerted to problems that might occur and presented with options to handle them, and were introduced to daily monitoring routines. Two initial interviews were conducted under direct supervision. Subsequent interviews were monitored once per week by co-principal investigators, Professors Mary Page and Nancy Washington.

Each pair of interviewers, one male and one female, was given a list of randomly selected addresses whose occupants were to be contacted in the randomized order in which they appeared on the list. Male and female interviewer teams visited identified households together. For eligible households agreeing to participate, husbands and wives completed the measures in separate rooms in the presence of the same sex interviewer.

## Results

In evaluating the basic hypothesis of this study, ratings of internalized racism by husbands and wives were used to predict ratings of marital satisfaction by husbands and wives.

For husbands' ratings of marital satisfaction, a multiple regression strategy entering internalized racism scores of husbands and wives as predictors revealed a significant overall effect ($F$ (1, 94) = 4.12, $p <$ .05), suggesting that internalized racism is predictive of marital satisfaction for husbands. The question, given overall significance, is whether husbands's and wives' internalized racism contributed equally or differentially to husbands' marital satisfaction. Evaluating the magnitude of component slopes associated with the regression of husbands' and wives' internalized racism on husbands' marital satisfaction revealed that the effect is significant for husbands ($t = -2.03$, $p < .03$) but not wives ($t = -.65$, $p > .05$). In accounting for husbands' marital satisfaction, then, husbands' but not wives' internalized racism is statistically significant: husbands reporting more internalized racism reported less marital satisfaction.

Parallel analyses were conducted for wives. The prediction of wives' marital satisfaction from husbands' and wives' internalized racism scores approached significance ($F$ (1, 94) = 3.55, $p < .06$). At the component level, internalized racism of wives ($t = -1.89$, $p < .03$) but not husbands ($t = -.25$, $p > .05$) is significant in accounting for marital satisfaction reported by wives. The finding that marital satisfaction reported by wives is significantly predicted by internalized racism of wives but not husbands is structurally similar to the pattern just noted for husbands. The correlation between marital satisfaction for wives and husbands was moderate, .56 ($p < .01$).

Although prediction equations for husbands' and wives' marital satisfaction corroborated the basic hypothesis of this study, the amount of variance in marital satisfaction captured by internalized racism is not altogether remarkable. The multiple $R$ for the prediction of husbands' satisfaction is .20 ($R^2 = 4\%$) and the multiple $R$ for wives' satisfaction is .19 ($R^2 = 3.6\%$). Suspicions arise therefore over the possibility that the internalization-satisfaction relationship is spuriously mediated through a third variable causally connected to both. We reasoned that socioeconomic status, a variable linked empirically to marital satisfaction and internalized racism, could well function in this way. This alternative was evaluated using a hierarchical regression strategy. In predicting marital satisfaction under this procedure, Hollinghead's (1975) four-factor index of socioeconomic status was first entered into the equation, followed by husbands' and wives' internalized racism that were entered as a block. In neither equation was the role of internalized racism significant after controlling for the effects of socioeconomic status. This result is not inconsistent with the hypotheses of spuriously mediated effect; this is, the relationship between internalization and satisfaction may be "caused by" socioeconomic standing. Examination of partial *betas* indicated a direct relationship between socioeconomic status and marital satisfaction and an inverse relationship between socioeconomic status and internalized racism.

## Discussion

The hypothesis that internalized racism is inversely related to marital satisfaction was partially supported by the results of this study. In particular, husbands reporting more internalized racism tended to report less marital satisfaction just as wives reporting more internalized racism tended to report less marital satisfaction. Marital satisfaction of wives was not affected directly by internalized racism of husbands, nor was marital satisfaction of husbands affected directly by internalized racism of wives. However, since the correlation between marital satisfaction of husbands and wives was moderate (.56), it is possible that the effect of internalized racism of one spouse on marital satisfaction of of the other is mediated through a three-link explanatory chain: (a) internalized racism of spouse A affects spouse A's marital satisfaction; (b) spouse A's marital satisfaction affects spouse B's marital satisfaction; and (c) internalized racism of A has an indirect effect on spouse B's marital satisfaction through its direct effect on A's marital satisfaction that affects B's. Although not specifically evaluated in this study, clarification of direct and indirect effects of internalized racism would add considerably to the nomological understanding of this construct. In this connection, it is also possible that spouse A's internalized racism affects spouse B's marital satisfaction through other proximal mediators such as A's personality—level of self-esteem or depression. It could be the case, for example, that internalized racism affects level of depression (Tomes & Brown, 1986) that consistently has been linked to marital quality (Heins, 1978; Coyne, Kahn, & Gotlib, 1987). It is also possible that marital satisfaction between spouses is influenced not only by internalized racism but also by socioeconomic status that may be correlated with both. As important as efforts to clarify conditions under which internalization has an effect are efforts to establish boundary conditions beyond which it has no effect. For example, it appears that whereas internalized racism influences personality and attitudinal variables of a wide range (Taylor, in press), it does not appear to influence communication efficiency or instrumental resourcefulness in intimate settings (Grundy, 1988).

    That the internalization-satisfaction relationship may be spuriously mediated by socioeconomic status is cause for alarm. As structural disadvantagement increases, internalized racism increases as marital satisfaction decreases, an implication of special seriousness in an economy where the socioeconomic gap between Black and White is widening at an accelerating rate. Results of this study identify the processes through which structural factors may have selectively deleterious effects on Black marriages.

    Finally, we raise the question of why low socioeconomic status has a negative impact on internalized racism and marital satisfaction. Does underschooling, unemployment, or underemployment "cause" identification with slave culture—"Blacks are just not as smart as Whites"? Do these cognitions "cause" feelings of exasperation and resignation that stifle or crush hopes of upward mobility, recursively producing lower socioeconomic outcomes as self-fulfilling prophecy? Does underschooling, unemployment, or underemployment "cause" displacement of frustrations originating outside the home onto relationships inside the home? Do these cognitions and displacements diminish hopes of the young whose cognitive and affective development are influenced by experiences of their parents? Is there implied here a virulent strain of social Lamarckism contributing to the growing underclass in Black America? Answers to these research questions could yield clues on how to enhance the viability of Black families in America.

## References

Asbury, C. A., Adderly-Kelly, B., & Knuckle, E. P. (1987). Relationships among WISC-R performance categories and measured ethnic identity in Black adolescents. *Journal of Negro Education, 56,* 172-183.

Banks, J. (1981). *Multiethnic education: Theory and practice.* Boston: Allyn & Bacon.

Bond, C. R., & McMahon, R. J. (1984). Relationships between marital distress and child behavior problems, maternal personal adjustment, maternal personality, and maternal parenting behavior. *Journal of Abnormal Psychology, 93,* 348-351.

Brown, A. B. (1979). *Black consciousness prototypes: A profile analysis of the Developmental Inventory of Black Consciousness (DIB-C).* Unpublished doctoral dissertation, University of Pittsburgh, Pittsburgh, PA.

Coyne, J. C., Kahn, J., & Gotlib, I. H. (1987). Depression. In T. Jacob (Ed.), *Family interaction and psychotherapy* (pp. 509-533). New York: Plenum.

Cross, W. E. (1971). The Negro-to-Black conversion experience: Toward a psychology of Black liberation. *Black World, 20,* 13-37.

Cross, W. E. (1980). Modes of psychological Nigrescence: A literature review. In R. L. Jones (Ed.), *Black psychology* (2nd ed.) (pp. 81-98). New York: Harper & Row.

Cross, W. E., Parham, T. A., & Helms, J. E. (in press). The stages of Black identity development: Nigresence models. In R. L. Jones (Ed.), *Black psychology* (3rd ed.). Berkeley, CA: Cobb & Henry.

Denton, S. E. (1985). *A methodological refinement and validation analysis of the Development Inventory of Black Consciousness (DIB-C).* Unpublished doctoral dissertation, University of Pittsburgh, Pittsburgh, PA.

Ellison, E. S. (1983). Issues concerning parental harmony and children's psychosocial adjustment. *American Journal of Orthopsychiatry, 53,* 74-79.

Floyd, F., & Markman, H. (1985). Observational biases in spouse interaction: Toward a cognitive/behavioral model of marriage. *Journal of Consulting and Clinical Psychology, 51,* 450-457.

Goldberg, W. A., & Easterbrooks, M. A. (1984). Role of marital quality in toddler development. *Developmental Psychology, 20,* 504-514.

Grier, W. H., & Cobbs, P. M. (1968). *Black rage.* New York: Basic Books.

Grundy, C. (1988). *Effects of internalized racism on marital quality in Black couples.* Unpublished master's thesis, University of Pittsburgh, Pittsburgh, PA.

Heins, T. (1978). Marital interaction in depression. *Australian and New Zealand Journal of Psychiatry, 12,* 269-275.

Hollingshead, A. B. (1975). *Four factor index of social status.* Unpublished manuscript.

Koren, P., Carlton, K., & Shaw, D. (1980). Marital conflict: Relations among behavior, outcomes, and distress. *Journal of Consulting and Clinical Psychology, 48,* 460-498.

Locke, H. J., & Wallace, K. M. (1959). Short marital-adjustment and prediction tests: Their reliability and validity. *Marriage and Family Living, 21,* 251-255.

Milliones, J. (1973). *Construction of the Developmental Inventory of Black Consciousness.* Unpublished doctoral dissertation, University of Pittsburgh, Pittsburgh, PA.

Spencer, M. B. (1986, January 30). *Minority children and mental health: Old perspectives and new proposals.* Workshop presentation sponsored by the National Institutes of Mental Health, "Minority Children and Mental Health," Atlanta, GA.

Taylor, J. (1980). Dimensionalizations of racialism and the Black experience: The Pittsburgh project. In R. L. Jones (Ed.), *Black psychology* (2nd ed.) (pp. 384-400). New York: Harper & Row.

Taylor J. (in press). Cultural conversion experiences: Implications for mental health research and treatment. In R. L. Jones (Ed.), *Advances in Black psychology* (Vol. 3). Berkeley, CA: Cobb & Henry.

Taylor, J., & Grundy, C. (in press). Measuring Black internalization of White stereotypes about Blacks: The Nadanolitization Scale. In R. L. Jones (Ed.), *Handbook of tests and measurements for Black populations* (Vol. 2). Berkeley, CA: Cobb & Henry.

Taylor, J., & Jackson, B. (in press a). Factors affecting alcohol consumption in Black women: Part I. *International Journal of the Addictions.*

Taylor, J., & Jackson, B. (in press b). Factors affecting alcohol consumption in Black women: Part II. *International Journal of the Addictions.*

Taylor, J., Wilson, M., & Dobbins, J. (1972). *Nadanolitization Scale.* Pittsburgh, PA: University of Pittsburgh, Institute for the Black Family.

Terrell, F., Taylor, J., & Terrell, S. (1980). Self concept of juveniles who commit Black on Black crimes. *Corrective and Social Psychiatry, 26,* 107-109.

Tomes, E., & Brown, A. (1986). *Psychological factors and depression among Black women of low socioeconomic status.* Unpublished manuscript, University of Pittsburgh, Pittsburgh, PA.

# Coping With Provider Role Strain: Adaptive Cultural Resources Among Black Husband-Fathers

## PHILLIP J. BOWMAN*
*University of Illinois at Urbana-Champaign*

This study investigated provider role strain and adaptive cultural resources as predictors of global family satisfaction in a national sample of Black husband-fathers ($N$ = 372). Multiple classification analysis revealed that provider role strain predictors had a significant negative effect on family satisfaction, with the harmful effect of objective difficulty being exacerbated by subjective reactions. In line with a role strain-adaptation model, cultural resources had offsetting positive effects with kinship bond and religious belief emerging as especially powerful predictors. In support of a buffering hypothesis, kinship bond eliminated harmful effects of both husband and father role discouragement. However, kinship bond failed to mitigate the harmful effect of objective employment difficulty. Findings not only provide important insight into the social psychology of role strain and adaptation, but also have relevance for clinical practice and public policy.

Psychologists and other social scientists have focused considerable attention on difficulties experienced by Black males in major life roles (Bowman, 1989; Evans & Whitfield, 1988; Gary, 1981; Staples, 1982; Wilkinson & Taylor, 1977). National data clearly document the serious problems that Black males face in educational, employment, and family roles (W. Allen & Farley, 1985; Farley & Allen, 1987; Wilson, 1987). Unfortunately, however, most existing research is descriptive rather

I would like to thank Ms. Judy Tolliver and Arnita Althaus for clerical assistance with this manuscript. Thanks are also due to University of Michigan's Program for Research on Black Americans.

Research for this article was undertaken with funding from the National Research Council and the Ford Foundation. At the time of this writing, Dr. Bowman was a visiting Senior Research Fellow with the University of Michigan's Institute for Social Research. He is currently an Assistant Professor of Psychology and Afro-American Studies at the University of Illinois, 603 East Daniel, Champaign, IL 61820. Correspondence regarding this article should be sent to Phillip J. Bowman at the above address.
*EDITORS' NOTE: Currently at Northwestern University.

than explicitly theory-driven and predictive. The fundamental nature, antecedents, and consequences of difficulties experienced by Black males in valued social roles remain ill understood and controversial. Research on Black males in social roles has most often been guided by a *pathology model* that views psychological and/or cultural deficits as the pivotal causes of dysfunctional behaviors.

## Beyond Pathology

The predominance of pathology research has resulted in Black males, especially in family roles, being depicted primarily as deviant or deficient (Bowman, 1989). Emphasis has been on Black fathers who are either absent from their families (Hetherington, 1966; Hendricks & Fullilove, 1983; Shinn, 1978), inadequate family providers (Coles, 1978; Liebow, 1967; Price-Bonham & Skenn, 1979), or marginally involved in other aspects of family life (Daniels, 1986; Dietrich, 1975; Schultz, 1978; Taylor, 1978). Despite these detailed examinations of Black fathers who are deserters or victims, we still know very little about responsible Black husband-fathers who somehow cope with discouraging provider role barriers (Bowman, 1985, 1989, in press; Jackson, 1978; McAdoo, 1988). Going beyond the pathology paradigm, the present study of Black husband-fathers in a national sample investigates how indigenous cultural resources facilitate adaptive coping with provider role strain. A more *Africentric* approach emphasizes the adaptive value of familial, religious, and other ethnic orientations as individuals cope with chronic strain in major life roles. In a critical review of literature on Black males, Bowman (1989) found that researchers have begun to formulate alternatives to the pathology model that provide a more balanced, meaningful, and accurate body of knowledge.

## Alternative Research Perspectives

As shown in Table 10.1, studies on Black fathers tend to emphasize one of four distinct themes—*pathology, oppression, coping,* or *ethnicity.* These four competing research approaches differ in two essential ways: (1) the degree of emphasis on maladaptive *or* adaptive behavioral patterns, and (2) the degree of emphasis on internal *or* external causal factors in the analysis of these behavioral patterns. Similar to pathology research, *oppression* studies focus on maladaptive rather than adaptive experiences of Black fathers. However, rather than reduce the blame to psychological or

**TABLE 10.1** Research Perspectives on Black Fathers

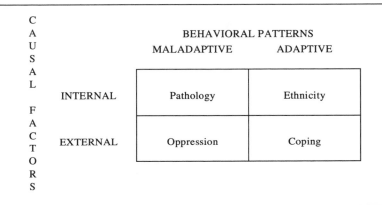

Note: From "Research perspectives on Black men" by P. J. Bowman. In R. L. Jones (Ed.), *Black Adult Development and Aging* (p. 119), 1989, Berkeley, CA: Cobbs & Henry. Copyright 1989 by R. L. Jones. Reprinted by permission.

cultural deficits, external institutional barriers are focused on as the root causes of difficulties faced by Black fathers (Gary, 1981; Liebow, 1967; Staples, 1982). In contrast to problem- oriented pathology and oppression research, coping studies focus on successful Black fathers who somehow take advantage of existing opportunities (Billingsley, 1968; Cazenave, 1979, 1981; Taylor, 1981). Finally, *ethnicity* researchers not only focus on successful Black fathers, but also emphasize the pivotal influence of indigenous cultural strengths in fostering adaptive familial behaviors (Ashante, 1981; Hill, 1971; Tinney, 1981).

## Role Strain-Adaptation: An Integrative Model

A growing literature of the *social psychology of role strain and adaptation* provides a systematic basis for linking essential elements from oppression, pathology, coping, and ethnicity models within a coherent research framework (Barnett & Baruch, 1985; Baruch & Barnett, 1986; Bowman, 1988, 1989, in press; L. I. Pearlin, 1983; L. I. Pearlin, Lieberman, Menaghan, & Mullan, 1981; Sarbin & Allen, 1969). Within a role strain-adaptation paradigm, the four distinct research orientations on Black fathers are not necessarily incompatible. Two basic notions in this integrative approach are (1) *that oppressive provider role barriers can result in either pathological or adaptive coping* and (2) *that indigenous ethnic or cultural resources can facilitate adaptive coping.* Role Strain involves both objective difficulty in a valued social role, and subjective reactions to such difficulty, that impede one's achievement of valued goals. *Normative* role strains are produced periodically by either role transitions, stressful events, or other problems that occur as individuals face adjustments in major life roles (V. Allen & Vande Vliert, 1981; Felner, Faber, & Primavera, 1980; Goode, 1960). However, *chronic* role strains can be produced either by personal limitations, or by external environmental barriers, or by conflicts at the person-environment interface (Kahn, Wolfe, Quinn, Snoek, & Rosenthal, 1964; Merton, 1968; L. I. Pearlin & Lieberman, 1979; L. I. Pearlin et al., 1981). *Role adaptation* refers to the process through which individuals mobilize accessible resources, or fail to mobilize them, in efforts to cope with role strain (S. Cohen & Wills, 1985; Kessler, Price, & Wortman, 1985; Menaghan, 1983; L. E. Pearlin & Schooler, 1978; Sarbin & Allen, 1968).

The specific *role strain-adaptation model* guiding the present study builds on an ongoing program of research (Bowman, 1984, 1985, 1988, 1989, in press; Bowman & Howard, 1985; Bowman, Jackson, Hatchett, & Gurin, 1982). Several premises regarding provider role strain and cultural adaptation are illustrated in Figure 10.1. First, *socially structured inequalities increase provider role strain which, in turn, reduces psychological well-being and family life quality* (arrows A and B). Among Black fathers, harmful psychosocial consequences of economic displacement and marginality are mediated by provider role strain (Bowman, 1985, 1988; Wilson, 1987). In addition to objective employment difficulty, provider role strain also includes role perceptions such as discouragement that may further impede adaptive coping.

*Indigenous ethnic patterns within African American communities may reaffirm adaptive cultural resources that, in turn, enhance psychological well-being and family life quality* (arrows C and D). Thus, among Black fathers, positive psychosocial effects of ethnicity may be mediated by a set of cultural resources (Bowman, 1989, in press; Hill, 1971). While flexible family roles represent an objective cultural resource, subjective cultural resources include such variables as strong kinship bonds, para-kin bonds, ethnic coping orientations, and religious or spiritual beliefs. Specific measures of these cultural strengths are employed in the present study to explore their adaptive value for Black husband-fathers. In a reciprocal manner, these adaptive cultural resources may be reinforced by social inequalities while also promoting

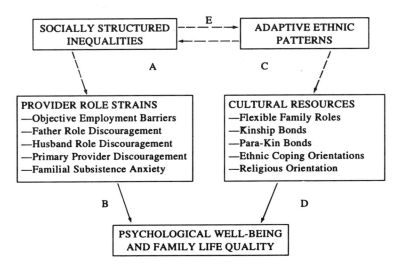

**Figure 10.1.** Interrelationships Among Major Classes of Variables in Provider Role Strain-Cultural Resource Model.

collective struggle to change such inequalities (arrows E). Rather than mere reactions to oppression, *Africentric* studies note that such cultural resources represent unique African forms that have been transmitted across the generations (Ashante, 1981; Baldwin, 1981; Berry & Blassingame, 1982; Herskovits, 1935; Nobles, 1974, 1988; Sudarkasa, 1980, 1988).

The hypotheses investigated in the present study make specific predictions about (1) *harmful effects* of objective and subjective dimensions of provider role strain on global family life quality, (2) *adaptive effects* of objective and subjective cultural resources, and (3) how adaptive cultural resources might *moderate harmful effects* of provider role strain. Each hypothesis regarding predictions of family life satisfaction is guided by findings from an earlier study on Black husband-fathers that investigated provider role strain predictors of global life happiness (Bowman, 1985). The earlier study found that the negative effect of husband role discouragement explained more variance in global happiness than did the objective employment barriers or other subjective reactions (father role discouragement, primary provider discouragement, or family subsistence anxiety). Thus, *husband role discouragement* is hypothesized to be a better predictor of family life quality than other dimensions of provider role strain. Religious orientation had a stronger enhancing effect on global happiness than flexible family roles or other subjective cultural measures of close kinship bond, para-kin bond, or ethnic coping orientation. Hence, *religious belief* is hypothesized to be a better predictor of global family life quality than are any of the other four cultural resources. It is also hypothesized that the most powerful cultural resource should reduce the negative effect of provider role strain dimensions on family life quality.

## Method

The data analyzed to test the above hypotheses were collected from a national cross-section sample of the Black adult population living in the continental United States. This sample was drawn according to a multistage, area probability sampling procedure designed to ensure that every Black household in the nation had the same chance of being selected for the interview (Kish, 1965). Detailed information is also available on the data collection procedures, characteristics of the sample, specific survey instruments, and public access to these national data (Bowman, 1983; Jackson & Gurin, 1987; Jackson, Tucker, & Bowman, 1990). Specialized screening techniques were developed to produce a national sample that more accurately represents all noninstitutionalized Black adults than in past studies. Highly trained interviewers completed 2,107 face-to-face interviews during 1979-1980 for a response rate of 67.1%. The majority of the sample resided in the South (53%) followed by the North Central (22%), Northeast (19%), and West (6%). Twenty percent lived in rural areas and a full 80% were urban residents. The respondents ranged in age from 18 to 101 years; 1,810 were females and 797 males. This study focuses specifically on 372 Black men who were both fathers and husbands.

### MEASURES

Data were collected through a carefully designed two-hour interview schedule that yielded a wide range of measures in several major areas—psychological well-being, life stress, employment experience, family, support networks, cultural patterns, and social background. Special focus group techniques and extensive pretesting increased the cultural sensitivity and quality of each measure. The specific dependent, independent, and control variables used in this multivariate study are described below.

## DEPENDENT VARIABLES

To measure global family life quality, respondents were asked: How satisfied are you with your family life, that is, the time you spend and the things you do with members of your family? Respondents were coded on a 4-point Likert-type scale that ranged from 1 ("very dissatisfied") to 4 ("very satisfied"). Although a single item, studies have shown this satisfaction measure to be a useful indicator of general family life quality; family satisfaction also correlated well with other global quality of life indicators (i.e., Andrews & Withey, 1974).

## INDEPENDENT VARIABLES

The two major sets of independent variables included five provider role strain predictors and five cultural resource predictors, which were measured as follows:

*Provider Role Strain. Objective employment difficulty:* Respondents were coded into a five-level employment status variable with the following categories: (1) High paying job, (2) Low paying job, (3) Not interested in job, (4) Hidden unemployed, (5) Officially unemployed. *Father role discouragement:* Respondents were asked, "Given the chances you have had, how well have you done at being a good father to your children? Do you think you have done very well, fairly well, not too well, or not well at all?" *Husband role discouragement:* "How have you done at being a good husband to your wife? Do you think you have done very well, fairly well, not too well, or not well at all?" *Primary provider discouragement:* "How well have you done in taking care of your family's wants and needs? Do you think you have done very well, fairly well, not too well, or not well at all?" *Family subsistence anxiety:* "How much do you worry that your total family income will not meet your family's expenses and bills? Would you say you worry a great deal, a lot, a little, or not at all?"

*Coping Resources. Flexible family roles:* Respondents were asked, "How many people in your household including yourself give money to support your household?" *Kinship bond:* "Would you say your family members are very close in their feelings to each other, fairly close, not too close, or not close at all?" *Para-kin bond:* "Not counting your husband/wife/partner, do you have a best friend? Do you have any friends that you feel very close to?" *Ethnic coping orientation:* "In this country if Black people do not get a good education or job, is it because (1) they haven't had the same chances as Whites in this country, or (2) they have no one to blame but themselves?" *Religious orientation:* "How religious would you say you are—very religious, fairly religious, not too religious, or not religious at all?"

*Control Variables. Age:* Respondents were categorized 18–34 years old, 35–54 years old, and those 55 and older: *Region:* Four categories included the southern, north central, northeastern, and western United States; *Urbanity:* Three categories included rural, small city/suburban, and metropolitan areas.

## DATA ANALYSIS PROCEDURE

Multiple classification analysis (MCA), in conjunction with one-way analysis of variance, is employed to investigate the relationships hypothesized in this study (Andrews, Morgan, Sonquist, & Klem, 1973). MCA is a form of multiple regression that estimates the separate and multiple effects of the various predictors (i.e., provider role strains, cultural resources) on global family life quality. For example, MCA estimates the magnitude of the separate effect of husband role discouragement, before (*Eta* coefficient) and after (*Beta* coefficient) controlling for other provider role strain dimensions. *F* tests are also calculated to evaluate the statistical significance of each predictor. The multiple correlation coefficient (*R*) estimates the joint effect of each set of predictors (i.e., provider role strain, cultural resource predictors).

## Results

### PROVIDER ROLE STRAIN AND GLOBAL FAMILY SATISFACTION

Results of the multiple classification analysis of husband role discouragement and other provider role strain predictors on global family life quality are shown in Table 10.2. Data are presented on the singular effect of each provider role strain predictor (*Eta* and *Beta* coefficients) along with relevant class frequencies and means. The *Eta* coefficients and *F* tests reveal that husband role discouragement (.30, $p < .001$), father role discouragement (.28, $p < .001$), primary provider discouragement

**TABLE 10.2** Multiple Classification Analysis of Family Life Quality by Provider Role Strain Predictors[a]

|  | N | Class Mean | Eta | Beta |
|---|---|---|---|---|
| Provider Role Strain Predictors |  |  |  |  |
| Objective Employment Barriers |  |  | .23** | .10[.16] |
| High paying job | 134 | 2.42 |  |  |
| Low paying job | 129 | 2.41 |  |  |
| Officially unemployed | 14 | 2.29 |  |  |
| Hidden unemployed | 27 | 2.63 |  |  |
| Not in labor force | 48 | 2.83 |  |  |
| Father Role Discouragement |  |  | .28*** | .15[.13] |
| Doing very well | 271 | 2.58 |  |  |
| Not doing very well | 81 | 2.15 |  |  |
| Husband Role Discouragement |  |  | .30** | .11[.13] |
| Doing very well | 250 | 2.61 |  |  |
| Not doing very well | 102 | 2.18 |  |  |
| Primary Provider Discouragement |  |  | .27*** | .10[.13] |
| Doing very well | 210 | 2.62 |  |  |
| Doing fairly well | 130 | 2.29 |  |  |
| Not doing well | 12 | 2.08 |  |  |
| Family Subsistence Anxiety |  |  | .13 | .07[.08] |
| Don't worry at all | 139 | 2.59 |  |  |
| Worry a little | 121 | 2.41 |  |  |
| Worry a lot | 35 | 2.43 |  |  |
| Worry a great deal | 57 | 2.40 |  |  |
| Control Variables |  |  |  |  |
| Age |  |  | .29*** | .19 |
| 18-34 years old | 113 | 2.24 |  |  |
| 35-54 years old | 141 | 2.52 |  |  |
| 55 years and older | 97 | 2.73 |  |  |
| Region |  |  | .09 | .02 |
| South | 190 | 2.52 |  |  |
| North Central | 81 | 2.38 |  |  |
| Northeast | 57 | 2.49 |  |  |
| West | 23 | 2.57 |  |  |
| Urban City |  |  | .15* | .09 |
| Rural | 89 | 2.61 |  |  |
| Small city/suburb | 100 | 2.40 |  |  |
| Metropolitan | 161 | 2.48 |  |  |

$R$ (adjusted) = .38[.36]
$R^2$ (adjusted) = .14[.13]
a. Partial coefficients [*Betas*] and multiple coefficients [*Rs*] within brackets represent effects within the more restricted model including only the provider role strain predictors.
*$p < .05$
**$p < .01$
***$p < .001$

(.27, *p* > .001) and objective employment difficulty (.23, *p* < .01) all had statistically significant effects on global family satisfaction. Only the level of anxiety over family economic subsistence failed to reach statistical significance (*Eta* = .13).

Since the zero-order coefficients (*Etas*) for the four significant provider role strain dimensions are similar in magnitude, the *Beta* coefficients provide additional insight into their relative effects. *Beta* coefficients in the brackets ([ ]) show that the effect magnitude of each provider role strain predictor is reduced when effects of the other predictors are controlled. This reduction suggests overlap among the provider role strain predictors, but the similar magnitude of these *Beta* coefficients also indicates that they combine somewhat equally in explaining 13% ($R^2$) of the variance in global family satisfaction. The introduction of selected control variables adds very little to the overall prediction ($R^2$ = .14), despite the statistically significant bivariate coefficients for both age (*Eta* = .29, *p* < .001) and urbanity (*Eta* = .15, *p* < .05).

An examination of the cell means indicates, as expected, that official unemployment is clearly linked to lower levels of satisfaction with family life. Moreover, subjective indicators of provider role discouragement also show linear effects with various perceived role difficulties systematically decreasing the level of global family satisfaction. For example, global family satisfaction was higher if husband-fathers reported doing very well in meeting the needs of their *children* (mean (M) = 2.58), *wives* (*M* = 2.61) and *family* (*M* = 2.62) than if they perceived difficulty in these three provider role areas (*M*s = 2.15, 2.18, and 2.08 respectively). Unexpectedly, and without statistical significance, husband- fathers who worried a great deal about family economic subsistence were only slightly lower in global family satisfaction (*M* = 2.40) than those who did not worry at all (*M* = 2.59).

## CULTURAL RESOURCES AND
## GLOBAL FAMILY SATISFACTION

Findings on the relative effects of religious belief and other cultural resources on global family satisfaction appear in Table 10.3. The *Eta* coefficients indicate that family closeness (.21, *p* < .001) and religious belief (.16, *p* < .01) were the only cultural resources with statistically significant effects on global family satisfaction. Husband-fathers who were members of "very close" families expressed higher levels of

**TABLE 10.3** Multiple Classification Analysis of Family Life Quality by Informal Coping Resource Predictors[a]

|  | Class N | Mean | Eta | Beta |
|---|---|---|---|---|
| Informal Coping Resource Predictors |  |  |  |  |
| Flexible Family Roles |  |  | .06 | .08[.08] |
| One family provider | 128 | 2.42 |  |  |
| Two family providers | 209 | 2.50 |  |  |
| Three or more providers | 19 | 2.53 |  |  |
| Kinship Bonds |  |  | .21*** | .16[.19] |
| Not too close | 19 | 2.37 |  |  |
| Fairly close | 112 | 2.31 |  |  |
| Very close | 226 | 2.57 |  |  |
| Para-Kin Relations |  |  | .05 | .04[.06] |
| No close friend | 63 | 2.48 |  |  |
| Close friend | 53 | 2.55 |  |  |
| Best friend | 240 | 2.54 |  |  |
| Ethnic Coping Orientation |  |  | .09 | .07[.07] |
| Individual blame | 115 | 2.56 |  |  |
| System blame | 240 | 2.44 |  |  |
| Religious Orientation |  |  | .16** | .08[.12] |
| Not too religious | 56 | 2.25 |  |  |
| Fairly religious | 169 | 2.49 |  |  |
| Very religious | 131 | 2.55 |  |  |
| Control Variables |  |  |  |  |
| Age |  |  | .29*** | .25 |
| 18-34 years old | 111 | 2.23 |  |  |
| 35-54 years old | 142 | 2.38 |  |  |
| 55 years and older | 103 | 2.71 |  |  |
| Region |  |  | .08 | .02 |
| South | 189 | 2.51 |  |  |
| North Central | 82 | 2.38 |  |  |
| Northeast | 60 | 2.50 |  |  |
| West | 25 | 2.48 |  |  |
| Urban City |  |  | .15* | .12 |
| Rural | 90 | 2.63 |  |  |
| Small city/suburb | 101 | 2.38 |  |  |
| Metropolitan | 164 | 2.45 |  |  |

$R$ (adjusted) = .31[.22]

$R^2$ (adjusted) = .10[.05]

a. Partial coefficients [*Betas*] and multiple coefficients [*Rs*] within brackets represent effects within the more restricted model including only the informal coping resource predictors.

*$p < .05$

**$p < .01$

***$p < .001$

global family satisfaction ($M = 2.57$) than their counterparts who reported that their families were only "fairly close" ($M = 2.31$) or "not too close" ($M = 2.37$). The class means on religious belief revealed a similar pattern with the very religious expressing the greatest level of global family satisfaction ($M = 2.55$), followed by the fairly religious ($M = 2.49$) and the not too religious ($M = 2.25$). The slightly higher family satisfaction among husband-fathers in households with more than one provider ($Eta = .06$), or who had a close friend ($Eta = .05$), or who blamed Blacks rather than the system for inequalities ($Eta = .09$) did not reach statistical significance.

The relatively powerful independent effect of family closeness remained even after partialling out effects of other cultural resources ($Beta = .19$) and selected control variables ($Beta = .16$). Overlapping effects of family closeness, religious belief, age, and urbanity are suggested by the slightly lower family closeness *Beta* coefficient when contrasted with the corresponding *Eta* coefficient. Despite multicollinearity between family closeness and other predictors, this measure of kinship bond combined largely with religious belief to explain 5% ($R^2$) and with age and urbanity to account for 10% ($R^2$) of the variance in global family satisfaction. Thus, being a member of a very close family, being very religious, being older, and living in a nonurban community operated independently and additively to enhance global family satisfaction among husband-fathers.

FAMILY CLOSENESS: A MODERATOR OF
STRAIN-SATISFACTION RELATIONSHIPS

It was hypothesized that the most powerful cultural resource should reduce the deleterious effect of provider role strain on global family satisfaction. To evaluate this hypothesis, data in Table 10.4 estimate multiple and independent effects of provider role strain predictors separately for husband-fathers in close families versus less close families. Strong kinship bond, as measured by a very close family, reduced the multiple *R* as well as several *Eta* and *Beta* coefficients that indicate harmful provider role strain effects.

As hypothesized, the joint effects of the five provider role strain predictors on global family satisfaction emerged as less devastating if husband-fathers were members of very close ($R = .29$) rather than less close ($R = .40$) families. Comparing the *Beta* coefficients under the two conditions provides insight into specific provider role strain dimensions that accounted for the reduced multiple effect ($R$) within very close families. Very

**TABLE 10.4** Multiple Classification Analysis of Family Life Quality, by Provider Role Strain Predictors and Kinship Bonds

| Provider Role Strain Predictors | N | *Very Close Families* Class % Means | | Eta | Beta | N | *Not Very Close Families* Class % Means | | Eta | Beta |
|---|---|---|---|---|---|---|---|---|---|---|
| Objective Employment Barriers | | | | .22 | .15 | | | | .23 | .22 |
| High paying job | 71 | (34) | 2.54 | | | 49 | (38) | 2.35 | | |
| Low paying job | 71 | (34) | 2.54 | | | 58 | (45) | 2.26 | | |
| Officially unemployed | 9 | (5) | 2.44 | | | 5 | (3) | 2.00 | | |
| Hidden unemployed | 19 | (9) | 2.74 | | | 8 | (5) | 2.38 | | |
| Not in labor force | 38 | (18) | 2.84 | | | 10 | (8) | 2.80 | | |
| Father Role Discouragement | | | | .19 | .06 | | | | .35 | .25 |
| Doing very well | 180 | (81) | 2.63 | | | 90 | (69) | 2.49 | | |
| Not doing very well | 41 | (19) | 2.32 | | | 40 | (31) | 1.97 | | |
| Husband Role Discouragement | | | | .22 | .08 | | | | .37 | .21 |
| Doing very well | 169 | (76) | 2.65 | | | 80 | (62) | 2.54 | | |
| Not doing very well | 52 | (24) | 2.33 | | | 50 | (38) | 2.02 | | |
| Primary Provider Discouragement | | | | .24 | .16 | | | | .26 | .02 |
| Doing very well | 144 | (65) | 2.68 | | | 66 | (51) | 2.50 | | |
| Doing fairly well | 74 | (33) | 2.39 | | | 55 | (42) | 2.16 | | |
| Not doing well | 3 | (2) | 2.20 | | | 9 | (7) | 2.11 | | |
| Family Subsistence Anxiety | | | | .22 | .16 | | | | .15 | .17 |
| Don't worry at all | 94 | (43) | 2.72 | | | 45 | (34) | 2.31 | | |
| Worry a little | 72 | (33) | 2.42 | | | 49 | (37) | 2.41 | | |
| Worry a lot | 21 | (10) | 2.43 | | | 14 | (11) | 2.43 | | |
| Worry a great deal | 34 | (16) | 2.59 | | | 22 | (17) | 2.14 | | |

$R$ (adjusted) = .29
$R^2$ (adjusted) = .086

$R$ (adjusted) = .40
$R^2$ (adjusted) = .161

close families virtually eliminated the independent effects of both husband role discouragement (*Beta* = .08) and father role discouragement (*Beta* = .06), whereas the not-close family condition exacerbated the independent effects of both (*Betas* = .21 and .25 respectively). In a rather striking manner, the absence of very close family ties increased negative effects of both husband and father role discouragement. Harmful provider role strain effects within very close families were restricted to objective employment difficulty, primary provider discouragement, and anxiety about family economic subsistence. Interestingly, discouragement as a primary provider had a more negative effect when families were perceived as very close (*Beta* = .16) rather than not very close (*Beta* = .02). However, objective unemployment and family economic worries were negatively associated with family life satisfaction regardless of family closeness.

As shown in Table 10.4, a comparison of specific class means under very close versus not-close family conditions also suggests that family closeness may directly reduce subjective aspects of provider role strain, and directly enhance global family satisfaction. Husband-fathers within very close families were as likely as those in the not-close condition to be unemployed, but they were consistently less likely to experience subjective aspects of provider role strain. For example, only 35% within very close families reported primary provider discouragement (perceived that they were not doing very well in meeting the general wants and needs of their families) compared to a full 49% within less close families. Moreover, at each level of provider role strain, the global family satisfaction means are higher within very close families than they are within less close families.

## Discussion

The present findings support a role strain-adaptation model that emphasizes both harmful psychosocial effects of chronic role strain and mitigating effects of adaptive cultural resources (Bowman, 1984, 1985, 1989, in press; Bowman & Howard, 1985; Bowman et al., 1982). As hypothesized, global family satisfaction among Black husband-fathers was reduced by provider role strain but enhanced by indigenous cultural resources. By clarifying effects of specific dimensions of provider role strain, results go beyond traditional descriptive research on the family role difficulties of Black fathers (Coles, 1978; Hetherington, 1966; Liebow, 1967; Price-Bonham & Skeen, 1979; Shinn, 1978). Data also provide new insight into the manner in which specific cultural strengths operate in the role adaptation process (Hill, 1971; Manns, 1981; Tinney, 1984). In line with the conceptual model, it is important to note that the provider role strain and cultural resource effects may mediate the broader impact of macro economic and indigenous ethnic patterns. Provider role strain predictors may mediate the harmful psychosocial impact of structural economic dislocation experienced by Black males in post-industrial America (W. Allen & Farley, 1985; Bowman, 1988; Wilson, 1987). Moreover, cultural resource predictors may mediate the adaptive impact of African American ethnic patterns which have been transmitted across the generations (Ashante, 1981; Berry & Blassingame, 1982; Herskovits, 1935; Nobles, 1988; Sudarkasa, 1988).

Within the context of existing theoretical literature, present data provide a basis to better understand the social psychology of role strain and adaptation (Bowman, 1990a, 1990b; L. I. Pearlin, 1983; Sarbin & Allen, 1968). Findings help to clarify the basic nature and consequences of chronic strain in major life roles. Results support the notion that harmful effects of chronic role strain occur as objective difficulty combines with discouragement and other risky role perceptions (Baruch & Barnett, 1986; Bowman, 1984, 1989; R. Cohen, 1978; Feather & Davenport, 1981; L. I. Pearlin et al., 1981; L. E. Pearlin & Schooler, 1978). However, results are not entirely congruent with the earlier study of Black husband-fathers that focused on global happiness rather than on family satisfaction (Bowman, 1985). In the earlier study, low personal happiness was associated much more with husband role discouragement (perceived difficulty in providing for one's wife) than with other provider role strain dimensions. In contrast, the present study found that low family satisfaction was associated about equally with husband role discouragement and three other provider role strain dimensions—objective employment difficulty, father role discouragement, and family subsistence anxiety. Therefore, a broader array of provider role strain dimensions may reduce family satisfaction; husband role discouragement may especially erode personal happiness. Hence, various aspects of role strain may have differential effects depending on the specific outcome measure. Future inquiry needs to further clarify the manner in which various aspects of chronic role strain combine to increase risks for a wide range of maladaptive psychosocial outcome measures.

Results also identified cultural resources with particular power in the role adaptation process. The relatively powerful effects of family closeness and religious belief on global family satisfaction are consistent with a growing literature on the cultural strengths of African Americans (i.e., Berry & Blassingame, 1982; Hill, 1971; Nobles, 1988). These family and religious measures were also the most prominent cultural resources in the earlier study of global happiness among Black husband-fathers (Bowman, 1985). However, the relative effects of these two cultural strengths were reversed for the two distinct psychosocial outcomes. Although the earlier study found that religious belief was the most powerful predictor of personal happiness, the present data revealed that family closeness was more important to family life satisfaction. One explanation for these findings is resource-outcome specificity. For example, strong kinship bonds may be especially important for adaptive outcomes within the family life domain, whereas religious belief may be more critical for adaptive religion-related behaviors and psychological well-being. Despite their lack of significance in the present study, cultural resources such as multiple family earners, close friendships, and system blame ideology may be linked to other adaptive outcomes. To be sure, these and other measures of flexible family roles, para-kin bonds, and ethnic coping orientations have been found to have adaptive value (Bowman, 1989; Bowman & Howard, 1985; Hill, 1971; Stack, 1974). Findings suggest that future inquiry should further unravel the operation of kinship bonds and other subjective cultural resources. For example, close kinship bonds may not only be interrelated with other cultural resources, but also may act as a pivotal intervening variable in the role adaptation process. Religious belief may increase close kinship bonds, which, in turn, promote a range of adaptive coping outcomes. Our findings also support studies on adaptive coping resources that suggest that close kinship bonds (1) moderate or buffer harmful effects of chronic provider role strain, (2) directly reduce subjective aspects of provider role strain, and (3) directly facilitate adaptive psychosocial outcomes (House, 1981; Menaghan, 1983; Turner, 1983; Wheaton, 1983).

In partial support of a buffering hypothesis, close families clearly reduced harmful effects of both husband and father role discouragement, but failed to mitigate effects of objective unemployment. The fact that very close families only reduced harmful effects of role discouragement but not objective difficulty help to further clarify the operation of cultural resources in the role adaptation process. Hence, cultural resources may be less effective in reducing harmful effects of objective barriers per se, but very effective in reducing the additional harmful effects of role discouragement. This may occur because subjective cultural strengths can directly control provider role perceptions such as discouragement, but cannot directly control structural employment barriers. Future studies should utilize longitudinal data and multivariate techniques to better clarify how perceptions of control mediate complex resource-strain-outcome relationships (Baron & Kenny, 1986; S. Cohen & Wills, 1985). For example, buffering effects of cultural resources in the face of chronic role strain may be mediated by adaptive cognitions such as self-efficacy reaffirmation, situational attributions, and path-goal motivation (Bowman, 1990a, 1990b).

In summary, results from this study provide additional insight into the social psychology of role strain and adaptation. Moreover, the role strain-adaptation approach is especially useful for understanding how African Americans mobilize indigenous cultural resources to cope with discouraging institutional barriers in school, work, family, and other major life roles. In addition to their theoretical relevance, findings also have important clinical and policy implications. Clinical intervention for chronic role strain may find cognitive-behavioral modalities useful for reducing the harmful effect of role discouragement or self-blame attributions. However, innovative intervention strategies that reinforce, reaffirm, or mobilize indigenous cultural resources to foster adaptive rather than maladaptive modes of coping appear especially promising. Despite the virtues of such culture-based personal empowerment, primary prevention also requires educational, employment, and family policies to eradicate the objective structural barriers that place African Americans at such high-risk for chronic role strains.

## References

Akbar, N. (1979). African roots of Black personality. In W. D. Smith, K. H. Burley, M. H. Mosley, & W. M. Whitney (Eds.), *Reflections on Black psychology*. Washington, DC: University Press of America.

Allen, V., & Vande Vliert, E. (Eds.). (1981). *Role transitions*. New York: Plenum.

Allen, W. R., & Farley, R. (1985). The shifting social and economic tides of Black America, 1950-1980. *Annual Review of Sociology, 12,* 277-306.

Andrews, F. M., Morgan, J. N., Sonquist, J. A., & Klem, L. (1973). *Multiple classification analysis*. Ann Arbor, MI: Institute for Social Research.

Andrews, F. M., & Withey, S. B. (1974). Developing measures of perceived life quality: Results from several national surveys. *Social Indicators Research, 1,* 1-26.

Ashante, M. K. (1981). Black male and female relationships: An Afrocentric context. In L. E. Gary (Ed.), *Black men* (pp. 75-83). Beverly Hills, CA: Sage.

Baldwin, J. (1981). Notes on an Afrocentric theory of Black personality. *Western Journal of Black Studies, 5*(3), 172-179.

Barnett, R., & Baruch, G. K. (1985). Women's involvement in multiple roles and psychological distress, *Journal of Personality and Social Psychology, 49,* 135-145.

Baron, R. M., & Kenny, D. A. (1986). The moderate-mediator variable distinction in social psychological research: Conceptual, strategic and statistical considerations. *Journal of Personality and Social Psychology, 51,* 1173-1182.

Baruch, G. K., & Barnett, R. C. (1986). Consequences of fathers' participation in family work: Parents, role strain and well being. *Journal of Personality and Social Psychology, 51,* 983-992.

Berry, M. F., & Blassingame, J. W. (1982). *Long memory: The Black experience in America*. New York: Oxford University Press.

Billingsley, A. (1968). *Black families in white America*. Englewood Cliffs, NJ: Prentice-Hall.

Bowman, P. J. (1983). Significant involvement and functional relevance: Challenges to survey research. *Social Work Research, 19,* 21-26.

Bowman, P. J. (1984). A discouragement-centered approach to studying unemployment among Black youth: Hopelessness, attributions and psychological distress. *International Journal of Mental Health, 13,* 68-91.

Bowman, P. J. (1985). Black fathers and the provider role: Role, strain, informal coping resource and life happiness. In A. W. Boykin (Ed.), *Empirical research in Black psychology* (pp. 9-19). Washington, DC: National Institute for Mental Health.

Bowman, P. J. (1988). Post-industrial displacement and family role strains: Challenges to the Black family. In P. Voydanof & L. C. Majka (Eds.), *Families and economic distress.* Newbury Park, CA: Sage.

Bowman, P. J. (1989). Research perspectives on Black men: Role strain and adaptation across the adult life cycle. In R. L. Jones (Ed.), *Black adult development and aging.* Berkeley, CA: Cobbs & Henry.

Bowman, P. J. (1990a). Toward a cognitive adaptation theory of role strain: Relevance of research on Black fathers. In R. Jones (Ed.), *Advances in Black psychology.* Berkeley, CA: Cobbs & Henry.

Bowman, P. J. (1990b). Naturally occurring psychological expectancies: Theory and measurement in Black populations. In R. L. Jones (Ed.), *Handbook of tests and measurements for Black populations.* Berkeley, CA: Cobbs & Henry.

Bowman, P. J. (in press). Marginality, ethnicity and family life quality: A national study of Black husband-fathers. In H. McAdoo (Ed.), *Family ethnicity and diversity.* Newbury Park, CA: Sage.

Bowman, P. J., & Howard, C. S. (1985). Race-related socialization, motivation and academic achievement: A study of Black youth in three generation families. *Journal of the American Academy of Child Psychiatry, 24,* 134-141.

Bowman, P. J., Jackson, J. S., Hatchett, S. J., & Gurin, G. (1982). Joblessness and discouragement among Black Americans. *Economic Outlook U.S.A.,* Autumn, 85-88.

Cazenave, N. A. (1979). Middle-income Black fathers: An analysis of the provider role. *Family Coordinator, 28,* 583-593.

Cazenave, N. A. (1981). Black men in America: The quest for "manhood." In H. P. McAdoo (Ed.), *Black families* (pp. 176-185). Beverly Hills, CA: Sage.

Cohen, R. M. (1978). The effects of employment status change on self-attitudes. *Social Psychology, 41,* 81-93.

Cohen, S., & Wills, T. A. (1985). Stress, social support, and the buffering hypothesis. *Journal of Personality and Social Psychology, 48,* 393-407.

Coles, R. (1978). Black fathers. In D. Wilkinson & R. Taylor (Eds.), *Black male in America* (pp. 85-101). Chicago: Nelson-Hall.

Daniels, S. (1986). Relationship of employment status to mental health and family variables in Black men from single-parent families. *Journal of Applied Psychology, 71,* 386-391.

Dietrich, K. T. (1975). A reexamination of two myths of the Black matriarchy. *Journal of Marriage and the Family, 37,* 367-374.

Evans, B. J., & Whitfield, J. R. (1988). *Black males in the United States: An annotated bibliography from 1967 to 1987.* Washington, DC: American Psychological Association.

Farley, R., & Allen, W. R. (1987). *The color line and the quality of American life.* New York: Russell Sage.

Feather, N. T., & Davenport, P. R. (1981). Unemployment and depressive affect: A motivational and attributional analysis. *Journal of Personality and Social Psychology, 41,* 422-436.

Felner, R. D., Faber, S. S., & Primavera, J. (1980). Transitions and stressful life events: A model of primary prevention. In R. H. Price, R. F. Ketterer, B. C. Bader, & J.

Monahan (Eds.), *Prevention and mental health: Research, policy and practice.* Beverly Hills, CA: Sage.

Gary, L. E. (Ed.). (1981). *Black men.* Beverly Hills, CA: Sage.

Goode, W. J. (1960). A theory of role strain. *American Sociological Review, 11,* 483-496.

Hendricks, L. E., & Fullilove, R. E. (1983). Locus of control and use of contraception among unmarried Black adolescent fathers and their controls. *Journal of Youth and Adolescence, 12,* 225-233.

Herskovits, M. J. (1935). Social history of the Negro. In C. Murchinson (Ed.), *A handbook of social psychology* (pp. 207-267). London: Oxford University Press.

Hetherington, D. (1966). Effects of parental absence on sex-typed behavior in Negro and White males. *Journal of Personality and Social Psychology, 4,* 87-91.

Hill, R. (1971). *Strengths of Black families.* New York: Emerson Hall.

House, J. S. (1981). *Work stress and support.* Reading, MA: Addison-Wesley.

Jackson, J. (1978). Ordinary Black husbands: The truly hidden men. In M. E. Lamb (Ed.), *The role of the father in child development* (pp. 139-144). New York: John Wiley.

Jackson, J. S., & Gurin, G. (1987). *National survey of Black Americans, 1979-80* (Vols. I & II). Ann Arbor, MI: Institute for Social Research.

Jackson, J. S., Tucker, M. B., Bowman, P. J. (1990). Conceptual and methodological problems in survey research on Black Americans. In R. L. Jones (Ed.), *Advances in Black psychology* (Vol. 1). Berkeley, CA: Cobbs & Henry.

Kahn, R. L., Wolfe, D. M., Quinn, R. P., Snoek, J. D., & Rosenthal, R. A. (1964). *Organizational stress: Studies in interrole conflict and ambiguity.* New York: John Wiley.

Kessler, R. C., Price, R. H., & Wortman, C. B. (1985). Social factors in psychopathology. Stress, social support and coping processes. *Annual Review of Psychology, 31,* 531-572.

Kish, L. (1965). *Survey sampling.* New York: John Wiley.

Liebow, E. (1967). *Tally's corner: A study of street corner men.* Boston: Little, Brown.

Mack, D. E. (1978). Power relationships in Black families. *Journal of Personality and Social Psychology, 30,* 409-413.

Manns, W. (1988). Support systems of significant others in Black families. In H. P. McAdoo (Ed.), *Black families* (pp. 238-251). Beverly Hills, CA: Sage.

McAdoo, J. L. (1988). The role of Black fathers in the socialization of Black children. In H. P. McAdoo (Ed.), *Black families* (pp. 257-269). Newbury Park, CA: Sage.

Menaghan, E. G. (1983). Individual coping efforts: Moderators of the relationship between life stress and mental health outcomes. In H. B. Kaplan (Ed.), *Psychosocial stress: Trends in theory and research* (pp. 157-192). New York: Academic Press.

Merton, R. K. (1968). *Social theory and social structure.* New York: Free Press.

Moos, R. H. (1976). *Human adaptation: Coping with life stress.* Lexington, KY: Health.

Nobles, W. (1974). Africanity: Its role in Black families. *The Black Scholar, 5,* 10-17.

Nobles, W. (1988). African American family life: An instrument of culture. In H. P. McAdoo (Ed.), *Black families* (pp. 44-53). Newbury Park, CA: Sage.

Pearlin, L. E., & Schooler, C. (1978). The structure of coping. *Journal of Health and Social Behavior, 19,* 1-21.

Pearlin, L. I. (1983). Role strains and personal stress. In H. B. Kaplan (Ed.), *Psychosocial stress: Trends in theory and research* (pp. 30-32). New York: Academic Press.

Pearlin, L. I., & Lieberman, M. A. (1979). Social sources of emotional distress. In R. Simmons (Ed.), *Research in community and mental health.* Greenwich, CT: JAI.

Pearlin, L. I., Lieberman, M. A., Menaghan, E. G., & Mullan. (1981). The stress process. *Journal of Health and Social Behavior, 22,* 337-356.

Price-Bonham, S., & Skeen, P. (1979). A comparison of Black and White fathers with implications for parents' education. *The Family Coordinator, 28,* 53-59.

Sarbin, T. R., & Allen, V. L. (1968). Role theory. In G. Lindzey & E. Aronson (Eds.), *Handbook of social psychology* (pp. 488-568). Reading, MA: Addison-Wesley.

Schultz, D. A. (1978). Coming up a boy in the ghetto. In D. Y. Wilkinson & R. L. Taylor (Eds.), *The Black male in America* (pp. 1-7). Chicago: Nelson-Hall.

Shinn, M. (1978). Father absence and children's cognitive development. *Psychological Bulletin, 85,* 295-324.

Stack, C. (1974). *All our kin: Strategies for survival in the Black community.* New York: Harper & Row.

Staples, R. (1982). *Black masculinity: The Black man's role in American society.* San Francisco: Black Scholar Press.

Sudarkasa, N. (1980). African and Afro-American family structure: A comparison. *The Black Scholar,* 37-60.

Sudarkasa, N. (1988). Interpreting the African heritage in Afro-American family organization. In H. P. McAdoo (Ed.), *Black families,* 37-53. Newbury Park, CA: Sage.

Taylor, R. L. (1978). Socialization to the Black male role. In D. Y. Wilkinson & R. L. Taylor (Eds.), *The Black male in America* (pp. 1-6). Chicago: Nelson-Hall.

Taylor, R. L. (1981). Psychological modes of adaptation. In L. E. Gary (Ed.), *Black men.* Beverly Hills, CA: Sage.

Tinney, J. S. (1981). The religious experience of Black men. In L. E. Gary (Ed.), *Black men.* Beverly Hills, CA: Sage.

Turner, R. J. (1983). Direct, indirect, and moderating effects of social support on psychological distress and associated conditions. In H. B. Kaplan (Ed.), *Psychosocial stress: Trends in theory and research* (pp. 105-155). New York: Academic Press.

Wheaton, B. (1983). Stress, personal coping resources, and psychiatric symptoms: An investigation of interactive models. *Journal of Health and Social Behavior, 24,* 208-229.

Wilkinson, D., & Taylor, R. (1977). *The Black male in America.* Chicago: Nelson-Hall.

Willie, C. V., & Grennblatt, S. L. (1978). Four classic studies of power relationships in Black families: A review and look to the future. *Journal of Marriage and Family, 40,* 691-696.

Wilson, W. J. (1987). *The truly disadvantaged: The inner city, the underclass, and public policy.* Chicago: University of Chicago.

# African American Children

The most important challenge that African American children have is to develop into competent people with the ability to see themselves as valued human beings. This is indeed difficult to do in our present society for there is a pervasive societal preference for people whose attributes are not African in origin.

Attributional style refers to ways in which individuals understand both positive and negative events in their lives. A body of literature exists to document that certain patterns are associated with depression and other maladaptive states. Belgrave and her colleagues extend this work by investigating to what extent attributional style is related to self-esteem and academic performance.

Despite the various racial preferences and self-racial identity responses what we obtain, one fact must be kept in sharp focus: At no age has it been found empirically that the self-concept of a child is affected by the particular verbal expression of racial preference. One of the sad assumptions that exists in the literature and in the popular media is that African American children hate themselves and their racial group. This assumption has been reinforced by researchers who have been myopic in their approaches. A crucial error has been made by researchers who have not separately assessed the children's racial attitude and their concepts at the same time, using different instruments. Usually one measure is made of racial identity and then assumptions are made about the children's self-esteem. The Clark chapter provides convincing evidence that racial identity and self-esteem are not the same.

The myth of Black hatred has been perpetuated by even our own scholars. In their important ground breaking studies, the Clarks made this error, for they only looked at the race self-identity, but then went on to discuss the children's self-concepts. In other words, *there is no support for a self-hatred hypothesis.* The self-identity of African American children has a normal distribution at all ages. One will find children who feel very good about themselves and those who feel less than sure, but the vast majority of them will fall within the normal range of one standard deviation of the mean on all measurements. In other words, they will look as positively upon themselves as do all other groups of children in our society. These findings have been true at all levels of the economic scale and in all regions of the country.

We do know certain evidence that has been found repeatedly in empirical studies in the past. Children become aware of racial differences in people at the same time they become aware of gender differences, at about 2 to 3 years of age. They do not place a value on these group memberships; they just know that different people come in different sizes, colors, and sexes. They begin to develop racial self-identity as they become aware that they have traits in common with one of these racial groups at around 3 to 4 years. They immediately develop racial preference, and they place a value on such membership. They may acknowledge their Blackness, but at the same time will express a desire to be anything but Black. At that point these children realize that it is easier to be White, because most of their racial and ethnic reinforcements usually are oriented away from Blackness. School experiences and television reinforce this preference.

All of these developmental stages are completed by the time the child is 5—the age when tests have been administered. Therefore when an examiner asks the child what doll he or she prefers or which picture is nicer, inevitably the response is out-group oriented. Out-group orientations were reported in the Gopaul-Mc.Nicol chapter for children from all different social economic classes and even in Trinidad.

It has been well documented that it is possible to change the responses of children, at least temporarily. The Powell-Hopson chapter is a replication of the Clarks's study and an attempt to reinforce the pro-Black responses that children gave to a stimulus. They were successful in their endeavor. Will this temporary reinforcement of positive responses to Blackness have a lasting impact on how the child feels about his or her race identity? Or will more fundamental changes in the children's lives be needed, as is done in Muslim family groups or within the collectives of Ujamaa schools, to ensure that these children have positive African orientations that will enable them to transcend the societal preferences of racial membership. Both the findings of Gopaul-Mc.Nicol and Powell-Hopson et al. were the subject of considerable controversy when they were first presented at the 1987 meeting of the American Psychological Association. Some African American researchers raised important questions about appropriate methods for evaluating racial identity. The reader is encouraged to review these comments in the February, 1988, issue of *The Journal of Black Psychology*. Others focused their attention on this question—How can we provide the means that would enable children to develop a sense of racial identity that would promote optimal development?

# 11 Racial Group Concept and Self-Esteem in Black Children

## MAXINE L. CLARK*
*Wake Forest University*

The relationship of racial group concepts (racial preference and racial attitudes) to general and specific self-esteem in Black children was examined. The study also attempted to validate the belief of Nobles (1973) that racial group attitudes influence the Black American's concept of "self." The subjects were 210 Black children in grades three to six. A Black experimenter administered a variation of the Coopersmith Self-Esteem Inventory to measure general and specific self-esteem, and a measure designed after the PRAM II test to measure racial preference and racial attitude. Results indicated no linear relationships between racial group concepts and general or specific self-esteem, but more complex relationships were found. Significant grade-level differences were found, along with physical/appearance esteem, as the single best predictor of general self-esteem.

Various disciplines of social and behavioral science have investigated the development of self-esteem in Black children. Some researchers concerned with racial differences have found that White children have higher self-esteem than Black children (Long & Henderson, 1968; Richmond & White, 1971; Stabler, Johnson, & Jordan, 1971). Other findings indicate no racial differences (Beglis & Sheikh, 1974; Busk, Ford, & Schulman, 1973; Carpenter & Busse, 1969; Hare, 1977; Samuels & Griffore, 1979). Within the last 10 years a considerable number of studies have reported contradictory findings with Black children having higher self-esteem than White children (Bewley, 1977; Cicirelli, 1977; Harris & Stokes, 1978; Rosenberg & Simmons, 1972; Simmons, Brown, Bush, & Blythe, 1978). Since these findings were reported, several researchers have attempted to explain the elevated score of

This paper is based on a doctoral dissertation submitted to the University of Illinois, Champaign-Urbana. This research was supported (in part) by U.S. Public Health Service Grant No. HD-00244 from the National Institutes of Child Health and Human Development. Maxine L. Clark, Department of Psychology, Wake Forest University, Winston-Salem, NC 27109.
*EDITORS' NOTE: Currently at Virginia Commonwealth University.

Black children either by analyzing the measures used (Gray-Little & Applebaum, 1979) or by investigating specific traits that might account for the difference (Harris & Stokes, 1978; Heiss & Owens, 1972). Self-esteem studies have also focused on the impact of sex (Carpenter & Busse, 1969; O'Malley & Bachman, 1979; Rubin, 1978; Samuels & Griffore, 1979); of age (Beglis & Sheikh, 1974; Bewley, 1977; Gray-Little & Appelbaum, 1979), of school racial composition (Busk, Ford, & Schulman, 1973; Rosenberg & Simmons, 1972; S. Williams & Byars, 1970), of socioeconomic status (Hare, 1977; Rosenberg & Simmons, 1972), and of academic performance (McIntire & Drummond, 1977; Rubin, 1978; Simmons et al., 1978) on self-esteem. Several studies have investigated the relationship of racial preferences and racial attitudes on self-esteem. Many of the earlier studies were subject to measuring only racial preferences and racial attitudes and to interpreting White preferences and inaccurate skin-color perceptions by Blacks to imply impaired self-concepts and low self-esteem (Bunton & Weissbach, 1974; Goodman, 1970; Landreth & Johnson, 1953; Rice, Ruiz, & Padilla, 1974). This methodological error has been noted (McAdoo, 1973; Rosenberg & Simmons, 1972). Those studies that have measured both self-esteem and some aspect of racial group concepts (racial preferences, racial identification, or racial attitudes) have reported conflicting findings. Several studies (Butts, 1963; Porter, 1971; Ward & Braun, 1972) have found a positive relationship between self-esteem and racial preference; however, McAdoo (1973, 1978), who studied racial attitudes and self-concept in Black preschoolers, did not. In addition, Rosenberg (1979) found no relationship between the Black child's attitudes toward his race and his personal self-esteem, which he felt refuted the notion that group rejection could result in Black self-hatred. A review of the literature in the area of Black self-hatred can be found in Baldwin (1979).

In order to clarify the relationship between self-esteem, racial attitudes, and racial preferences, a theoretical model proposed by Nobles (1973) explaining the concept of *self* in Black Americans was adopted. Nobles (1973) viewed *self* as a social process identifying three components: the "I"—self-perceptions, the "Me"—internalized attitudes identified by Mead (1934); and the "We," which he defined as internalized perceptions one has toward a group and being part of the group. Following this conceptual framework, a model was proposed that would determine whether racial self-perception, specific self-esteem, and racial group concepts (racial preferences and racial attitudes) would influence the

**TABLE 11.1** Groups Formed by Interaction Between Three Components of Self

| *(I)*<br>*Racial Self-*<br>*Perception* | *(Me)*<br>*Specific*<br>*Self-Esteem* | *Racial*<br>*Attitude* | *(We)*<br>*Racial*<br>*Preference* | *Group*<br>*No.* |
|---|---|---|---|---|
| Correct | Positive | Positive | In-group | 1 |
| | | | Out-group | 2 |
| | | Negative | In-group | 3 |
| | | | Out-group | 4 |
| | Negative | Positive | In-group | 5 |
| | | | Out-group | 6 |
| | | Negative | In-group | 7 |
| | | | Out-group | 8 |

level of general self-esteem in Blacks. Racial self-perception refers to the ability to identify oneself with a racial group. Specific esteem (Me) is synonymous with the "self as object" dimension identified by earlier theorists (Cooley, 1902; Mead, 1934). This component concerns itself with the internalization of others' positive and negative values and attitudes about physical development and appearance, social interaction, personal characteristics, and academic/school esteem. The racial group attitude dimension (We) has two subcomponents: racial attitude and racial preference. Own-race attitudes can be evaluated as either positive or negative, whereas racial preference can be either in-group or out-group oriented. General self-esteem refers to one's overall self-evaluation. A distinction between general and specific self-esteem has been made by previous researchers (Hare, 1977; Rosenberg & Simmons, 1972). There are sixteen possible interactions between the three components, but this study is concerned only with those eight groups that indicated correct racial self-perceptions (see Table 11.1).

The main purpose of this study was to examine the relationship between racial group concepts (racial preference and racial attitudes) and general and specific self-esteem in Black children. In addition, the study explored the ability of racial group concepts to predict general self-esteem, in an attempt to validate Nobles' notion that group attitudes influence the Black American's concept of "self."

## Method

SUBJECTS

The subjects in this study were 210 Black male and female children. Forty-seven percent were attending three integrated schools, and the remaining 53% attended grades three through six in five desegregated elementary schools that were located in a Midwestern college town. There were 83 third and fourth graders, with a mean age of 9 years and 6 months, and 127 fifth and sixth graders, with a mean age of 11 years and 1 month. Eighty-six of the children were males and 122 were females. Seventy percent lived in low-income predominantly Black neighborhoods.

MEASURES

Self-esteem was measured by a 53-item test adapted from questions on the Coopersmith Self-Esteem Inventory and the Piers-Harris Children's Self-Concept Scale. Half of the items described positive attributes of self, and the other half described negative attributes of self. Six items measured general self-esteem (I feel good about myself, I wish I were different), and the remaining 47 items measured the following four dimensions of specific self-esteem:

Physical/Appearance: My hair is nice. I am good looking.

Social: My friends like my ideas. My family is disappointed in me.

Personal: I worry a lot. I stay with something until I finish it.

Academic/School: I am good in my school work. I forget what I learn.

The self-esteem measure was pretested, and was found to have a split-half reliability of .80 and an individual item reliability of .87 as measured by the Kuder-Richardson coefficient.

Racial preferences and racial attitudes were measured by a test designed after the Preschool Racial Attitude Measure II (J. Williams, Best, Boswell, Mattson, & Graves, 1975). This test was composed of 13 Black and White illustrated items: 6 to assess preference for own race, 6 to assess attitudes about own race, and the last item determined the child's racial self-perception. Each illustration displayed a Black person and White person who were similar except for color and facial dimensions. Zipitone was used for the coloration of the Black figures. A descriptive story including both negative and positive attributes accompanied each illustration.

> Racial Preference: These two men are starting a bakery. Which man would you like to work for?
>
> Racial Attitudes: One of these boys picks on other kids. Which boy picks on the other kids?
>
> Racial Self-Perception: Put a check by the child who looks most like your racial group.

## PROCEDURE

The Black children who participated in this study were taken from their classrooms and assembled in groups varying in size from 10 to 20 children. They were tested by a Black female experimenter and research assistant. The self-esteem measure was administered first, with the items given orally to the third and fourth graders. Afterwards, an illustrated response booklet for the Racial Attitude and Racial Preference Measure was distributed and the experimenter read aloud the twelve statements accompanying each illustration, instructing the students to answer by marking one of the figures in their booklets.

## SCORING

The child responded to each item on the self-esteem measure by marking whether it was "like me," "sometimes like me," or "unlike me" and given 2, 1, or 0 points, respectively, for all positive items. Negative items were scored in an inverse manner: 2 points for "unlike me," 1 point for "sometimes like me," and 0 points for "like me." A total of 12 points could be earned from the responses to general self-esteem questions. The remaining 47 specific esteem items were scored in the same manner, with a maximum total of 94 points. The median score was computed for the total sample and was subsequently used as the cutoff point to denote positive (60-94) or negative (0-59) scores on the specific esteem items.

There were three scores calculated from the Racial Attitude and Racial Preference Measure. The preference items were scored by giving 1 point for each Black choice, and then they were summed. A total of

6 points was possible, with 4 or above indicating a Black preference, and below 4 a non-Black preference. The racial attitude items were scored by giving 1 point if a Black was chosen for a positive attribute or was not chosen for a negative attribute. A total of 6 points was possible.

## ANALYSIS OF DATA

A 2 (Specific Esteem) by 2 (Racial Preference) by 2 (Racial Attitude) analysis of variance and a 2 (Grade) by 2 (Sex) by 2 (Specific Esteem) by 2 (Racial Preference) by 2 (Racial Attitude) analysis of variance for unequal $N$s were performed on the general self-esteem scores. Additional three-way analyses of variance were performed, substituting each of the four dimensions of specific self-esteem for the total specific score for the third and fourth grades. Multiple regression analyses were employed to determine the ability of the racial group concepts to predict general self-esteem.

## Results

A ceiling effect was established in the area of racial self-perception. There was 100% identification with the Black choices as the child that looked most like them.

The raw data were dichotomized into high and low groups and a 2 (Specific Esteem) by 2 (Racial Preference) by 2 (Racial Attitude) analysis of variance was performed on the general self-esteem scores. Specific esteem was the only significant main effect, $F(1, 202) = 23.82$, $p < .001$. A 2 (Grade) by 2 (Specific Esteem) by 2 (Racial Preference) by 2 (Racial Attitude) analysis of variance was performed on the general self-esteem scores to examine grade differences in general self-esteem. Specific esteem was significant, $F(1, 194) = 13.93$, $p < .001$, along with the four-way interaction between grade, specific esteem, racial preference, and racial attitude, $F(1, 194) = 4.16$, $p < .04$.

Separate 2 (Specific Esteem) by 2 (Racial Preference) by 2 (Racial Attitude) analyses of variance were performed on the general self-esteem scores by grade level. Specific esteem was the only significant main effect for the fifth/sixth grade group, $F(1, 119) = 20.39$, $p < .001$; however, specific esteem, $F(1, 75) = 3.86$, $p < .05$, and the three-way interaction between specific esteem, racial preference, and racial attitude were significantly related to the general self-esteem scores, $F(1, 75) = 4.41$, $p < .03$, for the third/fourth grade.

Four subscores were calculated from the specific esteem questions: physical/appearance, personal, social, and academic/school. The third/ fourth grade raw data were dichotomized into high and low groups for each specific esteem subscore. A 2 (Appearance) by 2 (Racial Preference) by 2 (Racial Attitude) analysis of variance was performed on the general self-esteem scores. The physical/appearance variable was significant, $F(1, 74) = 28.28$, $p < .006$. A 2 (Social) by 2 (Racial Preference) by 2 (Racial Attitude) analysis of variance performed on the general self-esteem scores resulted in the social variable being the only variable to significantly influence the level of general self-esteem, $F(1, 74) = 4.31$, $p < .04$. Similar analyses were attempted, including personal esteem and academic/school esteem, but several groups with missing $N$s complicated the analyses.

In order to assess the ability of the racial group concepts to predict the level of general self-esteem, separate multiple regression analyses with general self-esteem as the criterion variable and one of the four specific self-esteem scores, racial preference, and racial attitude as predictor variables for the third/fourth grade was performed (see Table 11.2). The most significant group of predictor variables were racial preference, racial attitude, and physical/appearance esteem ($R^2 = .33$, $p < .01$). The only single predictor of general self-esteem was physical/appearance esteem, $t(79) = 5.83$, $p < .05$. Social esteem ($R^2 = .15$, $p < .01$) and personal esteem ($R^2 = .09$, $p < .05$), when grouped with racial preference and racial attitude, were also significant predictor variables; nevertheless, they accounted for very little of the total variance in the general self-esteem scores. $T$-tests revealed that social esteem, $t(79) = 3.22$, $p < .05$, and personal esteem, $t(79) = 2.19$, $p < .05$, were significant single predictors of general self-esteem, while academic/school esteem was not. To further investigate the strength of the specific esteem variables as predictors of general self-esteem, regression coefficients were computed with the four specific esteem scores as predictor variables and general self-esteem the criterion variable for the total population (see Table 11.3). As expected, the specific esteem variables were predictors of general self-esteem $R^2 = .28$, $p < .001$; nevertheless, the only single predictor of general self-esteem was physical/appearance esteem $t(205) = 5.88$, $p < .001$.

Table 11.4 shows the eight interaction groups, their total $N$, and their mean general self-esteem scores for the total population, third/fourth and fifth/sixth grade levels. Twenty-five percent of the total sample were in Group 1 with high specific esteem scores, in-group racial

**TABLE 11.2** Regression Coefficients and Multiple Correlation Coefficients for General Self-Esteem With Racial Preference, Racial Attitude, and Four Specific Esteem Subtests as Predictor Variables, Third/ Fourth Grade

| Predictor Variable | Beta | t | $R^2$ |
|---|---|---|---|
| Racial Preference | .15 | 1.39 | |
| Racial Attitude | −.05 | −0.48 | |
| Physical/Appearance | .54 | 5.83* | |
| | | | .33** |
| Racial Preference | .22 | 1.75 | |
| Racial Attitude | −.12 | −0.94 | |
| Personal | .23 | 2.17* | |
| | | | .09* |
| Racial Preference | .24 | 1.93 | |
| Racial Attitude | −.15 | −1.24 | |
| Social | .34 | 3.22* | |
| | | | .15** |
| Racial Preference | .23 | 1.80 | |
| Racial Attitude | −.09 | −0.71 | |
| Academic/School | .12 | 1.05 | |
| | | | .05 |

*$p < .05$, **$p < .01$

preferences, and positive own-race attitudes. The next largest group was Group 5, composed of children with low specific esteem scores, in-group racial preferences, and positive own-race attitudes (20%). The distribution of the third/fourth grade was slightly different from that of the older group, with 61% of the third/fourth grade level in Group 1 and

**TABLE 11.3** Regression Coefficients and Multiple Correlation Coefficients for General Self-Esteem With Four Specific Esteem Subtests as Predictor Variables

| Predictor Variable | Beta | t | $R^2$ |
|---|---|---|---|
| Physical/Appearance | .39 | 5.88*** | |
| Personal | .12 | 1.56 | |
| Social | .11 | 1.32 | |
| Academic/School | .02 | 0.26 | |
| | | | .28*** |

***$p < .001$

**TABLE 11.4** Mean General Self-Esteem Scores by the Three-Way Interaction of Specific Esteem, Racial Attitude, and Racial Preference

| Specific Esteem | Racial Attitude | Racial Preference | 3rd & 4th M | % | 5th & 6th M | % | Total M | % | Group No. |
|---|---|---|---|---|---|---|---|---|---|
| High | Positive | In-group | 9.37 | 36 | 10.09 | 17 | 9.67 | 25 | 1 |
| | | Out-group | 11.00 | 1 | 10.00 | 3 | 10.16 | 3 | 2 |
| | Negative | In-group | 10.00 | 13 | 10.15 | 16 | 10.09 | 15 | 3 |
| | | Out-group | 7.00 | 4 | 10.07 | 10 | 9.50 | 8 | 4 |
| Low | Positive | In-group | 7.90 | 25 | 8.27 | 17 | 8.09 | 20 | 5 |
| | | Out-group | 7.00 | 1 | 8.71 | 6 | 8.50 | 4 | 6 |
| | Negative | In-group | 7.80 | 12 | 8.23 | 17 | 8.10 | 15 | 7 |
| | | Out-group | 8.70 | 7 | 7.88 | 13 | 8.10 | 11 | 8 |

5, while the fifth/sixth graders were most evenly distributed over the eight groups.

Product moment correlation coefficients were calculated for specific esteem racial preference, racial attitude, general self-esteem, and the four specific esteem subscores (see Table 11.5). Racial preference and racial attitude were significantly correlated with each other for the total population ($r = .48$, $p < .001$) and the third/fourth grade ($r = .55$, $p < .001$). The four specific esteem scores were correlated highly with total specific esteem, each other, and general self-esteem. The Physical/Appearance was most highly correlated ($r = .49$, $p < .001$) and academic/school esteem the least correlated ($r = .25$, $p < .05$) with general self-esteem. The racial group concepts (racial preference and racial attitude) were unrelated to self-esteem (specific and general).

## Discussion

The primary purpose of this study was to investigate the relationship of racial group concepts (racial attitudes and racial preferences) to general and specific self-esteem in Black children. The data indicate that no apparent relationship exists, a finding that is supportive of

**TABLE 11.5** Correlation Coefficients of Specific Esteem, Racial Preference, Racial Attitude, and Four Subscores of Specific Esteem Test

|  | Specific Esteem | Racial Preference | Racial Attitude | General Self-Esteem | Physical Esteem | Personal Esteem | Social Esteem | School Esteem |
|---|---|---|---|---|---|---|---|---|
| Specific Esteem | 1.00 | .05 | .02 | .43*** | .62*** | .85*** | .83*** | .69*** |
| Racial Preference | .08 | 1.00 | .55*** | .18 | .09 | .07 | .06 | −.08 |
| Racial Attitude | .04 | .48*** | 1.00 | .01 | −.03 | .06 | .12 | −.16 |
| General Self-Esteem | .48*** | .03 | .01 | 1.00 | .58 | .24* | .33** | .11 |
| Physical Esteem | .68*** | .11 | −.01 | .49*** | 1.00 | .33** | .33** | .20 |
| Personal Esteem | .82*** | .05 | .03 | .35*** | .37*** | 1.00 | .68*** | .51*** |
| Social Esteem | .83*** | .05 | .08 | .36*** | .42*** | .62*** | 1.00 | .49*** |
| School Esteem | .71*** | .04 | .01 | .25* | .30** | .46*** | .48*** | 1.00 |

Note: Correlations above the diagonal are for the third/fourth grade; those below are for total population.
*$p < .05$, **$p < .01$, ***$p < .001$

McAdoo (1973, 1978) and Rosenberg (1979). McAdoo (1973, 1978) reported Black children holding negative own-race attitudes and positive self-concepts, and concluded that Black children learn to compartmentalize their racial attitudes and prevent them from influencing self-evaluation. The present results raise serious questions concerning the construct validity of instruments employed by previous researchers who utilized racial preference or racial attitude measures to make implications about self-concept or self-esteem (Bunton & Weissbach, 1974; Rice, Ruiz, & Padilla, 1974). Other researchers have also questioned the past methodologies of racial preference research. Gordon (1976) indicated that many researchers utilized preference measures to assess self-concept in Blacks during 1939–1963, leading to much of the low self-concept results. Banks (1976) questioned the ability of many previous preference studies to statistically prove Black preference for White. The present findings are also contrary to the "Black self-hatred doctrine" posed so frequently by many previous social scientists (see Baldwin, 1979) by providing empirical data to negate the belief that Blacks who internalize negative racial group attitudes from the larger White society would inevitably possess negative self-evaluations.

A secondary purpose of this study was to assess the validity of Nobles's (1973) notion that racial group attitudes influence the Black American's concept of "self" by determining whether racial group concepts would predict general self-esteem. The data indicated that neither racial preference nor racial attitude was a significant predictor of general self-esteem. Nevertheless, partial support for Nobles' (1973) theory was gained by data from the third/fourth grade analysis of variance. The three-way interaction of specific esteem, racial preference, and racial attitude had more influence on the general self-esteem scores than the main effect of specific esteem. However, the regression analysis indicated that the proportion of the variance accounted for by racial preference (3%) and racial attitude (0%) was miniscule. These data might be interpreted to mean that the racial group concepts failed to make an appreciable influence on the Black child's general self-esteem.

The significant grade-level finding indicated that the racial group concepts had a greater effect on the level of general self-esteem in the third/fourth grade as compared with the fifth/sixth grade level. These results must be interpreted with caution because of the small *N* in several cells of the ANOVA. Perhaps, during the preadolescent age, preoccupation with social and personal factors increases, and racial concepts, which are clearly established, appear to be deemphasized in determining one's general self-esteem. The younger school age child, in contrast, having recently internalized racial attitudes, might use these attitudes more consciously in the formation of general self-esteem. Other researchers believe that cognition influences the age differences found in self-concept and racial preferences. Montemayor and Eisen (1977) interpreted their age differences in self-concept to indicate that young children view and describe themselves in very concrete terms, whereas adolescents describe themselves more abstractly. Semaj (1980) related cognition to racial constancy and felt that age facilitates the development of racial constancy, which, in turn, affects the child's racial preferences.

The breakdown of the specific esteem test into its subtests yielded additional information concerning the third/fourth grade. The specific esteem test had been designed to include questions centered in four major esteem areas: physical/appearance, personal, social, and academic/school. The results of this study tend to indicate that physical/appearance esteem was more highly correlated with general self-esteem than any other variable, including the total specific esteem score. When the subtest scores were substituted for the total specific esteem score and grouped with racial preferences and racial attitude as general self-esteem predictors, it appeared as though the most significant group of predictors was physical/appearance esteem, racial attitude, and racial preference. This finding implies that physical appearance was an important variable in the formulation of general self-esteem in Black children. Attitudes about physical appearance seemed to be more intense than attitudes about school performance, social acceptability, or personal attributes. This preoccupation with physical appearance may be indirectly related to the issue of race. One of the questions in this area was, "I wish I could change my skin color." Past research that focused on studying the attitudes about physical appearance held by Blacks has centered on skin color. Rosenberg and Simmons (1972) discussed the importance that physical appearance has in Blacks' self-evaluation. They felt that skin color has been established as one of the most central features of racial physiognomy. Ultimately, it appears that the high significance of physical/appearance esteem as a predictor of general self-esteem may hold some underlined significance in explaining the influence of racial concepts on self-esteem.

The academic/school items were not significant predictors of general self-esteem, a finding that is contradictory to many previous studies on self-concept and academic achievement (Bledsoe, 1967; Campbell, 1967; Epps, 1969), but supports the findings of Hare (1977), who found that school esteem was a significant predictor of general self-esteem in middle-class White children and not in Blacks. The academic/school esteem was not correlated with general self-esteem for the third/fourth grade; nevertheless, a significant correlation was achieved for the fifth/sixth grade. These results are supportive of the findings of Beglis and Sheikh (1974), who looked at age differences and self-concept development and discovered that younger children classified themselves by more basic units of identification, whereas the older children's classifications reflected the importance of school achievements and peer relationships.

In summary, the present results suggest that accurate implications about specific or general self-esteem cannot be attained by research that measures only racial attitudes or preferences. These two variables were not significantly correlated with either specific esteem or general self-esteem. Only partial support for the belief that racial group concepts influence Black children's general self-esteem was attained. The results of this study indicate that additional research in this area is needed in order to determine whether age influences the impact of racial group concepts on general self-esteem. The findings of physical/appearance as the best predictor of general self-esteem suggests that racial physiognomy may be a crucial variable in self-esteem development for Black children.

# References

Baldwin, J. (1979). Theory and research concerning the notion of Black self-hatred: A review and reinterpretation. *The Journal of Black Psychology, 5*(2), 51-97.

Banks, W. C. (1976). White preference in Blacks: A paradigm in search of a phenomenon. *Psychological Bulletin, 83*(6), 1179-1186.

Beglis, J. F., & Sheikh, A. A. (1974). Development of the self-concept in Black and White children. *Journal of Negro Education, 43*(1), 104-110.

Bewley, K. (1977). Self-esteem: The alternative to genetic inferiority. *Negro Educational Review, 28*(2), 95-99.

Bledsoe, J. (1967). Self-concept of children and their intelligence, achievement, interest and anxiety. *Childhood Education, 42,* 436-438.

Bunton, P. L., & Weissbach, T. A. (1974). Attitudes toward Blackness of Black preschool children attending community-controlled or public schools. *Journal of Social Psychology, 92,* 53-59.

Busk, P., Ford, L., & Shulman, L. (1973). Effects of schools' racial composition on the self-concept of Black and White students. *Journal of Educational Research, 67*(2), 57-63.

Butts, H. (1963). Skin color perception and self-esteem. *Journal of Negro Education, 32,* 122-128.

Campbell, P. B. (1967). School and self-concept. *Education Leadership, 24,* 510-515.

Carpenter, T. R., & Busse, T. V. (1969). Development of self-concept in Negro and White welfare children. *Child Development, 40*(3-4), 935-939.

Cicirelli, V. (1977). Relationship of socio-economic status and ethnicity to primary grade children's self-concept. *Psychology in the Schools, 14*(8), 213-215.

Cooley, C. H. (1902). *Human nature and the social order.* New York: Scribner.

Epps, E. G. (1969). Correlates of academic achievement among northern and southern urban Negro students. *Journal of Social Issues, 25*(3), 55-70.

Goodman, M. E. (1970). *Race awareness in young children.* London: Collier-Macmillan.

Gordon, V. (1976). The methodologies of Black self-concept research: A critique. *Journal of Afro-American Issues, 4*(3-4), 373-381.

Gray-Little, B., & Appelbaum, M. (1979). Instrumentality effects in the assessment of racial differences in self-esteem. *Journal of Personality and Social Psychology, 37*(7), 1221-1229.

Hare, B. (1977). Racial and socioeconomic variations in preadolescent area-specific and general self-esteem. *International Journal of Intercultural Relations, 1*(3), 31-51.

Harris, A., & Stokes, R. (1978). Race, self-evaluation and the protestant ethic. *Social Problems, 26*(1), 71-85.

Heiss, J., & Owens, S. (1972). Self-evaluation of Blacks and Whites. *American Journal of Sociology, 78*(2), 360-370.

Landreth, C., & Johnson, B. C. (1953). Young children's responses to a picture and insert test designed to reveal reactions to persons of different skin color. *Child Development, 24*(1), 63-79.

Long, G., & Henderson, E. (1968). Self-social concepts of disadvantaged school beginners. *Journal of Genetic Psychology, 113,* 41-51.

McIntire, W., & Drummond, R. (1977). Multiple predictors of self-concept in children. *Psychology in the Schools, 14*(3), 295-298.

Mead, G. H. (1934). *Mind, self and society.* Chicago: University of Chicago Press.

McAdoo, H. P. (1973). A different view of race attitudes and self concepts in Black preschool children. Urbana: University of Illinois. (ERIC Document Reproduction Service No. ED 102 035)

McAdoo, H. P. (1978). Self-concept in Black preschool children. In W. Cross & A. Harrison, (Eds.), *Third Conference on Empirical Research in Black Psychology.* Washington, DC: NIE.

Montemayor, D., & Eisen, M. (1977). The development of self-conceptions from childhood to adolescence. *Developmental Psychology, 13*(4), 314-319.

Nobles, W. (1973). Psychological research and the Black self-concept: a critical review. *Journal of Social Issues, 29*(1), 11-29.

Nobles, W. (1976). Extended self: Rethinking the so-called Negro self-concept. *The Journal of Black Psychology, 2*(2), 15-24.

O'Malley, P., & Bachman, J. (1979). Self-esteem and education: Sex and cohort comparisons among high school seniors. *Journal of Personality and Social Psychology, 37*(7), 1153-1159.

Porter, J. D. (1971). *Black child, White child: The development of racial attitudes.* Cambridge, MA: Harvard University Press.

Rice, A. S., Ruiz, R. A., & Padilla, A. H. (1974). Person perception, self-identity, and ethnic group preference in Anglo, Black, and Chicano preschool and third-grade children. *Journal of Cross-Cultural Psychology, 5*(1), 100-108.

Richmond, B., & White, W. (1971). Sociometric predictors of the self-concept among 5th and 6th grade children. *Journal of Educational Research, 64*(9), 425-429.

Rosenberg, M. (1979). Group rejection and self-rejection. In R. Simmons (Ed.), *Research in community and mental health: An annual compilation of research* (Vol. 1). Greenwich, CT: JAI Press.

Rosenberg, M., & Simmons, R. C. (1972). *Black and White self-esteem: The urban school child.* Washington, DC: American Psychological Association.

Rubin, R. (1978). Stability of self-esteem ratings and their relation to academic achievement: A longitudinal study. *Psychology in the Schools, 14*(4), 503-507.

Samuels, D., & Griffore, R. (1979). Ethnic and sex differences in self-esteem in preschool children. *Journal of Genetic Psychology, 135*(1), 33-36.

Semaj, L. (1980). The development of racial evaluation and preference: A cognitive approach. *The Journal of Black Psychology, 6*(2), 59-79.

Simmons, R., Brown, L., Bush, D., & Blythe, D. (1978). Self-esteem and achievement of Black and White adolescents. *Social Problems, 26*(1), 86-96.

Stabler, J., Johnson, E., & Jordan, S. (1971). The measurement of children's self-concepts as related to racial membership. *Child Development, 42*(6), 2094-2097.

Ward, S., & Braun, J. (1972). Self-esteem and racial preference in Black children. *American Journal of Orthopsychiatry, 42*(4), 644-647.

Williams, J., Best, D., Boswell, D., Mattson, L., & Graves, D. (1975). Preschool racial attitude measure II. *Educational and Psychological Measurement, 35*(1), 3-18.

Williams, S., & Byars, H. (1970). The effect of academic integration on the self-esteem of southern Negro students. *The Journal of Social Psychology, 80*(2), 183-188.

# 12 Attributional Style and Its Relationship to Self-Esteem and Academic Performance in Black Students

**FAYE Z. BELGRAVE\***
**REGINALD S. JOHNSON**
*Howard University*
**CAROLE CAREY**
*University of Virginia*

The types of causal attributions made regarding successful and unsuccessful life events are related to a number of variables including depression and self-esteem. High self-esteem individuals tend to internalize their success outcomes and externalize their failure outcomes more than do low self- esteem individuals. The objective of this exploratory study was to investigate the relationship between attributional style and self-esteem and attributional style and academic performance in Black high school and college students. The results indicated that an internal attributional style for negative events was negatively associated with self-esteem. A stable attributional style for negative events was negatively associated with academic performance. An internal attributional style for positive events was negatively associated with academic performance. It was concluded that attributional style can be useful for understanding self-esteem and academic performance in this population.

Attributional style, a general tendency to make internal (versus external), stable (versus temporary), and global (versus specific) attributions for positive and negative events, has been found to be related to a number of variables. Abramson, Seligman, and Teasdale (1978) in a

The authors are grateful to Leah Corbin and Jamal Koram of the Upward Bound Program at the University of Virginia for their cooperation in this study.
Faye Z. Belgrave, Howard University, Center for Sickle Cell Disease, 2121 Georgia Avenue, N.W., Washington, DC 20059
Reginald S. Johnson, Howard University, Department of Psychology, Washington, DC 20059
Carole Carey, University of Virginia, Charlottesville, VA 22901
*EDITORS' NOTE: Currently at The George Washington University.

reformation of the learned helplessness model of depression proposed that attributing lack of control to internal factors leads to low self-esteem, whereas attributing lack of control to external factors does not. Attributing lack of control to stable factors should lead to helplessness, and attributing lack of control to global factors should lead to wide generalizations of helplessness across many situations. In a test of this model Seligman, Abramson, Semmel, and Baeyer (1979) found that depressed college students, compared to nondepressed college students, attributed bad outcomes to internal, stable, and global causes. Depressed students, compared to nondepressed students, reported external and unstable attributions for good outcomes. In another test of this model Metalsky, Abramson, Seligman, Semmel, and Peterson (1982) found that college students with an internal or global attributional style of negative outcomes experienced a depressive mood response when given negative feedback about performance (i.e., low grade), whereas students with an external or specific attributional style for negative outcomes were invulnerable to depressive mood reactions.

Feather (1983) found that depression and self-esteem were linked to attributional behavior. The more depressed subjects tended to give higher internal, stable, and global ratings for the causes of bad events, but their ratings for the causes of good events were more in the direction of external, unstable, and specific attributions. The reverse pattern was found for subjects with higher self-esteem. Ickes and Layden (1978) found that high self-esteem individuals appear to internalize their success outcomes and externalize their failure outcomes for a particular task more than do low self-esteem individuals who make relatively more internal attributions to negative events and external attributions to positive events.

In a test of the effect of attributional style on performance following failure, Ickes and Layden (1978) found that the subsequent performance of subjects who were predisposed to internalize their negative outcomes became worse following a failure. No impairment of performance was found for subjects predisposed to externalize their negative outcomes. Since this effect was found to be independent of self-esteem, the authors speculated that performance impairment previously attributed to self-esteem may really be due to attributional style. This finding suggests that a history of unsuccessful performance is more likely to lead to continual impairment or lower performance for individuals who internalize failure relative to those who externalize failure.

Of interest in this study is how attributional style can be used to help understand achievement and self-esteem in Black students. Research done in the area of Black motivation and achievement has pointed to a number of cognitive factors useful for explaining motivation and achievement (Boykin, Franklin, & Yates, 1979). Attributional style as a cognitive factor has not been investigated in a Black population. It is not known to what extent previously mentioned findings would apply to a Black population.

The purpose of this study was to explore the relationship between attributional style and self-esteem and attributional style and academic performance in Black students. It addressed the following questions:

1. What is the relationship between attributional style and self-esteem in Black students?
2. What is the relationship between attributional style and academic performance in Black students?

## Method

### SUBJECTS

*High School Sample.* Forty-six students enrolled in the Upward Bound Program at the University of Virginia served as subjects. The Upward Bound Program provides academic support and counseling to 10th, 11th, and 12th grade students identified as low income and with potential for education beyond high school. These students meet twice a month during the school year and for 6 weeks during the summer. The mean age of these students was 16.

*College Sample.* Forty-three students enrolled in three classes with predominately Black enrollments at the University of Virginia served as subjects. The responses of White students who filled out the questionnaire were not used. The mean age of these students was 20.

### MATERIALS

*Attributional Style Questionnaire.* This instrument (Peterson et al., 1982) was used to measure students' tendencies to attribute outcomes to internal (versus external), stable (versus unstable), and global (versus specific)[1] factors. Respondents are asked to vividly imagine themselves in twelve hypothetical situations. They then answer questions about the

cause of this event. The following is an item from the questionnaire
(Peterson et al., 1982, pp. 291, 292):

YOU MEET A FRIEND WHO COMPLIMENTS YOU
ON YOUR APPEARANCE.

1. Write down the one major cause _____
2. Is the cause of your friend's compliment due to something about you or
   something about the other person or circumstances? (Circle one number)

   Totally due to
   the other person                                        Totally due
   or circumstances   1   2   3   4   5   6   7   to me
3. In the future when you are with your friends, will this cause again be
   present? (Circle one number)

   Will never again                                        Will always
   be present         1   2   3   4   5   6   7   be present
4. How important would this situation be if it happened to you? (Circle one
   number)

   Not at all                                              Extremely
   important          1   2   3   4   5   6   7   important

The second question measures the extent to which the person makes
an internal versus external attribution (i.e., he or she sees the compliment as being due to himself or herself or to the other person). The third
question measures the extent to which the person perceives the cause
of the compliment as permanent rather than transient.

Twelve hypothetical events are presented in the questionnaire.[2] Half
are good events, and half are bad events. Half of the events are inter-
personal/affiliative, and half are achievement related. The reliability
and validity of the Attributional Style Questionnaire are satisfactory
(Peterson et al., 1982).

*Rosenberg's Self-Esteem Scale.* This is a 10-item scale designed to
assess global self-esteem. Respondents are asked to agree/disagree on
a 7-point scale to items. An example of a scale item is: "I feel I have a
number of good qualities." The reliability and validity of this instrument are acceptable (Rosenberg, 1965).

*Personal Data Sheet.* The personal data sheet was used to obtain
demographic information including sex, year in school, ethnic identification, and grade point average.

PROCEDURE

A questionnaire including the personal data sheet, the Attributional Style Questionnaire, and the Self-Esteem Scale was given to groups of students. Students were asked to be completely honest and were assured of confidentiality. In order to ensure that high school students completely understood how to respond to the Attributional Style Questionnaire, they were given two sample items prior to filling it out.

## Results

Composite internality and stability scores were computed for each respondent by totaling the internality and stability items. Separate composite internality and stability scores were also computed for the positive and the negative events. The following composite measures of attributional style were available: (a) Internality, (b) Internality for positive events, (c) Internality for negative events, (d) Stability, (e) Stability for positive events, and (f) Stability for negative events. A composite self-esteem score was also computed.

### High School Sample

*Attributional Style and Self-Esteem.* Pearson correlation revealed a significant negative relationship between internality and self-esteem ($r = -.37, p < .01$) with an internal attributional style associated with lower self-esteem. This significant relationship between internality and self-esteem is due to the highly significant relationship between an internal attributional style for negative events and self-esteem ($r < -.48, p < .001$). Respondents who made casual internal attributions for negative events scored lower on the self-esteem measure. The relationship between self-esteem and an internal attributional style for positive events was not significant.

The stability measure did not relate to self-esteem.

*Attributional Style and Academic Performance.* Academic performance as measured by grade point average was not significantly correlated with the composite internality measure. There was a significant negative relationship between an internal attributional style for positive events and grade point average ($r = -.26, p < .05$). Students who made internal attributions for positive events tended to have lower grade point averages. The relationship between an internal attributional style for negative events and grade point average was not significant.

The stability measure was marginally related to academic performance in a negative direction ($r = -.19$, $p < .10$). The attribution of stability for an event was associated with lower grade point average. This marginally significant relationship is due to the significant negative relationship between a stable attributional style for negative events and grade point average ($r = -.24$, $p < .05$). Respondents who indicated that the causes of negative events are relatively stable tended to have lower grade point averages. A stable attributional style for positive events was not related to grade point average.

The relationship between stability and internality was significant ($r = -.37$, $p < .01$), and the relationship between self-esteem and grade point average was significant ($r = -.25$, $p < .05$).

### College Sample

*Attributional Style and Self-Esteem.* The results indicated that there was a significant negative correlation between internality and self-esteem ($r = -.34$, $p < .01$). As with the high school sample, students who made more casual internal attributions tended to score lower on the self-esteem measure. Internal casual attributions were examined for both positive and negative events and the resulting correlations revealed self-esteem to be marginally related to an internal attributional style for positive events ($r = -.23$, $p < .10$) and significantly related to an internal attributional style for negative events ($r = -.39$, $p < .01$). Those students who made more internal causal attributions for negative events scored lower on the self-esteem measure.

The stability measure was not related to self-esteem.

*Attributional Style and Academic Performance.* Grade point average was marginally related to attributions of internality in the negative direction ($r = -.19$, $p < .10$). This marginally significant relationship is accounted for by the stronger relationship between an internal attributional style for positive events and grade point average ($r = -.35$, $p < .01$). As was the case with the high school sample, students who made internal attributions for positive events tended to have lower grade point averages. Grade point average was not related to an internal attributional style for negative events.

Grade point average was marginally related to attributions of stability ($r = -.23$, $p < .10$) in a negative direction. This negative relationship is due to the stronger relationship between a stable attributional style for negative events and grade point average ($r = -.26$, $p < .05$). Students who tend to feel that the causes of negative events are enduring had lower grade point averages. The relationship between a stable attributional style for positive events and grade point average was not significant.

Internality was significantly associated with stability ($r = .42$, $p < .01$). The relationship between self-esteem and grade point average was significant ($r = .26$, $p < .05$).

## Discussion

The results of this study indicate that certain attributional styles are related to self-esteem and academic performance in Black high school and college students. The findings for high school and college students do not differ.

Students who have a tendency to attribute internal causality for negative events are more likely to have lower self-esteem. This finding is consistent with those studies using non-Black subjects (Feather, 1983; Ickes & Layden, 1978). This finding suggests that interventions aimed at changing Black self-esteem also take into account attributional style.

The finding that academic performance is associated with attributions of stability for negative events is also consistent with other research done using non-Black subjects. Students who indicated that a negative event was stable and enduring were more likely to have lower academic performance. It is important that students with such an attributional style be taught that negative events may not endure. Negative behavior attributed to stable causes can be expected to lead to an exacerbation of the condition. The feeling that this is a permanent problem is likely to make the person feel more helpless and unable to change. On the other hand, attributing poor performance or negative behavior to temporary factors is likely to make the person less anxious and also able to improve subsequently. A study by Dweck (1975) demonstrated that attributing failure to lack of effort as opposed to ability results in subsequent improvement.

A study by Wilson and Linville (1982) used an attributional intervention to change subjects' attributions for their problems from stable to temporary causes. In this study the academic performance of students who were concerned about their grades was changed by changing the attributions for their problem from stable to unstable causes. College students were led to believe that their lower performance was temporary and that it was expected to get better. Subsequent behavior measures indicated that these students did better than a control group.

The finding that internal attributions made to positive events was negatively associated with grade point average appears to be somewhat inconsistent with the other results of this study and the findings from previous studies. It would appear that individuals with high academic performance would be more likely to internalize success and externalize failure. The reverse would appear to be true for the low achieving student (Ickes & Layden, 1978).

One possible explanation for the finding that academic performance is negatively associated with an internal attributional style for positive events is that Blacks who experience success recognize that significant others have contributed. This explanation is derived from the African philosophical orientation of "we" as opposed to "I" (Akbar, 1979; Nobles, 1980). One of the defining characteristics of an Afrocentric philosophy versus an Eurocentric philosophy is the concept of "weness." Hence the achievements of the individual are due to significant others. This orientation may have been exaggerated in the sample used in this study. Both Upward Bound students and students attending predominately Black classes may have a heightened sense of "weness" relative to other groups. Looked at from this perspective, the negative relationship between students' internal attributions for positive events and grade point average becomes clearer. Blacks who do well academically may recognize that their success is due in part to the contributions of others. With such an orientation, one would expect successful performance to be related to an external attributional style. More research with other indicators of performance is needed in order to further clarify this relationship.

In summary, the results of this study indicated that an internal attributional style for negative events is associated with low self-esteem in Black youths. A stable enduring attributional style for negative events is associated with lower academic performance. An attributional style for internalizing positive events is negatively associated with academic performance. These findings provide another cognitive framework for beginning to understand Black self-esteem and academic performance.

The objective of this exploratory study was to determine the usefulness of attributional style as a cognitive factor for understanding Black self-esteem and achievement. The study met its objective in determining these relationships. Since the findings were very similar in a high school and college sample, it is felt that the results are generalizable to Black youths. The major limitation of this study is that it is correlational, and cause and effect can not be determined. For example, individuals who continually perform low academically are more likely to see this as a stable event because it has indeed occurred in the past. However, an attributional style aimed at making stable attributions for successful performance is likely to exacerbate failure. Future studies aimed at using attributional techniques to modify performance and affective states such as self-esteem should prove helpful in evaluating the overall usefulness of this line of research.

## Notes

1. The global attributional style factor was not examined in this study.
2. The wording of two of the statements was changed slightly for high school students.

## References

Abramson, L. Y., Seligman, M. E. P., & Teasdale, J. D. (1978). Learned helplessness in humans: Critique and reformulation. *Journal of Abnormal Psychology, 87,* 49-74.

Akbar, N. (1979). African roots of Black personality. In W. A. Smith, K. H. Burlew, M. H. Mosley, & W. M. Whitney (Eds.), *Reflections on Black psychology.* Washington, DC: University Press of America.

Boykin, W., Franklin, A. J., & Yates, J. F. (1979). *Research directions of Black psychologists.* New York: Russell Sage.

Dweck, C. S. (1975). The role of expectations and attributions in the alleviation of learned helplessness. *Journal of Personality and Social Psychology, 31,* 674-685.

Feather, N. T. (1983). Some correlates of attributional style: Depressive symptoms, self-esteem, and protestant ethic values. *Personality and Social Psychology Bulletin, 9,* 125-135.

Ickes, W., & Layden, M. A. (1978). Attributional styles. In H. J. Harvey, W. Ickes, & R. F. Kidd (Eds.), *New directions in attribution research* (Vol. 2). Hillsdale, NJ: Lawrence Erlbaum.

Metalsky, G. I., Abramson, L. Y., Seligman, M. E., Semmel, A., & Peterson, C. (1982). Attributional styles and life events in the classroom: Vulnerability and invulnerability to depressive mood reactions. *Journal of Personality and Social Psychology, 43,* 612-617.

Nobles, W. (1980). African philosophy: Foundations for Black psychology. In R. L. Jones (Ed.), *Black psychology* (2nd ed.). New York: Harper & Row.

Peterson, C., Semmel, C. P., Baeyer, V. C., Abramson, L. Y., Metalsky, G. I. & Seligman,
    M. P. (1982). The attributional style and questionnaire. *Cognitive Therapy and
    Research, 6,* 287-299.
Rosenberg, M. (1965). *Society and the adolescent self-image.* Princeton, NJ: Princeton
    University Press.
Seligman, M. E. P., Abramson, L. Y., Semmel, A., & Baeyer, V. C. (1979). Depressive
    attributional style. *Journal of Abnormal Psychology, 88,* 242-247.
Wilson, T. D., & Linville, P. W. (1982). Improving the academic performance of college
    freshmen: Attribution therapy revisited. *Journal of Personality and Social Psychol-
    ogy, 42,* 367-376.

# 13 Implications of Doll Color Preferences Among Black Preschool Children and White Preschool Children

**DARLENE POWELL-HOPSON**
**DEREK S. HOPSON**
*Clinical Psychologists*
*Middletown, Connecticut*

Years after the "Black is beautiful" movement there remains a preference for white among Black and White preschool children. Black children have learned to reject their ethnic group as a consequence of pervasive negative stereotypes promoted by the media, teachers, parents, and the broader society. This article examined implications of previous research in 1985, which employed the Clark doll test (Clark & Clark, 1940), with the addition of a treatment intervention including learning principles of modeling, reinforcement, and color meaning word associations (Powell-Hopson, 1985). It was demonstrated that racial preferences among children could be changed at least temporarily. Pretest percentages showed that a majority of Black and White preschoolers chose a white doll when asked preference questions. In contrast, intervention posttest measurement revealed a significant percentage of preschoolers chose a black doll. We as scientists and clinicians have the tools to foster development of healthy positive self-images in youth, in particular Black children.

American racism has a long history of punishment, restriction, and oppression of the Black American. Within this context young Black children have encountered many challenges to their development of self-pride and a positive Black identity. Wilson (1978) noted that despite the "Black is beautiful" revolution American racism remains similar today as evidenced by continuation of a preference for White including "belief in its inherent rightness and the hatred of Black and belief in its inherent wrongness" (p. 83).

Correspondence concerning this article should be address to Darlene Powell-Hopson and Derek S. Hopson, Clinical Psychologists, 547 Main Street, Middletown, CT 06457.
© 1992 The Association of Black Psychologists.

The Joint Commission on Mental Health of Children (1970) issued a report on the mental health needs of children in the 1970s indicating that discrimination can have damaging effects on the psychological adjustment and self-esteem of young children and adolescents. In particular, it appears that through racial prejudice the Black child is subjected to derogatory views and negative self-images not only projected by the media, but also by teachers, parents, and the broader society. As an early experience, this provides for the child's growing knowledge of how the Black American is viewed in the country. Clark (1955) and Stevenson and Steward (1958) noted that many Black children learn to reject their own racial or ethnic group and adopt the cultural norms, values, and negative judgments about their group.

The development of racial prejudice (in particular inferiority of Black people) is a gradual learning process that appears in early childhood and is reliably assessed at age 3 (Wilson, 1978). Drs. Kenneth and Mamie Clark (1939) developed the "doll" test to measure children's racial awareness and preferences. They demonstrated that not only does a child's racial awareness begin around age 3, but also that children are aware of the advantages as well as negative attributes assigned to White and Black racial groups. In their study, eight different requests were made including "give me the doll that: (a) you like to play with or the doll you like best, (b) is the nice doll, (c) looks bad, (d) is a nice color, (e) looks like a White child, (f) looks like a colored child, (g) looks like a Negro child, (h) look like you." The results of the above experiment revealed that 67% of the Black children preferred white dolls to play with, 59% as the nice doll, and 60% for the doll having a nice color. In contrast, 59% chose the brown doll as being the one that looks bad. The five-year-olds in the study chose the white doll 75% of the time in response to the preference question. When measuring race awareness, there was a 61% correct race choice for the three-year-old children and 93% for the seven-year-old children.

The negative effects of racial prejudice on younger children, more specifically, the preference of white and rejection of black as reported by Clark and Clark (1939), have endured over several decades (Clark & Clark, 1940; Landreth & Johnson, 1953; Powell-Hopson, 1985; Taylor, 1966; Teplin, 1976). In contrast, several experimental procedures aimed a modifying racial attitudes or preferences have met with some promising results (Best et al, 1975; Edwards & Williams, 1970; McAdoo, 1970; McMurty & Williams, 1972; Shanahan, 1972). Outcomes of these studies further support the fact that childhood racial prejudices include a learning process that occurs through observation, imitation, actual experiences, rewards for prejudicial behavior, and direct teaching (Wilson, 1978). The implications of a study conducted by Powell-Hopson (1985), who employed the Clark doll test technique with the addition of a treatment intervention involving the learning principles of modeling, reinforcement, and color meaning word associations, are discussed.

One hundred and five Black preschoolers and 50 White preschoolers were presented with dolls that were exactly alike except for skin color and hair texture. The children were instructed to choose a doll to play with in groups of five. They were then individually asked the preference questions: "Give me the doll that . . . (a) you want to be, (b) you like to play with, (c) is a nice doll, (d) looks bad, (e) is a nice color, (f) you would take home if you could?" Two Black researchers (male and female) asked the children the preference questions.

In the pretest 65% of the Black children chose the white doll to play with, and 75% of the White children chose the white doll to play with. For the Black children, the 6 preference questions responses ranged from 60%–78% in favor of the white doll with 76% choosing the black doll as the doll that looked bad. For the White children, preference responses ranged from 62%–82% choosing the white doll, with 82% choosing the black doll as the doll that looked bad. The children in the segregated classrooms favored the white doll more than did the children in integrated classrooms. Fifty percent of the children in integrated classrooms chose the black doll as the doll that they wanted to play with and the doll that "is a nice doll." Thirty-one percent of the children in segregated classrooms chose the black doll as the doll that "is a nice doll." In two programs a high percentage (53 and 67) of the Black children chose the black doll in the pretest. Only 28% of the Black children and 16% of the White children said they had a black doll at home.

The second part of the study involved an intervention developed by the two researchers. In the intervention the children who chose a black doll were reinforced (verbally praised) and allowed to sit up front with the researchers. The children who chose white dolls had to sit in the back. The researchers chose black dolls themselves and modeled pro-Black responses to the preference questions. A story was read depicting Black children positively. In the story a Black male child and a Black female child are portrayed as the smartest and best in their class. The researchers also asked the children to hold up the black dolls and repeat positive adjectives such as "pretty, nice, handsome, clean, smart, good," and "we like these dolls the best." The dolls were never referred to as black or white.

The children were asked to put the dolls away and after 15 minutes they were asked to select a doll to play with in groups of 5, and afterwards the children were individually readministered the preference questions. Posttest results generated after the direct teaching behavior modification program indicated 68% of the Black children chose the black doll to play with, as did 67% of the White children. For the Black children, preference responses ranged from 69%–71% in favor of the black doll. For the White children, preference responses ranged from 62%–66% in favor of the black doll. Only 27% of the Black children chose the black doll as the doll that "looks bad," whereas 42% of the White children chose the black doll.

Seventy-two percent of the Black children in integrated classrooms and 67% in segregated classrooms chose the black doll to play with. For Black children in integrated classrooms preference responses ranged from 72%–89% in favor of the black doll, and for children in segregated classrooms preference responses ranged from 56%–68%. Overall, the children in integrated classrooms were more positive about the black doll than the children in segregated classrooms. These results are not expected to generalize beyond the experimental situation.

A debriefing session involved explaining to the children that neither doll was better than the other. In classrooms with all Black children each was told that the black doll was make to look like Black people and that it was "beautiful just like you." A debriefing was also held with the teachers to explain the purpose of the study and emphasize the need for building positive identities with Black children.

During the study, some of the spontaneous comments the children made indicated an awareness of prevailing social values and attitudes attached to race and skin. One Black child shouted: "Wait, let me get one; there aren't going to be any white ones left." Another Black child insisted he was white, and in an effort to prove it he demanded that the researchers look at the palm of his hand. Another child said: "Black is dirty." Still, another child said that White people have a lot of money. One White child who was not allowed to sit up front began to kick the chairs of the children in front of him. Another child shouted out loud that; "the white one is the good one." These conflicts and rejections of Blackness are directly related to the messages children receive from their environment. In the controlled experimental environment where black preferences were reinforced and modeled, Black children and White children chose the black doll. This clearly demonstrates the power of social learning theory principles and direct teaching.

It is interesting to note that some of the children who were from Black Muslim background chose the black doll very emphatically in the pretest. This may be the result of the direct cultural teaching they receive, which counteracts the impact of White American society's projections of negative Black images. Unfortunately, most children associate being White with success, beauty, and power. Children also hear associations such as "evil witches are black and angels are white" or "the bad guy wears black and the good guy wears white."

The study did not indicate that the children wished they were White, but it did indicate their awareness of society's preferences. Furthermore, these preferences result from conditioning and are susceptible to change (although isolated) through intervention. The fact that the researchers were Black role models appeared to have a definite positive impact on the children's attitudes and choices. Many of the children wanted to change their choice of doll after observing the researchers choose black dolls and after hearing the story depicting Black children in positive terms.

In two classrooms where a majority of the Black children chose the black doll in the pretest, the teachers had implemented formal and informal cultural experiences relating to issues of black identity. Here, one teacher was Black and the other White indicating that the race of the teacher was not as important as attitude and commitment to teaching racial pride to Black children.

In contrast, in one of the programs a Black teacher had a white Cabbage Patch doll in a classroom with all Black children, and this doll was the children's favorite. Still, in another classroom a Black teacher was highly concerned that this particular study may be teaching the children differences between Black and White despite the fact that the dolls were never referred to as black or white and pro-Black was not presented an anti-White. Of course, this teacher was not familiar with the Clarks' study (1939), which clearly demonstrated that as young as age 3 children are aware of racial differences and associated meanings or values.

Parents, educators, and mental health professionals need to take an active approach in building positive self-images of Black children. Perpetuation of negative stereotypes or active rejection of Blacks by Whites has enabled racism in its worse form to continue as long-standing in the broader American society. Dixon and Foster (1971) noted that racial prejudice not only threatens the integrity and development of Blacks but also impairs the ability of Whites to understand and learn to accept cultural differences of other racial groups.

It is apparent that all children need to be educated about the positive contributions of Black Americans in areas such as science, politics, business, athletics, arts, music, literature, and entertainment. Parent education programs can assist parents in developing their child's racial pride and acceptance of others. We must begin as early as preschool age to expose children regularly to Black Americans in positions of authority and power. In addition, children can be provided positive role models through class trips to environments, activities, and engagements that are controlled, produced, managed, or contributed to by Black people. Every child should be able to identify and talk about Blacks of earlier times and of the present. They should know who Martin Luther King, Jr., Harriet Tubman, George Washington Carver, Malcolm X were, as well as who Jesse Jackson is.

In conclusion, American society has still much work ahead in the area of fostering healthy, positive, self-images in youth, in particular, Black children. We have identified several methods readily available, which include basic learning principles that can be implemented in the various segments in our society such as the school system, media, and at home.

## References

Best, D. L., Smith, S. C., Graves, D. J., & Williams, J. E. (1975). The modification of racial bias in preschool children. *Journal of Experimental Child Psychology, 20,* 193-205.

Clark, K. B. (1955). *Prejudice and your child.* Boston: Beacon.

Clark, K. B., & Clark, M. P. (1939). The development of consciousness of self and the emergence of racial identification in Negro pre-school children. *Journal of Social Psychology, 10,* 591-597.

Clark, K. B., & Clark, M. P. (1940). Skin color as a factor in racial identification of Negro preschool children. *Journal of Social Psychology, S.P.S.S.I. Bulletin, II,* 159-169.

Dixon, V. J., & Foster, B. G. (1971). *Beyond Black or White: An alternate America.* Boston: Little, Brown.

Edwards, C. D., & Williams, J. E. (1970). Generalization between evaluative words associated with racial figures in preschool children. *Journal of Experimental Research in Personality, 4,* 144-155.

Joint Commission on Mental Health of Children. (1970). *Crisis in child mental health: Challenge for the 70's.* New York: Harper & Row.

Landreth, C., & Johnson, B. C. (1953). Young children's responses to a picture and insert test designed to reveal reactions to persons of different skin color. *Child Development, 24*(1), 63-79.

McAdoo, J. L. (1970). *An exploratory study of racial attitude change in Black preschool children.* Unpublished doctoral dissertation, University of Michigan.

McMurty, C. L., & Williams, J. E. (1972). The evaluation dimension of the affective meaning system of the preschool child. *Developmental Psychology, 6,* 238-246.

Powell-Hopson, D. (1985). *The effects of modeling, reinforcement, and color meaning word associations on doll color preferences of Black preschool children and White preschool children.* Unpublished doctoral dissertation, Hofstra University.

Shanahan, J. K. (1972). *The effects of modifying black-white concept attitudes of Black and White first grade subjects upon two measures of racial attitudes.* Unpublished doctoral dissertation, University of Washington.

Stevenson, H. W., & Stewart, E. C. A. (1958). A developmental study of race awareness in young children. *Child Development, 29,* 399-410.

Taylor, R. G. (1966). Racial stereotypes in young children. *Journal of Psychology, 64,* 137-142.

Teplin, L. A. (1976). A comparison of racial/ethnic preferences among Anglo, Black, and Latino children. *American Journal of Orthopsychiatry, 46,* 702-709.

Wilson, A. N. (1978). *The developmental psychology of the Black child.* New York: United Brothers Communications System.

# 14 Racial Identification and Racial Preference of Black Preschool Children in New York and Trinidad

SHARON-ANN GOPAUL-Mc.NICOL
*Hempstead, New York*

In 1947 Kenneth Clark studied racial identification and racial preference in Black preschool children by using the "Doll Test" experimental procedure. Clark found that the majority of the children showed a preference for the white doll and rejected the brown doll, but chose the brown doll as the one that "looks bad."

This study, conducted in 1986, examined racial identification and racial preference in 191 Black preschool children in New York and Trinidad. The same Clark Doll Test procedure was used. The dolls were identical in every respect except skin coloring. In the Clark study the dolls were identical in skin coloring and hair coloring. Trinidad was selected in order to determine whether the results would be different if the children were from a culture where the majority of the people were Black and where the leading role models were Black.

Even though 40 years have elapsed since Clark and Clark (1947) did their study, the results of the study reported here are very similar in that a substantial majority of Black preschool children in both New York and Trinidad evidenced preference for the white doll, and identified with the white doll. Even most of the dark-skinned Black children chose the white doll as looking like them and as the nice doll. However most of the children chose the black doll as "looking bad." The results of this study are also similar to the majority of studies cited in the literature.

What was particularly interesting in the results of this study is that although social class differs on measures of intelligence in favor of middle and upper classes, with respect to racial identity social class was

Correspondence concerning this article should be addressed to Sharon-ann Gopaul-Mc.Nicol, 109 Holly Avenue, Hempstead, NY 11550.

not a factor in doll preference since the socioeconomic status of children yielded no significant differences.

What was particularly disturbing were the spontaneous remarks made by the children. "I don't like being Black; I will be rich if I am like the white doll," were some of the comments uttered by the Black children. Piaget and Weil (1951) described the child's notion of nationality and identity as a dual process of cognitive and affective development. In other words, at the same time a child learns to handle concepts and absorb factual knowledge about them, he also develops affective dispositions. Piaget emphasized that evaluations of or attitudes toward others are initially egocentric, but subsequently egocentricity is replaced by acceptance of family and finally on wider societal values. Thus, the child's development of an attitude is seen as a process of social and observational learning. The results of this study and those of previous studies suggest that the atmosphere in which children live and the values passed on to them in school and in the media are powerful influences in attitude formation. The total volume of what enters into the formation of attitudes by way of social inheritance is much greater than the child's personal experience at home. Black children are constantly bombarded with images that suggest to them that their race is not the preferred race. Except in the spheres of entertainment and athletics, when Black children look around them they find few role models with their skin color who have important prestigious positions in this society. They see mainly White models in advertisements and as heroes of stories. Even today cartoons still usually portray the savage and the evil as the Black man. Naturally the little Black child will want to identify with what represents good, and thus he forms an attitude and a way of thinking that essentially favors White. Thus it is understandable that when asked "Which doll looks like you?" they experience difficulty in identifying with their own race. When the children made those comments and showed a preference for the white doll, they were probably reflecting the prevailing social attitude, and that is, to be powerful, beautiful, economically successful, and more socially accepted, one ought to be White.

A question raised by this study is why did the Trinidadian children evidence such a strong White preference. The answer may lie in the perception of White supremacy fostered by an English-colonial education system. It is evident that a White-bias permeates every facet of the cosmopolitan population—educational, economical, and social. Although the standard textbooks in the Trinidad schools rarely ever purposely humiliate any of the groups that comprise the population, the majority of textbooks fail to deal positively with the contributions made by various races to the growth and development of Trinidad. The average child may well assume that the development of Trinidad is solely the result of a Northern European or even an Anglo-Saxon heritage. This conception deprives many children of their share in the pride that comes from being an integral part of Trinidad.

Another possible explanation is that many teachers in the schools still show favoritism to the light-skinned Black children and the White children.They choose them to carry out more prestigious responsibilities such as classroom presidents. A young child may associate such positions with being powerful. The Black child then looks up to the White and light-skinned children, pairing skin color with prestige. It is important to remember that the teacher is perhaps the most important arbiter of the child's educational experience. Therefore, the perspective that he/she brings to the tasks and the assumptions, beliefs, and standards of comparisons that color this perspective will crucially influence the child's view. To a large extent the child identifies with the teacher (who is one of the most significant others in his life), uses the teacher as a model, and internalizes the values that the teacher embodies. Thus the emotional and evaluative feedback from the teacher may support or undermine the child's feelings of self-worth.

Another possible explanation for the White preference responses evidenced by the Trinidadian children is the media. The television is probably the most important purveyor of contemporary culture, and this medium is predominantly White. The very same programs that are shown in North America and Europe are shown in Trinidad with the same White bias.

It should be noted that although black dolls are more available both in New York and in Trinidad, most of the children did not have black dolls at home. This suggests that parents may be implicitly guiding their children's experience. When Black parents only buy white dolls for their children, they may not have explicitly stated "we prefer white dolls," but the implication is that white dolls are better to play with. Without conscious or intentional teaching on the part of the parents, children begin to incorporate in their value-systems the attitudes of their parents, and their behavior becomes a microcosm of the parents' behavior.

Change requires the involvement of all institutions. Parents have to play a more active role in monitoring the television shows and the movies that the children watch since these images are internalized by the children. Parents should manifest their displeasure about the lack of positive Black role models in the media, especially on television. Parents must look at the books that their children read both at school and at home, and must question and discuss with their children the subliminal messages— for instance, witches are Black and angels are White.

Educational institutions should focus more on the achievements of Blacks as part of an integrated curriculum, rather than separating Black history from the general curriculum. Teachers must have formal and informal cultural programs that are related to Black identity issues and stress positive aspects of Black life.

In addition, mental health professionals ought to address these issues. They ought to engage in research that can aid in promoting self-esteem and self-acceptance in Black children. Short interventions that are half hour in duration or involve only one session are not enough to overcome such influences. The fact that most of the twelve children who had participated in the Powell-Hopson (1985) study did not maintain their Black preference when they were participants in the Gopaul-Mc.Nicol (1986) study, but had reverted to white doll preference and selection, suggests that short-term interventions are insufficient. Research is needed that will examine the effects of a treatment intervention that can be part of the classroom curriculum for a longer period of time—for example, a school year. In addition, psycholinguists should begin addressing the biases in the language. Phrases like "Black Sunday" and "Black Magic" further perpetuate the negative self-image that the children embrace.

In summary, the results of this study suggest that there has been little change in the racial attitudes of Black preschool children over the past 40 years. The need for greater participation by parents, educators, and society at large in the promotion of racial pride and self-acceptance in Black children is as urgent today as at any time in our history.

## References

Clark, K. B., & Clark, M. P. (1947). Racial identification and preferences in Negro children. In T. M. Newcomb & E. L. Hartley (Eds.), *Readings in social psychology.* New York: Holt, Rinehart & Winston.

Gopaul-Mc.Nicol. (1986). *The effects of modeling, reinforcement, and color meaning word association of Black preschool children and White preschool children in New York and Trinidad.* Unpublished doctoral dissertation, Hofstra University.

Piaget, J., & Weil, A. (1957). The development in children of the idea of the homeland and of relations with other countries. *International Social Science Bulletin 3,* 561-578.

Powell-Hopson, D. (1985). *The effects of modeling, reinforcement, and color meaning word associations on doll color preferences of Black preschool children and White preschool children.* Unpublished doctoral dissertation, Hofstra University.

# Cognitive and Measurement Issues

Testing and measurement in the field of psychology owe a great deal to the early work of Galton and his students and their attempts to bring the structure of quantification to the early principles of variation in natural science. The application of a universal standard to the patterns of variation in nature has come to be what we know as normality, represented by the normal distribution. The firm establishment of this standard, along with the identification of certain aberrations, provided the foundation of quantitative procedures for the analysis of observational data and for the assessment of variations in nature, in particular. From the beginning of this work early theorists and investigators focused their attention on human variations and psychologists focused especially on variations in human mental characteristics.

Even the early work in this area was fraught with controversy, in part because of its implications for classification and ultimately because of the potential social, political, and economic compartmentalization of human individuals. This controversy has extended to the comparison of groups, defined by any and all of the customary demographic features. But chiefly within American psychology, this comparison has centered on race.

It is not surprising, therefore, that the majority of work on the psychology of African Americans regarding this topic area has been critical and deconstructive. That is, the response of scientists specializing in the study of African American populations has been one of skeptical reexamination of the principles and the technology of psychological testing and measurement. The chapters in this section represent the kind of critical work that has challenged the early, and still as yet unrefined, paradigms for the measurement of psychological differences in African Americans, with a view toward scientific reform.

The chapter by Hilliard reviews a major event in the challenge to the political ramifications of testing. The review of the historical case in California that stopped the use of intelligence tests for the classification and educational tracking of African American children brings this scientific effort into practical focus. Grubb draws our attention to an overlooked aspect of the evidence on group differences in intelligence: the similarity that obtains across racial groups in the lower ranges of the traditional measures. And Wyche and Novick, in their chapter, summarize the implications of recent revisions of the American Psychological Association's standards for testing and the impact those standards have on African American educational, occupational, and health-care opportunities.

Modern cognitive psychology reflects something of a compromise between early introspectionism and its behavioral antagonists. While cognition is inherently internal and subjective, its manifestations can be measured in overt responses to mental tasks. The study of these processes in African American populations has been slower in its development than similar work in virtually any other subdiscipline in psychology. The chapters contained in this volume provide an introduction to the kinds of efforts that have been undertaken in African American Psychology to bridge the gap in understanding cognition in this underresearched group.

Part of the reason for the absence of work in this area is the fact that research in cognition has been conceived largely as a pure, or basic, research enterprise. Although it has overlapped with studies of educational performance, the study of cognition per se has often ignored African American populations unless they were the subject of applied educational research. The resulting dependency on comparative methodologies and comparative conceptual models has left many fundamental questions about cognitive functioning in African Americans unasked. The chapters in this section articulate some of those questions along with the applied implications that follow from the answers.

Smith and Drumming report on research into a classical paradigm for the study of thinking processes: How do individuals carry out deductive procedures of reasoning? In their analysis of how African Americans perform this formal task of logical derivation and decision making, the authors cite both similarities and differences with earlier research on White populations. Shade, in her chapter, focuses particularly on the unique aspects of the perceptual orientations of African Americans. One implication of that research involves the effects that such a cognitive style may have on educational performance. This particular topic is reviewed and evaluated critically in Willis's chapter, which incorporates the work of Shade and many others. Another implication of Shade's analysis pertains to the applicability of universal theories of cognitive functioning and development to African American populations in particular.

# 15 IQ and the Courts: *Larry P. v. Wilson Riles* and *PASE v. Hannon*

## ASA G. HILLIARD III
### *Georgia State University*

This paper presents a brief history and a comparative analysis of two recent major Federal court cases on standardized IQ testing and Black children. It includes a discussion of some major implications of the two court decisions and a pending appeal. Finally, shortcomings of the two court battles are cited and suggested future directions for IQ psychometry and education are suggested.

In 1971, the National Association for the Advancement of Colored People supported a class action suit against Wilson Riles, Superintendent of Public Instruction for California, the California Sate Department Board of Education, and the San Francisco School Board over the placement of the following Black children into classes for the mental retarded: Darryl Lester, Sylvia Marie Walker, James Lanigan, Michael Sears, and John Harvey. The Bay Area Association of Black Psychologists led by Drs. William Pierce and Harold Dent, reexamined children who had been placed into classes for the educable mentally retarded (EMR) using the same tests as had been used before, but varying procedures to establish rapport. They found none of the children to be retarded. The case came to trial in 1977 and was decided in favor of the Plaintiffs in Judge Robert F. Peckham's 9th District Federal Court in San Francisco in 1980. This case is known as *Larry P. v. Wilson Riles.*

A similar class action suit was initiated in Chicago by a group of parents. It was called Parents in Action on Special Education (PASE). The case is referred to as *PASE v. Hannon,* Hannon being the Superintendent of Schools in Chicago at the time.

In both cases, it was alleged that standardized IQ tests were primarily responsible for the placement of the children in EMR classes and that

Asa G. Hilliard, Department of Educational Foundations, Georgia State University, Atlanta, GA 30303 the standardized IQ tests were racially and culturally biased against Black children, causing them to be placed inappropriately in EMR classes.

In San Francisco, Judge Robert Peckham ruled in favor of the Plaintiffs against the use of IQ tests. In Chicago, Judge John F. Grady ruled in favor of the Defendants and for the IQ tests, as he modified them. The San Francisco decision is being appealed. The Chicago case is not being appealed.

The final decision may come at the Supreme Court level. It will be a landmark decision, since it could result in the extension of the California ban on the use of IQ tests to place Black children into EMR classes. Even without a final decision, professional practice in the use of IQ tests in education is being carefully reevaluated (Holtzman, Heller, & Messick, 1980; Wigdor & Garner, 1982). Without IQ tests, new ways for determining EMR placements would have to be created, or the whole EMR classification might need to be reevaluated to determine its educational utility and benefit.

It is the purpose of this paper to provide an overview of the cases, to present a comparison of them, and to analyze the extent to which these cases address the complete range of essential issues associated with IQ testing and Black children for educational purposes.

At issue for Black children is the matter of appropriate and meaningful assessment. In the background hangs the old issue of the genetic capacity of Black people (Jensen, 1980). Also at issue is the validity of IQ psychometry for education, public credibility for psychologists, and perhaps even the validity of special education pedagogy.

The existing IQ testing system as used in education is a *ranking* and *classification* system. It is not a *diagnostic* and *remedial* system. If remediation of learning difficulties or low academic achievement is possible (Feuerstein, 1979, 1980), a major shift in professional orientation and practice is required. If remediation of such things as educable mental retardation (EMR) is not possible, then the burden of proof for the benefits of such sorting remains with advocates of such a system. In the absence of demonstrable benefits, one must question the use of such a system.

## The Cases

When Judge Robert F. Peckham found for the plaintiffs in the case of *Larry P. v. Wilson Riles* in the United States Federal District Court in San Francisco, he found IQ tests to be biased against Black children:

We must recognize at the outset that the history of the I.Q. test, and of special education classes built on I.Q. testing, is not the history of neutral scientific discoveries translated into education reform. It is, at least in the early years, the history of racial prejudice, of Social Darwinism, and of the use of the scientific "mystique" to legitimate such prejudices. (Peckham, 1979, p. 8)

In another United States Federal District Court in Chicago, in a similar case, Judge John F. Grady found for the defendants. He rendered a decision that IQ tests, though somewhat biased, would have no appreciable effect on placement decisions: "I conclude that the possibility of the few biased items on these tests causing an EMR placement that would not otherwise occur is practically non-existent" (Grady, 1980, p. 101).

A close examination of both written opinions will show that IQ psychometry actually lost in both cases. First, it lost when Judge Robert F. Peckham found the tests to be culturally and racially biased against Black children. In doing so, he appeared to be persuaded by the testimony of the plaintiffs' expert witnesses. In the *PASE v. Hannon* case, although Judge John F. Grady ruled for the defendants, he did so only after declaring a plague on both pro and con houses of the expert witnesses. Moreover, Judge Grady took the extraordinary step not only of rejecting expert opinion, but, by doing so, demonstrating a basic lack of respect for the professional expertise in the field by taking the position that his lay opinion about IQ tests was actually superior to both sets of professional opinion. The Peckham decision was a model of judicial restraint. Although Judge Peckham was not persuaded that IQ tests were valid for Black children, he did not move beyond that position and attempt to establish a professional remedy for the difficulties. Indeed, in his decision he made explicit his uneasiness about having to enter the domain that should be left to professionals:

A second essential caveat is that there should be no illusion about our capacity as a court to require educational systems to transcend societal inequalities and provide Black children generally with the kind of skills necessary for educational and social advancement in our country. That would take a major commitment, not a court order. We are perfectly aware of the complexity and interrelationship of educational problems, and indeed of the danger that an attack on EMR classes, in the absence of effective remedial education, could even hurt those individuals who, despite the aims and approach of EMR classes in general, actually benefited from what appears in retrospect to have been misplacement. Nevertheless, that consideration cannot allow us to sanction a labeling process that unjustifiably blames educational failure on the ostensible mental retardation of Black children and dooms disproportionate numbers of Black children to a program designed to keep their performance below normal. (Peckham, 1979, p. 102)

Judge Grady expressed no such hesitation. Not only did he feel himself competent to make an item-by-item assessment of the presence or absence of cultural bias in IQ testing, but in the act of doing so, he placed into the public record the actual items on one of the Wechsler intelligence tests, making them publicly available for the first time. The net result of both decisions is that IQ testing was not known to make a contribution to education that would be convincing to a lay judge. Judge Peckham rules that IQ test were biased based on his view of the testimony that was presented. Judge Grady rejected basic IQ testimony and made himself, a lay judge, superior to professional practice by "fixing the tests"!

### The Essence of the Decisions

In the case of *Larry P. v. Wilson Riles,* six important points emerged from Judge Robert F. Peckham's decision. They are as follows:

1. The Judge assumed that the actual differences in intellect between Blacks and Whites should be expected to be zero. Judge Peckham found no compelling evidence to justify any other assumption, although the California State Department of Education officials expressed a different view.

A number of key state officials in addition testified that they were familiar with Professor Jensen's writings and they would not rule out the genetic explanation for disparities between White children in IQ scores and EMR enrollment.

IQ tests can only be explained as the product of the impermissible and scientifically dubious assumption that Black children as a group are inherently less capable of academic achievement that White children.

Key officials in the State Department of Education, moreover, actually corroborated this explanation. They testified that they believed the over-enrollment of Black and Chicano children in EMR classes accurately reflected the incidence of mental retardation among those children. (Peckham, 1979, pp. 42, 88)

In the Chicago case, apparently the witnesses were able to agree on a zero difference among groups: "Defendants agreed with the plaintiffs that there is no evidence to support a hypothesis that Blacks have less innate capacity than Whites" (Grady, 1980, p. 92).

2. Judge Peckham ruled that IQ tests were both racially and culturally biased.

3. Judge Peckham actually expressed the opinion that the tests were not valid for Black children, but no compelling evidence was cited to establish the validity (except predictive validity) of IQ tests for White or other children.

4. Serious questions were raised, in the Judge's opinion, regarding the validity of special education pedagogy, the "treatment" that is supposed to be rendered to children who are identified by the tests as educable mentally retarded. No empirical evidence was presented of specific benefit for children because of placement of children into classes for the educable mentally retarded:

> Whatever the future, however, it is essential that California's educators confront the problem of the widespread failure to provide an adequate education to underprivileged minorities such as the Black children who brought this lawsuit. Educators have too often been able to rationalize inaction by blaming educational failure on an assumed intellectual inferiority of disproportionate numbers of Black children. That assumption without validation is unacceptable and is made all the more invidious when "legitimated" by ostensibly neutral, scientific IQ scores. We have refused to allow the continuation of EMR policies consistent only with that assumption, and it is hoped that this will clear the way for more constructive educational reform. (Peckham, 1979, pp. 109-110)

> In the words of Fred Hanson, a special education consultant and one of the key state administrators, "slow learning must be caused by limited intellectual capacity". . . . These classes are not meant for remedial instruction. . . . Further, the curriculum was not and is not designed to help students learn the skills necessary to return to the regular instructional program. To quote again from the state handbook, "The primary instructional goals for the mentally retarded are set forth in the Education Code, Section 6902 as 'Social Adjustment' and 'Economic Usefulness.' These primary goals should include physical health and development, personal hygiene and

grooming, language and communication skills, social and emotional adjustment, basic home and community living skills, and citizenship. Every classroom activity should contribute in some meaningful way to achieving these goals. . . . The educational goals for the educable mentally retarded are not reading, writing, and arithmetic per se; if these skills are accepted as the primary goals, the EMR students should remain in regular classes where academic skills are emphasized. (Peckham, 1979, p. 17)

5. The Judge expressed the opinion that the California State Department of Education was guilty of systematic and continuing negligence in the face of constant challenges to the validity of IQ testing for cultural minority populations:

> In addition, while the SDE (State Department of Education) has dutifully collected the reports legally required from school districts about local disproportionate enrollment and it has required local boards to comply with the law and explain the variances, these reports have been treated in a manner calculated to maximize tolerance of minority disproportion. First the SDE interpreted statutory requirements of a report when there is a variance of "15% or more from the percentage of such children in the district as a whole" to mean that a district was "entitled" to 15 free percentage points added to the minority representation in the population. Parity, therefore, was not even sought, and the literal reading of the statute meant that a district with 2% Black children in the population could have 17% Black enrollment in EMR classes. A district with 85% Black children would in turn be allowed 100% of the EMR enrollment. Beyond these remarkably tolerant interpretation . . . the SDE never evaluated the adequacy of the local explanation for the disproportion and never sought to utilize the data or explanations to obtain a sounder understanding of the problem, much less to work toward a solution. (Peckham, 1979, pp. 90-91)

> The facts permit but one inference, and the State has not offered evidence that permits any other inference. Despite the admitted problems with the IQ tests, and despite disproportionate enrollments which have even been condemned by the Legislature, the SDE's actions reveal a complacent acceptance of those disproportions, and that complacency was evidently built on easy but unsubstantiated assumptions about the incidence of retardation or at least low intelligence among Black children. Coupled with the affirmative decision to adopt a requirement of particular IQ tests in 1969, that complacent acceptance must be seen as a desire to perpetuate the segregation of minorities in inferior, dead-end, and stigmatizing classes for the retarded. (Peckham, 1979, p. 91)

6. The Judge virtually begged professionals to do their homework in such a way that the case could be taken out of the court arena.

Judge Grady explicitly stated that he was unimpressed by expert witnesses on either side of the question:

> The testimony, standing alone, does not preponderate in either direction. I have seen cases in which one set of experts is clearly more credible than the others and will, by their demeanor, appearance, credentials, and the reasonableness of their testimony, carry the day. This is not such a case. None of the witnesses in this case has so impressed me with his or her credibility or expertise that I would feel secure in basing a decision simply on his or her opinion. In some instances, I am satisfied that the opinions expressed are more the result of doctrinaire commitment to a preconceived idea than they are the result of scientific inquiry. I need something more than the conclusions of the witnesses in order to arrive at my own conclusions. (Grady, 1980, p. 8)

He appeared to feel quite comfortable that he could find culturally biased items on his own by a simple process of inspection:

> It is obvious to me that I must examine the tests themselves in order to know what the witnesses are talking about. I do not see how an informed decision on the question of bias could be reached in any other way, for me to say that the tests are either biased or unbiased without analyzing the test items in detail would reveal nothing about the tests but only something about my opinion of the tests. . . . I have said enough to indicate my belief that an analysis of the tests is essential. I will now proceed to that task. (Grady, 1980, pp. 8–9)

Having "repaired" the damage which he perceived, Judge Grady was apparently of the opinion that his "revised Wechsler" was valid. Consequently, at that point we actually had a new IQ test in Chicago, the *Grady-Wechsler!*

## The Limitations of the Two Court Cases

Neither the *Larry P. v. Wilson Riles* nor the *PASE v. Hannon* cases offered an opportunity for a true test of the validity of IQ tests:

> We do not address the broader questions of whether these IQ tests are generally valid as measures of intelligence, whether individual items are

appropriate for that purpose, or whether the tests could be improved. (Grady, 1980, pp. 91–92)

Even if they had, traditional professional criteria for validity determination are inadequate, since whole categories of relevant data are never developed or brought to bear on the process of establishing test validity. Because of the way in which the initial *Larry P. v. Wilson Riles* complaint was developed, no real attention was paid to the *weakness in the validity criteria*. In the case of *Larry P. v. Wilson Riles,* Black children were retested by Black psychologists on the same IQ instrument after the Black psychologists made certain adjustments to account for the cultural background of the children, and to ensure the establishment of rapport between examiner and examinee. Since the results were different for the children on the second administration of the same test, it was alleged that the tests were culturally biased against Black children. By choosing to select the dimension of the cultural bias as the basic basis for challenging the validity of the IQ tests in the *Larry P. v. Wilson Riles* and *PASE v. Hannon* cases, the plaintiffs in both cases virtually guaranteed a narrowly restricted domain within which the validity battle would be fought. I regard this as unfortunate, since, while it is my opinion that the cultural bias is not the root problem with standardized IQ tests, cultural bias is but the symptom of the more deeply rooted problem of test *validity* itself. Do standardized IQ tests actually measure mental functions or the ability to learn in any or all populations?

In order to gain some appreciation for the vastness of the relevant domain that is excluded from cultural bias and *instructional validity* determination at present, we may focus on categories of missing data. Some of them are as follows:

1. *No data on treatment ("school").* The absence of a systematically developed operational definition of "school" or "instruction" in studies of the validity of IQ tests leaves a critical variable in the study of test validity uncontrolled. Such data as do exist of variations in the quality of instructional treatment among teachers and among schools indicate that wide variation exists. These variations in treatment (teaching quality) may be sufficient to explain virtually all of the differences between cultural groups that psychometrists find when measuring IQ differences, especially if we include data both on school and on certain other major environmental treatments such as television exposure and

economic opportunity. The major point is that IQ test makers and advocates do not deal with these variables at all.

**2.** *No data on language and the application of linguistic criteria in test development.*

In the fifties, the United States Government spent millions of dollars developing systems for machine translation of Russian and other languages. After years of effort on the part of some of the most talented linguists in the country, it was finally concluded that the only reliable, and ultimately the fastest, translator is a human being deeply conversant not only with the language but with the subject as well. The computers could spew out yards of print-out but they meant very little. The words and some of the grammar were all there, but the sense was distorted. That the project failed was not due to lack of application, time, money, talent, but for other reasons, which are central to the theme of this chapter.

The problem lies not in the linguistic code but in the context, which carries varying proportions of the meaning. Without context, the code is incomplete since it encompasses only part of the message. This should become clear if one remembers that the spoken language is an abstraction of an event that happened, might have happened, or is being planned. As any writer knows, an event is usually infinitely more complex and rich than the language used to describe it. Moreover, the writing system is an abstraction of the spoken system and is in effect a reminder system of what somebody said or could have said. In the process of abstracting, as contrasted with measuring, people take in some things and unconsciously ignore others. This is what intelligence is: paying attention to the right things. (Hall, 1977, pp. 86-87)

The use of a common language, specifically common English, is the essential vehicle for interrogation, responding, and interpretation of *standardized* IQ test scores. *Therefore, an understanding of the science of linguistics, particularly in this case as it applies to the language of African Americans, is vital to any "science" of intellectual measurement that is dependent upon language,* especially as such language varies from the general language of Americans. *It is a gross scientific error to ignore the application of cultural linguistic principles to the analysis of interrogation, responding, and interpretation in standardized IQ testing.*

3. *No data on culture.* Like language, culture (which includes language) is a category of systematic scientific study. The existence of culture, the principles of its operation, and the existence of specific cultural configurations such as African American culture, including its variations, is well known to students of culture or to students of African American culture. Abundant empirical data exist that must be taken into account systematically when examining interrogation, responding, and interpretation of IQ data, which essentially are narrow cultural data. Test makers do not do this. There is no evidence that they can.

4. *No data on the impact of IQ on instruction.* The present limited justification for the use of IQ testing is made through an appeal to predictive validity. The gaping deficit in such an approach is that no empirical data exist to demonstrate that the systematic and correct use of IQ tests (predictive validity or not) results in instructional benefits to children. This is a fundamental error, since even if a weak predictive association exists between IQ and school achievement, the pedagogical value of doing IQ testing must be demonstrated by reference to data on improved academic outcomes for children as a consequence of the use of IQ tests.

5. *No data on the impact of special education.* During the trial, the benefits of special education were *assumed* by the defendants, not demonstrated. No empirical data were presented to show that the assignment of children to EMR (EMH in Chicago) classes on the basis of IQ tests or any other measure resulted in a better educational outcome for such children. Therefore, the absence of validity data on "EMR"/ "EMH" instructions links with the absence of a pedagogically valid application for IQ tests.

6. *No data on the impact of successful teaching.* Given the fact that no operational definition of "school" treatment was given, it should not be surprising that no recognition was given to the fact that the quality of general teaching that is available to various children varies widely in quite systematic ways, ways that are associated with the cultural background of students. The actual validity of IQ tests can never be known in the face of psychometric ignorance regarding variations in the quality of teaching, EMR or "regular," to which various children are exposed who are to be compared on IQ test scores. We must have validity and reliability data on pedagogical treatments.

7. *No data on early sensory-motor development of African and African American children.* Any systematic review of the literature on the sensory-motor development of African and African American children will reveal a remarkable phenomenon, which must be explained, especially in view of the negative perception of the learning abilities of Black children that is held by some writers. The repeated finding in the literature is that African and African American children exceed the norms on tests of sensory-motor (both physical and cognitive) development during the first two years of life. At the time that the basic "culturally neutral" tests are changed, the early advantage of African and African American children appears to decline. Were we in possession of systematic data on language and culture, it is my opinion that this apparent decline could be explained quite easily. As early sensory-motor tests change to linguistically biased IQ tests, tests that are based on the language of middle America, we witness a change from relatively culture-neutral to more culture-bound standardized assessment that creates a distortion in the comparisons of culturally different groups. To be valid, tests must be linguistically appropriate.

8. *No experimental studies of differential "treatment" of educable mentally retarded.* A rigorous validity test of standardized IQ measures could be conducted by taking a random sample of children who are identified by tests as educable mentally retarded and providing such children with systematic instructional treatment of a known high quality. A unique type of opportunity to examine "predictive validity" would then be presented. At present, predictive validity coefficients are earned by leaving everything in the school environment essentially free to vary (i.e., no reliability or validity data on "school"). Given the fact that the opportunities of different cultural groups in the United States can be documented to be systematically and distinctly different in quality, it is a scientific error to ignore the potential impact of such differential treatment on the instructional setting. Until the effects of differential treatments are ruled out by the use of experimental controls, no scientific answer to the cultural bias question can be given.

It should be clear from this list of neglected categories that testing the IQ tests for validity cannot be accomplished in ignorance of the data that must be generated within each of these categories. It should also be clear from the above why the charge of cultural bias in both IQ testing cases should have been the more basic charge that there was a lack of *instructional validity* for IQ tests. Clearly, the definitive court case on academic treatment in IQ testing has yet to be developed, and did not exist in either the *Larry P. v. Wilson Riles* or the *PASE v. Hannon* case.

## Why IQ Testing Cannot Be Fixed for School Use

As indicated above, the problems with IQ testing are far more grave than cultural bias, and the injuries resulting from their use extend beyond Black children. The real question is whether IQ testing contributes anything of significant value to the instructional and/or learning processes, such that we are better off with them than without. Up to now, responses to criticisms about IQ tests have generated the search for "culture-free," "culture-fair," "non-biased," "non-discriminatory," and "alternative" tests of intelligence. Indeed, the language of Judge Peckham's remedy calls for such tests. One problem with such searches is that there seems to be an implicit assumption that whatever is wrong with IQ tests can be remedied by considering the tests in isolation from the instructional process that they are expected to serve. The problem is seen essentially as one restricted to and dealing solely with traditional psychometrics. This is unfortunate, since it is the link or the question of the existence of a valid interaction between psychometrics and pedagogy that must be examined. This means that at least as much systematic attention must be paid to pedagogy as to psychometrics in any valid validation study.

The science of "mental measurement" may well be separated from the use of standardized IQ tests in school. It is possible that improvements in the science of mental measurement may occur without a direct practical application for pedagogy. It is also possible, and has been demonstrated many times (Feuerstein, 1980; Freire, 1973; Fuller, 1977), that pedagogy can be drastically improved without reference to IQ testing at all. In other words, IQ testing in no way has been demonstrated to be either a prerequisite for successful instruction, or even facilitative of instruction. If mental measurement is to mean anything at all for pedagogy, then psychometry is drastically in need of a paradigm shift. The need for such a paradigm shift should become obvious when we consider the problems with standardized IQ testing below:

1. The goal of IQ testing is wrong. The primary justification for the use of IQ testing in schools presently is to improve the "prediction of a

child's future academic performance." As long as our present notion of predictive validity looms as large as the goal of psychometry in education, it is unlikely that the valuable tools of psychology for pedagogy can ever be brought to play in the educational situation. The acceptance of a predictive validity model in psychometry is also the acceptance of a notion of static intellectual stratification among the general population that is to be matched by static pedagogical stratification with the psychometrist performing in the role of fortune-teller.

2. The assumptions of IQ psychometry are wrong. As mentioned above, the assumptions are that members of the population can and need to be ranked by intellect, and that such ranks are relatively stable. This is an article of faith, not science.

3. Present IQ psychometry suffers from the absence of an articulated concept of and operational definition of "teaching" or "school." Without such a concept and definition, adequate validity studies cannot be designed.

4. Present IQ psychometry suffers from the absence of a validated body of teaching practice. Valid systematic pedagogy is a prerequisite to the determination of valid pedagogical psychometry. For example, it does little good to prescribe "special education" to "educable mentally retarded children" when "special education" may be equally as varied in validity as well as strategies as "regular education."

5. Present IQ psychometry suffers from the fact that it has no valid link to instruction and never has had one.

6. Present IQ psychometry suffers from inadequate ancient criteria for determining test validity. At present a test is considered "valid" if there is agreement with similar tests, or if there is internal agreement within the test itself, or if the test appears to be related to future academic performance. However, if the assumption underlying psychometry and pedagogy is changed from one of static learner and static learning conditions to changing learner and changing learning conditions, then radical changes are required in the concept both of validity and reliability. If effective teaching is expected to change the academic achievement of learners, then the expectation associated with present instrumentation must change. The new expectation is that predictive validity

would be destroyed in many cases. Effective teaching can and does mean that the traditionally predicted outcomes for learners may not match actual attainment. Similarly, under conditions of effective pedagogy, the "reliability" of present instrumentation would also be destroyed. The concept of reliability is associated with stability in scores; and yet effective pedagogy is directed toward producing an instability, or more precisely, a change, in achievement scores—even taking into account the comparisons among rates of change among learners. Clearly, for present IQ instrumentation, existing definitions of validity and reliability are totally inadequate if the educability rather than the ineducability of general population is assumed.

7. The problem definition with present IQ testing is wrong. As indicated above, it is neither "non-biased," "non-discriminatory," "culture-fair," "culture-free," nor "alternative" testing which we seek. We seek *valid* testing, *valid in the sense that a positive contribution is made to instructional outcomes.* Each of these present problem definitions represents defensive tinkering with the IQ system without a basic willingness to engage in evaluation and change in the system itself.

## What Is Needed in Mental Measurement

1. We need to change the goal. The goal in mental measurement must be to change the course of expected educational outcomes for children beyond what would be expected without psychometric intervention. Such a change in the goal for psychometry is associated with the need for companion goals in psychological and education treatment.

2. We need valid links between psychometry and pedagogy.

3. We desperately need a reconstruction of the concept and the criteria for test validity.

4. We need a reconstruction of the concept and criteria for test reliability.

5. To accomplish such drastic changes as implied in the above will require a redefinition of competency for psychometricians.

6. We need a drastic change in the role of psychometrists.

A review of the literature on mental measurement through the use of standardized IQ tests reveals what appears to be a studied unwillingness to confront certain types of issues. Unfortunately, these are the very issues that are critical when considering challenges to the validity of IQ tests as they are used in schools. Among these apparently forbidden issues are the following: What is the relationship of language to intellect? For example, what is "vocabulary"? What is it about vocabulary that makes it a measure of intellect? Is there a universal intellectual vocabulary? Similarly, we may examine cultural assumptions which ought to be made explicit. For example, what is "general information"? Is there a universal general information? What I am pointing to here is the absence of an articulated rationale for the inclusion of certain categories within IQ tests as well as the absence of a rationale for utilizing restricted versions of a particular language as the sole vehicle for interrogation, responding, and interpretation. Furthermore, it appears to be an invasion of taboo territory to ask psychometrists for an articulated description of the criteria that they use for item construction. There is a general willingness to look at the way different subjects respond on items that have been constructed, but not to look at the rationale for item construction in the first place. Finally, beyond the factor analytically derived notion of *g,* present mental testing through IQ instruments gives information that causes discussants to be vague and amorphous in describing the mental functions that can or cannot be performed by test-taker. Basically, IQ psychometry has given attention to areas in which it feels comfortable, but studiously avoids the tough areas. At one time it could have been said that there were minimal data to be consulted in such areas. However, that is far from true at this time. One can only read the apparent resistance to use such data or ignorance of the existence of such data as a fundamental deficiency in contemporary psychometry. It is most unfortunate that these were not the matters that were on trial in either the *Larry P. v. Wilson Riles* or *PASE v. Hannon* cases.

At this time, Wilson Riles and Henry P. Gunderson have filed an appeal to the opinion of Judge Peckham. Essentially, the appellants' position is but a rehash in slightly more detail of data that were presented at the trial. Appellants contest, without data, the ruling that IQ tests are culturally biased. In doing so, appellants appear to insist upon the very narrowly restricted meaning of the test bias that has been alluded to earlier:

> Appellant took the position that in judging bias in a test, one must use the legitimate, recognized definition of test bias, embraced by those who

design and use tests, namely, its predictive validity; that when the test of predictive validity is applied, the IQ tests are not biased, and that they will predict equally well for Blacks and Whites the likelihood of success or failure in mastering the public school curriculum; that the EMR program is a benefit to pupils who are failing in school and require more individualized attention; that it need not be a permanent placement for the pupil who makes progress under that regimen; that periodic re-evaluations minimize the risk of misclassification, and that children are only placed in the program when they meet all the eligibility criteria, including parental consent. (Peckham, 1981, p. 12)

If one takes the elements of the paradigm for criticism, which I have suggested earlier, it is clear that appellants have done little more than to give the routine response to any criticism of IQ tests. As I have indicated, their whole argument rides on *predictive validity.*

As one reads the appellants' brief, especially where plaintiffs' witnesses are quoted selectively, it is not clear from the interpretation presented that defendants understood the testimony of plaintiffs' witnesses. Certainly the inferences that are drawn do not, in my opinion, represent the essence of plaintiffs' testimony. Moreover, the citations represent no systematic argument, but rather what appears to be random potshots at straw people who are created by the defendants' twisted interpretation of plaintiff's comments. One example may suffice:

Respondents, on the other hand, contend that the IQ test is not relevant because the classroom is not the only arena in which to display intelligent behavior. The ghetto drug pusher's business acumen is intelligent behavior. Knowing who Charlie Parker is . . . is intelligent behavior (RT208). Respondents want public school oriented definition of EMR to take into account many facets of human behavior which may be valuable, which have no relevance for the public schools. (Peckham, 1981, p. 13)

I assume that intelligent functioning is independent of the particular content. I assume further that an IQ test is designed to be a measure of intelligent functioning. At the same time, I recognize that public school systems operate with particular academic content, which will be quite distinct, in some cases, from experiential content, which one may find in a variety of other public settings. No argument need be made that the content of any particular outside setting must be a part of the school experience, e.g., that the "ghetto drug pusher's business acumen" should be taught in the public schools. Surprisingly, the State seems unable to distinguish arguments about mental competence from arguments about curricular content. I certainly would not argue for the social desirability of drug pushing, nor for the academic relevance to the school curriculum of the drug pusher's experience. But the legal, social, moral, or curriculum content problems associated with the drug pusher are quite distinct from the matter of intellectual functioning. If IQ testing is supposed to be simultaneously a measure of intellectual functioning and a measure of social desirability, moral values, legal action, etc., then such intent should be specified in the technical literature. Perhaps the inability of school people to distinguish intellectual from socially desirable behavior is one of the contributing factors to the low level of performance for many students in the public schools, since they may be being treated for the wrong "malady."

The appellants' brief is poorly organized, with citations of partial testimony of a variety of the State's witnesses on a variety of topics. Nothing new appears in this material. The State, led by such experts as Gossman and Humphreys, in its appeal has maintained its position that IQ tests are valid, leaving us with the inescapable conclusion that there is, as IQ tests describe, not only a 15-point difference in the average of IQ scores between Black and White populations, but that there is a comparable difference in inherent mentality as well.

Apparently stung by Judge Peckham's criticism that the State Department of Education was negligent in this matter, the opinion of the defendants offers weak citations regarding steps that it says were taken to respond to the charges of cultural bias. In doing so, it leans heavily on the master plan for special education that was developed by the State of California. Unfortunately, the master plan speaks to the issue of "mainstreaming," but does not speak to the issue of the disproportionate representation of Blacks in classes for the educable mentally retarded. Furthermore, the State actually makes the claim in its brief that EMR placement is beneficial for the children who are so placed. It does so without any presentation of data that have been arrived at systematically. Neither are there systematic data to support the State's contention that significant numbers of students are returned to the mainstream as a result of excellent special educating and EMR classes.

There are several other things in the State's brief. However, in general it is little more than a mishmash of citations that do not address the basic issues in the case, issues that have been described previously in this chapter. In making the appeal, Wilson Riles et al. appear to be quite satisfied with the status quo, having argued in essence that it was simply meant to be. We see no forecasts on the part of the State to show that it expects that it or anyone else has the capability to ensure essential equity in the academic achievement of Black and White students. After all the words have been cleared away, the meaning of the position taken by State Superintendent of Public Instruction Wilson Riles and his co-defendants is that they believe that the Black children are intellectually deficient, and not simply educationally behind.

## Conclusion

The fundamental issues in IQ psychometry have yet to be addressed. The *Larry P. v. Wilson Riles* and *PASE v. Hannon* cases simply serve as symptoms of the grave difficulties that exist in applied mental measurement in education. It took court cases to bring minimal problems with the IQ system to the surface, problems such as "cultural bias." What will it take to cause the profession itself to anticipate and avoid future difficulties by developing a focus now on the root problems associated with mental measurement applied to pedagogy? Just as defenders of IQ psychometry should find little to be happy about with the decision of Judge Grady, which apparently went in favor of the defendants, so should the whole field of psychology fail to find comfort in restricting its attention to the superficial issues that were addressed in the court cases.

Judge Peckham saw the problem, but also wisely saw that a judge could speak merely to the legal aspects of such a problem, insisting upon constitutional guarantees of equal protection of the laws. Unlike Judge Grady, Judge Peckham knew that the actual reconstruction of professional practice ultimately can come only from enlightened professionals. That can happen only when the basic issues are on the table. Up to now, this has not been the case.

The split decision in these two court cases exposes a part of the problem. IQ psychometry has suffered a knockout since it was unable to demonstrate significant benefit for students. The basic problem with IQ psychometry is that the whole field rests on fundamentally erroneous assumptions about the abilities of learners and the nature of teaching. Clients have a right to expect a great deal from anyone who poses as a scientist or professional in psychology or education. As knowing professionals, our validity criteria for testing and teaching should be even more stringent than those found among the general public. Anointing or legitimating the obvious in education is hardly professional level work. Psychometrics must make a positive contribution to pedagogy.

Unfortunately, the standardized IQ tests are still on trial. One can hardly imagine a federal court trial to determine whether a missile launch from Cape Canaveral would be able to reach the moon. Even if such a trial was conducted, one would certainly not imagine a lay judge feeling competent enough to reject the opinion of space specialists and to construct his or her own spacecraft. I believe that this could be due to the fact that a fundamental respect for the achievements of space scientists has been built upon a demonstration of their competent performance. The chapter of competent performance has yet to be written in the story of psychometry and pedagogy.

## References
## (and Selected Bibliography)[1]

*Alleyne, M. C. (1980). *Comparative Afro-America.* Ann Arbor, MI: Karoma.
*Angoff, W. H. (1971). Scales, norms, and equivalent scores. In R. L. Thorndike (Ed.), *Educational measurement.* Washington, DC: American Council on Education.
*Bever, T. G. (1972). Perceptions, thought, and language. In J. B. Carroll & R. O. Freedle (Eds.), *Language, comprehension, and the acquisition of knowledge* (pp. 99-112). Washington, DC: Winston.
*Cole, M., & Scribner, S. (1973). *Culture and thought.* New York: John Wiley.
*Cronbach, L. J. C., & Drenth, P. J. D. (Eds.). (1972). *Mental tests and cultural adaptations.* Paris: Mouton.
Feuerstein, R. (1979). *The dynamic assessment of retarded performers.* Baltimore, MD: University Park Press.
Feuerstein, R. (1980). *Instrumental enrichment.* Baltimore, MD: University Park Press.
Freire, P. (1973). *Education for critical consciousness.* New York: Seabury.
Fuller, R. (1977). *In search of the IQ correlation.* Stonybrook, NY: Ball-Stick-Bird Publications.
Grady, J. F. (1980). Parents in Action on Special Education (PASE), an incorporated Association; Lue B. B., on her own behalf and as the next friend of Barbara B.; and Onollie J., on her own behalf and as the next friend of Angela J., on behalf of themselves and all other persons similarly situated, Plaintiffs, v. Joseph P. Hannon, individually and in his capacity as General Superintendent of Schools in Chicago et al. No. 74C3586, in the Norther United States District Court for the Northern District of Illinois, Eastern Division, 1980.
Hall, E. T. (1977). *Beyond culture.* Garden City, NY: Anchor.
*Hilliard, A. G. (1981). I.Q. thinking as catechism: Ethnic and cultural bias or invalid science. *Black Books Bulletin, 7*(2) 99-112.
Holtzman, W. H., Heller, K. & Messick, S. (Eds.). (1980). *Placing children in special education: A strategy for equity.* Washington, DC: National Academy Press.
Jensen, A. (1980). *Bias in mental testing.* New York: Free Press.
*Kamin, L. (1974). *The science and politics of IQ.* New York: John Wiley.

[1]Selected bibliographic references are indicated by an asterisk.

*Mandler, J. M., & Stein, N. L. (n.d.). *The myth of perceptual defect: Sources and evidence.* Unpublished manuscript. University of California at San Diego, and Washington University.

*Orasanu, J., MacDermott, R. P., & Boykin, A. W. (1977, September/October). A critique of test standardization. *Social Policy,* pp. 61-67.

Peckham, R. F. (1979). Larry P. by his guardian ad litem, Lucille P. et al., Plaintiffs, v. Wilson Riles, Superintendent of Public Instruction for the State of California et al., Defendants, in the United States District Court for the Northern District of California, No. C-71-2270RFP, 1979.

Peckham, R. F. (1981). Larry P., by his guardian ad litem, Lucille P.; M. S. by his guardian ad litem, Joyce S.; M. J., by his guardian ad litem, Theresa J.; John by his guardian ad litem, Mary H., Sylvia M., by her guardian ad litem, Sylvia W.; R. L., by his guardian ad litem, Salina F., Plaintiffs-Appellees, v. Wilson Riles, Superintendent of Public Instruction for the State of California, Defendant-Appellant, Henry P. Gunderson et al. Defendants. Court of Appeals Docket No. 80-4027, Appellant's Opening Brief. United States Court of Appeals for the Ninth Circuit, 1981.

*Rand, Y., Tannenbaum, A. J., & Feuerstein, R. (1979). Effects of instrumental enrichment on the psychoeducational development of low-functioning adolescents. *Journal of Educational Psychology, 71*(6), 751-762.

*Shuy, R. (1977). Quantitative language data: A case for and some warnings against. *Anthropology and Education Quarterly, 1*(2), 78-82.

*Smith, E. (1978). *The retention of the phonological, phonemic, and morphophonemic features of Africa in Afro-American ebonics* (Seminar Series Paper). Fullerton, CA: California State University at Fullerton, Department of Linguistics.

*Stewart, M. (1981). *Melanin and sensori-motor intelligence.* Doctoral dissertation, George Peabody College of Education, Vanderbilt University.

*Tryon, W. W. (1979). The test-trait fallacy. *American Psychologist, 4*(5), 402-406.

*Turner, L. D. (1969). *Africanisms in the Gullah dialect.* New York: Arnold Press.

*Valentine, C. A., & Valentine, B. (1975, March). Brain damage and the intellectual defense of inequality. *Current Anthropology, 16*(1), 117-150.

*Vass, W. K. (1979). *The Bantu-speaking heritage of the United States.* Los Angeles: University of California, Center for Afro-American Studies.

Wigdor, A. K., & Garner, W. K. (Eds.). (1982). *Ability testing: Consequences and controversy.* Washington, DC: National Academy Press.

# 16 Intelligence at the Low End of the Curve: Where Are the Racial Differences?

**HENRY JEFFERSON GRUBB***
*Western Psychiatric Institute & Clinic*
*University of Pittsburgh School of Medicine*

Countless studies have pointed to the fact that Black-Americans score approximately one standard deviation below White-Americans, as groups, on standardized tests of intelligence. Certain interpretations of this oft recorded difference suggest that the Black race is inherently inferior, genetically, on this dimension of human performance. If this argument were correct, we could expect to see proportionately more Blacks identified as mentally retarded than Whites (in relation to their total population). This study analyzed data on Black and White population figures for (1) total population in three Western states and (2) mentally retarded populations in those same states. The results do not uphold the genetic-based assumptions. There was (1) no significant difference between the percentage of Blacks in the total population and the percentage of Blacks in the mentally retarded sample; (2) no difference between the percentage of Whites in the total population and the percentage of Whites in the mentally retarded sample; and (3) no difference between the Black to White total population ratio and the Black to White mentally retarded sample ratio. These results would suggest that the average lower performance of normal Black subjects on standardized IQ tests is not genetically linked and/or that the normal bell-shaped distribution of IQ scores can no longer be assumed to be a true model of the Black populations' test tapped intellectual behavior. Either truth would present problems for the racial-genetic viewpoint.

One of the great still unsolved problems today in psychology and education is the difference in intelligence test performance between the races. Blacks as a group consistently score about 1 standard deviation below similarly constructed White samples. Many explanations for this difference have

Henry J. Grubb, Department of Psychology, Box 21970A, East Tennessee State University, Johnson City, TN 37614-0002 (Current address)
This paper was presented to the Society for Cross-Cultural Research, Isle Verde, Puerto Rico, February 1985.
© 1992 The Association of Black Psychologists ·
*EDITORS' NOTE: Currently at Behavioral Consultants, Johnson City, Tennessee.

been proposed, including test-item bias (Taylor, 1976; Sewell, 1979), the test situation itself (Saigh, 1981; Terrell, Terrell, & Taylor, 1980), environmental differences in living conditions (Herzog, Newcomb, & Cisin, 1972), cultural deficiencies in the Black home and rearing practices (Greenberg & Davidson, 1972), and genetic viability (Jensen, 1969, 1977).

This short report is an examination of the validity of genetic-heritability explanation put forth by Jensen (1969) through the focusing in on those members of our American society labelled "mentally retarded," specifically those requiring constant supervision and care. This group includes those labelled profoundly (IQ $\leq$ 25) and severely (25 < IQ $\leq$ 40) retarded plus the lower range of the moderately retarded group (40 < IQ $\leq$ 48).

It has now been repeatedly demonstrated that random selected groups of Whites and Blacks matched for age and formal schooling score approximately 1 standard deviation apart on standardized IQ tests, Whites superior to Blacks. It is also assumed, based on intraracial analysis of data (mostly on White groups) that intelligence, as measured by IQ tests, is distributed through the population according to that described by the normal probability curve.

Figure 16.1 shows the typical racial group response pattern on standardized tests of intelligence such as the Wechsler scales (Wechsler, 1981). The mean of the White group is at 100, while the mean Black score is recorded 1 standard deviation below the majority group—at 85. According to probability statistics, half of each group (selected randomly) should score below their respective means, 15.9% should score below −1 standard deviation from their respective mean, and only 2.3% of each population should be recorded as greater than −2 standard deviations below the norm. As Figure 16.1 demonstrates, only 15.9% and 2.3% of the White population would score at or below an IQ equal to 85 (−1 White standard deviation) and 70 (−2 White standard deviations) respectively. Since the Black group's mean is already equal to an IQ of 85, the 15-point standard deviation adjusts so that 15.9% of Blacks receive an IQ score equal to or less than 70 (−1 Black standard deviation) and 2.3% would receive a score equal to or below 55 IQ points.

Since approximately two thirds of any random sample falls within + or −1 standard deviation of mean of its population, and slightly more than 95% of the same sample will be found between + or −2 standard deviations, it is easy to see why most studies involving differential statistics will be conducted on groups falling within these ranges, especially the initially described limits (+ or −1 standard deviation). Such studies have *proven* the efficacy of utilizing the bell-shaped curve in describing IQ performance.

The problem with studies examining racial group differences (or even individual differences) in this "middle group" is that much of the interor intrarace differences on IQ tests can be accounted for, either empirically or hypothetically, by evoking an environmental explanation. Up to a half standard deviation can be accounted for by demographic variables. Factors such as sex, socioeconomic status, father's occupation, and region of residence have already been shown to decrease the difference between Black and White IQ scores on standard IQ tests by about one-half standard deviation (Jensen, 1971; Reynolds & Nigl, 1981). Matching groups on these and other commonly found social, economic, and cultural differences can reduce the gap to six or seven IQ points on the Wechsler scales.

Even though stratification matching often can reduce the gap between racial groups, the difference remains statistically significant. This ability to reduce the gap has caused some environmentalists to suggest that there are more subtle "environmental" differences between the two groups that are not presently quantifiable but none the less are in existence and at work, keeping the Black child from performing at a level equivalent with his or her White counterpart. Flynn (1980) has labelled this unknown source of variance a blindfold and states:

> . . . the environmentalist . . . posit what I have called a blindfold and what Jensen calls a factor X: a factor which is present in one population and not in the other and which affects all individuals in one population and none in the other; and which must have an equal or constant effect on all members of the population in which it is present. And once we have falsified every specific candidate for the role of factor X, a genetic hypothesis is highly probable . . . (p. 53)

Mackenzie (1984), summarizing the genetic argument illustrated in the above quoted statement writes:

> In short, if there is relatively little environmental variance (i.e., high heritability) in IQ within racial groups, then the environmental factors needed to account for substantial IQ differences between racial groups must be ones that, although having a strong effect on IQ, are relatively uniform within each group. It is difficult even to imagine any credible environmental factors that meet these requirements, and no satisfactory ones have ever been proposed. Therefore, it can reasonably be concluded that the sources of race differences in IQ are most likely to be genetic. The genetic hypothesis can win the day by default, on the basis of the weakness of its opponent, without having to survive any independent tests of its own. (p. 1221–1222)

**TABLE 16.1** Number of Developmentally Disabled Clients in California, Colorado, and Nevada by Race

| Race of Client | Total Clients |
|---|---|
| All Races | 6,742 |
| White (including Spanish-American) | 5,956 |
| Black | 437 |
| Other & Unknown | 349 |

Source: Individualized Data Base Project of the Pacific State Hospital, Pomona, CA (as of June 30, 1975). Data obtained from the President's Committee on Mental Retardation, Washington, DC 20201.

This assessment has been correct since candidates for factor X have even included "the *flavor* of race relations" which is hypothesized as "sap(ping) the intellectual strength of minority groups" (Watson, 1970, p. 104).

The object of this paper is not to deal with the merits of such environmental arguments, but to more closely examine the hereditarian position by empirical examination of data and comparing such data with what would be predicted based on genetic theory.

## Method

### SUBJECTS

The subjects of this study were the 6,742 developmentally disabled clients enrolled in federal assistance programs in the three western states of California, Colorado, and Nevada, originally compiled by the Individualized Data Base Project. Pertinent information from that study is summarized in Table 16.1. In Table 16.2 are the number of various racial group members for the same three states.

### PROCEDURE

The percentage of total retarded citizens of California, Colorado, and Nevada was determined by dividing the total counted in the Individualized Data Base Project (IDBP) by the total number of residents in those respective states. The percentage of White retardates to the total White population and the percentage of Black retardates to the total Black population were calculated in like fashion.

The percentage of Whites and Blacks in the general population and the retarded population of the three-state region was also calculated.

**TABLE 16.**2 Racial Composition of California, Colorado, and Nevada

| States | All Races | White | Black | Other & Unknown |
|---|---|---|---|---|
| California | 19,953,134 | 17,761,032 | 1,400,143 | 791,959 |
| Colorado | 2,207,259 | 2,112,352 | 66,411 | 28,496 |
| Nevada | 488,738 | 488,177 | 27,762 | 12,859 |
| TOTAL | 22,649,131 | 20,321,501 | 1,494,316 | 833,314 |

Source: Information obtained from Bureau of the Census; 1970 figures.

**TABLE 16.**3 Breakdown of Blacks and Whites in California, Colorado, and Nevada by Percentage of Developmentally Disabled to General Citizenry

| Race | Total Population | Retarded Population | % Retarded Population |
|---|---|---|---|
| Total | 22,649,131 | 6,742 | .030 |
| White | 20,321,501 | 5,956 | .029 |
| Black | 1,494,316 | 437 | .029 |

**TABLE 16.**4 Breakdown of Races in California, Colorado, and Nevada by Percentages in Two Populations

| Population | Total | White | % White | Black | % Black |
|---|---|---|---|---|---|
| General | 22,649,131 | 20,321,501 | 89.723 | 1,494,316 | 6.598 |
| Retarded | 6,742 | 5,956 | 88.342 | 437 | 6.482 |

Finally the ratio of Blacks to Whites in the developmentally disabled population and general citizenry were derived. All this information is presented in Tables 16.3, 16.4, and 16.5.

Based on the percentages of the total and White retarded populations in these three states, a cut-off score was determined for IQ inclusion in the developmentally disabled group. Finally the percentage of Blacks predicted by racial genetics to be under their respective curve was contrasted to the actual number and percentage found in this study.

**TABLE 16.5** Ratio of Black to White in the Different Populations

| Population | Total | White (W) | Black (B) | Ratio B:W = B/W |
|---|---|---|---|---|
| General | 22,649,131 | 20,321,501 | 1,494,316 | .074 |
| Retarded | 6,742 | 5,956 | 437 | .073 |

## ANALYSIS AND RESULTS

The percentage of the total population in California, Colorado, and Nevada that was included in the Individualized Data Base Project (IDBP) as developmentally disabled was 0.03; this same figure was obtained for the White and Black racial groups (see Table 16.3). Based on the Normal Probability Curve, 0.03% of the general and White population would receive an IQ $\leq$ 48, and therefore, we may assume that those people included in IDBP were below this ceiling (refer to Figure 16.1). It is interesting that at this extreme end of the intellectual spectrum, there are no White-Black differences, whereas according to the normal curve of Black intellectual abilities (Figure 16.1), one would expect to find 0.68% of the general Black population scoring at 48 or below on standardized IQ tests.

Since the percentage of Blacks in the retarded population of the three western states is slightly lower (nonsignificantly) than the percentage of Blacks in the general population of the same region (and the obverse applied to the White race) (Table 16.4), while the ratio of Blacks to Whites remains the same for both populations (Table 16.5), it cannot be stated that the observed results are an artifact of the data's having been obtained from two data pools. According to all the reasoning of racial-genetics, approximately 0.68% of the total Black citizenry in California, Colorado, and Nevada, of 154,014 Black persons should have been identified by the IDBP (Figure 16.1). This "called-for" result would have been equal to 1 standard deviation and represented a $t$-score difference equal to the significant difference of .01 found between the racial groups in the central regions of the intellectual curve.

## Discussion

This report has attempted to verify the racial-genetic theory concerning Black-White IQ-differences by analyzing available data on the

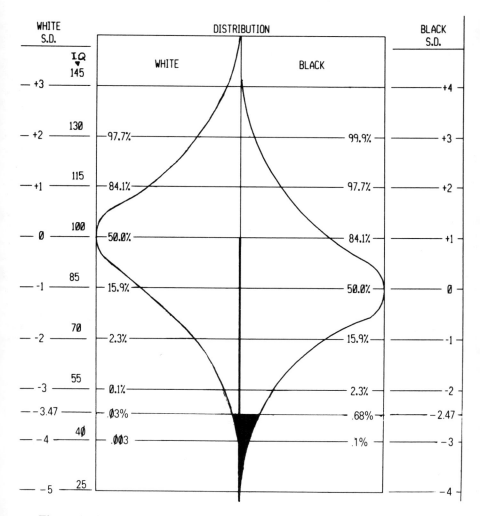

**Figure 16.1.** Normal Probability Curve Distribution of IQ Scores by Race

occurrence of the profoundly and severely retarded in each racial group. If IQ is inherited in the same fashion as height or other known inherited traits, its distribution through each group should be in accordance with probability statistics, and the difference in group performance at any

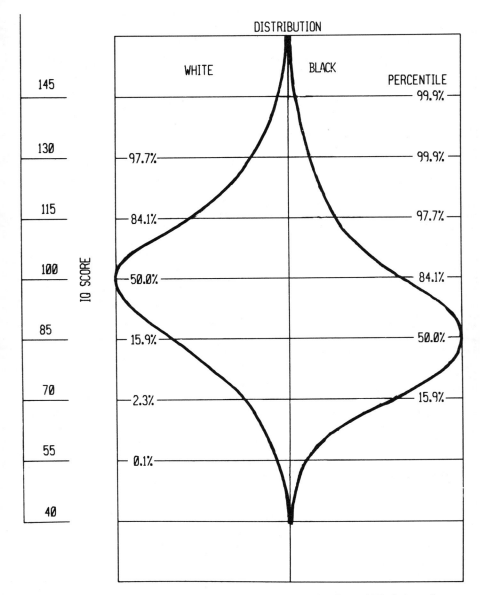

**Figure 16.2.** Reconstructed Probability Curve Distribution of IQ Scores for Blacks Compared to the Normal Probability Curve Distribution for Whites

cut-off score should be predictable. The data in this paper confirmed these assumptions when the total population of the three target states was analyzed as well as the White population (see Table 16.3). The assumptions of the hereditary viewpoint, as regards the Black race (based on IQ information focused around the group's measure of central tendency), was, however, not upheld in this study but would lead one to reject this line of reasoning.

It would appear that for those least affected by education, culture, and the environment, the profoundly/severely retarded, there are no racial differences. The Black race at the low end of measured intellect seems to conform to the normal probability curve of the general (and White) population (Figure 16.2). These results cannot be explained, as they were not predicted, by the hereditarian viewpoint.

These results can be explained from an environmental standing if we consider the noneducable mentally retarded as uninfluenced by Jensen's factor X, whereas those able to learn are influenced by it. It is still true that as yet this factor has been undefined and its nature or name is not the reason for this discourse; let it be known that such a factor could theoretically explain the skewness of the Black probability curve (would even predict such skewness of the Black probability curve).

Finally, although this paper does not deal with the high end of the curve, preliminary data from high IQ societies, presently being analyzed by the author, suggest that the Black group's representation past the general (and White) population + 2 1/2 standard deviation mark (IQ 137) is equivalent to that of the majority group (see Figure 16.2). This type of result would certainly not be expected from a hereditarian perspective.

Many authors have recently called for some compromise between the two positions endorsed by the nurturist and naturalist. Maybe by examining the extremes of intelligence we will be better able to define the proportion of heredity versus environment that goes into defining the difference in Black and White groups on measures of IQ.

## References

Flynn, J. R. (1980). *Race, IQ and Jensen.* London: Routledge & Kegan Paul.

Greenberg, J. W., & Davidson, H. H. (1972). Home background and school achievement of Black urban ghetto children. *American Journal of Orthopsychiatry, 42*(5), 803-810.

Herzog, E. Newcomb, C., & Cisin, I. H. (1972). But some are more poor than others: SES differences in a preschool program. *American Journal of Orthopsychiatry, 42*(1), 4-22.

Jensen, A. R. (1969). How much can we boost IQ and scholastic achievement? *Harvard Educational Review, 39,* 1-123.

Jensen, A. R. (1971, September). How much can we boost IQ and scholastic achievement? *Atlantic Monthly,* pp. 43-64.

Jensen, A. R. (1977). An examination of cultural bias in the Wonderlic personnel test. *Intelligence, 1,* 51-64.

Mackenzie, B. (1984). Explaining race differences in IQ: The logic, the methodology, and the evidence. *American Psychologist, 39*(11), 1214-1233.

Reynolds, C. R., & Nigl, A. J. (1981). A regression analysis of differential validity in intellectual assessment for Black and White inner city children. *Journal of Clinical Child Psychology, 10,* 176-179.

Saigh, P. A. (1981). The influence of religious symbols on the digit span performance of Roman Catholic elementary school students. *Journal of Clinical Psychology, 37,* 851-855.

Sewell, T. E. (1979). Intelligence and learning tasks as predictors of scholastic achievement in Black and White first-grade children. *Journal of School Psychology, 17,* 325-332.

Taylor, H. P. (1976). IQ heritability: A checklist of methodological fallacies. *The Journal of Afro-American Issues, 4*(1), 35-49.

Terrell, F., Terrell, S. L., & Taylor, J. (1980). Effects of race of examiner and type of reinforcement on the intelligence test performance of lower class Black children. *Psychology in the Schools, 17,* 270-272.

Watson, P. (1970, July 16). Society at work: How race affects IQ. *New Society, 16,* 102-105.

Wechsler, D. (1981). *Manual for the Wechsler intelligence scale-revised.* New York: Psychological Corporation.

# 17 Standards for Educational and Psychological Testing: The Issue of Testing Bias From the Perspective of School Psychology and Psychometrics

**LAMONTE G. WYCHE**
*Howard University*
**MELVIN R. NOVICK**
*The University of Iowa*

This article examines the various ways in which the problem of testing bias in the context of some contemporary educational, legal, and societal developments can and cannot be addressed by developments in test standards. It reiterates the contention that school psychologists should utilize differential assessment strategies in formulating decisions regarding school age Black children.

The general charge to the Joint Committee to Develop Standards for Educational and Psychological Testing was to revise the document titled *Standards for Educational and Psychological Tests* (APA, AERA, NCME, 1974).* For a discussion of the history of test standards see Novick (1981). The charge to the Standards Revision Committee (SRC) specified that the new standards should be a statement of technical requirements for sound professional practice and not a social action prescription. It was understood that the Standards must be responsive to current social, legal, and political concerns, but it was also agreed that the Standards should focus on the professional practice of testing in these areas, and on the documentation necessary to assess the soundness

The authors of the article were members of the Committee to Develop Standards for Educational and Psychological Testing: however, the views expressed herein do not necessarily reflect the consensus of the Committee.
LaMonte G. Wyche, School of Education, Department of Psychoeducational Studies. Howard University, Washington, DC 20059.
Melvin R. Novick. Lindquist Center for Measurement, The University of Iowa, Iowa City, IA 52240.

of such testing. Such documentation would make it easier for others to address social, legal, and political concerns from a sound technical basis. In order to have the widest possible counsel and review from potential users of the document, an outreach procedure involving over 150 advisors was implemented. The purpose of this procedure was to bring the concerns of a wide variety of persons to the Joint Committee. Hence, each committee member consulted extensively with appointed advisors in particular areas on issues that needed to be addressed by the new Standards.

The revision of the Standards in the area of test bias is important to developing ethical strategies for sound professional practice. The issue of test bias is one of primary concern to most school personnel, especially school psychologists. Bersoff (1979) observed that the greater awareness of possible test bias has come about primarily because of two factors: (a) legal proceedings challenging the disproportionate placement of certain racial/ethnic groups into special education classes, particularly those for the "retarded," and (b) federal mandates, including regulations contained in P. L. 94–142, that require testing in the child's primary language, and a social developmental study that includes an assessment of the child's adaptive behavior and cultural background.

One of the biggest problems involving testing bias is deciding exactly where the bias exists. From one point of view, the "bias" may be inherent in the test items themselves: for example, given the student's language and/or experiential background, it may be unreasonable to assume that he/she would possess the requisites for answering correctly (Hilliard, 1970). From another point of view it may reside in the test user's views regarding the nature of those learned abilities (aptitudes and achievements) considered critical for school success and/or expectations pertaining to a child's performance before, during, and after testing. Bias may result from the fact that the school environment may tend to reflect the values/beliefs of the core culture (Flaugher, 1978). In such a situation, test items or data that predict how well a student will perform in that environment may be perceived as biased; behaviors considered important to the parents or child may be useful if they do not possess some relevance for school functioning. Finally, the bias may be distal rather than proximate, resulting from prior conditions of economic and/or educational disadvantage or discrimination.

The problem of deciding where the bias resides puts school psychologists in an awkward situation. In most instances, there is a need to ascertain the reasons for a child's learning problems. Consequently, the professional school psychologist will administer tests that have documented reliability and criterion-related validity for predicting school performance in the standard curriculum, thus legitimizing their educational usefulness. However, the test user, to avoid possible "bias," may also wish to administer a test that has less direct relationship to school performance. The latter procedure is followed to reduce the adverse effects of living in a cultural/experimental milieu that may not introduce or nurture concepts, skills, abilities, and behaviors that undergird a child's school-related learning. Such a test might be thought of as being on the aptitude end of the aptitude-achievement continuum. In such a "reduced bias" approach to testing, the test user hopes to obtain information that has some utility for educational planing, but reduces the effects of dissimilar experiences and the strong "middle-class" emphasis that allegedly pervades the more common learning aptitude and achievement tests. To put it another way, the strategy is to use a test that measures capacity or potential (an aptitude test) rather than proficiency (an achievement test). From this point of view, of course, the bias in the use of the achievement test is not in the test itself, but in its use as a measure of aptitude. We should therefore generally speak of testing bias rather than test bias.

In the world of work, if we want to assess how well a person can play the violin, we sample his/her present skills and then make a judgment regarding his/her current level of proficiency. If the degree of proficiency is low, we try to train him/her to reach the desired level within a reasonable amount of time. The main focus is on the skill to be learned. Unless evidence is presented to the contrary, an assumption is made that no factors are operating that could cause a person to encounter undue problems in learning how to play the violin. A contrary assumption is sometimes made in schools where lack of present achievement is sometimes interpreted without reference to background information to conclude that some students cannot learn as opposed to have not yet learned.

In school situations, if we want to assess the ability of a child from an experientially "different" cultural environment to read, it may seem desirable not only to give a standard test in reading readiness, but also to give another test instrument that does not penalize him/her by requiring skills, concepts, and/or abilities he/she has not had an opportunity to learn.

The situation becomes more complicated by external factors. For example, if a child's chances for success in the regular educational program are low, there may be a recommendation for placement in a special education class. But this presents the school with a problem. Legally, it is safer to the school district for a child to struggle along in a regular class than for the district to place him/her in a special class to obtain additional assistance. Why? Because as soon as the child enters a special class, the districts potentially bear the responsibility of a law suit because of misdiagnosis.

Sometimes schools try to solve the problem by having children tested by "culturally oriented" psychologists. In these instances, there may be a better chance of assessing a child's abilities by eliminating possible language or cultural "biases." But this is a limited solution. In most classrooms, formal English is the language spoken and the school environment reflects the core culture of "middle-class" values, beliefs, and life-styles. To say that schools should not be this way takes us from reality to the realm of philosophical speculation.

The chief value of using reduced bias testing lies in avoiding an incorrect diagnosis of retardation. This label is probably the one that carries the greatest amount of social stigma. Although the reduced bias testing may assist in determining the students who may not benefit most from available special education services, it does not resolve the issue of planning appropriate educational experiences in the classroom or providing the specific kind of required remediation. Early Childhood and Head Start programs have provided partial, not total, answers.

The question, then, is how might this issue of testing bias in educational assessment be best resolved? Several partial solutions to the problem have been proposed and will be considered here. Some of these were treated in the test standards. Others could not be treated. Standards are to contain a clear statement of the technical requirements for the test user in explicit behavioral terms. This makes it easier for practicing school psychologists, for example, to use the revised Standards in ways that will be meaningful. This may aid in eliminating some poor testing practices.

Second, language was provided that would encourage test users in public education to obtain information about experientially different school-aged Black children from a variety of sources, including rating scales, classroom observations, and developmental checklists. This procedure will prevent school personnel from developing a habit of placing too great a reliance upon standardized test results for educational decision making.

The third solution to the problem of testing bias is related to the second; it is to discourage any one person from making placement and/or program decisions. Public Law 94–142 requires participants at a multidisciplinary conference to reach a consensus regarding recommendations for services. A consensus implies that everyone present at the conference has an opportunity to present relevant information and then discuss various alternatives before the final recommendations are formulated. The problem may also be viewed in other ways. Novick (1982) has noted that whether an ability test is on the aptitude or on the achievement end of the ability continuum depends upon characteristics of the test taker. If the test taker has been coached, a test that might otherwise be thought of as an aptitude test becomes an achievement test. Because a higher percentage of White students than Black students are coached on tests such as the SAT this may be a matter of concern.

It may also be a matter of concern whenever a supposed aptitude test is administered to test takers who do not have experiences assumed in test development. Two examples may be useful. A test of mathematics ability based on word problems should have a reading level substantially lower than that of the mathematics component of the test; otherwise the test cannot legitimately be called a mathematics test. It will be a test of mathematics and reading comprehension. A test of reading comprehension should deal with materials that are reasonably familiar to both genders and all cultural groups. Otherwise it becomes a test of reading comprehension and subject matter knowledge. Similarly a test of problem solving should not depend on a high level of ability on reading or mathematics achievement. In general, when dealing with test takers from cultural/linguistic minorities, a test that purports to measure some particular aptitude should not depend on high level achievements in areas that are unfamiliar to the test taker. The process of purifying a measure to assure that it does in fact measure what it purports to measure (e.g., aptitude as opposed to achievement) comes under the heading of construct validation and is the fourth partial solution addressable in Standards that is proposed here.

A fifth partial solution involves the recognition in Standards that test validation and treatment selection are intertwined. The validity of any test can be judged only with respect to specific possible treatments and the ultimate question of validity must relate to the comparative value of the proposed treatments. Consider four possible treatments.

1. Regular instruction
2. Remedial instruction pointed toward near-term transfer to regular instruction

3. Slower-paced instruction with lowered expectations
4. Faster-paced instruction with higher expectations

It is clear that the current level of learned ability is, in itself, inadequate data on which to make a judgment. Questions of construct validation mentioned earlier apply. But beyond this it must be recognized that the use of current levels of achievement in treatment selection must be moderated by an understanding of the previous opportunities afforded the student. A student whose current level of achievement is low but who has had prior educational disadvantagement and does well on a non-school-based measure might better be assigned to Treatment 2 rather than Treatment 3. A student with the same current level of attained ability, but without prior disadvantagement and a poor score on a non-school-based measure, might better be assigned to Treatment 3 rather than Treatment 2. Similar methodologies apply to the choices between Treatment 1 and Treatment 2, and Treatment 1 and Treatment 4. In technical terms the issue is one of different prediction. The central question is not whether or not the test has high criterion-related validity for specific treatments, but rather whether the test provided useful information in deciding among the available treatments or in formulating new treatments. The validation of such testing practices may need to focus heavily on the content and construct components of validity. If these issues are kept clearly in focus and the technical requirements given above are carefully met in test development and use, much of the poor practice seen in some testing applications can be eliminated.

The reader will perhaps have noted that we have discussed bias in testing but not fairness in testing. The former concept is a technical one, addressable in standards; the latter is a social/political issue of equal importance but no addressable in Standards according to the SRC charge. However, we note with satisfaction the recent statement by Humphreys (1983);

> Fairness is a matter of values, not of psychometrics. Their recommendation (Petersen & Novick, 1976) to modify the decision . . . on grounds of social utility is supportable policy on rational grounds. (p. 20)

We believe that this statement clearly suggests that questions of test fairness should be addressed in the appropriate arena with appropriate levels of government providing compensatory treatment to offset, to the extent possible, prior conditions of economic or social disadvantage.

# References

American Psychological Association, American Educational Research Association, and National Council on Measurement in Education. (1974). *Standards for educational and psychological tests.* Washington, DC: American Psychological Association.

Bersoff, D. (1979). Regarding psychologist testing: Legal regulation of psychological assessment in the public schools. *Maryland Law Review, 39,* 27-120.

Flaugher, R. (1978). The many definitions of test bias. *American Psychologist, 33,* 671-679.

Hilliard, A. (1970). *Language, culture, and assessment.* Paper presented at the National Institute of Education conference on the Ann Arbor Decision, Ann Arbor, MI.

Humphreys, L. G. (1983). [Letter to the Editor]. *The Educational Research, 12*(2), 20.

Novick, M. R. (1981). Federal guidelines and professional standards. *American Psychologist, 36,* 1035-1046.

Novick, M. R. (1982). Educational testing: Inference in relevant subpopulations. *Educational Researcher, 11,* 4-10.

Petersen, N. S., & Novick, M. R. (1976). An evaluation of some models for culture-fair selection. *Journal of Educational Measurement, 13,* 3-29.

# 18    On the Strategies That Blacks Employ in Deductive Reasoning

## WILBUR I. SMITH
## SAUNDRA T. DRUMMING
*Florida A & M University*

Over the past two decades, Wason's Four-Card Selection Task has attracted such a large amount of research and has generated such varied, interesting, and controversial results that it has come to be regarded as a standard paradigm for looking at how people reason deductively. Nevertheless, this article, which replicates Griggs and Cox's (1983) second experiment with a sample of 192 undergraduate college students, reports the first systematic study of the strategies that Black Americans use in the selection task. The results largely parallel those reported by Griggs and Cox as well as those that have been reported by other researchers. Still, the present results do differ in a number of ways from prior findings. We report an atypically high rate of accuracy for the standard version of the selection task. Also, the effect of problem content on processing strategy is curiously small, and its structure is unprecedented. On balance, the results of this study challenge monolithic notions of cognitive development that universally ascribe deficits in reasoning ability to Blacks. Some Blacks, notably those researched here, appear to acquire conceptual rules for logical reasoning that are as powerful and as fallible as any developed by people in Western, literate societies. Future research should explore the etiology of individual differences in reasoning ability and proclivities among Blacks.

In his *genetic epistemology,* the Swiss psychologist, the late Jean Piaget (Beth & Piaget, 1966; Piaget, 1972b), argued that the ability to reason deductively develops naturally and universally, maturing during adoles-

We thank Dr. Richard Griggs for sharing with us his view of and approach to research on human reasoning and for bringing to our attention several unpublished selection task studies. We also thank Linda Blackshear, Jack Carson, Jr., and three anonymous reviewers for their insightful comments on an earlier draft of this article.

Correspondence concerning this article should be addressed to Wilbur I. Smith, Assistant Professor, School of Business and Industry, Florida A&M University, Tallahassee, FL 32307.

Coauthor Saundra T. Drumming is an Assistant Professor, School of Business and Industry, Florida A&M University, Tallahassee, FL 32307.

cence. Although initially attractive (cf. Johnson-Laird, 1982, p. 7), this view, with its attending commitment to a "mental logic" (Johnson-Laird, 1982, 1985), is no longer widely accepted (Halford, 1982; Johnson-Laird, 1985; Saxe, 1983; Wason, 1977). Deductive reasoning is now thought to be a cognitive skill just as playing chess is a cognitive skill (Gardner, 1985; Johnson-Laird, 1982, p. 22), and like any other cognitive skill, the ability to reason deductively is thought to be acquired through the life processes of socialization, maturation, and training (Gardner, 1985; cf. Halford, 1982; cf. Hock & Tschirgi, 1985; Johnson-Laird, 1982, 1985; cf. Sternberg, 1986). Thus, as Piaget (1972a) himself came close to admitting, whether a person masters the art of deductive reasoning is largely determined by the environment in which he or she develops. In particular, individuals who are reared in environments where formal reasoning is highly regarded, widely taught, and consistently rewarded will develop deductive reasoning skills that surpass those of individuals who are reared in environments where formal reasoning is less central (Cheng & Holyoak, 1985, p. 414; Curran, 1988; Dasen, 1984; Fischer & Silvern, 1985; Gardner, 1985; Gellatly, 1987; Johnson-Laird, 1982; Scribner, 1977).

Besides standing in stark contrast to Piagetian lore, the "skill" view of deductive reasoning entails the implication that Black Americans underdevelop their logical reasoning skills. For Blacks, in general, mature in environments where intuitive reasoning and social astuteness have proven to be more adaptive than formal logical reasoning (see Hale, 1981; Shade, 1982, 1987). Within such environments, according to the "skill" view, people would develop elaborate intuitive rules for reasoning but would not develop a facility for reasoning with the truth-functional rules of formal logic.

If this view is accurate, the adult Black should demonstrate a preference for intuitive reasoning strategies and should be uncommonly susceptible to the errors and fallacies that accompany their use. This article subjects this expectation to an empirical test. The central question addressed is: To what extent do Blacks in fact use intuitive reasoning strategies to the exclusion of logical reasoning strategies? In particular, we investigate the processing strategies that Black Americans use in Wason's (1966, 1968) celebrated four-card problem, commonly known as the "selection task." Before describing the method and results of the study, we provide an overview of prior selection task research. And following the Results section, in the Discussion, we examine the similarities and differences between the findings reported by Griggs and Cox (1983, Experiment 2) and this replication study. Along the way, we advance tentative explanations for any discrepancies between the findings of two studies, paying particular attention to how they reflect on the conventional wisdom about reasoning in Blacks.

## The Selection Task: An Overview

Allegedly perverse (see Wason, 1983), undeniably controversial (see L. Cohen, 1981 and accompanying commentaries), the selection task is a widely researched logical reasoning problem. It consists of a rule and an array of four labeled cards. The subject is required to test the rule with the cards. For example, the subject might be presented with the rule, "If there is an A on one side of a card, then there is an 8 on the other side," and four cards showing, respectively, A, K, 8, and 5. (The cards are lying on a flat, opaque table with only their up sides visible.) The subject knows from experience or is told that each of the four cards has a capital letter on one side and a single-digit number on the other. He or she has to decide which card(s) definitely must be turned over to find out whether the rule has been violated.[1]

The rule itself is an abstract, conditional sentence of the form *If P then Q*. Cards A and K are the antecedents of the rule, $P$ and $\bar{P}$ (read as "not *P*"), respectively. Cards 8 and 5 are, respectively, $Q$ and $\bar{Q}$ (read as "not *Q*"), the consequents of the rule. The correct solution is to turn over cards A and 5 (cf. Halford, 1982, p. 280; Wason, 1968, p. 273), because only cards pairing $P$ (true antecedent) and $\bar{Q}$ (false consequent) violate the rule (Harman, 1986; Klayman & Ha, 1987; Popper, 1961). In particular, if a 5 appears on the other side of A, the rule has been violated. The rule has also been violated if an A appears on the underside of the 5. The rule, on the other hand, has been explicitly complied with if an 8 appears on the underside of the A and something other than an A appears on the reverse side of the 5. As for cards K and 8, there is no reason to turn over either of them. The rule does not address their obverses, with the result that the status of the rule cannot be determined from the letters or numbers that appear on their other sides. Only cards A and 5 provide definitive information about the status of the rule.

Usually no more than 30% and often as few as 4% to 10% of adult subjects correctly solve the sample problem or others like it[2] (Cheng, Holyoak, Nisbett, & Oliver, 1986, p. 295; Manktelow & Evans, 1979, p. 477; Wason, 1983, p. 53). Even Ph.D. scientists err embarrassingly on the selection task (Dawes, 1975; Einhorn & Hogarth, 1978; Kern,

Mirels, & Hilshaw, 1983; Mahoney & Kimper, 1976; but see Tweney & Yachanin, 1985). The common finding *is* that nearly all subjects select the *P* card (A) but fail to select the *Q* card (5) and frequently compound that mistake by selecting the *Q* card (8) instead (Wason & Johnson-Laird, 1972, p. 173). The subjects, then, in general, affirm the consequent and withhold the contrapositive of the role (Wason, 1968, p. 274). They seem not to understand the necessity of attempting to disconfirm the rule. The reason why has been the subject of much speculation and research.

Wason (1966, 1968) and his colleagues (Johnson-Laird & Wason, 1970) initially attributed the difficulty of the selection task to the subject's conscious use of a processing heuristic biased toward confirmation. Anyone with such a bias, they argued, reasons incorrectly about the selection task; that is, he or she disregards the canons of formal logic.[3] Rather than turn over cards that provide potentially disconfirming information, the person selects cards that are likely to demonstrate the truth of the rule (cf. Evans, 1978, p. 104, and Reich & Ruth, 1982, p. 395). On rules with affirmative components, for example, anyone with a confirmation bias would choose either cards *P* and *Q* or just card *P* (Johnson-Laird & Wason, 1970). A series of early studies reported finding this pattern in subjects' card selections, providing empirical support for confirmation theory (see the reviews by Johnson-Laird & Wason, 1970, Wason & Johnson-Laird, 1972, and Evans, 1982).

This support was quickly undermined, however. Subsequent studies discovered that confirmation theory fails to account for subjects' card selections on rules with negative components (see Evans, 1982, pp. 162–165). For instance, contrary to the predictions of confirmation theory, a majority of subjects select cards *P* and *Q* on abstract rules of the form *If P then not Q* (Evans & Lynch, 1973, p. 392; Johnson-Laird & Wason, 1977, p. 154).

This and other shortcomings of confirmation theory led Evans (1972; Evans & Lynch, 1973) to offer an alternative. Card choices in the selection task, he argued, are linguistically determined or cued (Evans, 1975, 1983a). Specifically, subjects tend to unconsciously select the cards mentioned in the rule (Evans, 1983b, p. 139; 1984). "Matching" is the name Evans gave this tendency.

Matching, he (1984, p. 452) speculated, is a heuristic of the preattentive cognitive processes that select "relevant" information for analytical processing. Its purpose is to reduce the mental load of cognitive tasks (Griggs & Cox, 1983, p. 523; Yachanin & Tweney, 1982). This is accomplished within the selection task by redirecting the subject's attention. Instead of focusing the subject's attention on the logical structure of the conditional rule, the matching heuristic focuses attention on the topic of the rule: the named cards, ignoring negatives. Only those cards get encoded into short-term memory. As a result, the subject subsequently fails to select the $Q$ card—the most common error in the selection task—simply because he or she never thinks of it (Evans, 1983b, p. 139).

Even though Evans' matching explanation of selection task performance has not gone unchallenged (Van Duyne, 1973, 1974), it is a more fundamental explanation than confirmation theory of subjects' card choices (Evans, 1980, p. 231; see also Johnson-Laird & Wason, 1977), and it has proven to be an accurate predictor of card choices for abstract rules (see Gilhooly, pp. 93–95, and Halford, 1982, pp. 283–284).

However, neither Wason's confirmation theory nor Evans' matching theory satisfactorily accounts for subjects' card selections on "thematic" rules (G. Cohen, 1983, p. 181). A thematic rule is one that describes a meaningful relation between everyday objects or ideas (cf. Griggs, 1983, p. 18). An example of a thematic rule is, "If the person is drinking beer, then the person must be over 19." Throughout the early to middle 1970s, a number of studies (Bracewell & Hidi, 1974; Gilhooly & Falconer, 1974; Johnson-Laird, Legrenzi, & Legrenzi, 1972; Lunzer, Harrison, & Davey, 1972; Van Duyne, 1974, 1976; Wason & Shapiro, 1971) found a facilitative effect for thematic rules. Often more than 70% of subjects turned over the correct cards for these rules.

At first, the "realism" of thematic rules was thought to foster the use of the logically correct disconfirmation processing strategy (see Evans, 1982, ch. 9, and Griggs, 1983). After scrutinizing the cumulative evidence more closely, several psychologists (Griggs & Cox, 1982; Manktelow & Evans, 1979; Reich & Ruth, 1982) abandoned this idea. Facilitation, they observed, seems to occur only on thematic rules with which subjects have had prior experience and could recall specific counterexamples to. Now neither the realism nor the prior experience supposition appears tenable, inasmuch as some thematic rules for which subjects have experienced counterexamples do not facilitate reasoning.

Manktelow and Evans (1979) demonstrated this point. They conducted four experiments involving thematic rules about food, such as: "If I eat macaroni, then I do not drink champagne" and "If I do not eat pork, then I drink red wine." Most people should be familiar with the idea expressed in these rules (selecting drinks based on the food selection), and most people should have experienced specific counterexamples to Manktelow and Evans' food-drink rules. Yet, no facilitative effects were found in any of the experiments. Performances on the thematic rules showed the low rates of disconfirmation typically found with abstract rules. In fact, matching was the dominant strategy evident in the subjects' card selections for both thematic and abstract rules. To explain Manktelow and Evans' findings, Pollard (1981) questioned whether their food-drink rules were really thematic. Regardless, other failures (Griggs & Cox, 1982; Yachanin & Tweney, 1982; see also the review by Griggs, 1983) to find a facilitative effect for various types of thematic rules coupled with the findings of a facilitative effect for some rules with which subjects had not had any prior experience (e.g., Cheng & Holyoak, 1985; D'Andrade, described in Rumelhart, 1980) leave little doubt that neither realism nor prior experience alone is sufficient to produce complete insight into the selection task.

The prevalent belief today is that facilitation is observed only when the thematic rule successfully evokes an appropriate "pragmatic reasoning schema" (Cheng & Holyoak, 1985; Cheng et al., 1986; see also Rumelhart, 1980, and Wason & Green, 1984). Cheng and Holyoak (1985, p. 395) described such a schema as an abstract knowledge structure induced from ordinary life experiences with notions like "permission," "obligation," and "causation." It consists of a set of generalized, context-sensitive rules that are defined in terms of classes of goals and relationships to test goals (p. 395). Metaphorically, a pragmatic reasoning schema can be thought of as a rule-based mental model, which when evoked operates upon the active content of working memory to produce inferences. For instance, the permission schema, according to Cheng and Holyoak (1985, p. 397), consists of the following four cognitive rules:

Rule 1: If the action is to be taken, then the precondition must be satisfied.
Rule 2: If the action is not to be taken, then the precondition need not be satisfied.
Rule 3: If the precondition is satisfied, then the action may be taken.
Rule 4: If the precondition is not satisfied, then the action must not be taken.

Of the thematic rules that have produced facilitation to date, all but a few fit the permission schema (Cheng & Holyoak, 1985, p. 396). This powerful "schema describes a type of regulation in which taking a particular action requires [the] satisfaction of a certain precondition" (p. 396, and see the cognitive rules for the permission schema above). Thematic rules that contain the English modals "can" and "must" (or their synonyms) will probably evoke the permission schema and produce a facilitative effect (p. 396).

Griggs and Cox (1983, experiment 2) provided a useful illustration. They compared subjects' performance on the drinking-age problem, a permission-type thematic rule (Cheng & Holyoak, 1985, p. 397), to their performance on an abstract rule. The abstract rule involved letters and numbers on cards, such as: "If a card has a vowel on one side, then it has an odd number on the other." The drinking-age problem, developed by Griggs and Cox (1982), contained rules like, "If a person is drinking beer, then the person must be over 19." Griggs and Cox found a large facilitative effect. Sixty-two of 80 subjects correctly solved the drinking-age problem. Far fewer, 13 of 80, solved the abstract problem. There was little evidence of matching or confirmational strategies on the drinking-age rules. In contrast, 35% of subjects' selections on the abstract rules conformed to the confirmation strategy, and, although matching was not strongly evident, 19% of subjects' selections were predicted by matching theory.

Griggs and Cox's (1983) results support the schema interpretation of the facilitative effect of thematic rules. Even more persuasive evidence for the schema interpretation was provided by Cheng and Holyoak (1985). They tested the permission schema and found that performance on an abstract rule increased dramatically (from 19% correct to 61% correct) when it was recast as a permission-type rule.

The foregoing overview of the selection task research supports two general conclusions. On abstract rules, subjects tend to select the cards named in the rule (i.e., matching). This contrasts sharply with their selections on thematic rules where they tend to employ the logically correct disconfirmation strategy, provided the rule evokes a suitable pragmatic reasoning schema. However, on thematic rules that do not evoke reasoning schemata, the subjects display the same reasoning fallacies as they do on abstract rules.

Our aim in this study is to ascertain whether these conditions also apply to the reasoning strategies of Black Americans in the selection task. We particularly want to find out if Blacks, as the "skill" view implies, show extraordinarily high use of intuitive reasoning strategies such as confirmation and matching and extraordinarily low use of disconfirmation, the logical processing strategy.

# Method

## SUBJECTS

One-hundred-ninety-two students enrolled in lower-division undergraduate business courses served as subjects for course credit. One-hundred-eighty-seven of the subjects were Black Americans. Four of the remaining five were other American racial/ethnic minorities. A majority (103) of the subjects were female. None of the subjects had any prior experience with the selection task.

## DESIGN

Twenty-four subjects were randomly assigned to each of the eight conditions formed by combining Problem Type and Rule into a 2 × 4 between-subjects factorial experiment. The abstract problem and the drinking-age problem (Griggs & Cox, 1982) were the two levels of Problem Type. The levels of Rule were the four rules formed by permutating the negation operator "not" over the two components (antecedent and consequent) of a conditional rule (cf. Griggs and Cox, 1983, p. 523). These rules are *If P then Q, If P then not Q, If not P then Q,* and *If not P then not Q*. The verbal referents of the $\bar{P}$ (read as "not *P*") and $\bar{Q}$ (read as "not *Q*") components were chosen so that all four rules took on the semantic structure of the *If P then Q* rule (cf. Griggs & Cox, 1983, p. 528).

## TASK, MATERIALS, AND PROCEDURES

The subjects were tested individually at prearranged times over three consecutive days. Upon arriving at the testing site, each subject was given an oral overview of the task and was provided a booklet consisting of an instruction sheet, an answer sheet, and a sample card. The answer sheet presented the conditional rule (corresponding to the experimental condition) and the four rectangular boxes ("cards") from which the subject would make selections. For the abstract problem, the four boxes were labeled A, K, 5 and 8, uniquely ordered for each of the 24 subjects assigned to an abstract rule.

The instruction sheet contained the statement of the problem and instructions for completing the selection task. For the *If P then Q rule,* the abstract problem read as follows:

Imagine that you are an inspector for the Pica Flash Card Company. This company produces educational flash cards for children. All of its flash cards have a capital alphabetic letter on one side and a single-digit number on the other. (Take a look at the sample card.) Your job at the Pica Flash Card Company is to ensure that the production of flash cards conform to the following rule: If the card has an A on one side, then it has an even number on the other side.

Each of the boxes pictured on the second page of this booklet presents one side of four different flash cards. These flash cards were produced today. Your task in this experiment is to select the flash card or flash cards that you *definitely* need to turn over to determine whether or not the production rule has been violated. You are free to turn over as many of the flash cards that you feel is necessary, including turning over all of the flash cards or turning over none of the flash cards. Record your selection by drawing a large "X" on the flash card or flash cards that you would turn over.

The other three rules for the abstract problem contained negated components. The rule with the negated consequent (*If P then not Q*) *was,* "If the card has an A on one side, then it does not have an odd number on the other side." "If the card does not have a K on one side, then it has an even number on the other side," was the rule with the negated antecedent *(If not P then Q).* The rule with both components negated *(If not P then not Q)* was, "If the card does not have a K on one side, then it does not have an odd number on the other side."

Except for content, the drinking-age problem was constructed like the abstract problem. The four rectangular boxes on the answer sheet were labeled DRINKING BEER, DRINKING COKE, AGE 16 and AGE 22, in one of 24 unique orderings—a different order for each subject. The statement of the drinking-age problem for the *If P then Q* rule read as follows:

Imagine that you are a police officer on duty. It is your job to ensure that people conform to certain rules about drinking. The cards pictured on the second page of this booklet contain information about four people sitting at a table. On one side of the card is the person's age and on the other side of the card is what the person is drinking. (Take a look at the sample card.) Naturally, only one side of each card is visible in the picture. Here is a rule about drinking: If the person is drinking beer, then the person must be over 19.

Your task in this experiment is to select the card or cards that you *definitely* need to turn over to determine whether or not the rule is being violated. You are free to turn over as many of the cards that you feel is necessary, including turning over all of the cards or turning over none of the cards. Record your selection by drawing a large "X" on the card or cards that you would turn over.

The negated rules for the drinking-age problem were, "If the person is drinking beer, then the person must not be under 19," "If the person is not drinking Coke, then the person must be over 19" and "If the person is not drinking Coke, then the person must not be under 19." The subjects were allowed adequate time to complete the selection task. Most of them required less than 5 minutes. None required more than 15 minutes.

## Results

Table 18.1 displays the logical notation used to present the results. Panel A of the table relays the association between the four cards of the selection task and the logical symbols for representing them: $P$, $\bar{P}$, $Q$, $\bar{Q}$. In panel B, these logical symbols are used to illustrate for each of the four conditional rules in the selection task the card choices that conform to the three most widely researched processing strategies for reasoning: disconfirmation, confirmation, and matching. Confirmation and matching are faulty intuitive reasoning strategies. Disconfirmation is the correct processing strategy for the selection task. Subjects' card selections not conforming to any of these strategies are labeled "unaccounted for" in the results.

The subjects' actual card selections are classified as to processing strategy in Table 18.2. As is shown there, use of the disconfirmation strategy, indicated by the selection of cards $P$ and $\bar{Q}$, was significantly facilitated (i.e., increased) by the drinking-age problem. Sixty-five subjects selected cards $P$ and $\bar{Q}$ on the drinking-age rules, whereas less than half that number (30) selected these cards on the abstract rules ($\chi^2(1) = 12.8$, one-tailed, $p < .001$). Facilitation is evident on all but the *If P then not Q* rule. It is most pronounced on the *If not P then not Q* rule (*Binomial test,* one-tailed, $p < .001$), followed by the *If P then Q* rule ($\chi^2(1) = 4.4$, one-tailed, $p < .05$). Use of the disconfirmation strategy on the other two rules differed insignificantly between problem types ($\chi^2$ tests, $p > .05$).

Like the disconfirmation strategy, selection frequencies for the four individual cards of the selection task varied inconsistently between the drinking-age and abstract problems as Table 18.3 shows. The proportion of subjects that selected the $P$ card and the proportion that selected

**TABLE 18.1** Notation and Conventions Used in Presenting the Results

*A. Logical Symbols for the Cards of the Selection Task*

|  | Selection Task Card | |
|---|---|---|
| *Logical Symbol* | *Abstract Problem* | *Drinking-Age Problem* |
| $P$ (true antecedent) | A | DRINKING BEER |
| $\overline{P}$ (false antecedent) | K | DRINKING COKE |
| $Q$ (true consequent) | 8 | AGE 22 |
| $\overline{Q}$ (false consequent) | 5 | AGE 16 |

*B. Card Selections Conforming to Various Processing Strategies*

|  | *Processing Strategies*[a] | | |
|---|---|---|---|
| *Rule* | *Disconfirmation* | *Matching* | *Confirmation* |
| *If P then Q* | $P\overline{Q}$ | $PQ$ | $PQ$ or $P$ |
| *I P then not Q* | $PQ$ | $P\overline{Q}$ | $PQ$ or $P$ |
| *If not P then Q* | $P\overline{Q}$ | $\overline{P}Q$ | $PQ$ or $P$ |
| *If not P then not Q* | $PQ$ | $\overline{P}\overline{Q}$ | $PQ$ or $P$ |

a. A card selection that conforms to more than one processing strategy for a given rule is a "nonunique" selection.

the $\overline{Q}$ card are roughly equal for the problems ($\chi^2$ tests, $p > .05$). Selection of the $P$ card, on the other hand, varied significantly. Twenty-three subjects turned over the $P$ card on the abstract problem compared to just six on the drinking-age problem ($\chi^2(1) = 8.8$, one-tailed, $p < .01$). Of the four rules, only *If not P then not Q* accounts for a significant percentage of interproblem difference in the rate with which the $P$ card was selected (*Binomial test,* one-tailed, $p < .05$).

**TABLE 18.2** Frequencies With Which Subjects' Card Selections Conform to Various Processing Strategies for Each Rule and Problem

|  | *Abstract Problem* | | | | *Drinking-Age Problem* | | | |
|---|---|---|---|---|---|---|---|---|
| *Strategy* | $P{\to}Q$ | $P{\to}\overline{Q}$ | $\overline{P}{\to}Q$ | $\overline{P}{\to}\overline{Q}$ | $P{\to}Q$ | $P{\to}\overline{Q}$ | $\overline{P}{\to}Q$ | $\overline{P}{\to}\overline{Q}$ |
| Disconfirmation | 6 | 17 | 6 | 1 | 17 | 16 | 14 | 18 |
| Matching | 7 | 17(17)[a] | 0 | 4 | 0 | 16(16)[a] | 0 | 0 |
| Confirmation | 13(7)[b] | 1 | 4 | 4 | 2 | 4 | 5 | 1 |
| Unaccounted For | 5 | 6 | 14 | 15 | 5 | 4 | 5 | 5 |

Note: Maximum cell entry is 24. $P{\to}Q$ = If P then Q; $P{\to}\overline{Q}$ = If P then not Q; $\overline{P}{\to}Q$ = If not P then Q; $\overline{P}{\to}\overline{Q}$ = If not P then not Q.
a. The number within parentheses is the matching selections which conform to the disconfirmation strategy.
b. The number within parentheses is the confirmation selections which conform to the matching strategy.

**TABLE 18.3** Frequencies With Which Subjects Selected Individual Cards for Each Rule and Problem

| Rule | Abstract Problem | | | | Drinking-Age Problem | | | |
|------|----|----|----|----|----|----|----|----|
| | $P$ | $\overline{P}$ | $Q$ | $\overline{Q}$ | $P$ | $\overline{P}$ | $Q$ | $\overline{Q}$ |
| P→Q | 21 | 2 | 10 | 10 | 19 | 0 | 0 | 21 |
| P→$\overline{Q}$ | 21 | 1 | 4 | 21 | 21 | 1 | 2 | 17 |
| $\overline{P}$→Q | 22 | 9 | 15 | 17 | 19 | 3 | 3 | 16 |
| $\overline{P}$→$\overline{Q}$ | 12 | 11 | 10 | 12 | 19 | 2 | 3 | 20 |
| Total | 76 | 23 | 39 | 60 | 78 | 6 | 8 | 74 |
| Overall % | 79.2 | 24.0 | 40.6 | 62.5 | 81.3 | 6.3 | 8.3 | 77.1 |

Note: Maximum cell entry is 24. $P{\rightarrow}Q$ = If P then Q; $P{\rightarrow}\overline{Q}$ = If P then not Q; $\overline{P}{\rightarrow}Q$ = If not P then Q; $\overline{P}{\rightarrow}\overline{Q}$ = If not P then not Q.

Selection of the $Q$ card was also affected by problem type. Significantly fewer subjects selected this card on the drinking-age problem than on the abstract problem ($\chi^2(1) = 19.1$, one-tailed, $p < .001$). This relation holds for all but the *If P then not Q* rule where the selection frequencies are small (*Binomial tests*, one-tailed, $p > .10$).

A closer look at the subjects' performance on the drinking-age problem in Table 18.2 reveals a familiar pattern. While almost 20% (19/96) of their card selections are unaccounted for, a majority (65 of 96 or 67.7% conform to the disconfirmation strategy. Strikingly, selection of cards $P$ and $\overline{Q}$, the disconfirmation choice, is not mediated by rule ($\chi^2(3) = .5, p > .10$).

Confirmation, which accounts for 12.5% (12/96) of card selections, is the least evident strategy for the drinking-age problem. Evans' matching theory is a bit more successful than confirmation, predicting 16.7% (16/96) of card selections. However, when the matching selections that are predicted by the disconfirmation and confirmation strategies are excluded from the tally, matching does not account for any of the subjects' card selections. In addition, all four of the specific tests for matching outlined by Evans and Lynch (1973) failed when applied to the data in Table 18.3 ($\chi^2$ tests, one-tailed, $p > .10$). There, then, is little evidence for matching on the drinking-age problem.

Matching fares only marginally better on the abstract problem. It accounts for about 29% (28/96) of the subjects' card selections, 4% (4/96) if nonunique selections (those conforming to matching and to some other processing strategy for a given rule) are removed. One of the four Evans-Lynch tests for matching was accepted, however. As

Table 18.3 shows, more $\overline{P}$ cards were selected on abstract rules with negative antecedents than on rules with positive antecedents ($\chi^2(1) = 11.1$, one-tailed, $p < .001$). Still, overall, the evidence for matching is meager.

Confirmation accounts for an additional 23% (22/96) of card selections on abstract rules, and fully 41.7% (40/96) are unaccounted for. These notwithstanding, the surprise finding for the abstract problem is that slightly more than 31% (30/96) of the card selections conform to the disconfirmation strategy. This is a comparatively high percentage, almost double the 16.25% rate reported by Griggs and Cox (1983, Experiment 2), for example. Noteworthy though, the rate at which the subjects selected cards $P$ and $\overline{Q}$ on the abstract problem was uneven across rules ($\chi^2(3) = 18.3$, $p < .001$). More than 56% (17/30) of the disconfirmation choices occurred on the *If P then not Q* rule. For that rule, matching and disconfirmation choices are confounded, which makes explaining the selection of cards $P$ and $\overline{Q}$ difficult.

## Discussion

The central query of this study has been answered in the negative. The Black students who served as subjects did not demonstrate an abnormal preference for intuitive reasoning strategies. To the contrary, they appear to have approached the selection task in much the same manner as the non-Black subjects (R. A. Griggs, personal communication, August 1984) in the Griggs-Cox (Griggs & Cox, 1983, Experiment 2) study that was replicated here. On the drinking-age problem, our subjects employed the disconfirmation, confirmation, and matching strategies in roughly the same relative proportion that Griggs and Cox reported for their subjects. As did Griggs and Cox, we found that the drinking-age problem facilitated the selections of cards $P$ and $\overline{Q}$. For the abstract problem, Griggs and Cox found that 47.5% (including the biconditional-interpretation strategy) of subjects' selections were unaccounted for with regard to processing strategy (p. 531); we found the unaccounted for to be 41.7% (40/96). Matching was not strongly evident for the abstract problem in either the Griggs-Cox or the present study, but there was clear evidence of the disconfirmation and confirmation strategies in both studies.

In summary, we did not find the ineptness that Blacks are supposed to show in deductive reasoning. Whatever their developmental histories, these students apparently had acquired conceptual rules for logical reasoning that are as powerful and as fallible as any. And, as a result, they showed unexpectedly typical reasoning skills. Not to be overlooked, however, are important differences between our results and the results that Griggs and Cox reported. The facilitation we found for the drinking-age problem is quantitatively and qualitatively different from what they found. Moreover, we reported higher rates of disconfirmation on the abstract problem than they. These differences are explored more fully in the ensuing discussion, starting with the disconfirmation finding.

## DISCONFIRMATION STRATEGY
## ON THE ABSTRACT PROBLEM

Performance on the abstract version of the selection task is typically poor. Often no more than 10% of subjects select the correct cards for it (Wason, 1983). Of the 80 subjects in the Griggs–Cox study, merely 16.25% selected cards $P$ and $Q$ on the abstract problem. The subjects in the present study performed substantially better than that. Thirty of them (31.25%) correctly solved the abstract problem. In both Griggs and Cox's and our studies, a large percentage (between 53% and 57%) of the correct selections for the abstract problem occurred on the *If P then not Q* rule where disconfirmation and matching choices are identical.

Accounting for the relatively high rate with which our subjects selected cards $P$ and $\overline{Q}$ is problematic. Several possibilities exist. Perhaps the subjects we studied simply possessed greater reasoning skills than the subjects studied by Griggs and Cox. Although that is an intriguing possibility, we are mindful of the exploratory nature of this study and the frailness of its evidence, and, accordingly, we refrain from offering as venturous an explanation as individual differences for the results. Instead of individual differences, we think it more likely that methodological variations in our study account for the disparity in our findings.

First, unlike Griggs and Cox and most other researchers, we provided a context (i.e., a story line) for our abstract rules. The subjects were told that the rule applied to the production of flash cards. As such, the rule specified the required characteristics of a finished flash card. Though we did not intend it, perhaps this context evoked either the permission or obligation pragmatic reasoning schema. If so, the subjects would most likely have found the correct solution to the selection task more frequently than typically is found. Even though this explanation is consistent with our results, it is not completely satisfactory. Much higher rates of disconfirmation should have been observed if an appropriate reasoning schema had been fully evoked (see Cheng & Holyoak, 1985).

A more promising explanation concerns a slight variation in the construction of our rules. The abstract rules in the present study were more specific or concrete than Griggs and Cox's. Their *If P then Q* rule was, "If a card has a vowel on one side, then it has an odd number on the other side." Our corresponding rule was, "If the card has an A on one side, then it has an even number on the other side." These rules are syntactically identical, but they differ in the specificity of their antecedent terms: "vowel" versus "A."

For that reason, subjects in the Griggs-Cox study were required to make an inference not required of our subjects. Their subjects had to recall from long-term memory the definition of a vowel and retain the definition in short-term memory as they tested the rules. Our subjects had no such requirement. They had only to recognize the elements in the rule—a cognitively simpler task. Given that the processing strategy used in the selection task is somewhat sensitive to mental load (cf. Halford, 1982, p. 283; Wason, 1983; Wason & Green, 1984), the differences between Griggs and Cox's and our abstract rules may account for the differences found in solution rates.

## FACILITATIVE EFFECT OF THEMATIC CONTENT

The second unexpected finding of the present study concerns facilitation—the extent to which subjects selected cards *P* and *Q* more often on the drinking-age problem than on the abstract problem. We found significantly less facilitation that Griggs and Cox ($Z = 2.78$, one-tailed, $p < .01$). Two items contributed to this. Their subjects exhibited superior performance on the drinking-age problem. About 78% of the Griggs–Cox subjects correctly solved it compared to 67.7% in the present study. The other item is that our subjects performed much better than theirs on the abstract problem. Because of these two quantitative differences, there is a qualitative difference in the facilitation reported by the two studies.

Usually, thematic problems facilitate the use of the disconfirmation strategy by increasing the frequency with which subjects select the *Q* card. The selection of the *P* card typically differs little between problem types (see Evans, 1977). That happened in the Griggs–Cox study where 74 and 62 subjects selected the *P* card on the drinking-age and abstract problems, respectively. The frequencies with which their subjects selected the $Q$ card differed much more between the problems: 71 on the drinking-age problem compared to 44 on the abstract problem. We too found the selection of card $P$ to be invariant across problem types; 76 and 78 subjects selected the $P$ card on the abstract and drinking-age problems, respectively (Table 18.3). But our results for the $Q$ card were unlike Griggs and Cox's. As shown in Table 18.3, the subjects in the present study selected the $Q$ card 60 times on the abstract problem and 74 times on the drinking-age problem, an insignificant difference ($\chi^2(1) = 1.3$, one-tailed, $p > .10$). Thus, in contrast to Griggs and Cox, the facilitation reported in this study does not reflect increased selection of the $Q$ card. Instead, the facilitation observed occurred because the drinking-age problem suppressed the selection of irrelevant cards, $P$ and $Q$. These cards were selected significantly less often on the drinking-age problem than on the abstract problem. This is not a novel finding. Griggs and Cox reported such findings. What is unusual is that in the present study facilitation is completely accounted for by the reduction in the frequency with which these irrelevant cards were selected on the thematic rules.

## Conclusion

This study has examined the processing strategies that Black college students use in Wason's selection task. Only two unique findings are reported. The first is that methodological idiosyncrasies of the study either allowed or induced the subjects to exhibit uncommon deftness with the abstract version of the selection task, where slightly more than 31% of them employed the logically correct disconfirmation strategy. The second surprise finding pertains to facilitation. It is atypically small and its etiology is unprecedented—in that, the facilitation resulted solely from the low rates with which the irrelevant cards $P$ and $Q$ were selected on the thematic rules.

These unique findings notwithstanding, the present results fit comfortably within the overall pattern of selection task results that have been reported over the past 20 years. Subjects in this study displayed the same reasoning skills and fallacies as other subjects who have been studied. For that reason, this study has not carved nature at its joints. The psychological and philosophical issues addressed are not novel, and the empirical results are not revolutionary. Nevertheless, the present results contribute importantly to the selection task literature.

In particular, this study reaffirms the profound difficulty of the abstract version of the selection task and the relative ease of the thematic version. At the same time, this study extends the generality of the selection task literature to a subject population not previously covered. Foremost, the present results challenge the conventional wisdom about how Blacks think. There was no evidence of a culture-specific reasoning style in the data for the sample of Blacks studied, contrary to expectations (cf. Shade, 1982). Evidently, some Blacks, perhaps those from privileged socioeconomic backgrounds like the subjects in this study, acquire conceptual rules for reasoning which are no more intuitive and no less logical than any developed by people in Western, literate societies.

Follow-up studies should examine in detail the impact that the "Black experience" has on the development of reasoning and problem-solving skills. Over time, such analyses should provide a more adequate basis for evaluating the cognitive functioning of Black Americans, and may, like this study, present a more positive view of their thinking skills.

## Notes

1. Instructions in the selection task vary from study to study. Originally, the subject was asked to establish the "truth" or "falsity" of a rule (cf. Wason, 1966). To ask whether a rule had been "violated" became popular later (e.g., Reich & Ruth, 1982). Depending upon other experimental variables, the instructions may marginally affect the results obtained (Chrostowki & Griggs, 1985; Griggs, 1983; Valentine, 1985).

2. By "like" the sample problem is meant any abstract, conditional rule with an affirmative antecedent and consequent.

3. Klayman & Ha (1987) lucidly demonstrate that for some hypothesis testing tasks (e.g., 2-4-6 task [Wason, 1960]) the confirmation strategy is entirely appropriate (see also the paper by Tweney et al., 1980). The selection task is not among them. From a normative view, confirmation is always an incorrect strategy to employ in the selection task (Klayman & Ha, 1987, p. 221).

## References

Beth, E. W., & Piaget, J. (1966). *Mathematical epistemology and psychology.* Dordrecht, Holland: D. Reidel.

Bracewell, R. J., & Hidi, S. E. (1974). The solution of an inferential problem as a function of the stimulus materials. *Quarterly Journal of Experimental Psychology, 26,* 480-488.

Cheng, P. W., & Holyoak, K. J. (1985). Pragmatic reasoning schemas. *Cognitive Psychology, 17,* 391-416.

Cheng, P. W., Holyoak, K. J., Nisbett, R. E., & Oliver, L. M. (1986). Pragmatic versus syntactic approaches to training deductive reasoning. *Cognitive Psychology, 18,* 293-328.

Chrostowski, J. J., & Griggs, R. A. (1985). The effects of problem content, instructions, and verbalization procedures on Wason's selection task. *Current Psychological Research and Reviews, 4*(2), 99-107.

Cohen, G. (1983). *The psychology of cognition* (2nd ed.). London: Academic Press.

Cohen, L. J. (1981). Can human irrationality be experimentally demonstrated? *Behavioral & Brain Sciences, 4,* 317-370.

Curran, H. V. (1988). Relative universals: Perspectives on culture and cognition. In G. Claxton (Ed.), *Growth points in cognition.* London: Routledge & Kegan Paul.

Dasen, P. R. (1984). The cross-cultural study of intelligence: Piaget and the Baoulé. *International Journal of Psychology, 19,* 407-434.

Dawes, R. M. (1975). The mind, the model, and the task. In F. Restle, R. M. Shiffrin, N. J. Castellan, H. R. Lindman, & D. B. Pisoni (Eds.), *Cognitive theory Volume I* (pp. 119-129). Hillsdale, NJ: Lawrence Erlbaum.

Einhorn, H. J., & Hogarth, R. M. (1978). Confidence in judgment: Persistence of the illusion of validity. *Psychological Review, 85,* 395-416.

Evans, J. St. B. T. (1972). Interpretation and matching bias in a reasoning task. *Quarterly Journal of Experimental Psychology, 24,* 193-199.

Evans, J. St. B. T. (1975). On interpreting reasoning data—A reply to Van Duyne. *Cognition, 3,* 387-390.

Evans, J. St. B. T. (1977). Toward a statistical theory of reasoning. *Quarterly Journal of Experimental Psychology, 29,* 621-635.

Evans, J. St. B. T. (1978). The psychology of reasoning: Logic. In A. Burton & J. Radford (Eds.), *Thinking in perspective: Critical essays in the study of thought processes* (pp. 90-110). London: Methuen.

Evans, J. St. B. T. (1980). Current issues in the psychology of reasoning. *British Journal of Psychology, 71,* 227-239.

Evans, J. St. B. T. (1982). *The psychology of deductive reasoning.* London: Routledge & Kegan Paul.

Evans, J. St. B. T. (1983a). Linguistic determinants of bias in conditional reasoning. *Quarterly Journal of Experimental Psychology, 35A,* 635-644.

Evans, J. St. B. T. (1983b). Selective processes in reasoning. In J. St. B. T. Evans (Ed.), *Thinking and reasoning: Psychological approaches* (pp. 135-163). London: Routledge & Kegan Paul.

Evans, J. St. B. T. (1984). Heuristic and analytic processes in reasoning. *British Journal of Psychology, 75,* 451-468.

Evans, J. St. B. T., & Lynch, J. S. (1973). Matching bias in the selection task. *British Journal of Psychology, 64,* 391-397.

Fischer, K. W., & Silvern, L. (1985). Stages and individual differences in cognitive development. *Annual Review of Psychology, 36,* 613-648.

Gardner, H. (1985). *Frames of mind: The theory of multiple intelligences.* New York: Basic Books.

Gellatly, R. H. (1987). Acquisition of a concept of logical necessity. *Human Development, 30,* 42-47.

Gilhooly, K. J. (1982). *Thinking: Directed, undirected and creative.* New York: Academic Press.

Gilhooly, K. J., & Falconer, W. A. (1974). Concrete and abstract terms and relations in testing a rule. *Quarterly Journal of Experimental Psychology, 26,* 355-359.

Griggs, R. A. (1983). The role of problem content in the selection task and in the THOG problem. In J. St. B. T. Evans (Ed.), *Thinking and reasoning: Psychological approaches* (pp. 16-43). London: Routledge & Kegan Paul.

Griggs, R. A., & Cox, J. R. (1982). The elusive thematic-materials effect in Wason's selection task. *British Journal of Psychology, 73,* 407-420.

Griggs, R. A., & Cox, J. R. (1983). The effects of problem content and negation on Wason's selection task. *Quarterly Journal of Experimental Psychology, 35A,* 519-533.

Hale, J. (1981). Black children: Their roots, culture, and learning styles. *Young Children, 36,* 37-50.

Halford, G. S. (1982). *The development of thought.* Hillsdale, NJ: Lawrence Erlbaum.

Harman, G. (1986). *Change in view: Principles of reasoning.* Cambridge: MIT Press.

Hock, S. J., & Tschirgi, J. E. (1985). Logical knowledge and cue redundancy in deductive reasoning. *Memory & Cognition, 13*(5), 453-462.

Johnson-Laird, P. N. (1982). Ninth Bartlett memorial lecture. Thinking as a skill. *Quarterly Journal of Experimental Psychology, 34A,* 1-29.

Johnson-Laird, P. N. (1985). Deductive reasoning ability. In R. J. Sternberg (Ed.), *Human abilities: An information-processing approach* (pp. 173-194). New York: Freeman.

Johnson-Laird, P. N., Legrenzi, P., & Legrenzi, M. S. (1972). Reasoning and a sense of reality. *British Journal of Psychology, 63,* 395-400.

Johnson-Laird, P. N., & Wason, P. C. (1970). A theoretical analysis of insight into a reasoning task. *Cognitive Psychology, 1,* 134-148.

Johnson-Laird, P. N., & Wason, P. C. (1977). A theoretical analysis of insight into a reasoning task. In P. N. Johnson-Laird & P. C. Wason (Eds.), *Thinking: Readings in cognitive science* (pp. 143-157). Cambridge: Cambridge University Press.

Kern, L. H., Mirels, H. L., & Hinshaw, V. G. (1983). Scientists' understanding of propositional logic: An experimental investigation. *Social Studies of Science, 13,* 131-146.

Klayman, J., & Ha, Y. (1987). Confirmation, disconfirmation, and information in hypothesis testing. *Psychological Review, 94,* 211-228.

Lunzer, E. A., Harrison, C., & Davey, M. (1972). The four-card problem and the generality of formal reasoning. *Quarterly Journal of Experimental Psychology, 24,* 326-339.

Mahoney, M. J., & Kimper, T. P. (1976). From ethics to logic: A survey of scientists. In M. J. Mahoney (Ed.), *Scientists as subject: The psychological imperative* (pp. 187-193). Cambridge, MA: Ballinger.

Manktelow, K. I., & Evans, J. St. B. T. (1979). Facilitation of reasoning by realism: Effect or non-effect? *British Journal of Psychology, 70,* 477-488.

Piaget, J. (1972a). Intellectual evolution from adolescence to adulthood. *Human Development, 15,* 1-12.

Piaget, J. (1972b). *The principles of genetic epistemology.* London: Routledge & Kegan Paul.

Pollard, P. (1981). The effect of thematic content on the "Wason Selection Task." *Current Psychological Research, 1,* 21-29.

Popper, K. R. (1961). *The logic of scientific discovery.* New York: Science Editions.

Reich, S. S., & Ruth, P. (1982). Wason's Selection Task: Verification, falsification and matching. *British Journal of Psychology, 73,* 395-405.

Rumelhart, D. E. (1980). Schemata: The building blocks of cognition. In R. S. Spiro, B. C. Bertram, & W. F. Brewer (Eds.), *Theoretical issues in reading comprehension* (pp. 33-58). Hillsdale, NJ: Lawrence Erlbaum.

Saxe, G. B. (1983). Piaget and anthropology. *American Anthropologist, 85,* 136-143.

Scribner, S. (1977). Modes of thinking and ways of speaking: Culture and logic reconsidered. In P. N. Johnson-Laird & P. C. Wason (Eds.), *Thinking: Readings in cognitive science* (pp. 143-157). Cambridge: Cambridge University Press.

Shade, B. J. (1982). Afro-American cognitive style: A variable in school success. *Review of Educational Research, 52,* 219-244.

Shade, B. J. (1987). Ecological correlates of educative style of the Afro-American children. *Journal of Negro Education, 56,* 88-89.

Sternberg, R. J. (1986). Toward a unified theory of human reasoning. *Intelligence, 10,* 281-314.

Tweney, R. D., Doherty, M. E., Wormer, W. J., Pliske, D. B., Mynatt, C. R., Gross, K. A., & Arkkelin, D. L. (1980). Strategies of rule discovery in an inference task. *Quarterly Journal of Experimental Psychology, 32,* 109-123.

Tweney, R. D., & Yachanin, S. A. (1985). Can scientists rationally assess conditional inferences? *Social Studies of Science, 15,* 155-173.

Valentine, E. R. (1985). The effect of instructions on performance in the Wason Selection Task. *Current Psychological Research and Reviews, 4*(3), 214-223.

Van Duyne, P. C. (1973). A short note on Evans' criticism of reasoning experiments and his matching bias hypothesis. *Cognition, 2,* 239-242.

Van Duyne, P. C. (1974). Realism and linguistic complexity in reasoning. *British Journal of Psychology, 65,* 59-67.

Van Duyne, P. C. (1976). Necessity and contingency in reasoning. *Acta Psychologica, 40,* 85-101.

Wason, P. C. (1960). On the failure to eliminate hypotheses in a conceptual task. *Quarterly Journal of Experimental Psychology, 12,* 129-140.

Wason, P. C. (1966). Reasoning. In B. Foss (Ed.), *New horizons in psychology I* (pp. 135-151). Harmondsworth, Middlesex: Penguin.

Wason, P. C. (1968). Reasoning about a rule. *Quarterly Journal of Experimental Psychology, 20,* 273-281.

Wason, P. C. (1977). The theory of formal operations—A critique. In B. Geber (Ed.), *Piaget and knowing* (pp. 119-135). London: Routledge & Kegan Paul.

Wason, P. C. (1983). Realism and rationality in the selection task. In J. St. B. T. Evans (Ed.), *Thinking and reasoning: Psychological approaches* (pp. 44-75). London: Routledge & Kegan Paul.

Wason, P. C., & Green, D. W. (1984). Reasoning and mental representation. *Quarterly Journal of Experimental Psychology, 36A,* 597-610.

Wason, P. C., & Johnson-Laird, P. N. (1972). *Psychology of reasoning: Structure and content.* London: B. T. Batsford Ltd.

Wason, P. C., & Shapiro, D. (1971). Natural and contrived experience in a reasoning problem. *Quarterly Journal of Experimental Psychology, 23,* 63-71.

Yachanin, S. A., & Tweney, R. D. (1982). The effect of thematic content on cognitive strategies in the four-card selection task. *Bulletin of the Psychonomic Society, 19*(2), 87-90.

# 19

# Is There an Afro-American Cognitive Style? An Exploratory Study

## BARBARA J. SHADE
*University of Wisconsin-Parkside*

This study examined the possibility of a unique Afro-American cognitive style. One hundred seventy-eight ninth grade students stratified by race, sex, and achievement level were administered three cognitive style tasks. Results revealed a significant difference between Afro- and Euro-American students in their perceptual orientation to the environment. It is suggested that this difference may influence the performance patterns reported on nonverbal measures.

In recent years several scholars (Hale, 1982; Jenkins, 1982; White, 1984) have suggested that Afro-Americans have a unique cognitive style that influences their participation in the learning process. Although the idea seems to have intuitive support, it has not been tested empirically. This study was designed to explore this possibility.

Cognitive style is a culturally induced way in which individuals organize and comprehend their world. Although it is a construct often viewed with skepticism, it is beginning to gain credence as more attention is focused upon individual differences in processing information.

The assumptions made about cognitive style seem to emanate from findings of studies of one dimension, i.e., that of field independence-field dependence. However, this stylistic preference represents only one of several dimensions represented by the construct. As Watchel (1972) and Vernon (1973) pointed out, cognitive style refers to a pattern of strategies. This pattern includes not only perceptual style as measured by field articulation studies, but also the examination of preferences in conceptual differentiation as well as interpersonal interaction. Thus, to determine a particular cognitive style requires the examination of the consistency of performance in more than one arena. Therefore, to

Barbara J. Shade, Division of Education, Box 2000, University of Wisconsin-Parkside, Kenosha, WI 53141 explore the possibility of an Afro-American cognitive style, it was deemed necessary to examine group variations in all three of the psychological processes embodied in the concept.

## Method

### SAMPLE

One hundred seventy-eight (178) ninth grade students were randomly selected from two urban school districts in Southeastern Wisconsin. Within the sample 92 were Afro-American and 86 were Euro-American. The sample selected was stratified by achievement level and sex. The choice of the use of ninth grade students was based upon studies by Witkin, Goodenough, and Karp (1967) that indicated that cognitive style seems to be relatively stable between the ages of 14 and 17. In addition, a review of the literature found no significant differences between Afro- and Euro-Americans on any of the cognitive style dimensions prior to grade three or after age 19.

The students selected for this study attended the same schools, generally lived in the same neighborhoods, and, from all indications, seemed to be relatively close in socioeconomic status. Thus, the social ecology for both groups was assumed to be basically the same with the exception of their racial/cultural orientation.

### PROCEDURES

Following the selection of the students, parents and students were contacted by letter to explain the study and to secure permission and participation. Students who agreed to participate were tested during their study hall periods and all instruments and tasks were administered in a one-hour time frame by previously trained assistants.

### INSTRUMENTS

Vernon (1973) pointed out that cognitive style is best conceived as a superordinate construct involving perceptual, intellectual, and social domains. Three instruments representing each of the areas were selected. The tasks were chosen based upon previous use with culturally diverse populations, ease of administration, and previous use in the study of cognitive style. Following a review of the literature on each instrument and several pilot studies, the following instruments were

**TABLE 19.1**  An Analysis of Variance of Group Differences on Three Cognitive
Style Measures

|  | Mean | Mean Square | FH Ratio | Significance Level |
|---|---|---|---|---|
| Embedded Figures |  |  |  |  |
| Afro-American | 6.52 | 373.01 | 15.70 | .0001 |
| Euro-American | 9.42 |  |  |  |
| Object Sorting Task |  |  |  |  |
| Afro-American | 14.88 | 9.96 | 0.32 | N.S. |
| Euro-American | 14.40 |  |  |  |
| Myers-Briggs Type Indicator |  |  |  |  |
| Afro-American | 6.34 (ESTP) | 148.303 | 5.11 | .025 |
| Euro-American | 8.17 (ESTJ) |  |  |  |

selected: the Group Embedded Figures Test to measure perceptual differentiation style preferences; the Clayton-Jackson Object Sorting Task as a measure of preferences in conceptual differentiation; and the Myers-Briggs Type Indicator as a measure of social interaction style.

Although the results in a previous study (Shade, 1983) revealed a difference between ethnic groups on all three measures, a significant difference was not evident on the Object Sorting Task in this sample. A highly significant difference emerged in an analysis of variance between Afro- and Euro-Americans on the Group Embedded Figures Test (Table 19.1). These findings were confirmed in a discrimination analysis that revealed that the Group Embedded Figures Test discriminated between the racial groups correctly at least 86% of the time.

Although the significance level was not as high as the researcher preferred ($p = .025$), a difference was also found between Afro- and Euro-American students on the Myers-Briggs Type Indicator. The numbers represented by the means in Table 19.1 represent one of 16 different personality types in which four different bipolar dimensions are combined. The difference in this sample occurred on the Judging vs. Perceiving dimension of the scale with Afro-Americans being more perceptive, whereas Euro-Americans were more judging. This suggested that Afro-Americans in this sample tended to be more spontaneous, flexible, open-minded and less structured in their perceptions of people, events, and ideas and Euro-Americans in this sample appeared to be self-regulated, judgmental, and less open-minded.

## Discussion

The finding of a significant difference in field articulation on the Group Embedded Figures Test and on the judging/perceiving dimension of the Myers-Briggs Type Indicator seems to suggest that the perceptual process is the primary dimension in which Afro-Americans demonstrate a unique preference. It is recognized that it is difficult to separate the perceptual process from the process of cognition in general (Arnheim, 1969). Current literature on modality preferences suggests that this might be a fruitful approach in that different groups seem to have different preferences for obtaining and learning information (NASSP, 1981). Thus, the findings represented by this study may lead to further exploration of the Serpell (1976) and Wober (1966) hypotheses that studies of cognitive style are actually studies of the differences in visual information processing.

The possibility of a cultural variation in visual information processing has been examined for international samples but is not one that has been explored within the framework of American culture. If, through additional study, it can be found that Afro-Americans visually transform and interpret pictorial images based upon their own cultural interpretation, a reexamination will need to be made of the use of pictorial representations in the assessment of cognitive functioning.

## References

Arnheim, R. (1969). *Visual thinking*. Berkeley: University of California Press.

Hale, J. (1982). *Black children: The roots, culture and learning style*. Provo, UT: Brigham Young University Press.

Jenkins, A. H. (1982). *The psychology of the Afro-American: A humanistic approach*. Elmsford, NY: Pergamon.

National Association of Secondary School Principals. (1982). *Learning styles and brain behavior*. Reston, VA: Author.

Serpell, R. (1976). *Cultural influences on behavior*. London: Methuen.

Shade, B. J. (1982). Afro-American cognitive style: A variable in school success. *Review of Educational Research, 52*, 219-244.

Shade, B. J. (1983). *Afro-American patterns of cognition (Final report)*. Madison: University of Wisconsin, Center for Education Research.

Vernon, P. E. (1973). Multivariate approaches to the study of cognitive styles. In J. Royce (Ed.), *Multivariate analysis of psychological theory*. New York: Academic Press.

Wachtel, P. L. (1972). Field dependence and psychological differentiation: Reexamination. *Perceptual and Motor Skills, 35*, 179-189.

White, Joseph L. (1984). *The psychology of Blacks: An Afro-American perspective*. Englewood Cliffs, NJ: Prentice-Hall.

Witkin, H. A., Goodenough, D. R., & Karp, S. A. (1967). Stability of cognitive style from childhood to young adulthood. *Journal of Personality and Social Psychology, 7*, 291-300.

Wober, M. (1966). Sensotypes. *Journal of Social Psychology, 70*, 181-189.

# 20

# Learning Styles of African American Children: A Review of the Literature and Interventions

## MADGE GILL WILLIS
*Atlanta, Georgia*

A review of theories, research, and models of the learning styles of Black children reveals that Black children generally learn in ways characterized by factors of social/affective emphases, harmony, holistic perspectives, expressive creativity, and nonverbal communication. Underlying these approaches are assumptions that Black Americans (African Americans) have been strongly influenced by their African heritage and culture, and that Black children's learning styles are different—but not deficient. Implications for intervention include recommendations for instructional interventions, curriculum organization, assessment, and suggestions for future research.

The field of African psychology is growing with theories and research about personality (Baldwin, 1981; Williams, 1981), the family (Nobles, 1985), and models for research (L. King, Dixon, & Nobles, 1976). With the increasingly large numbers of African American children who are not successful in school, more attention needs to be devoted to developing methods and processes by which they can effectively learn, achieve, and be empowered. The construct of learning style seems to be an appropriate one for studying the instructional process.

Polce (1987) provided an overview of learning styles in terms of cognitive, affective, physiological, and environmental factors. Although sociocultural factors are listed as having an effect on learning style, no mention is made of how this impacts upon children from different cultures. Black psychologists, educators, and sociologists have presented evidence that the culture of African Americans is a distinct one that socializes Black children to survive in American society in a way that is (and must be) different from the way that White children are

---

Correspondence concerning this article should be addressed to Madge G. Willis, 4540 Cascade Road, Atlanta, GA 30331.

socialized (Boykin & Toms, 1985; McAdoo & McAdoo, 1985; Nobles, 1974). This African American cultural influence affects cognition and learning style, attitude, behavior, and personality (Hale-Benson, 1986; Hilliard, 1976).

Before knowing where to go, it is important to know where we have been and what has been done in the area. This article examines several sources of research, observations, descriptions, and dimensions that characterize the cognitive functioning and learning styles of African American children. First, the underlying assumptions that most characterizations make about Black children's learning styles will be discussed. Second, the characteristics of their learning styles will be described. Finally, suggestions for future research and development as well as implications for interventions involving curriculum, instruction, and assessment will be offered.

## Assumptions

There are four major assumptions underlying the integrated model presented here. The first is that learning style is an important dimension to consider in a child's school experience (Polce, 1987). *Learning style* can be defined as a way of perceiving, conceptualizing, and problem-solving. Learning style is a preference for the way of interacting with and responding to the environment (Polce, 1987). The second assumption is that culture affects cognition, attitude, behavior, and personality (Hale-Benson, 1986; Hilliard, 1976; Neisser, 1986). Assumption three is that African Americans are strongly influenced by their African heritage and culture (Hale-Benson, 1986; Nobles, 1986). Last, but perhaps most important, is that tacit assumption that the differences between Black and White children's cognitive functioning and learning styles are simply that—*differences*—and not deficits. Various organizations are recognizing that Black children are different, but not deficient, and that they have unique strengths and learning needs that should be addressed in the schools (National Alliance of Black School Educators [NABSE], 1984; National Association of School Psychologists [NASP], 1985). Supporting data are offered for this last assumption because there is sometimes a tendency among Blacks to shy away from acknowledging some differences for fear that the differences would be misinterpreted as weaknesses.

There is support for the different-not-deficient assumption from a social as well as a biological perspective. In terms of the social view,

Hilliard (1976) stated that there is compelling evidence to support the assumption that dichotomous learning patterns or styles are found at all intelligence levels. There is, then, no correlation between style and ability. He stated, "Every style is necessary, valuable and useful in human experience if society is to function fully" (p. 43).

Support for the lack of biological deficiencies in African Americans' cognitive abilities can be found in studies comparing Black and White infants and toddlers. The consistent results are that African and African American children from birth to about three years of age score higher than European and White American children on tests of development and intelligence. Gordon (1982) and Hale-Benson (1986) provided excellent reviews of these studies and raise questions as to whether this "precocity" of Black children is genetic, environmental, or affected by the changing nature and content of the tests. Arthur Jensen (1969) urged further study to determine the factors involved as he, rather ironically, found "brain wave patterns in African newborn infants [that] show greater maturity than is usually found in the European newborn child. . . . This finding especially merits further study since there is evidence that brain waves have some relationship to IQ . . . and since at least one aspect of brain waves . . . has a very significant genetic component." (p. 87). There is irony in Jensen's finding that a positive genetic factors exists that may at least partially account for "precocious" Black intelligence. However, some African American researchers have recognized such factors as a manifestation of a physiological strength for people of color and are studying it intensely. King, Adams, and Barnes (1987) and H. Adams and King (1988) have presented research on the enabling and enhancing effects of melanin on cognition, memory, and various other psychological and biological processes. They offered additional support for the position that African American children's differences should not be interpreted as physiological or genetic deficiencies but, rather, can possibly be sources of strengths.

## Black Learning Styles

The field of African Psychology is a developing one in terms of formalized theories and conceptual models. As with most theoretical foundations and models, observation and analysis of behaviors form the initial data base. These types of data, along with constructs and paradigms from African philosophy and culture, have generated the conceptualization of Black learning styles described in this article (Hilliard, 1987; Nobles, 1986).

As Polce (1987) defined it, learning style encompasses cognitive elements, perception, affective correlates, physiological factors, and environmental factors. Similarly, Boykin (1983), Nobles (1985), and others characterized Black life and cultural style as very holistic, in that all parts of a person's thinking, feeling, behaving, and being are inextricably interdependent and connected. Therefore, in a learning situation, a Black child's verve, spirituality, time perspective, and expressive individualism are usually all involved. These qualities are part of the nine dimensions that Boykin (1983) described that are expressed by Blacks and that have their origins in the African belief system that has influenced contemporary African American culture. They are:

1. *Spirituality*—a belief that powers greater than man exist and are at work.
2. *Harmony*—man and his environment are interdependently connected; this applies to living in harmony with nature rather than trying to control it and to integrating the parts of one's life into a harmonious whole.
3. *Movement*—a rhythmic orientation to life that may be manifested in music and dance as well as in behavior and approach.
4. *Verve*—the psychological aspect of the movement dimension; involves a preference to be simultaneously attuned to several stimuli rather than a singular, routinized, or bland orientation; energetic, intense.
5. *Affect*—emotional expressiveness and sensitivity to emotional cues; integration of feelings with cognitive elements.
6. *Communalism*—interdependence of people; social orientation.
7. *Expressive individualism*—focus on a person's unique style or flavor in an activity; spontaneity; manifested in a unique tilt of a hat, a walk, a jazz musician's rendition.
8. *Orality*—importance of information learned and transmitted orally; call and response pattern.
9. *Social time perspective*—time is viewed in terms of the event rather than the clock; for example, an event begins when everyone arrives.

Although Boykin did not specifically describe these as learning style dimensions, they can be observed in children in learning situations, and Boykin did offer strategies for curriculum modifications based on these dimensions.

Shade (1982) reviewed studies comparing Blacks and Whites on various dimensions and found differences similar to those that Boykin observed. The dimensions reviewed included:

• *Worldview*—greater cautiousness, suspiciousness, and apprehension among Blacks, as measured by the 16 PF and understood as the result of living in an urban society with a history of racial prejudice.

• *Social cognition*—in their perception of people. Blacks had more of an affective focus as opposed to a physical focus; in social interactions Blacks focused more on the people and Whites focused more on the task demands of the situation.

• *Stimulus variety*—similar to Boykin's *verve.*

• *Conceptual tempo*—refers to whether a person is more reflective or impulsive; Shade found a lack of evidence to support the commonly held assumption that Blacks are more impulsive; noteworthy is the role of the wise elders in traditional African society who are often described as very reflective thinkers.

• *Field dependence/independence*—Witkin's (1977) construct; field dependent persons need cues from the environment, they prefer external structure, are people-oriented, are intuitive thinkers, and remember material in a social context; field independent persons develop structure themselves, can pull out cues embedded in a context, prefer to work alone, are object- and task-oriented, and are analytical thinkers; Blacks were found to be more field dependent and Whites were more field independent.

Looking at cognitive style as involving perceptual, intellectual, and social domains, Shade (1986) used tests from each of these domains to compare Black and White high school students. Although previous research found differences in all three domains (Shade, 1983a), the 1986 study found no differences on the object-sorting task that measured the intellectual (conceptual) domain but did find significant differences between Blacks and Whites on the social and perceptual measures. Using the Group Embedded Figures Test, Shade found Black students to be more field dependent in terms of their perception. On the Myers-Brigg Type Indicator, Blacks were found to be more spontaneous, flexible, open-minded, and less structured in their perceptions of people, thoughts, and events (higher on P). White students tended to be more self-regulated, judgmental, and less open-minded (higher on J). Shade (1983b) also looked at whether there was a difference in achievement for students with different learning styles and found similar results.

Again, using the Group Embedded Figures Test and the Myers-Brigg, Shade found that high achievers were more field independent, object-oriented, rational/logical processors, and were analytical, linear thinkers. The low achievers were field dependent, person-oriented, and perceptual/sensory processors. Although almost equal numbers of Blacks and Whites were included in the study, the racial composition of the different achievement levels was not specified. Therefore, it is not clear how much of the learning style difference was due to racial/cultural factors. Shade concluded that there appears to be a learning style that may facilitate school achievement. That style, according to other conceptualizations, is similar to White students' preferred style, whereas the style of low achievers is similar to Black students' preferred style. This leads to many implications and questions about the role of instruction in the success of Black students.

Hilliard (1976) posited a continuum of behavioral styles that involved many of the characteristics described above. He made a similar comparison of schools as they are and schools as they could be. The current situation of most schools is, as Shade (1983b) found, similar to White students' learning styles. Hilliard labeled this style atomistic-objective. It is manifested by breaking down an experience into its parts or atoms, separating oneself from the experience (similar to field independence), preferring regularity, environmental control, and objectivity by placing little value on the meaning of an event. At the other end of the continuum is the synthetic-personal style that is characteristic of Black learners. Users of this style seek to synthesize or bring together divergent experiences in order to obtain the essence or gist of the experiences. They prefer experimentation, improvisation, and harmonious interaction with others and the environment. These characteristics are consistent with his vision of schools as they could be. Table 20.1, excerpted from Hilliard (1976), shows the two styles of schools.

Schools currently exist with instruction broken into separate, independent subject areas, standardized testing, uniform curricula, and interactions between student and workbook emphasized, all of which are manifestations of the atomistic-objective style. This follows a historical pattern as the American industrial revolution involved mass production of uniform parts in a routinized, precise process, and the current computer infusion continues this type of linear, analytical style. The synthetic-personal style is exemplified under "School as it could be" and includes characteristics such as creativity, divergent thinking, affective, people-focused opportunities. Hale-Benson (1986) incorporated many of these characteristics in her early childhood curriculum and program, which suggested that schools with these traits can really be created.

Hilliard's concept of behavioral style was pervasive in that it exists in other types of life experiences such as religion, music, and language (Hilliard, 1976). He offered descriptions of each style in these areas as support for the validity of the style dimension.

Cooperation is a behavior pattern that can be considered a survival strategy developed in America, where working together and sharing were necessary for Blacks in order to succeed in a society with racial discrimination. Or it can be considered a carryover from African culture where communal life is the social norm. A proverb from Uganda is, "Intelligence is like fire, when it goes out you can get it from your fellow man" (Wober, 1974). This proverb also highlights the practical and concrete nature as well as the communal and cooperative aspect of intelligence and learning processes in that society. Cooperation is an important dimension in African American children's learning style. Research has found that cooperative learning groups, in which small, heterogenous ability groups work together on learning tasks and activities, are particularly effective for Black students (Slavin & Oickle, 1981).

Language or communication style is a specific aspect of cognitive or learning style with characteristics that follow along the same lines as those described above for general cognitive styles. There are several excellent reviews and descriptions of African American communication, along with implications for school instruction. (Brooks, 1985; Dandy, in press; Taylor & Lee, 1987)

These Black-White polarities described by Boykin, Hilliard, and Shade are not dissimilar to what other researchers have found when investigating learning styles among students without reference to race or sex. Witkin's (1977) field dependence/independence and Cohen's (1969) relational/analytic styles divided learners into categories with many of the same qualities as synthetic-personal/atomistic-objective. The primary differences in typologies seem to be the underlying assumptions about which factors influence each style's development and subsequently affect the tone, flavor, and emphasis of the specific characteristics observed. For example, Cohen stated that the development of analytic versus relational style is determined by the amount of structure in a person's primary groups, particularly the family. Boykin's perspective of a cultural and racial origin of Black learning styles incorporated family but with a focus on different aspects than did Cohen's.

Not all Black children demonstrate all of the characteristics described in Boykin's, Hale-Benson's, or Hilliard's typologies and models. What

**TABLE 20.1** The Learning Style of the School

| *School as it is in general* | *School as it could be* |
| --- | --- |
| Rules | Freedom |
| Standardization | Variation |
| Conformity | Creativity |
| Regularity | Novelty |
| Memory for specific facts | Memory for essence |
| Normality | Uniqueness |
| Precision | Approximate |
| Atomistic | Global |
| Egocentric | Sociocentric |
| Convergent | Divergent |
| Controlled | Expressive |
| Universal meanings | Contextual meanings |
| Direct | Indirect |
| Cognitive | Affective |
| Isolation | Integration |
| Scheduled | Targets of opportunity |
| Object-focused | People-focused |
| Constant | Evolving |

Note: Excerpted from *Alternatives to IQ testing: An approach to the identification of gifted minority children* (p. 41) by A. G. Hilliard, 1976. San Francisco: San Francisco State University. Excerpted by permission.

is characterized here are the ends of the continuum of learning style. Placement along the continuum depends on factors such as variations in the types of socialization that occur in the family (i.e., how much parents identify with mainstream American versus African American culture, what types of options they perceive they have in their lives, their ability to adapt to the requirements of various institutions, and numerous other complex factors) (McAdoo, 1981). The individual person's ability and desire to develop various behavior repertoires is another critical factor in where they fall along the continuum of learning styles. Wober (1967) suggested that Africans (and logically, African Americans also) may vary their cognitive style response according to the specific situation. Hilliard (1976) stated that although there are strong relationships between style and cultural or ethnic group, a person can learn and integrate elements of other styles with his or her basic style. He defined a gifted person as "one who has integrated and harmonized the polar dispositions within himself or herself" (p. 43). This is an example of the biculturality that is seen as a reality for African Americans in this society (Boykin & Toms, 1985).

In summary, the observations, theories, and research about Black children's learning style can be integrated into four groupings of characteristics:

1. *Social/affective:* people-oriented, emphasis on affective domain, social interaction is crucial, social learning is common.
2. *Harmonious:* interdependence and harmonic/communal aspects of people and environment are respected and encouraged, knowledge is sought for practical, utilitarian, and relevant purposes, holistic approaches to experiences, synthesis is sought.
3. *Expressive creativity:* creative, adaptive, variable, novel, stylistic, intuitive, simultaneous stimulation is preferred, verve, oral expression.
4. *Nonverbal:* nonverbal communication is important (intonation, body language, etc.), movement and rhythm components are vital.

Some essential issues are: How can the construct of learning style be developed further from an Africentric perspective? How can this construct be applied to the educational experience of African American children?

## Future Directions

The theory-building, research, and applications that have been done in the area of African American learning styles have only begun to uncover the tip of the iceberg. Questions that need to be addressed include:

1. What are the processes involved in the synthetic-personal learning style? Is it analogous to Feuerstein's (1979) model of the processes involved in analytic or atomistic-objective thinking, but in an Africentric manner consistent with the style? Azibo (1988) suggested formulating and describing cognitive style using African personality traits and constructs, a path that seems most appropriate. Also, what is the process by which learning styles are learned and can be taught?

2. What are the normative data on behaviors such as physical development, activity levels, etc., on African American children? How does this relate to hyperactivity diagnoses, teacher expectations, and classroom discipline? Hale-Benson (1986) and Gordon (1982) discussed the behavioral expectations of dependency, docility, and submissiveness that schools have and how that creates a conflict in that the normal activity level and independence of many Black children is greater than the normal levels for most White children. Labels of hyperactivity are often placed on Black children because of the different expectations of

normal behavior. Hale-Benson suggested that research on physical development norms for Black children would aid teachers in determining appropriate expectations.

3. What are the best practices in assessment that include looking at the total world of the student? Hilliard (1976) differentiated between the two fundamental questions that are asked in assessments: (1) Do you know what I know? and (2) What is it that you know? Too often question one is emphasized and question two is treated minimally, if at all. However, in looking at students with various cultural backgrounds, the second question may be the most important one. More implementation of assessment procedures that ask the child what it is that he knows and then tie that information into appropriate curricular and instructional practices is needed.

4. What kinds of applications of learning styles to specific instructional techniques such as teaching reading, math, etc., are appropriate? What is the appropriate evaluative research to determine the effectiveness of these techniques?

5. What would a model school or independent school or program that implements these theories and applies the research be like? How can they be established and evaluated?

These are just a few of the paths to be explored in the process of developing this area. As these questions are answered, undoubtedly, more will appear.

## Implications for Interventions

Because African Americans tend to be a practical, utilitarian people, this author feels the need to also suggest some paths for a more immediate application of the current knowledge of African American learning styles.

The current trend toward pluralism and multicultural education in the schools may help schools more easily accept the notion of an African American learning style. Not only instructional methods, but also curriculum, class management, classroom organization, and assessment methods can be involved in interventions appropriate for improving the school achievement of Black children. These types of interventions may be most appropriate for educators, school psychologists, and other professionals working directly with students and/or consulting in the schools.

It is noted that these interventions are not suggested as the easy nor the sufficient solution to African American children's learning difficulties in the schools. Achievement is a complex issue, and sensitivity to learning style is only one aspect of it. Other critical aspects that must be addressed in a comprehensive program for African American achievement include teacher expectations and cultural synchrony (Irvine, 1990). Irvine discussed how teacher expectations are a very significant factor in African American children's school achievement. Low expectations by teachers usually lead to a self-fulfilling prophecy cycle of failure by the students. Irvine (1990) and Nobles (1990) also posited that an understanding and incorporation of the content and processes of students' culture and cultural styles is another critical component in students' achievement. Irvine labeled this latter concept *cultural synchrony*, and includes in it cognitive style as well as language/communication style. With these points in mind, the awareness of cognitive learning style is seen as an avenue for developing interventions that will help facilitate the school achievement of African American children.

## Instructional/Curricular Interventions

Boykin (1983) emphasized the early school years as starting points for appropriate instruction and stated that research gives support to the position that educational modifications that are congruent with Black learning styles have had positive results. Slavin (1977) and Slavin and Oickle (1981) found a greater increase in Black students' academic performance when cooperative learning groups were used. Similarly, Treadwell (1975) found group academic counseling to be more effective than individual counseling with Black students. When teachers used instructional techniques that involved more stimulus variety, greater verve, and rhythmic, verbal interactions, the Black students performed better than they did with traditional techniques (Boykin, 1982; Piestrup, 1973; Rohwer & Harris, 1975). As mentioned previously, there needs to be continued research on the effectiveness of these types of interventions. Additional interventions that are illustrations of the African American learning style are described below.

Involving movement, particularly rhythmic movement (as in creating rap songs of science or social studies facts or using self-talk in working through math problems), is appropriate.

Social interaction and opportunities for social learning in peer groups and cross-age groups should be encouraged along with cooperative learning groups. Hale-Benson (1986) stressed peer tutoring and small group learning. Often this is more effective than the one-to-one teacher-student instruction that is commonly prescribed by educators for low achievers.

Holliday (1985) emphasized the teacher-student interactions as critical to a child's learning. She recommended that observations and consultation about teacher-student interactions be a part of the basic assessment procedure for students with learning problems since social interactions are a crucial part of the learning experience for African American teachers and students.

Many studies have documented that teacher talk comprises the overwhelming majority of verbal communication in the classroom. The emphasis on oral expression in Black culture suggests that more student talk is particularly important in learning situations. The role of Black dialect in learning the mainstream dialect has not yet been totally clarified. Most researchers agree that Black children need to learn to fluently communicate in the mainstream dialect. This can be accomplished without negating or labeling Black dialect as inferior or wrong. Again, once a child feels acceptance and respect for who and how he is, he is more willing and able to take on new and different challenges. Boykin (1983) cautioned that "stylistic inflexibility can result when . . . styles are dishonored by teachers" (p. 359).

Unfortunately, low self-concept and self-respect are too commonly seen among African American children. There are studies that have examined the relationship between self-concept/personal identity and group concept/identification (Looney, 1988; Spencer, Brookins, & Allen, 1985), and although the relationship is not yet clearly determined, there is generally agreement that positive group identification and a healthy sense of self are desired goals (Kunjufu, 1984). A pattern observed during the author's experiences in making school presentations on Black history was that most students, both Black and White, thought that the origin of Black people was in slavery. People who believe that their heritage and past were founded on such an abhorrent experience are certainly at risk for not developing a healthy sense of who they are. Because of the widespread portrayal of Africa as primitive, undeveloped, helpless, and poor, many Blacks do not want to accept any association with it. The historical facts about the complex societies and technologies developed in Africa are generally esoteric and not part of most people's knowledge base (James, 1976). However, it is for these reasons of miseducation about the history of African Americans that it needs to be comprehensively and accurately emphasized throughout the curriculum. The National Alliance of Black School Educators (NABSE) emphasized the need for awareness, knowledge, and respect for African and African American history and culture in the schools (NABSE, 1984). The *Baseline Essays* developed in the Portland, Oregon, Schools provide an excellent beginning for educators to learn about Africans in art, social studies, language arts, music, math, and science and then to incorporate this knowledge into the schools' curriculum (*African American Baseline Essays*, 1988).

Connected with positive self- and group concept are interventions that emphasize self-knowledge (Nobles, 1986) and relevance (Boykin, 1983). Nobles stated that new learnings must be related to what a person already knows and has experienced. It must be meaningful and useful to him/her. Boykin cited research that found that academic skills were more easily mastered when tasks were embedded in a context that was culturally familiar to the students. Reading programs that emphasize skill mastery along with creative writing and language experience stories composed by the students are often very effective (Delpit, 1988). The Success in Reading program (A. Adams, 1978) is an excellent one for this purpose. Kunjufu (1984) recommended the Cultural Linguistic Approach (CLA) developed at Northeastern Illinois University Center for Inner City Studies.

The division of knowledge into subject matter such as math, science, spelling, etc., is an analytic approach to learning skills. Usually, there are no connections among the subjects, and each subject has a separate curriculum. A more holistic approach to curriculum would minimally involve coordination among teachers and subjects so that, for example, by the time the vocational teacher is using measurements to build or create a project, the math teacher has taught measurement skills. At the more holistic end would be a curriculum that was centered around natural, logical topics of life that would fully integrate all academic skills whether taught by a single teacher or several teachers. For example, elementary students may be learning how to get to school or home from various places. Map skills, measurement, math skills to do the measuring or counting, social studies skills about neighborhoods, spelling and creative writing about feelings and experiences while going from place to place, songs about places or traveling or getting lost, and art projects to create collages and three-dimensional neighborhood models can be taught in a coherent and meaningful way. Some elementary schools incorporate this approach to a degree in their use of learning centers. This author was involved in a Saturday program that developed a holistic curriculum that incorporated the above approach. Informal data indicated greater motivation, interest, and achievement among the students (Willis, 1988).

As in most aspects of life, a balance is necessary. It is unrealistic to expect all schools with Black students to totally restructure their educational programs and practices to accommodate Black students' learning styles. However, it must also be clarified and emphasized that many of the recommended practices are effective for all children, and not just for Black children. Anderson (1988) stated that many other groups of color display learning behaviors similar to the styles described for Blacks. Goodlad and Oakes (1988) found that White students benefited from recommendations made in response to Black students' learning styles.

The necessary balance should also include modifications by students to become more adaptable to the school's teaching styles. Boykin (1983) suggested that behavioral patterns associated with mainstream American society should be introduced to Black children in appropriate contexts. His goal was to prepare Black children to become "culturally bistylistic and to learn to discriminate when one mode of expression might be more effective than the other" (p. 359).

Hilliard (1987) advocated the use of methods such as Feuerstein's (1979) Dynamic Assessment and Instructional Enrichment approach that involves specifically teaching the skills that are a part of the analytic or atomistic-objective learning style. Students who learn these skills do better in school because they have learned how to learn in the manner that the schools teach. With such models in mind, NABSE (1984) distinguished between remediation and mediation. They took issue with the phenomenon of labeling students as needing "re-mediation" when they have never received the initial mediation or teaching.

## Assessment Interventions

Hilliard (1983) stated that the goals of mental measurement need to be drastically changed. He described current IQ testing as having questionable validity and purpose and having no practical application to instruction. As a preferred approach, he advocated that the goal of mental measurement be to change what happens with students in a way that would not be possible without this type of intervention. Of course, this would also involve changes in the connection between testing and teaching, in the concepts of reliability and validity in the field of psychometry, and in the roles of testers.

Alternatives to traditional standardized testing involve intervention on another level. Models such as those developed and implemented in San Francisco (Dent, 1987), Chicago (Heaston, 1987), and Detroit

(Draper, Hamilton, & Jones, 1987) are just a few of the appropriate and effective ones. These examples of assessment that take into account the students' learning styles and society's politics involve looking at the student's learning and needs in the context of the regular classroom. More specifically, Dent (1987) developed a six-stage model that analyzes referral data for a pattern, analyzes and, where necessary, modifies the regular instructional program for the referred student and his classmates, assesses the student's home curriculum, and as a rarely reached last step, estimates the child's learning potential.

In Chicago, a process assessment paradigm was implemented that aims to identify the student's strengths and weaknesses and to develop an appropriate educational and adjustment program. When assessment is necessary, it focuses on the process of learning (as opposed to the outcome) and the modifiability of the learner (as opposed to labeling a fixed ability level) (Heaston, 1987). This paradigm involves much of the theory of Feuerstein's (1979) approach and is the basis of Detroit's special education reform program (Draper et al., 1987).

When traditional assessment is used with Black students, appropriate modifications in response to the students' learning style is recommended. Lidz (1981) offered many suggestions to improve assessment of all children, and several of them are particularly appropriate for Black students.

*Time* is a concept that has been identified as being perceived differently by Blacks and Whites. Therefore, the approach to timed test items will be different; and consequently, the actual performance of Blacks may not be reflective of the level of skill acquired. Testing the limits should be an automatic procedure on all timed tasks in order to get a more qualitative picture of the student's skills. The student's reaction to the fact that they are being timed may also provide qualitative information about their attitude to time constraints. Probe responses, especially those that seem not to be related to the question. Find double ceilings and basals to provide qualitative information. At the same time, research needs to be done on the effects of varying administration procedures for timed tasks and on developing and modifying tests without time limits.

The Wechsler Intelligence Scale for Children—Revised (WISC-R) is considered to be an extremely biased and limited test by many African American educators and psychologists (Hilliard, 1987). If the purpose of administering the test is to learn what is it that the child knows, it must be kept in mind that the WISC-R measures analytical, atomistic-objective cognition, generally penalizes creativity and expressive individualism, and has norms that are not directly applicable to most Black children. If the results of the test are to be used to mediate and remediate skills that the child has not mastered, as in Feuerstein's approach, then it may theoretically have some purpose. Unfortunately, the WISC-R is more commonly used to rank a child with respect to the standardization sample. For Black children, this is certainly not being judged by a jury of their peers and often has deleterious consequences for them.

Shade (1986) suggested that cognitive style is simply a difference in visual information processing. This perspective, along with her research findings, would suggest that Blacks interpret visual images differently than do Whites. This would have major implications for tests, including supposedly "culture-fair" tests, that involve analyzing visual information or completing visual perception tasks. Additional research is needed to further define this relationship.

## Conclusion

This article has provided a review of some of the literature on learning styles of African American children. It offers a historical basis for the existence of this approach to conceptualizing African American children's learning behaviors and suggests interventions for educators, school psychologists, and others working with children. The concept of African American learning models and styles is a relatively new perspective. Continuing research and model development, as described above, needs to be done to better understand how to improve the educational experience of Black children.

Some might say that since the integration of schools, effective pedagogy for African American children is something that now needs to be reestablished. There is irony but realism in that observation.

Education is a powerful tool for both subordination and freedom. Education is subordinating when it is unconnected to students' own experiences . . . and when it demands that students accept other people's interpretations of the world. Education is freeing when it helps students think about their own lives, when it gives them skills and conceptual frameworks that help them pursue their own concerns, and when it helps them examine the barriers that keep them from success and attainment of the good life. (Sleeter & Grant, 1986, p. 299)

# References

Adams, A. (1978). *Success in beginning reading and writing.* Santa Monica, CA: Goodyear.

Adams, H., & King, R. (1988, August). *New perspectives on creative states of consciousness, dreams, learning, melanin and memory.* Plenary session at the 21st Annual Convention of the Association of Black Psychologists, Washington, DC.

*African American Baseline Essays.* (1988). (rev. ed.). Portland, OR: Multnomah School District 1J.

Anderson, J. A. (1988). Cognitive styles and multicultural populations. *Journal of Teacher Education, 39*(1), 2-9.

Azibo, D. A. (1988). Understanding the proper and improper usage of the comparative research framework. *The Journal of Black Psychology, 15*(1), 81-91.

Baldwin, J. (1981). Notes on an Africentric theory of Black personality. *The Western Journal of Black Studies, 5*(3), 172-179.

Boykin, A. W. (1982). Task variability and the performance of black and white schoolchildren: Vervistic explorations. *Journal of Black Studies, 12,* 469-485.

Boykin, A. W. (1983). On academic task performance and Afro-American children. In J. R. Spencer (Ed.), *Achievement and achievement motives* (pp. 324-371). Boston: Freeman.

Boykin, A. W., & Toms, F. D. (1985). Black child socialization: A conceptual framework. In H. P. McAdoo & J. L. McAdoo (Eds.), *Black children: Social, educational and parental environments* (pp. 33-52). Beverly Hills, CA: Sage.

Brooks, C. K. (Ed.). (1985). *Tapping potential: English and language arts for the Black learner.* Urbana, IL: National Council of Teachers of English.

Cohen, R. (1969). Conceptual styles, culture conflict, and nonverbal tests of intelligence. *American Anthropologist, 71,* 828-856.

Dandy, E. B. (in press). *Black communications: Breaking down the barriers.* Chicago: African American Images.

Delpit, L. D. (1988). The silenced dialogue: Power and pedagogy in educating other people's children. *Harvard Educational Review, 58,* 280-298.

Dent, H. (1987). The San Francisco public schools experience with alternatives to IQ testing: A model for non-biased assessment. *The Negro Educational Review, 38,* 146-162.

Draper, I., Hamilton, A., & Jones, J. (1987). The Detroit public schools experience with alternatives to IQ testing: Major special education efforts. *Negro Educational Review, 38,* 173-189.

Feuerstein, R. (1979). *The dynamic assessment of retarded performers: The learning potential assessment device, theory, instruments and techniques.* Baltimore, MD: University Park Press.

Goodlad, J. I., & Oakes, J. (1988). We must offer equal access to knowledge. *Educational Leadership, 45*(5), 16-22.

Gordon, B. M. (1982). Towards a theory of knowledge acquisition for Black children. *Journal of Education, 164,* 90-108.

Hale-Benson, J. E. (1986). *Black children: Their roots, culture and learning styles* (2nd ed.). Baltimore, MD: Johns Hopkins University Press.

Heaston, P. (1987). The Chicago public schools experience with alternatives to IQ testing: The color of rubies. *Negro Educational Review, 38,* 163-172.

Hilliard, A. G., III. (1976). *Alternatives to IQ testing: An approach to the identification of gifted minority children (Final report).* San Francisco: San Francisco State University. (ERIC Document Reproduction Service No. EC 103 067).

Hilliard, A. G., III. (Ed.). (1987). Testing African American students [Special issue]. *Negro Educational Review, 38.*

Holliday, B. G. (1985). Towards a model of teacher-child transactional processes affecting Black children's academic achievement. In M. B. Spencer, G. K. Brookins, & W. R. Allen (Eds.), *Beginnings: The social and affective development of Black children* (pp. 117-131). Hillsdale, NJ: Lawrence Erlbaum.

Irvine, J. J. (1990). *Black students and school failure: Policies, practices and prescriptions.* New York: Praeger.

James, G. G. M. (1976). *Stolen legacy.* San Francisco: Julian Richardson Associates. (Original work published 1954)

Jensen, A. R. (1969). How much can we boost IQ and scholastic achievement? *Harvard Education Review, 39,* 1-123.

King, L., Dixon, V., & Nobles, W. (Eds.). (1986). *African philosophy: Assumptions and paradigms for research on Black persons.* Los Angeles: Fanon Research & Development Center.

King, R., Adams, H., & Barnes, C. (1987). *Neuropsychology, melanin and Black psychology.* Think Tank presentation at the 20th Annual Convention of The Association of Black Psychologists, Atlanta, GA.

Kunjufu, J. (1984). *Developing positive self-images and discipline in Black children.* Chicago: African American Images.

Lidz, C. S. (1981). *Improving assessment of school children.* San Francisco: Jossey-Bass.

Looney, J. (1988). Ego development and black identity. *The Journal of Black Psychology, 15*(1), 44-56.

McAdoo, H. P. (Ed.). (1981). *Black families.* Beverly Hills, CA: Sage.

McAdoo, H. P., & McAdoo, J. L. (Eds.). (1985). *Black children: Social, educational and parental environments.* Beverly Hills, CA: Sage.

National Alliance of Black School Educators. (1984). *Saving the African American child* (A report of the NABSE Task Force on Black Academic and Cultural Excellence). Washington, DC: Author.

National Association of School Psychologists. (1985, June). Advocacy for appropriate educational services for all children. *Communique,* p. 9.

Neisser, U. (Ed.). (1986). *The school achievement of minority children: New perspectives.* Hillsdale, NJ: Lawrence Erlbaum.

Nobles, W. W. (1974). African root, American fruit: The Black family. *Journal of Social and Behavioral Sciences, 20,* 52-63.

Nobles, W. W. (1985). *Africanity and the Black family: The development of a theoretical model.* Oakland, CA: The Institute for the Advanced Study of Black Family Life and Culture.

Nobles, W. W. (1986). *African psychology: Toward its reclamation, reascension and revitalization.* Oakland, CA: Insitute for the Advanced Study of Black Family Life and Culture.

Nobles, W. W. (1990). The infusion of African and African American content: A question of content and intent. In A. G. Hilliard, L. Payton-Stewart, & L. O. Williams (Eds.), *Infusion of African and African American content in the school curriculum: Proceedings of the First National Conference October 1989* (pp. 5-24). Morristown, NJ: Aaron Press.

Piestrup, A. (1973). *Black dialect interference and accommodation of reading instruction in first grade* (Monograph No. 4). Berkeley: University of California, Language Behavior Research Laboratory.

Polce, M. E. (1987). Children and learning styles. In A. Thomas & J. Grimes (Eds.)., *Children's needs: Psychological perspectives* (pp. 325-335). Washington, DC: National Association of School Psychologists.

Rohwer, W., & Harris, W. (1975). Media effects on prose learning in two populations of children. *Journal of Educational Psychology, 67,* 651-657.

Shade, B. J. (1982). Afro-American cognitive style: A variable in school success? *Review of Educational Research, 52,* 219-244.

Shade, B. J. (1983a). *Afro-American patterns of cognition (Final report).* Madison: University of Wisconsin, Center for Education Research.

Shade, B. J. (1983b). Cognitive strategies as determinants of school achievement. *Psychology in the Schools, 20,* 488-493.

Shade, B. J. (1986). Is there an Afro-American cognitive style? *The Journal of Black Psychology, 13,* 13-16.

Slavin, R. E. (1977). *Student team learning techniques: Narrowing the achievement gap* (Report No. 228). Baltimore, MD: Johns Hopkins University, Center for Social Organization of Schools.

Slavin, R. E., & Oickle, E. (1981). Effects of cooperative learning teams on student achievement and race relations: Treatment by race interactions. *Sociology of Education, 54,* 174-180.

Sleeter, C. E., & Grant, C. A. (1986). Success for all students. *Phi Delta Kappan, 68,* 297-299.

Spencer, M. B., Brookins, G. K., & Allen, W. R. (Eds.). (1985). *Beginnings: The social and affective development of Black children.* Hillsdale, NJ: Lawrence Erlbaum.

Taylor, O., & Lee, D. L. (1987). Standardized tests and African Americans: Communication and language issues. *The Negro Educational Review, 38,* 67-80.

Treadwell, V. (1975). Group and individual counseling: Effects on college grades. *Journal of Non-White Concerns, 5,* 73-82.

Turner, L. D. (1969). *Africanisms in the Gullah dialect.* New York: Arnold Press.

Williams, R. L. (1981). *The collective Black mind: An Afrocentric theory of Black personality.* St. Louis, MO: Williams & Associates.

Willis, M. G. (1988, October). *Making a difference: Afterschool tutorial and enrichment programs.* Paper presented at the 18th Annual Conference of the National Black Child Development Institute, Los Angeles.

Witkin, H. A. (1977). Educational implications of cognitive styles. *Review of Educational Research, 47,* 1-64.

Wober, M. (1967). Adopting Witkin's field-independence theory to accommodate new information from Africa. *British Journal of Psychology, 58*(1-2), 29-38.

Wober, M. (1974). Towards an understanding of the Kiganda concept of intelligence. In J. W. Berry & P. R. Dasen (Eds.), *Culture and cognition: Reading in cross-cultural psychology* (pp. 261-280). London: Methuen.

# Differential Approaches in Psychology

Psychology has expanded its focus to include so many content areas that growing numbers of subdisciplines have emerged. Consequently, you would need to know a psychologist's area of specialization these days to even grasp a basic understanding of his or her professional activities. Nevertheless, generally, these subdisciplines have two things in common. First, the areas have not done an adequate job of addressing topics unique to African Americans that might naturally fit within a particular area of specialization. Second, these areas have not adequately examined whether the patterns of relationships among critical attitudes, behaviors, or outcomes are the same for African Americans as they are in the samples in which the research was conducted.

One goal of this text is to bridge this gap. Earlier, research and theoretical issues were raised on topics such as cognition and psychological testing and the child. This section examines theory and research related to four subdivisions of psychology—personality, clinical, health, and social psychology.

Personality psychology focuses on stable characteristics that individuals demonstrate across a range of settings. Racial identity, although multidimensional in nature, is one such characteristic. Of the many important theories that exist about the development of racial identity, that of Joseph Baldwin and his colleagues stands out because of their efforts to conceptualize a healthy African American personality as one that affirms African American life and places a high priority on the survival of African American institutions and culture. Their chapter is useful to scholars who want to increase their understanding of how Afrocentricity relates to the psychology of African Americans. It also is useful for those embarking on research in this area because it describes the development of one of the major measures of racial identity, the African Self-Consciousness Scale.

The focus of clinical psychology has been upon the etiology, assessment, and treatment of psychopathology. Traditional assessment frameworks such as the Diagnostic and Statistical Manual (DSM-III-R) use a European worldview and behavioral style as the standard of normalcy. Consequently, there is growing evidence to attest to the increased rates of misdiagnosis among African Americans. Atwell and Azibo's chapter assumes that Eurocentric assessment methods are not appropriate for understanding whether African Americans have assumed psychological stances in regard to their African heritage that promote or interfere with the development of their mental health. Their treatise provides an alternative framework that mental health professionals might use to make decisions about the mental health of an African American client in particular, and all Africans in general. Similarly, Anna Jackson argues that traditional treatment methods are not sensitive to unique aspects of the interpersonal styles and worldviews of African Americans tied to our cultural heritage. She describes alternatives to traditional psychotherapy in this paper.

Social psychologists study the social determinants of behavior. Delay of gratification was originally conceptualized as a stable personality trait unaffected by social factors. A few highly publicized research projects were interpreted to suggest that African Americans manifest personalities less capable of delaying immediate gratification in order to pursue long-range goals that require persistence and sacrifice. Later, it became more apparent that decisions about delaying immediate gratification were the end result of a cognitive chain of perceptions and experiences influencing expectancies about the likelihood of future rewards. Moreover, as Banks and his colleagues describe, the research actually is unclear on whether Africans are less willing to delay gratification if existing research is examined comprehensively rather than selectively.

Health psychologists address the influence of both behaviors and health-related attitudes on health outcomes. Although health psychology has some common interests with clinical psychology, social psychological perspectives certainly have been useful in shaping some of the theoretical perspectives that have contributed to our understanding of health concerns. The chapter by Burlew, Butler, Lewis, and Washington is a case in point. Specifically, this chapter provides evidence that attrition is higher among females than males in mixed gender groups for African Americans in alcohol treatment programs and includes some discussion of why this might be so.

The other chapters in this section address the alarmingly high proportion of African Americans who suffer from certain health problems. The good news, however, is that one can alter susceptibility through behavioral change. Faye Belgrave's chapter provides a brief, but comprehensive, overview of why health psychology is such an important area for African Americans. It also discusses some concrete roles for health psychologists concerned about improving health outcomes among African Americans. Hypertension is certainly one example. Both the Clark and Harrell chapter and the chapter by Hector Myers and his colleagues provide health professionals with a good foundation for understanding how behavioral styles (Clark & Harrell) and life stress (Myers, Bastien, and Miles) are related to the alarming rates of hypertension among African Americans.

# 21 Assessment of African Self-Consciousness Among Black Students From Two College Environments

**JOSEPH A. BALDWIN**
**JAMES A. DUNCAN**
**YVONNE R. BELL**
*Florida A & M University*

This research investigated the relationship of social cultural setting and background characteristics to African self-consciousness (ASC) as measured by the ASC Scale. Two hundred fifty Black college students, half from predominantly Black Florida A&M University (FAMU) and half from predominantly White Florida State University (FSU), were administered the ASC Scale and a background questionnaire. The findings revealed that: (a) FAMU students obtained significantly higher ASC Scale scores than FSU students; (b) older students obtained significantly higher ASC scores than younger students; (c) upper level students obtained higher ASC scores than lower level students, and this effect was more pronounced for FAMU students than for FSU students; (d) students with Black Studies backgrounds obtained higher ASC Scale scores than did students without this experience, especially for the FSU students; (e) FAMU students with all-Black elementary school backgrounds obtained higher ASC Scale scores than did the other students. It concluded: (a) that the African self-consciousness construct appears to be an important factor in explaining differences in psychological functioning and behavior among Black students in different sociocultural settings; and (b) that Black sociocultural settings and pro-Black experiential emphases are probably facilitative of healthy Black personality functioning.

The significance of the construct of African self-consciousness, or some facsimile of it, to the assessment and full understanding of important African American behaviors has been given increasing emphasis in contemporary theory and research on the Black personality (Akbar,

Joseph A. Baldwin, James A. Duncan, and Yvonne R. Bell can be contacted at: Department of Psychology, Florida A&M University, Tallahassee, FL 32307.

1974, 1979; Azibo, 1983a, 1983b, 1983c; Baldwin, 1980a, 1980b, 1981, 1984; Baldwin & Bell, 1985; Curry, 1981, 1984; Gibson, 1984; Williams, 1981). It is assumed in these studies that a significant part of the variance in the psychological functioning and behaviors of African Americans can be accounted for in whole or in part by the Black personality construct of African self-consciousness.

African self-consciousness has been labeled and defined in a variety of ways by different theorists and researchers. Such terms as *psychological Blackness, Black consciousness, Black awareness,* and *Black self-concept* have all been used as an approximation, more or less, of the African self-consciousness construct. Most of these conceptions tend to agree that Black or African American (cultural) consciousness is central to normal and healthy Black personality functioning. Notwithstanding some variations, it is generally accepted in these conceptions that African self-consciousness, however it may be labeled, refers to the awareness and knowledge that African Americans have (possess and practice) of themselves as African people historically, culturally, and philosophically. The construct basically consists of positive Black identity, pro-Black beliefs, attitudes, priorities, awareness, knowledge, and practice by African Americans of the African philosophy and culture. Hence, African self-consciousness is a theoretical construct that attempts to explain the psychological functioning and behavior of persons of African descent from their own cultural perspective.

More or less consistent with this conceptual framework, the definition of the African self-consciousness construct as it is used in this research, and the underlying conceptual model, derives from the Black personality theory of Joseph Baldwin (1980a, 1981, 1984). Baldwin's model proposes that the Black personality comprises a complex biopsychical structure consisting of two core components: the African self-extension orientation and African self-consciousness. The African self-extension orientation represents the fundamental organizing principle of the Black personality system. It is a deep-seated, innate, and unconscious process. It is defined essentially as a spiritualistic transcendence in experience. This spirituality, or *Africanity* as it is also called, is the key ingredient that allows for "self-extension" to occur in Black psychological experience. The African self-extension orientation thus represents a biogenetically defined (i.e., inherent-permanent) psychological disposition or propensity that all Black people possess, and it can be inferred in all of the basic behaviors characteristic of Black people. The African self-extension orientation gives coherence, continuity, and most importantly, Africanity, to the basic behaviors and psychological functioning of Black people.

The African self-consciousness component of the personality derives from the African self-extension orientation and represents the conscious level process directing the spirituality of the Black personality system. It operates synonymous to the African self-extension orientation under "normal-natural" conditions. However, it is subject to social-environmental influences. The most important aspect of African self-consciousness is that it gives conscious direction and purpose to the Africanity thrust that defines the core of the Black personality system. It directs the African survival thrust of the Black personality. African self-consciousness, according to this theory, includes the following:

1. The recognition of oneself as "African" (biologically, psychologically, and culturally) and of what being African means as defined by African cosmology.
2. The recognition of African survival and proactive development as one's first priority value.
3. Respect for and active perpetuation of all things African African life and African institutions.
4. Having a standard of conduct toward all things "non-African," and toward those things, peoples, etc., that are "anti-African."

According to Baldwin's theory, deviations from this pattern of normal functioning in the African self-consciousness core of the personality are explained in terms of variations in the personal and institutional support systems characterizing the developmental and experiential life space of the individual. It is proposed that Black social settings possess more intrinsic Africentric reinforcements than non-Black settings. Both individual differences and collective behavior among African Americans can be explained from this Africentric framework. We can see then that African self-consciousness is a key dimension of the Black personality in Baldwin's theory. It directs as well as reflects the conscious level African survival thrust in Black people's normal-healthy functioning. It is also that aspect of the Black personality system that has good heuristic value and can thus be assessed and studied through empirical examination. Hence, research on African self-consciousness and the predictions generated from this construct will provide for an empirical analysis of the Black personality.

## Black Consciousness Research

Previous studies on Black consciousness have suggested the existence of a strong correlation between a variety of important African American behaviors and levels of Black or African self-consciousness (Azibo, 1983a, 1983c; Baldwin, 1983). Specifically, most findings in this area suggest a strong correlation between high levels of Black consciousness and positive or effective psychological functioning and behavior among Black people (Azibo, 1983a, 1983b, 1983c; Baldwin & Bell, 1985; Curry, 1981, 1984; Gibson, 1984; Hilliard, 1972; Parham & Helms, 1981; Williams, 1981).

In an investigation by Curry (1981, 1984), two measures were used to assess Black consciousness: (1) The African Cultural Ideology Scale (ACIS), designed to assess dimensions of the African worldview; and (2) The Subjective Values Inventory (SVI), a measure that elicits information about descriptive differences and similarities in the meaning of concepts. Curry administered these measures to 100 African Americans and 53 African-born Blacks who were students at Pennsylvania State University. The ACIS results were subjected to factor analysis that produced seven factors for both African Americans and African-born Blacks. Factors emerging for African Americans included: (1) pride in African heritage; (2) pride in personal qualities; (3) communalism; (4) preference for Black solidarity; (5) disillusionment with intercontinental Black solidarity; (6) dissatisfaction with integration; (7) moderate Black solidarity and communalism. The emerging factors for the combined groups included: (1) ambivalence between individuality and solidarity; (2) solidarity and group identification; (3) preserved individuality with an African identification; (4) ambivalent integrationism; (5) acceptance of African ideals; (6) socialist African self-assertiveness; (7) personal preference for autonomy. The results of the SVI indicated that African Americans and African-born Blacks perceive their relationship to their environment in terms of cooperative and interdependent social relations. These results were generally supported by the ACIS results. Curry concluded that her findings supported the belief that African Americans and African-born Blacks are far too similar to one another to ignore the interdependent interactions that exist between African descendants throughout the world.

Also, a couple of studies by Azibo (1983b, 1983c) generated significant positive correlations between Black consciousness and personal causation and pro-Black preferences. In one study (Azibo, 1983b), using content analysis of subjects' story protocols as a measure of personal causation (i.e., intrinsic-communal motivation) and Williams' Black Personality Questionnaire as a measure of Black consciousness, Azibo found Black consciousness to account for a substantial amount of variance in personal causation. Blacks with higher amounts of Black consciousness or psychological Blackness also evidenced more intrinsic-communal motivation in their story protocols. In another study, Azibo (1983b) found that Blacks obtaining higher scores on Williams' Black Personality Questionnaire also rated photographs of Black females as more attractive and more favorable than photographs of White females. Low scorers rated the Black and White photographs practically equivalent.

Finally, Gibson (1984) expanded upon Azibo's (1983a) findings on the relationship between Black consciousness and personal causation that was conceptualized in terms of internal-external locus of control (I-E). Gibson used the African Self-Consciousness (ASC) scale, an Africentric measure of Black consciousness, and a culturally sensitive (Africentric) measure of the I-E construct. The Africentric I-E measure defined externality in terms of collective efficacy and corporate responsibility consistent with the communal-holistic principles of African cosmology (Baldwin, 1980b; Dixon, 1976; Nobles, 1980), and it also emphasized item content relevant to African American everyday life experiences. Gibson administered the ASC scale and the Africentric I-E measure to 50 Black college students and found a significant positive correlation between ASC scale scores and external personal causation scores. Those students who obtained higher ASC scale scores also tended to be more externally (collective-communal) oriented in their explanations of causality and determinism in their lives than were the low ASC scale scoring students. Gibson speculated on the basis of her findings that perhaps African self-consciousness fosters Africentric attributions.

At the present time, there has been very little Africentric focused research (Baldwin & Bell, 1985; Gibson, 1984) that has specifically attempted to empirically assess African self-consciousness as it is defined by Baldwin's (1981) theory. It is vital, of course, that the instruments used to assess this critical aspect of the Black personality be derived from the construct itself. Thus, the ASC scale, which is based on the Africentric personality theory of Joseph Baldwin (1980a, 1981, 1984; Baldwin & Bell, 1985), was used to assess African self-consciousness in that study.

## Purpose of the Research and Hypothesis

As noted previously, it is asserted by authorities in this area that the Black personality, in terms of African self-consciousness, plays a significant role in generally all aspects of African Americans' psychological functioning and behavior. Given the perspective generated by the findings of African self-consciousness research to date, it seems worthwhile to further assess the relationship between African self-consciousness and other important behaviors and circumstances of African Americans. We are particularly interested in this study in examining degrees of African self-consciousness among Blacks in diverse social settings of American society.

The purpose of this research, then, is to examine the possible influence of diverse social settings and certain background characteristics on African self-consciousness in Black college students. Although this study is largely exploratory, it is expected that Black students from a predominantly Black university setting will possess a greater African self-consciousness than will Black students from a predominantly White university setting. This expectation is based on the general notion in Black personality theory that Blacks in a predominantly Black setting should be more socialized into the African American cultural reality and therefore have healthier Black personalities than Blacks do in a predominantly White setting (Baldwin, 1981, 1984; Williams, 1981). In a Black setting, one naturally comes into more frequent contact with other Blacks and should be exposed to a higher frequency of Africentric (Black-oriented) cultural activities and to more positive Black role models than would likely occur in a predominantly White setting. Hence, it is predicted that Black students from the predominantly Black setting will possess a higher degree of African self-consciousness in terms of higher ASC scale scores than will Black students from the predominantly White setting.

## Methods

### SUBJECTS

The subjects were 250 Black college students, 125 from Florida A&M University (FAMU) and 125 from Florida State University (FSU) in Tallahassee, Florida. The subjects from FAMU were enrolled in introductory psychology courses; the FSU subjects were acquired through the Black Student Union and Black studies classes. Regarding sex distributions, both groups had more females than males—FSU had 11 more females than FAMU, and FAMU had nine more males than FASU.

## INSTRUMENTS

The instruments used in this research consisted of the ASC scale developed by Baldwin and Bell (1982, 1985) and a background questionnaire developed by the authors. The ASC scale is a 42-item Black personality questionnaire designed to assess African self-consciousness. It comprises four competency and six expressive dimensions. The four competency dimensions are as follows: (1) awareness/recognition of one's African identity and heritage; (2) general ideological and activity priorities placed on Black survival, liberation, and proactive-affirmative development; (3) specific activity priorities placed on self-knowledge and self-affirmation, i.e., Africentric values, customs, institutions, etc.; (4) a posture of resolute resistance toward anti-Black forces and threats to Black survival in general. The six manifest or expressive dimensions cover the areas of education, family, religion, cultural activities, interpersonal relations, and political orientation (Baldwin & Bell, 1985).

The ASC scale items alternate from negative skewing toward African self-consciousness (where low scores index the construct) to positive skewing toward African self-consciousness (where high scores index the construct). Odd numbered items are negatively skewed for the African self-consciousness construct, and are scored as the reverse of their scaled values (i.e., an odd scaled value of 8 = 1, 7 = 2, 6 = 3, etc.), and even numbered items are positively skewed for the construct and are scored by computing their scaled scores directly. Responses occur on a four-point scaling system, ranging from strongly disagree to strongly agree responses. The final ASC scale score can be computed as either the total score (sum) or the mean total score (sum of scores/ number of items). The ASC scale can be individually or group administered in about 20 minutes. Preliminary testing of the scale has generated reliability coefficients in the 90s range (test-retest), and validity coefficients in the 70s range (Baldwin & Bell, 1985; Gibson, 1984).

A background questionnaire was also administered to these subjects. Among the background variables examined were sex, marital status, educational level, number of Black Studies courses, college major, place of birth, family size, family type, region of country during childhood, racial composition of childhood region, racial composition of childhood school, birthplace of parents, race of parents, occupation of parents, educational level of parents, childhood region parents reared in, and type of region parents reared in. This measure required about 10 minutes to complete.

PROCEDURES

The ASC scale and background questionnaire were administered to the students at the two universities under both individual and group testing arrangements. Instructions emphasized that there were no right or wrong responses and that responses were merely a reflection of the subject's own feelings. The subjects were allowed to look over the instruments and raise any questions they had before the testing began. All testing was administered by the same person. The FAMU data were obtained through regular psychology classes, and the FSU data were obtained from students enrolled in Black Studies classes and those attending Black student union meetings.

**Results**

The primary data in this research consisted of ASC scale mean total scores for each student from the two university settings, and frequencies of high and low ASC scale scores and of the various levels of the background variables. These data were analyzed using the chi-square, analysis of variance, and the $t$-test statistical procedures.

In the first analysis, the background data collected on the subjects were examined for significant trends relative to ASC scoring patterns. The scores on the ASC scale were divided into high and low ASC group categories. The high ASC group consisted of those subjects whose ASC scale mean scores were 5.0 and above, and the low ASC group consisted of those subjects whose ASC scale mean scores were 4.99 and below. The frequencies for the ASC scale groups × the background categories were analyzed using the chi-square ($\chi^2$) test. The data were analyzed in each setting separately. The results of the analysis for the FAMU (predominantly Black) setting revealed no significant differences in frequencies between the background variables and the ASC groups (although there were several tendencies in the direction of a significant effect, e.g., educational level, age, and childhood school). On the other hand, there were some significant differences indicated in the FSU (predominantly White) setting. These significant findings occurred in relation to the following variables: educational level × ASC, $\chi^2(4, N = 125) = 15.808$, $p < .01$; number of Black Studies courses × ASC, $\chi^2(1, N = 125) = 6.69$, $p < .01$; and categorical age (young/old) × ASC, $\chi^2(1, N = 125) = 10.033$, $p < .01$. These significant findings for the FSU data indicate the following: More FSU upperclassmen (juniors and seniors) obtained higher ASC scores than underclassmen (freshmen and sophomores). Similarly, more FSU students who were 20 years old and older obtained higher ASC scores than did younger students (19 years old and younger). Also, more FSU students who had taken one or more Black Studies courses obtained higher ASC scores than students who had not taken Black Studies courses.

The analysis of variance was used to examine the relationship between the two university settings and the background data based on ASC scale mean scores. This analysis determined whether any significant differences, in terms of main effects and interactions, occurred between these variables. The results are summarized in Table 21.1. These results revealed several significant main effects and two significant interactions. As can be observed, for analyses 1–6 and 8–11, a significant main effect was obtained for the setting variable. The ASC scale scores for the predominantly Black setting were consistently higher than for the predominantly White setting. There were also significant differences found in analyses 1, 3, and 4 for the background variables of age, educational level, and Black Studies courses. Specifically, analysis 1, age, indicates that older students obtained significantly higher ASC scores (mean $(M) = 5.33$) than younger students $(M = 5.06)$. The $t$-test was also computed on these data within each setting and again significant differences occurred between the younger and older students: FAMU $t(123) = 3.57$, $p < .001$ and FSU $t(123) = 3.45$, $p < .001$.

Analysis 3, educational level, indicates that upperclassmen $(M = 5.55)$ obtained significantly higher ASC scores than underclassmen $(M = 5.14)$. Analysis 4, Black Studies courses, indicates that students who had taken one or more Black Studies courses obtained significantly higher ASC scores $(M = 5.57)$ than students who had not taken any Black Studies courses $(M = 5.17)$. Further $t$-test analyses of these data within each setting did not yield any significant differences. Hence, only in the case of age were significant differences maintained within each setting.

Additionally, analyses 3 and 7 revealed significant interactions for the setting × background variables. For analysis 3, the setting × educational level interaction $(F(4, 250) = 4.357$, $p < .002)$ indicates that

**TABLE 21.1** ANOVA Summary Table on the Effects of the Two University Settings and the Background Variables on ASC Scale Scores

| | Source of Variation | (df) | F | P |
|---|---|---|---|---|
| 1 | Setting (A) | 1 | 6.497 | .01 |
| | Age (B) | 1 | 21.493 | .001 |
| | A × B | 1 | 0.401 | NS |
| 2 | Setting (A) | 1 | 5.232 | .02 |
| | Sex (B) | 1 | 0.002 | NS |
| | A × B | 1 | 1.607 | NS |
| 3 | Setting (A) | 1 | 11.109 | .001 |
| | Educational Level (B) | 4 | 7.855 | .001 |
| | A × B | 4 | 4.375 | .002 |
| 4 | Setting (A) | 1 | 5.045 | .01 |
| | Black Studies Courses (B) | 1 | 16.969 | .001 |
| | A × B | 1 | 0.326 | NS |
| 5 | Setting (A) | 1 | 5.617 | .02 |
| | Family Size (B) | 1 | 0.502 | NS |
| | A × B | 1 | 0.029 | NS |
| 6 | Setting (A) | 1 | 4.311 | .04 |
| | Childhood Community (B) | 3 | 1.137 | NS |
| | A × B | 3 | 0.907 | NS |
| 7 | Setting (A) | 1 | 3.530 | NS |
| | Childhood School (B) | 3 | 2.079 | NS |
| | A × B | 3 | 2.618 | .05 |
| 8 | Setting (A) | 1 | 4.154 | .09 |
| | Birthplace of Mother (B) | 3 | 1.374 | NS |
| | A × B | 3 | 0.750 | NS |
| 9 | Setting (A) | 1 | 5.073 | .02 |
| | Birthplace of Father (B) | 3 | 0.368 | NS |
| | A × B | 2 | 2.157 | NS |
| 10 | Setting (A) | 1 | 6.714 | .01 |
| | Types of Region of Mother (B) | 2 | 0.845 | NS |
| | A × B | 2 | 1.794 | NS |
| 11 | Setting (A) | 1 | 6.970 | .009 |
| | Types of Region of Father (B) | 2 | 0.442 | NS |
| | A × B | 2 | 1.577 | NS |

FAMU upperclassmen obtained higher ASC scale scores ($M = 6.36$) than either FSU upperclassmen ($M = 5.36$) or FSU underclassmen ($M = 5.03$), whereas FAMU underclassmen's ASC scores ($M = 5.25$) were only higher than FSU underclassmen. For analysis 7, the setting × childhood school interaction ($F(3, 249) = 2.618, p < .05$) indicates that FAMU students who attended an all-Black childhood school obtained

**TABLE 21.2** Cell Means for the Significant Interactions

|  |  | Setting | | Row |
|  |  | FAMU | FSU | Means |
| --- | --- | --- | --- | --- |
| Educational | Freshman | 5.26 | 5.04 | 5.11 |
| Level | Sophomore | 5.25 | 5.02 | 5.17 |
|  | Junior | 5.35 | 5.30 | 5.33 |
|  | Senior | 6.88 | 5.39 | 6.14 |
|  | Column Means | 5.50 | 5.26 |  |
| Childhood | All-Black | 5.92 | 5.11 | 5.68 |
| School | Majority Black | 5.40 | 5.20 | 5.30 |
|  | Evenly Integrated | 5.31 | 5.38 | 5.35 |
|  | Majority White | 5.34 | 5.24 | 5.28 |
|  | Column Means | 5.50 | 5.25 |  |

higher ASC scores overall ($M = 5.92$) than did the other FAMU students and all of the FSU students. Only the FSU students who attended evenly integrated childhood schools obtained marginally higher ASC scores ($M = 5.38$) than did FAMU students from similar backgrounds ($M = 5.31$). The means for these two interactions are presented in Table 21.2.

## Discussion

The hypothesis of this study predicted that the students from the predominantly Black university setting would exhibit a higher degree of African self-consciousness, in terms of higher ASC scale scores, than would students from the predominantly White university setting. The significant difference in ASC scores occurring between the FAMU and FSU students clearly supports this hypothesis. The FAMU students obtained significantly higher ASC scores than did the FSU students. These findings suggest that a predominantly Black academic setting may indeed have a more positive influence on African self-consciousness than does a predominantly White setting. At least this does appear to have been the case in these findings. Perhaps, as the underlying theory suggests, this effect might possibly be caused by a greater likelihood of the occurrence of pro-Black norms, social expectancies, and reinforcements in such a setting (Baldwin, 1981, 1984). Hence, the African self-consciousness behavior (i.e., pro-Black behavior) of Black students in a predominantly Black university setting could be more frequently or more strongly reinforced than might be the case in a predominantly White university setting. In other words, it is probably more socially acceptable in a predominantly Black setting for Blacks to display more "pro-Black consciousness" attitudes and behaviors than not. On the other hand, it would be more socially unacceptable in a predominantly White setting to display pro-Black consciousness attitudes and behaviors (or anything other than pro-White attitudes and behaviors). However, this is mere conjecture at this point since these notions were not directly tested in this study. Although we have no way of ascertaining why these differences actually occurred, it is noteworthy that they are most consistent with relevant theoretical formulations. Further study is needed to fully explain the meaning of this finding relative to the underlying theory.

At any rate, the significant relationships found between some of the background variables and ASC scale scoring patterns enabled us to clarify somewhat the nature of the African self-consciousness construct in these kinds of social settings. For example, a second major finding of this study revealed that significantly more students with Black Studies backgrounds obtained significantly higher ASC scores than did students without the experience. This finding suggests, as would be expected (Crawford, 1980), that Black Studies exposure more than likely helped to increase the level of cultural awareness, i.e., African self-consciousness, of those students with this experience. The fact that significantly more students in the predominantly White setting with this exposure obtained higher ASC scores than did their same-setting peers further indicates the strong positive influence of Black Studies exposure on African self-consciousness. Through the teaching of positive knowledge about the African and African American heritage and culture, and pro-Black experiences in general, Black Studies courses would appear to strengthen African self-consciousness in Black students. At least this appears to have been the case in this study.

A third major finding of this study revealed that FAMU students with predominantly Black elementary school backgrounds obtained higher ASC scores than did other FAMU students or FSU students from similar or dissimilar backgrounds. This finding suggests that substantially pro-Black elementary school experience could provide a more solid foundation for a stronger African self-consciousness development later in life. The differences in ASC scores associated with this finding could possibly be explained by the idea that African self-consciousness is best cultivated or nurtured when it is in a predominantly Black setting. Consistent with Baldwin's (1981, 1984) theory, Black institutions should naturally provide better supports and reinforcements for African self-consciousness development. On the other hand, integrated elementary schools could possibly have a more inhibiting or weakening and/or distorting effect on the African self-consciousness potential of the Black students so exposed. Although these are mostly speculations, as already noted, they are most consistent with the theoretical model undergirding this research.

Two other related findings of this research revealed that older students, and significantly more upper level college students, obtained significantly higher ASC scores than did younger, lower level students. Also, while the educational level difference was more pronounced for FAMU upper level students relative to FSU students, the age effects were equally true of both settings. These findings taken together suggest that the longer the length of time in college, and the older the student, both appear to have a positive effect on African self-consciousness, especially in a predominantly Black college setting. These findings further suggest that some primary and secondary school experiences (such as integrated school) might possibly have a more inhibiting or weakening affect on African self-consciousness in Black students (Baldwin, 1979) than does college experience. This explanation, when buttressed by the preceding one relating to predominantly Black elementary school experience, would seem to be quite tenable.

We are admittedly a little surprised at not finding any additional significant patterns among the variety of background variables examined. Although we strongly suspect that other aspects of significant variance probably lie within the background factors' area of focus, our measure apparently did not operate at the level of sensitivity necessary to ferret out some other suspected relationships in this area. Perhaps a background measure emphasizing more interpersonal and active social relations, as well as more culturally specific content, would provide the necessary sensitivity for discriminating other important patterns of relationships. Future research in this area should bring more clarity to this overall issue.

## IMPLICATIONS OF THE STUDY

The nature of this research was pioneering in conception and scope. As noted earlier, only a few relevant studies have been undertaken in this critical area of African American psychology (Azibo, 1983a, 1983c; Baldwin & Bell, 1985; Curry, 1981, 1984; Gibson, 1984). Beyond the studies by Baldwin and Bell (1982, 1985) and Gibson (1984), no previous research to our knowledge has explicitly assessed the construct of African self-consciousness as it is defined by Baldwin's (1981, 1984) theory, focusing on a collegiate sample from both predominantly Black and predominantly White settings. Therefore, a collegiate sample of this diversity has provided an opportunity to examine some important aspects of the applicability of the African self-consciousness construct across one example of the diverse social settings that characterize contemporary African American life. Some of this diversity was certainly represented by the two racial-cultural settings utilized in this study.

The findings of this research provide additional supporting evidence for the Africentric theory of Black personality advanced by Baldwin (1976, 1980a, 1981, 1984). We have observed in this study that social-environmental influences do appear to account for some of the variance in ASC scores. That is, the type of sociocultural settings that Blacks are in appears to influence the level of African self-consciousness that they manifest. As noted earlier, it may be speculated, based on these findings, that a predominantly Black sociocultural setting appears to have a more positive effect on the development of African self-consciousness in Black students than does a predominantly White setting. Hence, predominantly Black academic settings (and, perhaps predominantly Black experiences in general) apparently possess more intrinsic Africentric reinforcements and should probably be encouraged for Black students based on these findings. On the other hand, predominantly White or integrated academic environments may not be as strongly advisable based on these results (Baldwin, 1979, 1981, 1984). We recognize, however, that these findings are merely suggestive at this point, since the samples were not randomly drawn and the components of the two settings were not systematically examined. More definitive conclusions should await further evidence.

In addition, it might also be speculated based on the findings of this study that Black Studies curriculum exposure probably had a very positive effect on African self-consciousness development in the Black college students studied. Thus, Black Studies curricula for Black students should be encouraged according to these results. The findings of this research further seem to suggest that Black students, especially younger students, should probably begin to take Black Studies courses as early in their college training as possible to enhance their African self-consciousness. These findings also imply that the secondary school experiences of Black students may not sufficiently cultivate and reinforce African self-consciousness to the degree that they should. Perhaps the addition of Black Studies courses to the high school curriculum would help to rectify this possible developmental problem in Black students.

Although we strongly believe, as predicted by the theory (Baldwin, 1981, 1984), that other background factors probably exert a substantial influence on African self-consciousness, admittedly only a small number of these variables were found to have a relationship to ASC scores. Perhaps a revised background questionnaire emphasizing a more inter-personal/social learning and communal focus would allow us to discern other relevant background variables. It is hoped that further research in this direction will yield more fruitful results in this vital area of African self-consciousness research. This study also suggests that future research in this area might be focused on some of the specific ways in which predominantly Black and predominantly White settings act upon African self-consciousness in Black students—such as, what factors peculiar to a predominantly White setting might possibly influence variance in African self-consciousness. A similar question, of course, should be asked about predominantly Black settings.

CONCLUSIONS

A major conclusion that can be drawn from the findings of this research is that a predominantly Black academic setting correlates positively with African self-consciousness. That is, African self-consciousness appears to be stronger among Blacks in a predominantly Black academic setting than in a predominantly White academic setting. This study therefore suggests that a predominantly Black academic setting might represent a more healthy and positive environment for affirmative personality growth and development in African Americans. This study further suggests that perhaps the social integration movement in America, especially in the area of education, although possibly having some positive effects, may have also had some negative and unhealthy effects on the Black personality (Akbar, 1981; Baldwin, 1979, 1980b, 1984; Hale, 1982). A more systematic examination of this issue is no doubt needed. Relatedly, a second major conclusion that can be drawn from this study is that educational curricula specific to the Black experience also correlates positively with African self-consciousness. Thus, predominantly Black academic environments and perhaps educational experiences as well appear to have a more positive and facilitative effect on African self-consciousness, based on this research. More systematic research in this vital area should provide a more definitive empirical justification for the value of these settings and experiences to healthy Black personality.

## References

Akbar, N. (1979). African roots of Black personality. In W. D. Smith, K. H. Burley, M. H. Mosley, & W. M. Whitney (Eds.), *Reflections on Black psychology.* Washington, DC: University Press of America.

Akbar, N. (1981). Mental disorder among African Americans. *Black Books Bulletin, 7*(2), 18-25.

Akbar, N. (Luther X). (1984). Awareness: The key to Black mental health. *The Journal of Black Psychology, 1*(1), 30-37.

Azibo, D. A. (Donald F. Allen). (1983a). *African (Black) personality theory, status characteristics theory and perceived belief similarity: Which is predominante in dominance/reactance behavior?* Unpublished doctoral dissertation, Washington University in St. Louis.

Azibo, D. A. (Donald F. Allen). (1983b). Perceived attractiveness and Black personality: Black is beautiful when the psyche is Black. *The Western Journal of Black Studies, 7*(4), 229-238.

Azibo, D. A. (Donald F. Allen). (1983c). Some psychological concomitants and conse-quences of the Black personality: Mental health implications. *Journal of Non-White Concerns in Personnel and Guidande, 11*(2), 59-66.

Baldwin, J. A. (1976). Black psychology and Black personality: Some issues for consid-eration. *Black Books Bulletin, 4*(3), 6-11, 65.

Baldwin, J. A. (1979). Education and oppression in the American context. *Journal of Inner City Studies, 1,* 62-83.

Baldwin, J. A. (1980a). An Africentric model of Black personality. In *Proceedings of the Fourteenth Annual Convention of the Association of Black Psychologists.* Washing-ton, DC: The Association of Black Psychologists.

Baldwin, J. A. (1980b). The psychology of oppression. In M. Asante & A. Vandi (Eds.), *Contemporary Black thought.* Beverly Hills, CA: Sage.

Baldwin, J. A. (1981). Notes on an Africentric theory of Black personality. *The Western Journal of Black Studies, 5*(3), 172-179.

Baldwin, J. A. (1983). *The Black personality research project.* Unpublished research proposal, Florida A & M University, Pcychology Department.

Baldwin, J. A. (1984). African self-consciousness and the mental health of African Americans. *The Journal of Black Studies, 15*(2), 177-194.

Baldwin, J. A., & Bell, Y. (1982). *The African self-consciousness scale manual.* Tallahassee: Florida A & M University, Psychology Department.

Baldwin, J. A., & Bell, Y. (1985). The African self-consciousness scale: An Africentric personality questionnaire. *The Western Journal of Black Studies, 9*(2), 61-68.

Crawford, Z. (1980). *The effects of Black studies exposure on racial consciousness and Black self-concept.* Unpublished doctoral dissertation, Stanford University.

Curry, A. O. (1981). *An African worldview exploratory examination of traditional attitudes, values and personality correlates of Black African people.* Unpublished doctoral dissertation, Pennsylvania State University.

Curry, A. O. (1984). *An examination of traditional attitudes and values of Black African people: A study within an African world view.* Paper presented at the Seventeenth Annual Convention of the National Association of Black Psychologists, New York.

Dixon, V. J. (1976). World views and research methodology. In L. King, V. Dixon, & W. Nobels (Eds.), *African philosophy: Assumptions and paradigms for research on Black persons.* Los Angeles: Fanon Research & Development Center.

Gibson, V. (1984). *The relationship between African self-consciousness and personal causation in Black college students.* Unpublished master's thesis, Florida A & M University.

Hale, J. (1982). *Black children: Their roots, culture and learning styles.* Provo, UT: Brigham Young University Press.

Hilliard, T. (1972). Personality characteristics of Black student activists and non-activists. In R. L. Jones (Ed.), *Black psychology.* New York: Harper & Row.

Nobles, W. (1980). African philosophy: Foundation for Black psychology. In R. L. Jones (Ed.), *Black psychology* (2nd ed.). New York: Harper & Row.

Parham, T., & Helms, J. (1981). The influence of Black students' racial identity attitudes on preferences for counselor's race. *Journal of Counseling Psychology, 28,* 250-257.

Williams, R. L. (1981). *The collective Black mind: An Afrocentric theory of Black personality.* St. Louis, MO: Williams & Associates.

# 22 Diagnosing Personality Disorder in Africans (Blacks) Using the Azibo Nosology: Two Case Studies

IRENE ATWELL
*Christopher House, Trenton, NJ*
DAUDI AJANI YA AZIBO
*Department of African American Studies*
*Temple University*

A *nosology* is an organized system for diagnosing diseases, disorders, or pathologies, as opposed to their mere enumeration. The present study compared clinical diagnoses of two African (Black) clients using two distinct diagnostic systems, the Eurocentric DSM-III-R nosology and the Africentric Azibo Nosology. The theoretical and paradigmatic importance of the comparison is that in Eurocentric psychology and psychiatry the DSM-III-R nosology is the standard diagnostic tool, whereas in the Africentric psychology literature this Euro-standard has been challenged as inadequate regarding the diagnosis of personality disorder in Africans. The practical importance of the comparison is that 18 disorders peculiar to the African personality are found in the Azibo Nosology that have no precedent in the DSM-III-R nosology. Three questions are asked in this study: (1) Does the Azibo Nosology accurately reflect the real life conditions of Africans? (2) Can the Azibo Nosology be effectually employed by a therapist? And, (3) is the Azibo Nosology superior to the DSM-III-R on each of the preceding questions? Based on the results of the two case studies presented, the answer to the three questions appears affirmative. Recommendations for conducting psychological practice with African clients are offered.

Throughout the history of Eurocentric psychology and psychiatry the diagnosis of personality functioning in Africans has been noxious. This

Gratitude is due to the reviewers for their commentaries and to Ms. Nadia Kravchenko for typing this manuscript. This article is dedicated to the memory of Mr. Frank K. Miller, the second author's father, who joined the ancestors while this article was in preparation.
Correspondence regarding this article should be addressed either to Ms. Irene Atwell, M.Ed., Christopher House, Trenton, NJ 08609 or to Daudi Ajani ya Azibo, Ph.D., Department of African American Studies, Temple University, Gladfelter Hall, Philadelphia, PA 19122.

is especially true of the diagnosis of personality disorder where early Eurocentric practice advanced diagnostical gems like *drapetomania,* in which escape behavior of an enslaved African was considered a disease of the mind, and *dysaesthesia Aethiopica,* in which resistance to enslavement by an African was seen as a hebetude of mind (Thomas & Sillen, 1972, p. 2). This kind of pernicious misrepresentation of Africans' psychological functioning (a) continued as Eurocentric psychology matured (see Guthrie, 1976), (b) directly served the maintenance of White supremacy, (c) has been immeasurably damaging to the health and welfare of Africans (e.g., Bulhan, 1981; Collins & Camblin, 1982; Dent, 1982; Sullivan, 1981; Williams, 1972, 1974; B. Wright, 1982b; B. Wright & Isenstein, 1978), and (d) has facilitated a worldwide infamy regarding Africans that at present appears to be inexpungible.

Although Eurocentric psychology is mature at 112 years of age in 1991, its diagnosis of mental disorder in Africans remains detrimental in contemporary times. H. Myers and King (1980) reported statistics that showed a trend toward the disproportionate diagnosis of Africans as having more severe and more antisocial conditions. Some examples are acute and chronic brain syndromes, suicide (as conceived Eurocentrically, but see B. Wright [1981, 1985 ch. 2]), and unsocialized aggressive conduct disorder. Such conditions have poor prognoses. Does this state of affairs represent a valid phenomenon or the continued praxis of White supremacy maintenance in Eurocentric psychology? It is revealing that there is an alarming trend toward drug treatment and nonpsychiatric incarceration (removal) of the Africans so diagnosed, as H. Myers and King pointed out. B. Wright (1982a) also noted that the trend in treatment, when provided, was increasingly toward drug therapy.

Regarding personality order in Africans, Eurocentric psychology has, at best, obscured the matter. In Akbar's (1981) judgment, it was as late as 1951 that the first discussion emanating from the Eurocentric view of African personality that warranted serious attention was produced by Kardiner and Ovesey. Even so, theirs was akin to the standard negative and pejorative view that characterized the Eurocentric conception of the African personality (Azibo, in press a, in press b).

## African Psychology's Remedy

Considering that Eurocentric psychological practice obscures the order and malevolently distorts the disorder in African personality, it follows that etiological perspectives on (e.g., Nobles, 1986, ch. 1) and

intervention in (e.g., Azibo, in press c) African psychological functioning have been less than adequate. Historically, African psychologists'
response to this dismal state of affairs has been multifaceted: reactive
protest, capitulation, and the proactive production of alternatives, some
deriving strictly from an Africentric thought base and some not (see
Azibo, 1989a).

*The Azibo Nosology.* Regarding the diagnosis of African personality disorder, a profound alternative that is strictly Africentric and remedies the
problems discussed above has been advanced. It is the *Azibo Nosology.*
The unfamiliar reader should see the complete presentation of the Azibo
Nosology (Azibo, 1989b). What follows is a limited discussion designed
to provide a basic introduction to the nosology's structural pillars of correct
orientation, misorientation, and mentacide. The Azibo Nosology is

> a diagnostic system of ordered and disordered African (Black) personality
> functioning . . . [that] systematizes 18 of the disorders of the African per-
> sonality (a) with one another and (b) with the nosological system prevalent
> in Euro-American psychology (DSM-III). (Azibo, 1989b, p. 173)

The nosology itself is yoked to an Africentric conceptualization of
ordered or normal African personality. When an African's beliefs,
values, attitudes, and behaviors are oriented (a) to recognize himself or
herself as an African, (b) to prioritize African interests, survival, and
proactive development, (c) to respect and perpetuate all things that are
African, and (d) to support a standard of conduct that neutralizes people
and things that are anti-African, he or she is said to be correctly oriented.
"Correct orientation is described as genetic Blackness plus psychological Blackness . . . [which means] that conscious manifestation of African-
centered psychological and behavioral functioning in genetically Black
persons" (Azibo, 1989b, p. 182). This is normalcy for the African
personality, according to African personality theory (see Azibo, in press
a, in press b). For example, correct orientation as just presented is
virtually the same as African self-consciousness, the normalcy construct in Baldwin's advanced Africentric theory of Black personality
(see Baldwin, 1981, 1984). It has been contended that the sum total of
an African's psychological functioning, including that which is relevant
to the maintenance of the Race and the more mundane which may not
be race-maintenance relevant, can be properly construed within this
general African personality theory context (Azibo, 1983a, in press a).

It is from this context that the Azibo Nosology explains personality disorganization and disorder. The most fundamental disorder is Joseph Baldwin's concept of psychological misorientation. Indeed, it may be etiologically responsible for additional disorders—including both the mundane and race-maintenance relevant types. (This issue is discussed below in light of evidence from the case studies.) Misorientation, not to be confused with disorientation, is manifest when an African proceeds from or negotiates the environment with a conceptual base in which African-centered psychological and behavioral elements are not the operative ones. Rather, European-centered, Arab-centered, or other non-African-centered cognitive elements are operative in the conceptual base. An African so afflicted manifests an orientation to reality that does not promote the maintenance of his or her Race, but promotes instead the maintenance of the non-African group whose cognitive elements are operative in his/her psyche—including those that are anti-African! Hence the fundamentality of the misorientation concept and the sheer brilliance of Dr. Joseph Baldwin in the chosen nomenclature itself.

Because misorientation and correct orientation are relative matters of degree, *misorientation* is described as genetic Blackness minus psychological Blackness (see Azibo, 1989, pp. 184–185). Baldwin's African self-consciousness construct could be used instead of the psychological Blackness nomenclature. As pointed out elsewhere (Azibo, 1989b, in press b; Baldwin, 1984), particular types of misorientation can be distinguished (see Table 22.1).

Frequently, there are systematic workings that deplete an African's psychological Blackness/African self-consciousness or preclude its development. *Mentacide* is the name given for this multifarious systematic destruction that militates against correct orientation. Not only does mentacide produce misorientation by alienating the African from his or her correct orientation, but it can discombobulate the more mundane aspects of personality dealt with by the DSM-III-R as well (Azibo, 1989b).

Hopefully, it can be seen from this brief discussion of the Azibo Nosology's pillars (correct orientation, misorientation, and mentacide) that it is an attempt to deal sophisticatedly with personality disorder in Africans. It outright subsumes DSM-III-R type conditions and locates them relative to conditions of African personality disorder. Regarding the latter, the most up-to-date constructs and concepts are included. Eighteen of these disorders have been identified in the works of various theorists and practitioners. Sixteen of these are predisposed, and perhaps precipitated, by misorientation and mentacide.

Table 22.1 lists the disorders for a quick reference. The reader should note that the Azibo Nosology is a nosology, not a mere enumerative aggregation of concepts found in the literature. That is, the Azibo Nosology is designed to depict the systematic unfolding of disorder in the African personality. It should, therefore, provide a more accurate diagnosis than other nosologies.

The second author has received numerous personal communications from practicing clinicians that laud and attest to the nosology's clinical accuracy and viability. Also, in the Minority Mental Health Program (now discontinued) at Washington University and the MS program in community/school psychology at Florida A & M University the nosology has been incorporated into the graduate psychology curriculum thanks to the foresight of Drs. Robert L. Williams and Joseph A. Baldwin, respectively.

Such testimony provides encouragement regarding the usefulness of the Azibo Nosology. Clinical research, however, is needed to further buttress the compelling treatise that the Azibo Nosology represents. First of all, does it accurately reflect the reality of the African condition in real life? If yes, then does it lend itself to effectual employment by a therapist? And, on both questions, is the Azibo Nosology superior to the Eurocentric nosology that is called the DSM-III-R? The need for an answer to this question is acute: B. Wright (1982b) has argued an increasingly popular position about the DSM-III-R's efficacy as an insidious weapon used against Africans. It is likely that the concerns about the DSM-III-R are equally as applicable to the *International Classification of Diseases*. Two case studies will help answer these three question.

## First Case Study

Erica Jones is a 29-year-old, Black, single mother of three. She presented as lively, very attractive, and extremely motivated to respond.

*Reason for Entering Treatment.* Erica reported experiencing chest pains, shortness of breath, and palpitations of the heart. She was diagnosed with Panic Disorder. Upon initial contact, Erica went on to explain that she was being treated by her medical doctor for a multitude of complaints involving these symptoms and others. Erica elaborated that quite recently she had begun to experience chest pains so extreme that she had to be seen in hospital emergency rooms. However, her last two episodes of chest pains and other symptoms resulted in her being rushed

**TABLE 22.1** Personality Disorders Found in the Azibo Nosology

| Disorder | Theorist/Practitioner |
|---|---|
| Major Predisposing Disorders | |
|     1. psychological misorientation | Joseph A. Baldwin (1984) |
|     2. mentacide | Bobby Wright (1979; see Olomenji, 1985) |
|     3. alienating mentacide | Daudi Ajani ya Azibo (1989b) |
|     4. peripheral mentacide | Daudi Ajani ya Azibo (1989b) |
| Particular Types of Misorientation/Disorders Subclassed Under Misorientation (5-7) | |
|     5. Negromachy | Charles Thomas (1971) |
|     6. alien-self disorder | Na'im Akbar (1981) |
|     7. anti-self disorder | Na'im Akbar (1981) |
| Other Disorders of the African Personality | |
|     8. materialistic depression | Harun Black, Harold Braithwaite, Kevin Taylor (1980) |
|     9. individualism | See Vernon Dixon (1976, pp. 65-66) and Haki Madhubuti (1978, pp. 122-123) |
|     10. sexual misorientation | Daudi Ajani ya Azibo (1989b) |
|     10a. sex obsession | Frances Welsing (1988; see Azibo, 1989b) |
|     11. WEUSI anxiety | Robert L. Williams (1981) |
|     12. reactionary disorders | Daudi Ajani ya Azibo (1989; see Fanon, 1963, pp. 249-311) |
| Reactionary Disorders of Current Moment (13-15) | |
|     13. psychological brainwashing | Frantz Fanon (1963; pp. 285-289) |
|     14. psychological burnout | Daudi Ajani ya Azibo, 1989b; see Madhubuti, 1978, pp. 136-138) |
|     15. oppression violence reactions | Daudi Ajani ya Azibo (1989b) |
|     16. self-destructive disorders | Na'im Akbar (1981) |
|     17. organic disorders | Na'im Akbar (1981) |
|     18. theological misorientation | Daudi Ajani ya Azibo (1989b) |
| Disorder | |
|     18a. Jonestown syndrome | Frances Welsing (1981) |
|     18b. theological alienation | Daudi Ajani ya Azibo (1989b) |

to the emergency room where she was diagnosed as a possible heart attack victim. Later, that was ruled out. A series of tests was completed, with no medical explanation of why the chest pains and a variety of symptoms continued. Erica's doctor referred her to the Community Mental Health Center (CMHC), and she was diagnosed with Panic Disorder. She continued to manifest anxiety and the following symptoms:

shortness of breath, palpitations of the heart, trembling and shaking, stomach pain, chest pain, and feeling out of control.

As treatment progressed, it was learned that Erica's childhood was characterized by a series of irreconcilable themes and values. Erica and a younger sister were born into an interracial marriage: father Black and Protestant; mother White and Catholic. Erica reported that her parents divorced when she was about 6 years old. Her mother returned to Italy, leaving Erica and her younger sister to be reared by the paternal grandmother.

As treatment continued it was learned that:

1. Erica experienced significant loss with the sudden absence of her mother. Her grandmother alluded to the idea that the reason why Erica's mother left was due to the fact that she didn't want Black children. This created a sense of guilt, shame, low self-esteem, and no sense of worth.

   Then there would be times, according to Erica, that her grandmother told them to take pride in their Black heritage but not to be ashamed of being partly White. Again, this enhanced guilt and shame. It also caused significant conflict around which culture to identify with as each one, according to Erica's grandmother, did not want to accept her.

2. Although Erica's father and paternal grandmother were Protestants, they sent Erica and her sister to Catholic schools. Erica reported that the only belief that her grandmother and Catholicism agreed upon was that there was only one God. Issues concerning the form of worship became very salient and conflictual. This left Erica as a young girl and adolescent in the middle of a controversy that she had neither knowledge of nor power to resolve.

3. Erica's father remarried, fathered another child, and left Erica at age 12 to be parented primarily by her aging grandmother. It was thus substantiated that she was "unwanted." She reports that her father's interactions with her decreased sharply and he paid little attention to her ideas, behavior, or values.

4. Promiscuity was responded to very casually in her family. According to Erica, when female members in her family, including her younger sister, dated older men and became sexually involved and received gifts, significant family members were mute. Some had children out of wedlock with no great repercussions from the family. However, she recalls being verbally assaulted and eventually asked to leave the family home when her grandmother discovered that she was pregnant. Erica gave birth to her oldest son at age 16. There was significant conflict over the birth of her

son because he was fathered by an Italian. She returned to the family home when the child was approximately 8 months old. This occurred after living with the child's father, several different girlfriends, and finally, living in a shelter for a couple of weeks.

Erica tearfully remembered this episode in her life as one of the most demeaning, and yet, very significant. The father of her son supported her financially for approximately a year. Racial harmony became more difficult and racial strife was exacerbated as Erica could not align to a Black/White culture. Instead, she fluctuated between the two cultures. Her son's father eventually separated from her. This left her without income and forced her to stay with friends. She was permitted to return home, but only after neighbors and friends began to gossip about her situation and the possibility of the state intervening to file guardianship papers for her son because of nonpermanent and unstable residence.

Erica confided that she didn't understand why her family identified with the Black culture, since identification with Blackness was associated with shame, poverty, and discrimination. She had given them a grandchild who had White parentage, and no one seemingly accepted this child.

Erica had two more sons, only one fathered by a Black male. That child was placed in the care of a relative.

A salient factor in the treatment process with Erica was reviewing her original diagnosis and then determining the cause of her chest pains. After a significant period of time in treatment and great apprehension coupled with denial was overcome, Erica was able to reveal some covert issues. It became clear that Erica did not identify with the Black race: Her relationship with her father and his obvious regard toward Whites coupled with her grandmother's conflictual stance toward both races had left Erica with the conclusion "better to be White." It was salient that her father and grandmother seemed to agree that Whites had more opportunities to achieve success, access to better housing and job opportunities, and so forth.

It was important to discern the panic attacks as a symptom and to understand that her "misorientation" had led to "alienating mentacide." *Misorientation* is defined as

a psychological state in which an African operates "without an African-centered belief system . . . [s/he] proceeds with a cognitive definitional system that is non-Black . . . [and] depleted of concepts of psychological Blackness and . . . composed of alien (i.e., non-African) concepts [like] psychological Europeanism and psychological Arabism. (Azibo, 1989b, pp. 184–185; Baldwin, 1984)

Alienating mentacide

render[s] the African's psyche void of any pro-Black orientations to life . . . simultaneously [there is] an instilling of (a) a pro-European orientation that commands . . . acceptance and admiration of and allegiance to White persons and White-dominated society . . . and (b) the relative disparagement of all things African.[1] (Azibo, 1989, p. 186)

Panic attacks occurred when Erica was confronted with her own Blackness. Continued conflict around race, values, and beliefs caused apprehension, which inevitably manifested a multitude of symptoms. Relationships ended in turmoil and sometimes assaultive behavior. Reluctance to acknowledge her Black heritage or to give credence to any contribution made by African Americans like Benjamin Bannekar, Charles Drew, Harriet Tubman, Martin Luther King, Jr., Adam Clayton Powell persisted.

Her conflictual life-style of having children and never being married did not coincide with societal values and, thereby, continued to cause her great anxiety, guilt, and shame. This was evidenced by her not wanting her acquaintances to know that she had never married, and that her children had different fathers. As these issues were addressed, Erica would manifest symptoms of distress. Frequency of sessions was decreased over a 3-6 month period, but remained on the theme. It was crucial to be persistent and not to be dissuaded from the issue. The therapist found that after Erica had been in treatment over a 3- to 6-month period, her panic attacks were also a means to manipulate and to protect herself from reality. Through observation, the therapist was able to discern that any time someone introduced a topic or issue that was in conflict with Erica's reality, that she would begin to evidence symptoms. If closure did not occur on the threatening topic, more severe symptoms would be manifested, concluding in a panic attack.

*Treatment Strategy.* Treatment included helping Erica to discuss and identify who she was, and addressing the issues of race, biracial ethnicity, values, and beliefs. Significant reading was required like *The*

*Autobiography of Miss Jane Pittman, Manchild in the Promised Land,* and so forth.[2] Erica was encouraged to seek out Black exhibits and Black arts and to be prepared to discuss their significance in the ongoing sessions. She was also encouraged to read European and African history. This permitted her to get in touch with factual reality, while dismantling the perceived utopia of White society and providing her with a basis of something to be proud of regarding U.S. African American achievements and heritage.

After approximately one year in therapy, Erica was able to feel more comfortable with the idea of her nuclear family being interracially mixed. Additionally, she had achieved a healthy regard for each cultural group. Salient factors of (1) being recognized as Black by others, (2) her rejection of this identity, and (3) having a son who was readily identifiable as Black were not as difficult for Erica. She was able to understand that her continued ambivalence toward identifying with the Black race assisted in the manifestation of panic attacks.

Erica continues to learn more historical data concerning U.S. African culture. This provides her with additional support as she addresses and resolves her issues concerning "being Black in America."

## Second Case Study

Mary Johnson is a 9-year-old Black female. She presents as angry (passive-aggressive) and verbally repressed. Hygiene and grooming are fair.

Sarah Johnson (who shall be referred to as Ms. Johnson) is a 42- to 45-year-old Black mother of four children, Mary being the youngest. She meets a demanding schedule of work and church activities that leave minimal time for parenting or socializing. There is no father in the home since divorce occurred several years ago. The father has not been involved with the family for approximately five years.

*Reason for Entering Treatment.* Mary Johnson evidences conduct disorder in the classroom as well as an inability to control temper or to verbalize complaints or conflicts prior to exploding.

Initial contact with Ms. Johnson was tentative as she presented in a surly, angry manner. Her affect was flat as she verbalized frustration with her daughter's continued inappropriate behavior. Also, she was frustrated with a system that attempted to regulate and state "how she should discipline her child." Ms. Johnson verbalized animosity toward a system that had been ineffective in helping her aid Mary to control her temper and behavior, but was critical of the use of corporal punishment. Furthermore, Ms. Johnson was able to verbalize an implied distrust of all the "reports of misconduct" attributed to Mary since she reported that Mary was often teased and treated unfairly because of her darker complexion and strong African features like broad face, wide nose, and short, thick hair.

Throughout this initial narration of complaints and frustration, this 9-year-old girl sat silent and tense. She offered no rebuttal or opinion of her actions and behavior and spoke only when spoken to directly.

After meeting with the mother and daughter three times, the therapist took note of the following issues of contention:

> Identity: Who am I? What is the relationship between me and the larger U.S. culture? Did the posturing of supervising non-Blacks lead to significant concern and self-doubt regarding her own ability and level of authority?
>
> Sexuality: Male and female behavior—society's expectations.
>
> Race: Ashamed of color, illiteracy, ignorance concerning ethnicity.
>
> Parenting: Unsure of skills of self, appropriate way to teach love.

In the third family session, the therapist reviewed what had been misdiagnosed as a conduct disorder and reassessed it as an identity crisis, not only for the patient, Mary, but for the family. What this family had experienced in the Azibo Nosology would be "mentacide": The raping of the mind and spirit of a Black family in this case. The disorder of mentacide became so exacerbated that it began to evidence itself in Mary's behavior. (Additional diagnoses are given below.)

Mary began to touch male classmates' genitals. She had a need to confirm that the genders are different, but still human. She was asked, "Why would you touch a person in that specific area?" Initially, no response was given. Several sessions later, when she was alone with the therapist, she confided that she wanted to know what the difference was between girls and boys. Was she simply addressing sex and sexual organs? The therapist suggested NO! The therapist suggested that Mary needed to confirm gender differences and the role or position that gender permits in this society. In recent years, this society has espoused "openness" and "equal rights for women and minorities." However, there still remains a covert, implied message of what roles belong to whom. In other words, Mary's anger and frustration stemmed from an unknown factor that neither she nor her mother had influence over. What Mary did, the therapist suggests, was to attempt to confront or gain some form of clarity to the contradiction by touching the genital areas. Sessions around male and female child behavior ensued. However, the therapist took note that the mother was uncomfortable when discussion around male/female roles and behavior continued. Ms. Johnson was unsure of the following:

1. Correctness or appropriateness of her role as mother and female. Ms. Johnson verbalized conflict and guilt concerning having to leave her children in the home while she worked. Ms. Johnson's feminine/female role underwent a transformation from being mother/female = nurturer/supporter to mother/father = absolute authority. This transformation led to her being the only teacher of survival skills, values, and beliefs. Her method of teaching or conveying this was by strict discipline. This left minimal time to consider any gentler or nurturing aspect of role as mother/female.

2. Ms. Johnson, having been divorced for several years, had taken on the role of both mother and father. Having fused both roles into one, she had constricted parental guidance and supplanted it with only discipline. She ascribed to "spare the rod and spoil the child."

3. However, Ms. Johnson was quite pleased with her achievement at work. She was now at a supervisory level. This led Ms. Johnson to significant conflict. As she stated in so many words, had she sacrificed the parenting of her children for satisfaction at work?

4. Finally, Ms. Johnson was unable to discuss her ancestry, i.e., who she was, her family tree, where she came from. She evidenced signs of frailty around her own identity and role. She had no working knowledge of what it meant to be Black, but had conveyed to her children and, specifically, to Mary that indeed to be Black was something to be ashamed of and to work hard and overcome. Mentacide is apparent here. Because of Ms. Johnson's felt inferiority regarding being Black, she conveyed to Mary that the darkness of her skin was a handicap that had to be overcome. Her way (method) of teaching Mary survival skills was to encourage her to become more congruent with the larger U.S. culture and to emulate the traits thereof. Although Mary had informed her mother on several occasions that she felt abused by name-calling that was directed at her by other classmates, Ms. Johnson's response to Mary was "to pay no attention to the verbal abuse" and "do nothing or tell the teacher." However, this left Mary feeling unnurtured, unloved, confused, and without a source of reference of how to handle overt and covert acts of discrimination and bias. Name-calling like "spook," "spade," and "nigger" was hurtful to Mary. She responded to the pain by exhibiting assaultive and threatening behavior.

The therapist was able to assist mother and daughter at first separately, then in sessions together to discuss their Blackness and what it meant to them. It was important to address issues around being Black. That there was no need for shame had to be made clear. Both mother and daughter were given homework assignments to read on what African people had done in history, before and after the Mayflower.

Discussions around male and female roles, ethnicity, and values were significant in the treatment process of Ms. Johnson. From reading Black literature and learning about the history of her people, she was able to discuss pertinent conflicts that had angered her, but that she had never verbalized for fear of sounding foolish or unforgiving. Fears around self-doubt and inadequacy came spilling out as Ms. Johnson told of her own childhood on a plantation in Alabama. There, she was raised by a stepmother and father who constantly reminded her that she was Black, and that there was nothing she could do about it. She was able to tearfully relate how Blacks in the 1940s and 1950s always had to yield the right of way when they went to town. Because of the pervasive White superiority atmosphere and its continuing manifestation of anti-Black discrimination practices, violence toward Blacks, Ms. Johnson concluded, would remain prevalent. She felt that the best way to avoid it was to conform and to act in the manner that Whites felt was appropriate. So, most of the time they remained on the plantation. Additionally she related how the Blacks seemed to hate each other too. She was able to verbalize feelings of shame at being called "Black" as she was one of the darker children. Also, she expressed how she was told by family and peers that she would probably remain in the South and work because she was too Black (i.e., dark pigmentation).

From a diagnostic point of view, Ms. Johnson's misorientation is compounded by mentacide. Additionally, her misorientation includes the Negromachy condition (identified by Thomas, 1971) defined as confusion and doubt of self-worth pertaining to one's Blackness. The intergenerational transmission of African personality disorders is also apparent here.

After several sessions with Ms. Johnson, she was able to discuss some internal conflicts she felt about herself (self-doubt about her parenting and supervisory abilities) and the history of her people. As Ms. Johnson showed greater regard for herself and was impressed by the history of African people, Mary's behavior improved. Mary was encouraged to read about the contributions that African people had made throughout history. Both mother and daughter were encouraged to discuss different

Africans in history and how they felt about the contributions they had made and what role they had played. Mary was prompted to reconsider education: what it would mean for her and her family and her people. The therapist encouraged Ms. Johnson and Mary to share their new knowledge and insight with Mary's siblings at home, which Ms. Johnson and Mary informed the therapist they had been doing.

The therapist felt it was a salient factor for Ms. Johnson to share with Mary how her childhood had been, how she had felt, and how she had handled individuals calling her names because of her complexion. Ms. Johnson timidly agreed. The therapist provided support when needed, but permitted Ms. Johnson to tell her story to Mary with little interruption and to share with Mary why it was so important for her to do well in school.

Mary and Ms. Johnson were in treatment for several more months. They defined themselves in terms of Blackness and in being content with who they were. Mary's behavior continued to improve as she read more African literature, fiction and nonfiction. Genital touching abated. She determined that it was appropriate for her to have control over her temper and, for the most part, she did stop manifesting explosive behavior. She reported that when the other children began to realize that she was no longer ashamed of her color, most of the name calling stopped.

Ms. Johnson continued to need help in learning parenting skills. However, she had achieved a better perception about herself as she continued her quest for the history of her people. The last time the therapist heard from Mary, her goal was to become a nurse!

## Discussion

The interval between the initial advancement of the nosology (Azibo, 1982) and the first clinical study investigating it has been long. The results, which we would like to hope are irrefragable, have certainly been worth the wait. Regarding the 3 questions posed in the introduction, first it appears that the Azibo Nosology did indeed accurately reflect or map onto the real-life conditions of the clients. Additionally, the clients displayed some covert symptoms stemming from reaction to the hegemonic White supremacy that is ingrained in United States society. The Azibo Nosology facilitated the uncovering of these symptoms. The other nosology contributed to the masking or overlooking of these symptoms. These clients are negotiating real, relatively common life circumstances in the United States. They do not appear to be unduly atypical where African-United States clients are concerned. For example, quite similar issues and problems are apparent in many of the cases that Boyd-Franklin (1989) discussed.

Second, it is plain to see that the first author, who was the client's therapist, was able to effectually employ the nosology. Acquiring a thorough grounding in the understanding of the Azibo Nosology and related literature coupled with motivation to serve her people facilitated the therapist's effectual employment of the nosology. There were no inordinate or unduly difficult impediments inherent in the nosology that hindered its usage. On the contrary, the therapist is better able to assess disorder in the African personality through the utilization of the Azibo Nosology. This nosology provides a framework that lends itself to the examination of suppressed and covert issues peculiar to Africans. The Azibo Nosology permits the therapist to consider psychological misorientation as a major disorder in its own right and as the predisposing condition for DSM-III-R and other Azibo Nosology disorders.

Third, it would appear from the two case studies presented that the Azibo Nosology was superior to the Eurocentric DSM-III-R diagnostic system regarding (a) the accurate diagnosis of Africans' true psychological condition (mapping onto our real-life reality) and (b) its easy and effective employment. The informal shoptalk of many practitioners reveals dissatisfaction with what they consider to be the DSM-III-R's overly cumbersome and complicated nature. The Azibo Nosology is sophisticated enough to capture the fundamental reality of African personality disorganization and yet relatively uncomplicated to use. This is a major credit to this nosology (Azibo, 1989b, p. 205).

Whether the Africentric nosology yields a more accurate diagnosis of the psychological condition of Africans than does the Eurocentric nosology may be the most significant issue. The case studies demonstrate how DSM-III-R diagnoses can be overturned by diagnoses from the Azibo Nosology. This is a point to be taken in all seriousness. It appears that the DSM-III-R serves to mask and obscure the true nature of African personality disorganization, whereas the Azibo Nosology reveals and illuminates it: Erica Jones' condition was obscured by the DSM-III-R Panic Disorder diagnosis and was revealed by the Azibo Nosology diagnosis of misorientation with alienating mentacide. From the perspective afforded by the Azibo Nosology, it is apparent in the description of symptoms given in the First Case Study that additional major symptoms suggestive of Negromachy, alien- and anti-self disorders, and WEUSI anxiety were operative. Mary Johnson's DSM-III-R conduct disorder diagnosis hid the fundamental factor of the mentacide disorder undergirding the general misorientation that was the root cause of the manifest presenting problems. (See Azibo, 1989b, and Azibo, in press b, for discussion of the cited disorders and Table 22.1 for their listing.)

Given, as these case studies indicate, the inferior and obfuscatory diagnoses afforded by the DSM-III-R for problems African clients might suffer, it follows that an ensuing intervention effort would similarly be less than adequate. Although adjustment may be realized under these conditions, intervention ensuing from an Azibo Nosology diagnosis is oriented to eradicate all of the African personality disorders as well as any legitimate DSM-III-R type problems and to engender what Baldwin (1981, 1984) calls African self-consciousness or what Azibo (1989b) calls correct orientation/psychological Blackness (see Azibo, in press c). This is evident in the case studies where, in essence, the clients were provided "therapeutically-directed [psychological] Africanity development" as part of intervention. The second author has called for this before (Azibo, 1983, p. 64). Let us be reminded that Blackness (Africanity) is a tonic (Thomas, 1971).

## Recommendations

We offer five recommendations for conducting psychological practice with African clients based on the case study results. First, one must commit oneself to employ the Azibo Nosology as the base diagnostic system. It thus becomes the psychological helper's "Bible" and the Eurocentric nosologies like the DSM-III-R and the *International Classification of Diseases* are relegated to "hymnals" to be used only when a condition listed therein is not incongruous with the African social reality structure (see Azibo, 1989b). The therapist's case reports should forthrightly advance the Azibo Nosology diagnosis. A DSM-III-R diagnosis should also be written-up for two reasons: (a) if the suspected condition is not incongruous with the African social reality structure and (b) because the practical problems of hegemony elucidated elsewhere (Azibo, 1988) remains in effect. The authors are fully cognizant of laws throughout the United States requiring the Eurocentric diagnosis, especially for the therapist to receive third-party payments.

There are several gains that may obtain from advancing diagnoses from the Azibo Nosology. One is that practitioners would be forced to deal with the nosology as a legitimate classification system. Also it would further reinforce the Association of Black Psychologists as it moves seriously into the arena of sanctioning/certifying those who practice with African clients. Nobles (n.d.) has pointed out the immense potential of the Association. Another gain is the possibility of countering the practical problem of hegemony explained elsewhere (Azibo, 1988). Persons in appropriate positions of authority could require or somehow persuade practitioners to include diagnoses from the Azibo Nosology—if they wish to receive payment, or to receive referrals, and so on. From this, any number of developments could result, including the dismissal of the authority person who advocates usage of the Azibo Nosology if he or she is not shrewd.[3] If the practitioner refuses to use the Azibo Nosology or uses it ineptly, then maybe that would be grounds for terminating his or her services. The void could then be filled by an African Psychology practitioner with requisite competency. To sidestep termination and related administrative fallout, the practitioner-contractor might be persuaded to refer the client to an African Psychology practitioner for a diagnosis from the Azibo Nosology. Intervention consultation might also be arranged. This is an illustration of how "team practice" could be institutionalized. The advances in the African personality field necessitate these kinds of developments (see Azibo, in press c).

The second recommendation is to overcome "the naivete of the psychological helper" (Azibo, in press c) by becoming grounded in the African psychology discipline. Special emphasis must be placed on African personality theory and research. Some starter references might be Akbar (1981, 1985), Azibo (1989a, 1989b, in press a, in press b, in press c), Baldwin (1980, 1984, 1986, 1987, 1989), Jackson (1979), Karenga (1982, ch. 8), Nobles (1976, 1986), Semaj (1981), and Williams (1981).

Conducting additional research on the nosology is the third recommendation. More case studies, incidence and prevalence studies, and attempts to tackle the research issues identified in the presentation of the nosology (see Azibo, 1989b) must be forthcoming. Special mention must be given to the research issues posed by the "Baldwin Hypothesis." Dr. Joseph Baldwin, with input from colleagues Drs. Raeford Brown and Yvonne Bell, has argued at various professional meetings that a DSM-III-R type of disorder can obtain in an African only if he or she is already misoriented. That is, it is not possible for the African personality to suffer what might be a DSM-III-R type of malady unless psychological misorientation is or has been manifested. This is a provocative etiological perspective. And, our case study results are consistent with the Baldwin Hypothesis contention: in both cases a preexisting misorientation disorder(s) was a precursor to the condition diagnosed using the DSM-III-R. Azibo (in press b) addresses the Baldwin Hypothesis further. For now, it shall suffice to note the following:

(a) The Baldwin Hypothesis is presented here in its most general formulation. When, and if, it is put in writing by its original articulators, there may be caveats and particulars not mentioned here.

(b) Is the degree of psychological misorientation an operative variable regarding this hypothesis?

(c) Similarly, is the type of DSM-III-R disorder an operative variable here?

(d) What about persons who by most indications are correctly oriented (defined in Azibo, 1989b) with a high degree of African self-consciousness (Baldwin, 1981, 1984), but apparently suffer a disorder either of the DSM-III-R type or the Azibo Nosology? For instance, are there not persons suffering from sexual misorientation or depression who otherwise appear correctly oriented? The answer to this question was presumed affirmative in the initial publication of the nosology (Azibo, 1989b). The Baldwin Hypothesis plausibly counters, however, by contending that disorders in the otherwise correctly oriented African probably predated that person's attainment of correct orientation or African self-consciousness. In other words, because of the anti-African hegemony and oppression that is inherent in Eurocentric culture (see Baldwin, 1985; Richards, 1989), many Africans may bring disorders accrued under the Eurocentric order with them as they achieve African self-consciousness or psychological liberation.

The fourth recommendation is that clinicians and theorists attempt to discover additional disorders or syndromes within the logic system of the Azibo Nosology. It is expected that disorders as yet unidentified will be documented. The Azibo Nosology has shown the capacity to incorporate new disorders (Azibo, 1989b).

Development of Africentric psychotherapies that are oriented to induce the personality order state of correct orientation (and correct psychological and behavioral functioning if possible) to which the Azibo Nosology is yoked is the fifth recommendation. Belief Systems Analysis (Myers, 1988) and NTU Psychotherapy (Phillips, 1989) are promising. Research is important here too.

In conclusion, as the African psychological community takes up these recommendations, the African psychology discipline will grow and be further substantiated. It is inescapable as well that our theory, research, and practice will come on line with liberation dictates per Baldwin's (1989) and Azibo's (in press b) observations. The related work is part of the revitalization of the discipline as discussed by Nobles (1986). History in the making is unfolding by our own hands and at our own pace. Our Africentric discipline is becoming an effective counterpoise to the Eurocentric psychological systems (Azibo, 1989a). The post-Eurocentric period has dawned.

## Notes

1. *Arab* can be substituted for *European* and *White* here. The Arab world is equally guilty of inflicting misorientation and alienating mentacide on Africans who are unfortunate enough to fall under Arabic political and cultural influence.

2. The actual readings were Baldwin, James (1978), *Nobody Knows My Name;* Bedini, Silvio A. (1984), *The Life of Benjamin Banneker;* Brown, Claude (1965), *Manchild in the Promised Land;* Gaines, Ernest (1982), *Autobiography of Miss Jane Pittman;* Greenlee, Sam (1985), *The Spook Who Sat by the Door;* Haley, Alex (1977), *Autobiography of Malcolm X;* and *Golden Legacy Illustrated History Magazine,* Vol. 1–16 (1983).

3. This goes beyond paradigm shift to a power and money shift. Let's face it, it will be bloody, and casualties are forecast. Victory will be a function of stealth, cunning, execution, and tenacity. Dr. Bobby Wright's work in Chicago transforming the then Garfield Park Community Mental Health Center (now named after him) stands as a model.

## References

Akbar, N. (1981). Mental disorder among African Americans. *Black Books Bulletin, 7*(2), 18-25.

Akbar, N. (1985). Nile Valley origins of the science of the mind. In I. Van Sertima (Ed.), *Nile Valley civilizations* (African Studies Department, Beck Hall, Rutgers University, New Brunswick, NJ 08903).

Azibo, D. A. (1982). *Advances in Black personality theory and implications for psychology.* Unpublished monograph.

Azibo, D. A. (1983a). *African (Black) personality theory, status characteristics theory, and perceived belief similarity: Which is dominant in dominance/reactance behavior?* Unpublished doctoral dissertation, Washington University in St. Louis.

Azibo, D. A. (1983b). Some psychological concomitants and consequences of the Black personality: Mental health implications. *Journal of Non-White Concerns in Personnel and Guidance, 11*(2), 59-66.

Azibo, D. A. (1988). Understanding the proper and improper usage of the comparative research framework. *The Journal of Black Psychology, 15*(1), 81-91.

Azibo, D. A. (1989a). *African psychology in historical perspective and related commentary.* Manuscript submitted for publication.

Azibo, D. A. (1989b). African-centered theses on mental health and a nosology of Black/African personality disorder. *The Journal of Black Psychology, 15*(2), 173-214.

Azibo, D. A. (in press a). Advances in Black/African personality theory. *Imhotep: An Afrocentric review* (Dept. of African American Studies, Temple University, Philadelphia, PA 19122).

Azibo, D. A. (in press b). *Liberation psychology.* Trenton, NJ: African World Press.

Azibo, D. A. (in press c). Treatment and training implications of the advances in African personality theory. *The Western Journal of Black Studies.*

Baldwin, J. A. (1980). The psychology of oppression. In M. Asante & A. Vandi (Eds.), *Contemporary Black thought.* Beverly Hills, CA: Sage.

Baldwin, J. A. (1981). Notes on an Africentric theory of Black personality. *The Western Journal of Black Studies, 5*(3), 172-179.

Baldwin, J. A. (1984). African self-consciousness and the mental health of African Americans. *Journal of Black Studies, 15*(2), 177-194.

Baldwin, J. A. (1985). Psychological aspects of European cosmology in American society: African and European cultures. *The Western Journal of Black Studies, 9*(4), 216-223.

Baldwin, J. A. (1986). African (Black) psychology: Issues and synthesis. *The Journal of Black Studies, 16*(3), 235-249.

Baldwin, J. A. (1987). African psychology and Black personality testing. *The Negro Educational Review, 38*(2-3), 56-66.

Baldwin, J. A. (1989). The role of Black psychologists in Black liberation. *The Journal of Black Psychology, 16*(1), 67-76.

Black, H., Braithwaite, H., & Taylor, K. (1980). *Survival manual: First aid for the mind* (4th ed.). Atlanta: Institute for Collective African Consciousness (c/o Louis A. Ramey, West Mental Health Center, 3703 Bakersferry Road, Atlanta, GA 30331).

Boyd-Franklin, N. (1989). *Black families in therapy: A multisystems approach.* New York: Guilford.

Bulhan, H. (1981). Psychological research in Africa: Genesis and function. *Race & Class, 23*(1), 25-41.

Collins, R., & Camblin, L. D., Jr. (1982). The politics and science of learning disability classification: Implications for Black children. *Black Child Journal, 4*(1), 18-25.

Dent, H. (1982). Problems surrounding IQ tests: Discrimination/mental retardation vs. learning disabilities. In A. Harvey & T. Carr (Eds.), *The Black mentally retarded offender.* New York: United Church of Christ Commission for Racial Justice.

Dixon, V. (1976). World views and research methodology. In L. King, V. Dixon, & W. Nobles (Eds.), *African philosophy: Assumptions and paradigms for research on Black persons.* Los Angeles: Fanon Research & Development Center.

Fanon, F. (1963). *The wretched of the earth.* New York: Grove Press.

Guthrie, R. (1976). *Even the rat was white: A historical view of psychology.* New York: Harper & Row.

Jackson, G. G. (1979). The origin and development of Black psychology: Implications for Black studies and human behavior. *Studia Africana, 1*(3), 270-293.

Kardiner, A., & Ovesey, L. (1951). *The mark of oppression.* New York: World.

Karenga, M. (1982). *Introduction to Black studies.* Inglewood, CA: Kawaida Publications.

Madhubuti, H. R. (1978). *Enemies: The clash of races.* Chicago: Third World Press.

Myers, H. I., & King, L. M. (1980). Youth of the Black underclass: Urban stress and mental health. *Fanon Center Journal, 1*, 1-27.

Myers, L. (1988). *Understanding an Afrocentric world view: Introduction to an optimal psychology.* Dubuque, IA: Kendall/Hunt.

Nobles, W. (1976). Black people in white insanity: An issue for Black community mental health. *Journal of Afro-American Issues, 4,* 21-27.

Nobles, W. (1986). *African psychology: Toward its reclamation, reascension and revitalization.* Oakland, CA: Institute for the Advanced Study of Black Family Life and Culture.

Nobles, W. (n.d.). *Crisis in our soul: The restoration of the National Association of Black Psychologists.* Unpublished manuscript.

Olomenji. (1985, July). Mentacide: Rape of Black minds. *The Final Call, 5*(2), 22-26.

Phillips, F. (1989). *NTU Psychotherapy: Principles and processes.* Manuscript submitted for publication.

Richards, D. M. (1989). *Let the circle be unbroken: Implications of African spirituality in the Diaspora.* Self-published (D. M. Richards, Black Studies, Hunter College, New York City).

Semaj, L. T. (1981). The Black self, identity, and models for a psychology of Black liberation. *The Western Journal of Black Studies, 5,* 158-171.

Sullivan, O. R. (1981). Who's testing Black children and youth in the public schools? *Freedomways, 21*(2), 114-118.

Thomas, A., & Sillen, S. (1972). *Racism and psychiatry.* Secaucus, NJ: Citadel.

Thomas, C. W. (1971). *Boys no more: A Black psychologist's view of community.* Beverly Hills, CA: Glencoe Press.

Welsing, F. (1981). The concept and color of God and Black mental health. *Black Books Bulletin, 7*(1), 27-29, 35.

Welsing, F. (1988). Keynote address to the 1988 Convention of the Association of Black Psychologists [Videotape].

Williams, R. L. (1971). Abuses and misuses in testing Black children. *The Counseling Psychologist, 2,* 62-73.

Williams, R. L. (1974). Danger: Testing and dehumanizing of Black children. In G. Williams & S. Garfield (Eds.), *Clinical child psychology: Current practices and future prospects.* New York: New York Behavioral Publication.

Williams, R. L. (1981). *The collective Black mind: An Afrocentric theory of Black personality.* St. Louis, MO: Williams & Associates.

Wright, B. (1979). *Mentacide.* Unpublished manuscript.

Wright, B. (1981). Black suicide: (Lynching by any other name is still lynching). *Black Books Bulletin, 7*(2), 15-19.

Wright, B. (1982a). *Dr. Bobby E. Wright: The man and his mission* [Videotape]. The Atlanta Chapter of the Association of Black Psychologists.

Wright, B. (1982b). Black mental retardation as political dynamic. In A. Harvey & T. Carr (Eds.), *The Black mentally retarded offender.* New York: United Church of Christ Commission for Racial Justice.

Wright, B. (1985). *The psychopathic racial personality and other essays.* Chicago: Third World Press.

Wright, B. J., & Isenstein, V. (1978). *Psychological tests and minorities* (DHEW Publication No. ADM. 78-482). Washington, DC: Government Printing Office.

# A Theoretical Model for the Practice of Psychotherapy With Black Populations

ANNA MITCHELL JACKSON*
*University of Colorado School of Medicine*

This article reviews selected psychotherapy and personality models advanced by Black theoreticians and proposes a scheme developed by the author for the incorporation of African and African American frames of reference into clinical and consultative activities. Facilitative and nonfacilitative variables in the implementation of the model are discussed briefly.

Traditional clinical intervention strategies have been used with Black clients with varying degrees of effectiveness (Adams, 1979; Banks, 1972; Branch, 1977; Di-Angi, 1976; Griffith, 1977; A. Jackson, 1973; and Wilson, 1974). Indeed, clinical practices as they pertain to Black populations have been based primarily on European and American constructs (Baldwin, 1976; Nobles, 1972; G. Jackson, 1977; Offer & Sabashin, 1966). Black culture, if cited at all, often is evaluated as a variant of European culture.

Increasingly, Black theoreticians have questioned the application of traditional treatment approaches to Black populations, citing as evidence the lack of congruence of these practices with the Black experience, life style, and culture (Akbar, 1977; W. Allen, 1978; Amini, 1972; Buck, 1977; Leonard & Jones, 1980; G. Jackson, 1976). In addition to race and culture, systematic and systemic practices of racism also have been noted as important in researching inequities in client diagnosis, disposition, and treatment involvement (Griffith, 1976; A. Jackson, Berkowitz, & Farley, 1974; Thomas & Sillen, 1972; Warren, Jackson, Nugaris, & Farley, 1973).

Models of personality and treatment based on African and African-American frames of reference have been proposed as corrective

Presented in fuller version under the title, "The Practice of Psychology: A Black Perspective" at the Association of Black Psychology Convention, Cherry Hills, NJ, August 16, 1980.
Anna M. Jackson, University of Colorado Medical Center, 4200 East 9th Avenue, Box C-258, Denver, CO 80262.
*EDITORS' NOTE: Currently at Meharry Medical College.

mechanisms by certain theoreticians (Baldwin, in press; Jones, 1980; Toldson & Pasteur, 1975). The stated goals of these theories by and large is the incorporation of particular aspects of Black culture thought to be germane to the adaptive functioning of Black individuals. A treatment model proposed in this paper is based on similar referents. The purpose of the model is to clarify basic underlying values and behaviors believed to be essential to the understanding of behavioral dynamics and to potential positive treatment outcomes.

## Cultural Theories

Psychological theories provide a mechanism for understanding human behavior and for developing treatment models. However, theoretical formulations are germane only to the extent that the importance of culture is recognized and relevant cultural values incorporated (Hall, 1977). In this section, selected Black cultural theories will be examined and their potential relevance to treatment of Black individuals explored. These theories collectively emphasize the importance of African values and language structure in understanding Black behavior either as maintained intact or as modified by encounters with racial discrimination (Akbar, 1977; Baldwin, in press; G. Jackson, 1979; Jones, 1980; Toldson & Pasteur, 1975; Turner, 1969; Vaas, 1979).

Cultural theories in Black psychology are characterized generally by an emphasis on "wellness" or normality instead of psychopathology. The focus on normality in turn is based on an African value system. These theories are quite discrepant with existing psychological formulations about human behavior in general and Black behavior in particular (Baldwin, 1976; Chimezie, 1973; Nobles, 1972).

Prominent among the cultural values advocated by Black psychologists are those of group-centered behavior, strong kinship bonds, inherent feeling of cooperation and sharing, enhanced sensitivity to interpersonal issues, and an over-arching religious orientation that provides structure, direction, a philosophy of the interrelatedness of all things, and a comprehensive way of interpreting the universe and life (Mibiti, 1971; Nobles, 1972). Behaviors that deviate from these norms are perceived largely as erosions of Black identity or cultural values. The prescribed task when erosions of this nature occur is one of resocialization. Notably absent in reconstructive prescriptions are concepts of disordered development and a reliance on individual recompensation except as individual efforts are influenced by group goals or extended self-identity (Baldwin, 1976; A. Jackson,

1982; Mibiti, 1971; Nobles, 1976). In illustration of the type of synthesis and philosophy described above, the theoretical formulation of several Black psychologists will be reviewed.

A noted Black theoretician, Na'im Akbar (1977), has creatively combined religious and cultural beliefs with insightful observations of Black behavior. He has stressed the absence of competitive attitudes in his writings and a pervasive sense of caring and concern as core behavioral traits that characterize Black people. A "feeling" or affective orientation is also stressed by him. These core traits are perceived as instrumental in the adaptive functioning of Black individuals; traits that have permitted Black people to deal effectively and innovatively with the malignant form of racism experienced during and following slavery. The heightened sense of caring and empathy, in his opinion, also carries with it an obligation to help establish a more stress free and equitable environment. Cooperative efforts and respect for others are cardinal tenets in his theory. Based on his writings, his perception of human motivation appears to be that basic intentions and drives are benevolent in nature and that people are propelled largely by their desires to help others. Human potential seems to be conceptualized in terms of mastery. In keeping with a strong religious orientation, Akbar has also stressed the role of naturalness in human behavior, spirituality, and the holistic organization of man and the universe in theoretical presentations (1976, 1977).

In his theoretical formulations regarding the structure of Black personality, Joseph Baldwin (in press) has emphasized the biogenetic origins of Black character traits. Since Black personality traits are conceptualized as innate, culture specific, and unique, changes in basic characteristics can only occur through dilution of the African genetic structure itself. However, confusion regarding African values and Black identity can occur through the incorporation of beliefs discrepant with those previously held. When this occurs, "misorientation" results and a progressive loss of Blackness occurs. As the underlying structure for Blackness is genetically based in this theoretical system, "misorientation" can be readily reversed by resocialization. In this model, then, deviation from the norm is described as a maladjustment that can be conceptualized in terms of loss of contact with cultural roots. Although maladjustment can reach levels of moderate severity in this system, adjustment problems can be addressed effectively by the reestablishment of cultural linkage and by cognitive restructuring. No assumption is made about underlying or unconscious mechanisms in the development of maladjusted behavior.

The importance of biological and cultural underpinnings for Black behavior is underscored by Gerald Jackson (1976, 1977). He is also of the opinion that social and political influences shape behavioral responses. The influences of social and political forces are strongly alluded to in the prior theoretical systems discussed as well. G. Jackson conceptualizes the uniqueness of Black behavior along several dimensions. He describes socialization experiences that help in the solidification of group-centered behavior and parenting styles that help cultivate respect for age, cooperation, and role flexibility. Motivation is described as group-centered in his system. Cognition and problem solving are described as inductive in nature, a view that is supported by other Black psychologists. He emphasizes a need for increased political sophistication and influence.

The type of socialization experiences and cultural training that Jackson described results in unique cognitive and perceptual styles. Thomas (1980) reported a vigorous evaluation and screening component in her analysis of self-esteem and perception that insures a Black referent. This active process relies heavily on group consensual validation and facilitates reculturation. In keeping with the perspective the author (G. Jackson, 1979) described divergent thinking (inductive reasoning) as a pervasive problem-solving technique in Black adolescents. This cognitive style was thought to be characteristic of Black people in general.

The salient value of Black culture and life-style in treatment approaches have been addressed increasingly by Black psychologists (A. Jackson, 1982; Jones, 1980; Toldson & Pasteur, 1975) and varying assessments of the effects of racism and the impact of these experience and cultural beliefs on behavior (Jones, 1980). The incorporation of cultural values in treatment is advocated by many practitioners (Akbar, 1977; Baldwin, in press; A. Jackson, 1982).

Treatment implications that can be drawn from these theories are extensive. One possible treatment approach is described below. The tentative model developed by the author attempts to capture the essence of African and African American culture described previously and to incorporate these into a clinical treatment paradigm.

## Proposed Black Clinical Treatment Model

The Black clinical practice model proposed is one of collective action of Black professionals, of continuity of services, and of direct intervention within multiple systems. The concept is one of a service chain that encompasses the Black client, family members, the Black community, and political and economic systems in which the person is involved. The service chain is more extensive than usual, involving Black professionals from all spheres in keeping with the concept of collective responsibility, and involving change as a concept for all participants. In the proposed model, intervention would take place in multiple ways. The client's world-view, cultural environment, and situational context would be integral parts of the assessment procedure. These factors would be utilized in a coordinated way to dictate intervention strategies. The approach stresses systems interconnectedness, culture, group identity, belonging, and reciprocal benefit. As such, the emphasis becomes one of holistic health and prevention rather than disease or psychopathology.

In the Black clinical practice model, problems are assumed to have multiple origins and to require multiple approaches for solution. The treatment approach involves a widening sense of responsibility for the client and the Black community as well as for political and economic systems confronting the client. The components of the model are presented in Figure 23.1.

The Black clinical practice model is composed of seven basic modules—the Black helping person, the Black client and family, Black professionals, the Black community, Black culture, political and economic systems, and the general environment. All modules are essential components in the model, but the primary units are envisioned as Black helping professional(s), and the Black client and family since these are likely to be the initial components involved. However, the importance of systems, group focus, and networks are recognized as crucial components in treatment. The initial role of the helping professional is one of understanding the problems that have developed in the system, to help the client understand the difficulty, and ultimately, to facilitate behaviors that will lead to better functioning involving multiple relationships within the system. Closer approximation to Black culture is assumed as a necessary goal at some point in treatment. The concentration is on growth or change of individual perception, behavior, and cognition as well as upon possible environmental structuring and change. Change is effected in reaction to assessed personal and cultural values.

The model also takes into account the importance of political and economic factors on behavior. Change of any kind must involve factors that influence behavior and the quality of life. To concentrate on only one aspect of the model, the client and family, to the exclusion of other aspects, is to risk incompleteness and ineffectiveness.

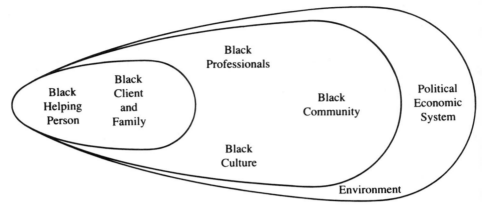

**Figure 23.1.** Proposed Black Clinical Practice Model

Another important facet of the model is the close working relationships among Black professionals—Black professionals from widely different backgrounds. It is envisioned that inclusion of Black professionals from diverse backgrounds will be a systematic means of effecting change across a broad spectrum of behaviors and systems and will permit a reinstitution of "groupness" that has been eroded by time, history, and social and political circumstances.

Race, Black identity, and Black culture are cornerstones of the model. These factors have spanned time, history, and circumstance to perpetuate a sense of uniqueness as a people and as an individual member of the racial group. Synchrony among all of these factions, then, may be viewed as optimal adjustment or optimal mental health. Effective operational behavior within systems, networks, and environments is seen as enhancing optimal adjustment.

Within the framework of the Black clinical practice model, the Black helping professional becomes an integral part of the network and family resources of the individual. To enhance therapeutic effectiveness, concepts of individual, group, family, and multiple impact therapies may be utilized within the confines of overlapping community, cultural, and political network systems.

Despite the seemingly logical nature of the model and consistency with described Black cultural values, numerous barriers to implementation exist. Some major barriers are discussed below.

### Barriers to Implementation of the Clinical Practice Model

Theoretically the proposed Black clinical practice model is consistent with existing concepts of Black culture and psychotherapeutic approaches. However, notwithstanding the logical nature of the model itself, the final proof must be practical implementation.

Implementation of the Black clinical practice model would entail open-ended involvement on the part of helping Black professionals, requiring creative funding mechanisms and supportive networks. These could prove to be sizable deterrents to implementation. Considerable risk-taking behaviors would be involved on the part of helping professionals as well as the abandonment of acquired personal economic and political advantages.

In addition to the factors mentioned below, another sizable barrier to the development of the Black clinical practice model is the vast variability of Black people. Black people differ in perspectives, perceptions, and personality even though basic cultural values and behavioral styles are postulated (and observed). Because this is likely, the Black helping professional must make assessments of the client on many different dimensions. Assessment might involve actual participant observation for a period of time in the social and family environs of the client.

Credibility poses still another barrier to implementation. Skepticism about motivation and competency may impede client involvement and therapist effectiveness. Although this is a traditional barrier to treatment involvement, distrust of Black helping professionals takes on special significance. In certain instances Black professionals may be seen as extensions of White institutions and as indistinguishable from White professionals. This could be because of inferred similarities in employment settings and educational and clinical experience. Also, internalization of pervasive opinions about the competency of Black people may negatively influence the formation of trusting relationships.

Societal, political, and individual factors in the implementation process are potentially the largest barriers of all. In societal structures where power is determined by race, there are always problems of influence and control over crucial life experiences for both therapist and client. Social and political structures set real limits on goals.

Yet certain aspects of the Black clinical practice model can be implemented. Emphasis can be placed, for example, on family and group procedures. Psychotherapy with Black clients can include family members and other significant persons on a routine basis. Also the range of Black consultants can be expanded to include anthropologists, sociologists, economists, urban planners, and lawyers. Community development and education can be consistently emphasized as well. Nevertheless, actual implementation of the treatment model in all of its aspects will require extensive deliberation and study. Although formidable, this appears to be a goal worthy of pursuit. Without alternative clinical practice procedures, traditional approaches will continue to be used. Given the continuation of traditional approaches as central clinical practices, past difficulties in treatment, in involvement, and outcome are predictable.

## Conclusion

The need to develop treatment models and personality theories consistent with the cultural values and life experiences of Black people has been advocated by Black theoreticians. Activities in this area have increased in recent years. The theoretical Black clinical practice model proposed in this article is an attempt to embellish this line of discourse and to spur creative efforts at refinement and implementation.

## References

Adams, P. L. (1979). Dealing with racism in bi-racial psychiatry. *Journal of the American Academy of Child Psychiatry, 9,* 33-43.

Akbar, N. (1976). *The community of self.* Chicago: Nation of Islam Office of Human Development.

Akbar, N. (1977). *Natural psychology and human transformation.* Chicago: World Community of Islam.

Allen, S. (1971). The African heritage. *Black World, 20*(3), 14-18.

Allen, W. R. (1978). The search for applicable theories of Black family life. *Journal of Marriage and the Family, 40*(1), 117-129.

Amini, J. M. (1972). *An African frame of reference.* Chicago: Institute of Positive Education.

Baldwin, J. A. (1976). Black psychology and Black personality: Some issues for consideration. *Black Books Bulletin, 4*(3), 6-11, 65.

Baldwin, J. A. (in press). *Afrikan (Black) personality: From an Afrocentric framework.* Chicago: Third World Press.

Banks, H. C. (1972). The differential effects of race and social class helping. *Journal of Clinical Psychology, 28,* 90-92.

Branch, T. S. (1977). Race and therapist status as variables in the therapeutic process (Doctoral dissertation, University of Washington, 1976). *Dissertation Abstracts International, 37*(7-B), 3597.

Buck, M. (1977). Peer counseling from a Black perspective. *The Journal of Black Psychology, 3*(2), 107-113.

Chimezie, A. (1973). Theorizing on Black behavior: The role of the Black psychologist. *Journal of Black Studies, 4*(1), 15-28.

Di-Angi, P. (1976). Barriers to the Black and White therapeutic relationship. *Perspectives in Psychiatric Care, 14*(4), 180-183.

Griffith, M. S. (1976). Effects of race and sex of client on duration of outpatient psychotherapy (Doctoral dissertation, University of Colorado, 1975). *Dissertation Abstracts International,* 1976, *36(8-B),* 4157.

Griffith, M. S. (1977). The influence of race on the psychotherapeutic relationship. *Psychiatry, 40*(1), 27-40.

Hall, E. T. (1977). *Beyond culture.* Garden City, NY: Anchor.

Jackson, A. M. (1973). Psychotherapy: Factors associated with the race of the therapist. *Psychotherapy: Theory, Research and Practice, 10,* 273-277.

Jackson, A. M. (1979). Performance on convergent tasks by Black adolescents. In W. D. Smith, A. K. Burlew, M. H. Mosley, & W. M. Whitney (Eds.), *Reflections on Black psychology,* Lanham, MD: University Press of America.

Jackson, A. M. (1982). Psychosocial aspects of the therapeutic process. In S. M. Turner & R. T. Jones (Eds.), *Behavior therapy and Black populations: Psychosocial issues and empirical findings.* New York: Plenum.

Jackson, A. M., Berkowitz, H., & Farley, G. K. (1974). Race as a variable in the treatment involvement of children. *Journal of American Academy of Child Psychiatry, 13*(1), 20-31.

Jackson, G. G. (1976). The African genesis of the Black perspective in helping. *Professional Psychology, 7*(3), 363-367.

Jackson, G. G. (1977). The emergence of a Black perspective in counseling. *Journal of Negro Education, 46*(3), 230'253.

Jackson, G. G. (1979). The origin and development of Black psychology: Implications for Black studies and human behavior, *Studia Africana, 13,* 271-293.

Jones, A. C. (1980). *A conceptual model for treatment of Black patients.* Personal correspondence.

Leonard, P., & Jones, A. C. (1980). Theoretical considerations for psychotherapy with Black clients. In R. C. Jones (Ed.), *Black psychology* (2nd ed.). New York: Harper & Row.

Mbiti, J. S. (1971). *African religions and philosophy.* Garden City, NY: Anchor.

Nobles, W. (1972). African philosophy: Foundations for Black psychology, In R. L. Jones (Ed.), *Black psychology.* New York: Harper & Row.

Nobles, W. (1976). Extended self: Rethinking the so-called Negro self-concept. *The Journal of Black Psychology, 2*(2), 15-24.

Offer, D., & Sabshin, M. (1966). *Normality: Theoretical and clinical concepts of mental health.* New York: Basic Books.

Thomas, A. (1980). *A reinterpretation of the development of Black self-esteem.* Dissertation proposal.

Thomas, A., & Sillen, S. (1972). *Racism and psychiatry.* New York: Brunner/Mazel.

Toldson, I. C., & Pasteur, A. B. (1975). Developmental stages of Black self-discovery: Implications for using Black art forms in group interaction. *Journal of Negro Education, 44*(2), 130-138.

Turner, L. D. (1969). *Africanisms in the Gullah dialect.* New York: Arnold Press.

Vass, W. K. (1979). *The Bantu-speaking heritage of the United States.* Los Angeles: University of California, Center for Afro-American Studies.

Warren, R. C., Jackson, A. M., Nugaris, J., & Farley, G. K. (1973). Differential attitudes of black and white patients toward treatment in a child guidance clinic. *American Journal of Ortho Psychiatry, 43*(3), 384-393.

Wilson, W. (1974). Effective therapeutic variables with the black client. *Dissertation Abstracts International, 35*(6-B), 3044-3045D.

# 24 Delayed Gratification in Blacks: A Critical Review

**W. CURTIS BANKS***
**GREGORY V. McQUATER****
*Social Learning Laboratory*
*Educational Testing Service*
**JENISE ROSS ANTHONY**
*Institute for Urban Affairs and Research*
**WANDA E. WARD*****
*University of Oklahoma*

Research on the delay of gratification in Blacks was critically reviewed. The methodology typically employed to investigate this construct involves offering the individual a choice of obtaining either a small, immediate reward or a large, delayed reward. Contrary to previous reports, it is argued here that the evidence divides published studies into those demonstrating overall patterns of nonpreference for delayed versus immediate rewards and those demonstrating overall or partial patterns of preference for delayed rewards among Blacks. Little empirical evidence is provided in the literature of a tendency for Blacks to prefer immediate gratification, or of the relationship of such behavior to other personality characteristics.

The delay of gratification has been conceptualized as the ability to forgo immediate opportunities to satisfy impulses in favor of alternative opportunities that are more remote in time, but often of greater objective value. As such, the ability is one that is believed to distinguish those individuals who succeed and prosper by hard work, thrift, and self-control from those who are susceptible to the temptations of short-term gains and impulsivity. This conceptualization has lent itself to an analysis of

W. Curtis Banks, Social Learning Laboratory, Educational Testing Service, Princeton, NJ 08541.
Gregory V. McQuater, Department of Human Development and Family Studies, Cornell University, Ithaca, NY 14850.
Jenise Ross Anthony, Howard University, 2900 Van Ness Street, N.W., Washington, D.C. 20008.
Wanda E. Ward, University of Oklahoma at Norman, Norman, OK 73069.
EDITORS' NOTES: *Currently at Howard University, **Currently at PepsiCo Corporate Division, ***Currently at National Science Foundation.

class differences in sociopsychological functioning (Davis & Dollard, 1940; Drake & Cayton, 1945; Schneider & Lysgaard, 1953), of cultural differences that distinguish national groups (Mischel, 1961b), and of race differences in personality characteristics (Lessing, 1969; Mischel, 1958; Price-Williams & Ramirez, 1972; Strickland, 1972).

Davis and Dollard (1940) and Schneider and Lysgaard (1953) argued that the lower class is characterized by "minimum pursuit of education," "low aspirations," a "readiness to engage in physical violence," and "free sexual gratification (as through intercourse)" (p. 143). In contrast, they described the middle class as characterized by a "deferred gratification pattern" of postponed intercourse, delayed economic independence (from parents), and thrift, all of which contribute to their relative achievement, economic success, and social responsibility.

Similarly, a number of more recent studies have contributed to an empirical validation of Drake and Cayton's (1945) and Davis and Dollard's (1940) impressionistic observations about the inability to delay gratification among Blacks. Experimental research has been aimed at establishing the relationship of immediate gratification preferences to academic success (Lessing, 1969), achievement motivation (Mischel, 1961a), social responsibility (Mischel, 1961a, 1961c), and psychopathology (Unikel & Blanchard, 1973) in that population. Moreover, certain theorists (e.g., Rainwater, 1970) have conjectured that such an "orientation toward immediate gratification (p. 230) is a result of a sense of impotence, unstable interpersonal relationships, and a disinclination to think about the future" (see also Pettigrew, 1964). A great deal of this line of theorizing is related directly to the empirical literature concerning father-absence (Mischel, 1958; 1961b), trust (Price-Williams & Ramirez, 1974; Seagull, 1966; Strickland, 1972), locus of control (Strickland, 1972; Zytkoskee, Strickland, & Watson, 1971), and conceptions of time (Mischel, 1961c).

Past reviews have devoted little critical attention to the body of evidence that relates to this fertile area of theorizing about Black populations (see Mischel, 1966; Renner, 1964). Consequently, much of what recent theorists have inferred from past research and conjectured regarding "a preference for smaller, immediate rewards" among Blacks (Mischel, 1966, p. 125), stands in marked contrast to the actual data. The accumulated evidence largely refutes rather than supports the construct validity of immediate gratification preference among Blacks. Accordingly, with minor exception the evidence fails even to substantiate that such preference characterizes the behavior of that population.

## Delayed Versus Immediate Gratification Preferences

Systematic experimental research into delayed gratification began with Black subject populations in the Carribean (Mischel 1958, 1961c). Mischel had observed informally in the context of a village in Trinidad what earlier social observers had remarked upon in different settings (e.g., Drake & Cayton, 1945). It appeared to Mischel and to his casual informants that a marked tendency obtained in Trinidadian Blacks toward immediate gratification (see Mischel, 1971). This seemed in striking contrast to the behavior of a native East Indian population that was characterized by self-deprivation and the postponement of gratification.

In an attempt to verify this cultural observation, Mischel devised a simple paradigm in which subjects were asked to make a choice between two alternative rewards for their participation in an experiment. Subjects could choose to receive a small reward to be presented immediately by the experimenter, or a larger, more valued reward to be presented somewhat later by the experimenter. In his initial investigation with 35 Black 7- to 9-year-olds (both sexes) and a comparative sample of 18 East Indians, Mischel (1958) offered the alternative of a one-cent candy immediately or a ten-cent candy after one week.

Sixty-seven percent of the Indian children selected the larger, delayed reward; 33% chose the smaller, immediate reward. This pattern did, indeed, differ from that of the Black sample, who chose the larger, delayed alternative less often (37%) than the smaller, immediate alternative (63%). Neither of these patterns of choice in itself, however, could be characterized as preferential. In his sample of 18, Mischel's East Indian subjects would have needed to choose at a rate exceeding 70% to reject the null hypothesis of chance ($p = .05$) selection of the large, delayed alternative (see Table 24.1). More germane to the present discussion, Blacks were equally nonpreferential in their selections, their 63% of choices for the small, immediate reward failing to exceed the rate required (66%) at the 95% level of confidence by simple $z$-test.

In a somewhat later investigation Mischel (1961b) engaged 69 Black children from Trinidad and 69 Black children from Grenada, aged 8 to 9 years. These children were offered a choice similar to that offered the earlier sample, a two-cent candy immediately or a ten-cent candy a week later. Fifty-three percent of the Trinidadian Black sample chose the two-cent candy; 47% chose the ten-cent alternative. This pattern conformed to chance. Of the Grenadian Blacks, only 24% chose the small, immediate alternative, whereas 76% clearly preferred the larger

**TABLE 24.1**  Criterion Percentages for Significant* Choice Behavior in Favor of Immediate or Delayed Reward

| *Total Number of Subjects Making Choices* | *Criterion %* |
|---|---|
| 20 | 71 |
| 30 | 67 |
| 40 | 65 |
| 50 | 64 |
| 60 | 63 |
| 70 | 62 |
| 80 | 61 |
| 90 | 60 |
| 100 | 60 |
| 125 | 59 |
| 150 | 58 |
| 200 | 57 |

*Deviation from chance frequencies, significant at the .05 level.

delayed reward at a rate that rejects the null hypothesis of chance, but in the direction of delay-preference.

Another sample of Trinidadian Blacks, this time ranging in age from 12 to 14, was engaged by Mischel (1961c) in a study of the relationship between immediate preferences and delinquency. Within the overall sample of 206 children, 68% selected a twenty-five-cent candy to be received in one week over a five-cent candy to be received immediately (32%). This pattern of clearly significant ($p = .05$) preference for the larger delayed reward also obtained for that subsample of the overall group who were classified as nondelinquents. Nondelinquent children from a large elementary government school selected the twenty-five cent candy 74% of the time, clearly significant within that group of 136. The delinquent subsample from a boy's industrial school selected the immediate reward 44% of the time, and the delayed reward 56%, a pattern that did not depart from binomial chance.

This same pattern of inconsistent findings has been replicated in a range of variations on Mischel's initial paradigm. For instance, a sample of 112 Black Trinidadian 11- to 14-year-olds was presented with one actual reward choice and two hypothetical queries (Mischel, 1961a). Subjects could select either a ten-cent candy to be received immediately or a twenty-five-cent candy to be received in one week. In addition, they indicated either their agreement or disagreement with each of the following self-descriptive statements: "I would rather get ten dollars right now than have to wait a whole month and get thirty dollars then"; "I would rather wait to get a much larger gift much later rather than get a smaller one now." On the basis of their three responses the children were assigned to consistent delay (3 delay responses), inconsistent delay (2 or 1 delay responses) and consistent immediate (0 delay responses) groups. Combining those who made two or three delay responses, 49% of the children can be said to have made delay choices. Using those who made either one or no delay responses, the combined nondelay (or immediate) groups totaled 51% of the overall sample. These rates of choice are obviously the same as chance. Even taking the consistent delay ($n = 37$) and the consistent immediate ($n = 30$) groups only, the dichotomy of choice would be 55% and 45%, respectively. Although these frequencies are in the direction of preference for the larger, delayed reward, they do not depart from statistical chance for a sample of 67.

Strickland (1972) offered a different reward choice to 171 American Black children, aged 11 to 13 years. Following the completion of a questionnaire, the children were offered a choice between one 45-rpm record immediately or three 45-rpm records to be received in three weeks. Overall, 55% of the children selected the one record immediately, 45% selected to wait for the three records in three weeks. These frequencies again conform to chance, indicating nonpreference.

A series of four choices between small, immediate, and large, delayed rewards was presented to fourth-graders in a midwestern city. Hertzberger and Dweck (1978) asked 19 Black male and 15 Black female children to choose between one nickel immediately or three nickels in one week, two nickels immediately or five nickels in one week, two nickels immediately or three nickels in one week, a small candy bar immediately or a medium-sized candy bar in one week. Each child made all of these choices without knowing which of them would be the "real one" to determine the actual gift. Across the four choices, females selected the larger delayed alternative 53%, 47%, 53% and 54% of the time, respectively; males chose that alternative at rates of 63%, 58%, 58%, 58% respectively. None of these was different from chance.

Price-Williams and Ramirez (1974) presented their sample of 60 Black fourth graders with these questions: "Suppose you could get $10 now or wait a month and get $30, which would you take?" "If you could get a small 5¢ candy bar now, or wait a month and get a bigger 25¢

candy bar, which would you take?" "If you could get a small present now, or take a bigger one a month later, which would you take?") The first question was entirely hypothetical, whereas the latter two were accompanied by a tangible display of the alternatives and resulted in the child's actually receiving the chosen alternative. In response to the first query 18% of the children indicated a choice of the immediate $10, while 82% indicated a choice of the $30 to be obtained later. Thirty-three percent chose the smaller immediate candy bar, and 67% chose the larger, delayed one. Finally, 37% chose the smaller gift, and 67% chose to wait for a larger, more attractive alternative. All of these frequencies were, in fact, significantly different from chance and in the direction of delayed gratification preference.

Extending the strategy of presenting purely hypothetical verbal queries, Lessing (1969) devised seven items that related to choice situations (e.g., "If wearing ugly braces would make my teeth look prettier later on, I would put up with looking awful for a year or two"). Eight-eight Black eighth- and eleventh-graders responded with either agreement or disagreement to each of the seven items and were scored zero or one for each immediate versus delayed response, respectively. The possible range of scores was 0 to 7 indicating from low to high delayed gratification preference, and the overall mean for the sample was 5.16. Using an estimate of the standard deviation of the scores, calculated from the reported analysis of variance results, would yield a $t$-value greater than 7.00 when the obtained mean is compared with a 3.50 scale midpoint. It can, therefore, be surmised that these Black subjects responded significantly in a delayed gratification direction.

In a somewhat ambiguous report of delayed gratification choices of 68 Black third-graders in Syracuse, New York, Seagull (1966) described two subsamples—one which was "unclassifiable" as to socioeconomic status, and one which was "classifiable." All children were offered a choice between one Hershey bar immediately and two Hershey bars to be obtained after waiting one week. Seagull reported that among the "unclassifiable" Blacks, 51% chose the immediate alternative, and 49% chose the delayed; these frequencies do not differ from chance. But among Seagull's "classifiable" group, 24% chose the immediate and 76% chose the delayed candy bars, indicating significant preference for the larger, albeit postponed reward.

Taken together these reports offer little substantiation of past impressionistic conjectures about the inability to delay gratification among Blacks. Clearly the majority of evidence reveals a pattern of nonpreference for either smaller immediate or larger delayed rewards within that population. At the same time, a considerable accumulation of evidence suggests quite the opposite of immediate preferences. Lessing (1969), Mischel (1961b, 1961c), Price-Williams and Ramirez (1974), and Seagull (1966) reported choice patterns among American, Trinidadian, and Grenadian Blacks that reflect a preference for delayed gratification. Against these findings only three studies within the experimental research literature support the notion that Blacks exhibit immediate reward preferences. Mischel (1958) found that his entire (albeit small) subsample of Black Trinidadian children who reported their fathers as not living at home ($n = 10$) chose the immediate reward alternative. Similarly, he reported in a later study (Mischel, 1961b), that a subsample of "father-absent" Trinidadian Blacks ($n = 23$) preferred the immediate, smaller reward at a rate (74%), which exceeded chance. Mischel interpreted both these observations in terms of trust, reasoning that the absence of a father may have undermined the confidence of these children in any promises made by authority figures. Strickland (1972) attempted to lend support to this thesis in a study of the effects of the promise-maker's race, and found that her sample of Black children ($n = 84$) preferred the immediate reward (67%) when the experimenter was White.

One possible interpretation of these overall results, therefore, may be that some Blacks do prefer immediate rewards some of the time, and that the aggregate trend of chance-like responding conceals a genuinely consistent response pattern in two distinct preference groups. Although the major burden of this argument in behalf of immediate preference in Blacks is borne by the discriminating construct of father absence (or trust), a broader body of validative research, speaks to this general line of reasoning. It may be appropriate, then, to turn to an analysis of that correspondent evidence before concluding our assessment of the status of delayed gratification in Blacks.

## Trust and Father-Absence

In one of the very earliest experimental studies of delayed gratification Mahrer (1956) examined the hypothesis that acquired expectancies determine an individual's willingness to forgo immediate rewards in favor of postponed alternatives. Accordingly, Mahrer presented lower socioeconomic children with experimentally manipulated experiences of fulfilled and unfulfilled promises of delayed reinforcements. On subsequent trials, those children subjected to expectancy disconfirmations chose the delayed rewards less often than children who had experienced confirmation of expected rewards. What is more, the effect of experimentally controlled trust was highly specific to the identity of the agent of past experience. That is, acquired expectancies were specific to the agent from whom they were learned; disconfirmed expectancies in the context of one agent did not affect later delayed reward choices in the context of a new agent.

Precisely what identifying characteristics of agents serve to establish the specificity or generality of acquired expectancies is not clear. In Mahrer's investigation, agents were all identical in race and sex, yet the specific experiential differences that distinguished them for subjects were sufficient to cue discriminant responding. Mischel (1958) conjectured that sex alone may be sufficient, however, to cue generalization of expectancies; and he hypothesized that a White American male might evoke distrust in children whose confidence in authority had been undermined by an absent Black father. Two experiments were directed at a test of this hypothesis.

In his investigation of Trinidadian Blacks and East Indians, Mischel (1958) asked children, "Does your father live at home with you?" Those who answered "no" were assigned to a "father-absent" group, comprised of ten such Black respondents and one East Indian. Although the sample of one East Indian did not permit inference, Mischel reported a unanimous tendency among "father-absent" Blacks to select an immediate reward, a trend that distinguished them significantly from "father-present" Black children. Moreover, with that investigation both father-absence and relative selection of overall immediate rewards distinguished the overall sample of Blacks from the overall sample of Indians, and Mischel reasoned that the resultant discouragement of trust among Blacks could explain the observed cultural-racial differences in behavior.

In a specific test of this hypothesis, Mischel (1961b) examined father-absence and delayed gratification in larger samples of Trinidadian Black, Grenadian Black, and Trinidadian East Indian children. The results were conclusively negative. Trinidadian Blacks differed significantly from Grenadians in their selection of delayed rewards, but the groups were undifferentiated in the incidence of father-absence. Neither did Grenadian Blacks differ from Trinidadian East Indians in the incidence of father-absence, though they differed significantly in preference for delayed rewards. Furthermore, in two separate replications with large samples of eleven-to-fourteen-year-old Trinidadian Blacks alone, no relationship obtained between father-absence and delayed- or immediate-reward preferences.

Pursuing a different line of reasoning, Strickland (1972) argued that within a given cultural context certain identifying characteristics of agents may cue expectancies in different directions. For American Blacks, White agents may be those for whom peculiarly negative expectancies have been acquired, the resultant distrust leading to an unwillingness to delay gratification in a choice situation. Her results confirmed this hypothesis be revealing a significantly greater proportion of Black children selecting delayed rewards offered by a Black experimenter as compared with a White experimenter. However, Price-Williams and Ramirez (1974) found that spontaneous verbalizations of trust were more frequent in White than in Black children even though the race of the experimenter was matched to the race of the subjects.

It might seem that immediate reward preference among Blacks would derive from experiences primarily with powerful White social agents whose unfulfilled promises evoke distrust and uncertainty. This argument, of course, is quite distinct from that advanced by Mischel. It is also distinct from the body of evidence which reveals nonpreference and delayed-preference as predominant in Blacks.

Although specific experiences may have significant potential for shaping expectancies and resultant behaviors, Blacks may show a certain resilience which defies the generalization of effects. For example, Seagull (1966) reported that an experimental manipulation of trust, similar to that of Mahrer's (1956), significantly affected preferences for immediate and delayed rewards among Black third-graders. However, he also observed a recurring pattern of delaying behavior in "lower working class . . . Negro children who are overly trusting even in the face of repeated disconfirmation" (p. 350), prompting him to conclude that "delay choice was a situationally determined variable," often defying "consistently broken promises" (p. 351) in that population.

## SOCIAL RESPONSIBILITY

Early experimental research also sought to establish the inability to delay gratification as a factor in social deviancy. Mischel (1961c) compared juvenile delinquents with controls from a population of Trinidadian Blacks. He reported that a significantly larger proportion of delinquents than of controls selected a five-cent candy to be received immediately. However, the proportion of juvenile delinquents choosing the smaller, immediate reward was actually smaller than the proportion choosing the larger, delayed alternative, although both proportions conformed to chance for that group. Futhermore, juvenile delinquents who chose the immediate reward were undifferentiated on Harris' (1957) measure of social responsibility from juvenile delinquents who chose the delayed rewards. Finally, when reward choices were combined with verbal responses to two hypothetical queries, the resultant pattern of "delay" responses permitted the classification of "consistent delayers" and "consistent nondelayers." Only these extreme subgroups of the juvenile delinquent sample were different on the Harris measure.

In a similar investigation, Trinidadian lower- and lower-middle-class Black children were given one actual and two hypothetical choices between immediate and delayed rewards, and they responded to the Harris measure of social responsibility (Mischel, 1961a). Taken together, those children who gave 2 or 3 delay responses had higher social responsibility scores than those children who gave 1 or 0 delay responses.

Unikel and Blanchard (1973), however, failed to find any differences in delayed-reward choices between Black delinquents classified as psychopathic and those classified as nonpsychopathic. They also reported that Black psychopathics "manifested no significant difference in preference for delayed rewards as the delay interval increased" (p. 60). These findings are in direct contrast to Mischel's hypothesis that the time perspectives among juvenile delinquents affect delayed reward choices (1961c), or that social responsibility among Blacks is related to delay behavior.

ACHIEVEMENT

Early theorists argued that the ability to delay gratification is a critical factor in distinguishing those who persevere in hard work toward valuable long-range goals. Mischel (1961a) hypothesized that achievement motivation (*n* Achievement), as measured by fantasy expressions (McClelland, Atkinson, Clark, & Lowell, 1953), is a central aspect of the personality of socioeconomically and academically successful persons, and that the construct validity of delayed reward choices should be reflected in a positive association between that behavior and *n* Achievement. He predicted that individuals who are high in delayed reward preference would be those who "have learned to like work" (p. 544), and, in turn, are those who are high in *n* Achievement. In a sample of 112 Black Trinidadian eleven- to fourteen-year-olds this association did significantly obtain. The Pearson correlation between number of delayed reward choices (across three queries) and $n$ Achievement scores was .27.

Whether such association establishes the validity of delayed-reward choices as a construct implicated in actual academic and economic success is quite another matter. Considerable argument has been advanced against the ability of the $n$ Achievement measure itself to predict achievement outcomes for Blacks or distinguish them from other customarily successful populations in American society (e.g., Katz, 1967). In fact, a more direct test of the hypothesized relationship between delayed reward preference and achievement was carried out by Lessing (1969). That investigation measured delay preferences with seven hypothetical items reflecting choice situations (see p. 48). She correlated the resultant scores with the grade point averages for her combined Black and White eighth- and eleventh-grade samples, obtaining a Pearson coefficient of .23. However, she reported that the apparent influence of delayed gratification upon academic achievement "was solely by means of the variance shared with IQ" (p. 160).

## LOCUS OF CONTROL AND ACQUIESCENCE

One final way in which past research has attempted to establish the construct validity of immediate gratification preference in Blacks is through its association with an individual's confidence in his ability to assert initiative and to control his reinforcement outcomes. Mischel (1961a) hypothesized that preference for immediate rewards would, therefore, be positively related to acquiescence in Blacks. Lessing (1969), Strickland (1972), and Zytkoskee, Strickland, and Watson (1971) hypothesized that such preferences would be positively related to an external locus of control, or a sense of powerlessness in Blacks.

Mischel asked his sample of Black Trinidadian youngsters to imagine that he (Mischel) was thinking of something with which they might agree or disagree. Without his indicating exactly what he was thinking, subjects were asked to indicate whether they believed they would agree (by indicating yes) or disagree (by indicating no). Those children who were high in delayed-reward choices more often indicated disagreement than children who were high in immediate reward choices. The validity of this measure of acquiescence, however, was unsubstantiated.

In a series of studies that employed a more generally validated measure, Strickland and her associates have found no association in

Blacks between external locus of control and preference for immediate rewards. The locus of control scores in the Nowicki-Strickland[1] 40-item instrument were virtually identical for Black eleven- to thirteen-year-olds choosing immediate or choosing delayed rewards. Similarly, Zytkoskee, Strickland, and Watson (1971) found little correlation ($r = .09$) between the Bialer Locus of Control Scale (Bialer, 1961) and their five-item measure of immediate- versus delayed-reward preference in a sample of 76 Black ninth-graders. Furthermore, Lessing (1969) found that Blacks were significantly differentiated by a measure of locus of control, but they were not differentiated by a measure of delayed gratification preference.

## Conclusions

In recent years, a rather explicit trend has emerged from the critical analysis of research into personality and social behavior in Blacks. Conventional paradigms, the constructs whose validity they were aimed at establishing, and the phenomena they are designed to reveal, appear to have benefited from far more heuristic momentum than the empirical evidence would justify. The inability to delay gratification in Blacks can be counted among White-preference, external locus of control, and lack of motivation in this respect. Notwithstanding the characterization offered of Blacks in much of the published literature (Mischel, 1971; Pettigrew, 1964; Rainwater, 1970), experimental data largely represent Blacks either as preferring delayed gratification or as indifferent toward immediate versus delayed rewards. Five investigations (Hertzberger & Dweck, 1978; Mischel, 1958, 1961a; Strickland, 1972; Unikel & Blanchard, 1973) show Black samples as either entirely or primarily nonpreferential toward the delay of gratification. Five (Lessing, 1969; Mischel, 1961c, 1961b; Price-Williams & Ramirez, 1974; Seagull, 1966) reveal either entire samples or subsamples of Blacks as preferring delayed rewards. In only three instances of published research (Mischel, 1958, 1961b; Strickland, 1972) have relatively limited subsamples of Blacks displayed a preference for immediate rewards.

The meaning of such a trend is not immediately apparent. Taken together, the evidence may reflect a relatively consistent tendency among Blacks to distribute themselves normally around a central tendency of nonpreference for delayed gratification. On the face of it, such a trend could not reject the thesis that orientations among Blacks toward delayed gratification may underlie certain aspects of dysfunctional individual and social behavior. Going even further, it may be argued that the occasional selection by some Blacks of immediate reward alternatives is itself a behavior that differentiates those individuals from others, in the direction of dysfunctionality. In this sense the overall nonpreferential trends could conceal a theoretically meaningful dichotomy of preference among Blacks.

These interpretations could be substantiated by a strong and consistent convergence of the construct validative evidence. On one hand, Blacks as a group might be characterized by a lack of motivation to achieve, by negative self-concept, low aspirations, or a sense of powerlessness; but none of these generalized characterizations can be empirically substantiated. On the other hand, those Blacks who prefer immediate rewards may be peculiarly unsuccessful, irresponsible, socially untrusting, or subjectively powerless relative to other Blacks; the accumulated data scarcely sustain this hypothesis either.

Preference for immediate rewards has occasionally distinguished Black children of father-absent homes from those of father-present homes (Mischel, 1958). More often it has not (Mischel, 1961b). This failure of father-absence consistently to distinguish delayed gratification preferences might rest largely with its rough approximation to the more specific variable of trust. Yet theorists have never been clear about precisely what cues evoke trust in Blacks (cf. Price-Williams & Ramirez, 1974; Strickland, 1972) or whether such sentiments, when aroused, play a significant role in the behavior of Blacks in the real world (Seagull, 1966). Mischel's finding suggested that the sex of the rewarding agent is sufficient to cue learned distrust; Strickland argued rather that the agent's race was the critical feature; and Price Williams and Ramirez's results suggest that neither is necessary or sufficient. Seagull strongly argued that for those most likely to feel distrust, it might not matter anyway.

Although Blacks who prefer immediate rewards may be more acquiescent than others (Mischel, 1961a), they do not perceive themselves as less capable of controlling their reinforcement outcomes (Strickland, 1972; Zytkoskee, Strickland, & Watson, 1971). They may display less achievement in their fantasy expressions (Mischel, 1961a), but such expressions may not distinguish them from high achievers (Katz, 1967) nor may such gratification preferences influence their actual success (Lessing, 1969). With respect to social responsibility, it is paradoxical that the same characteristic that distinguishes between normal and juvenile delinquent youngsters (Mischel, 1961c) fails to distinguish individual differences in either measured social responsibility attitudes (Mischel, 1961c) or psychopathology (Unikel & Blanchard, 1973) within delinquent populations.

That the phenomenon of delayed gratification choices in Blacks has attained so equivocal a status is likely due to limitations in both its theoretical and methodological development. Early discussions reflected a status of theoretical indecision over the appropriate framework from which to approach the important questions. Mischel (1958), for example, appealed to such psychodynamic constructs as ego strength and such social learning constructs as expectancies, and to such antecedents as father-absence and time perspectives. But perhaps even more critical to the development of research in this area was the initial decision to proceed with a paradigm in which a sensitivity to reward latency was to be inferred from choices between alternatives that confounded that variable with reward quantity.

From the nature of choices made by subjects within the standard delayed gratification paradigm, it is impossible to distinguish preference for immediate alternatives from preference for small ones, or preference for delayed rewards from preference for large ones. A complete factorial design would, of course, have obviated this dilemma. Yet it was not explored. Quite apart from considerations of ego strength or expectancies, one might imagine that indifference toward the alternative rewards is fully to be expected. The net values of small, albeit immediate, and delayed, albeit large, rewards may, upon minor assumptions, be conjectured to be equal. Some recent research confirms this hypothesis (McQuater, 1980; Ward, 1976; Banks, McQuater, Pryor, & Salter[2]) as well as its implications for choice behavior across the full range of delay and quantity permutations.

The most valuable aspect of the delayed gratification paradigm, in fact, may be its amenability to analyses of some of the most basic processes which govern the values of incentive stimuli for human behavior. In this regard, the predominance of nonpreferential responding in Blacks may serve as a logical point of departure for the analysis of the component features of incentive stimuli, and the rational manner in which their subjective significance bares upon motivation and behavior. In that light, the limitations of past research findings for establishing the construct validity of delayed gratification seem possibly irrelevant. Far from disturbing, the status of nonpreference for delayed gratification in Blacks would potentially seem both coherent and heuristic for future research on reinforcement processes in Black behavior.

## Notes

1. Strickland, B. R., & Nowicki, S. (1971, September). *Behavioral correlates of the Novicki-Strickland locus of control for children*. Paper presented at the meeting of the American Psychological Association, Washington, DC.
2. Banks, W. C., McQuater, G. V., Pryor, J., & Salter, B. (1976). *The effect of reward amount, delay interval, and work on incentive value*. Unpublished manuscript.

## References

Bialer, I. (1961). Conceptualization of success and failure in mentally retarded and normal children. *Journal of Personality, 29,* 303-320.

Davis, S., & Dollard, J. (1940). *Children of bondage*. Washington, DC: American Council on Education.

Drake, S., & Cayton, H. R. (1945). *Black metropolis*. New York: Harcourt Brace.

Harris, D. B. (1957). A scale for measuring attitudes of social responsibility in children. *Journal of Abnormal and Social Psychology, 55,* 322-326.

Hertzberger, S. D., & Dweck, C. S. (1978). Attraction and delay of gratification. *Journal of Personality, 46*(2), 215-227.

Katz, I. (1967). The socialization of academic motivation in minority group children. *Nebraska Symposium on Motivation, 15,* 133-191.

Lessing, E. (1969). Racial differences in indices of ego functioning relevant to academic achievement. *The Journal of Genetic Psychology, 115,* 153.

Mahrer, A. (1956). The role of expectancy in delayed reinforcement. *Journal of Experimental Psychology, 52,* 101-105.

McClelland, D. C., Atkinson, J. W., Clark, R. A., & Lowell, E. L. (1953). *The achievement motive*. New York: Appleton-Century-Crofts.

McQuater, G. V. (1980). Delay of gratification: A theoretical and methodological address (Doctoral dissertation, Princeton University, 1980). *Dissertation Abstracts International, 41-03,* 1162B. (University Microfilms No. 80-1866-4)

Mischel, W. (1958). Preference for delayed reinforcement: An experimental study of a cultural observation. *Journal of Abnormal Social Psychology, 56,* 57-61.

Mischel, W. (1961a). Delay of gratification, need for achievement, and acquiescence in another culture. *Journal of Abnormal and Social Psychology, 63*(3), 543-552.

Mischel, W. (1961b). Father-absence and delay of gratification. Cross-cultural comparisons. *Journal of Abnormal and Social Psychology, 63*(1), 116-124.

Mischel, W. (1961c). Preference for delayed reinforcement and social responsibility. *Journal of Abnormal and Social Psychology, 62,* 1-7.

Mischel, W. (1966). Theory and research on the antecedents of self-imposed delay of reward. In B. A. Maher (Ed.), *Progess in experimental personality research, 3.* New York: Academic Press.

Mischel, W. (1971). *Introduction to personality*. New York: Holt, Rinehart & Winston.

Pettigrew, T. F. (1964). *A profile of the Negro American*. New York: Van Nostrand.

Price-Williams, D. R., & Ramirez, M. (1974). Ethnic differences in delay of gratification. *Journal of Social Psychology, 93,* 23-30.

Rainwater, L. (1970). *Behind ghetto walls: Black family life in a federal slum*. Chicago: Aldine.

Renner, K. E. (1964). Delay of reinforcement: A historical review. *Psychological Bulletin, 61*(5), 341-361.

Schneider, L., & Lysgaard, S. (1953). The deferred gratification pattern: A preliminary study. *American Sociological Review, 18,* 142-149.

Seagull, A. A. (1966). Subpatterns of gratification choice within samples of Negro and White children. *Papers of the Michigan Academy of Science, Arts, and Letters, 51*(2), 345-351.

Strickland, B. R. (1972). Delay of gratification as a function of race of the experimenter. *Journal of Personality and Social Psychology, 22*(1), 108-112.

Unikel, I. P., & Blanchard, E. B. (1973). Psychopathy, race, and delay of gratification by adolescent delinquents. *Journal of Nervous and Mental Disease, 156*(1), 57-60.

Ward, W. E. (1976). *The use of internal-external locus of control and delay of gratification constructs in explaining Black behavior.* Unpublished senior thesis, Princeton University.

Zytkoskee, A., Strickland, B. R., & Watson, J. (1971). Delay of gratification and internal versus external control among adolescents of low socio-economic status. *Development Psychology, 4*(1), 93-98.

# 25

# Gender Differences in the Participation of African Americans in Alcoholism Treatment

## A. KATHLEEN HOARD BURLEW
## JACQUELINE BUTLER
## NINA LEWIS
## KENNETH WASHINGTON
*University of Cincinnati*

This research examined the relationship of gender to treatment utilization in alcoholism programs among African Americans. It was predicted that completion and participation rates for males would exceed the rates for females in a program utilizing a mixed-sex treatment group format. The subjects included 148 individuals participating in a treatment program designed for African Americans. The findings revealed that females were less likely to complete the program and attended proportionately fewer group and individual sessions than males. Some implications of the findings for planning treatment programs for African American women are also discussed.

Alcoholism and other substance abuse continue to occur in increasing rates in this society. According to national surveys, about one-third of the U.S. population over age 18 fits the classification of moderate to heavy drinkers. Moreover, alcohol is involved in approximately one-half of all accidental deaths, suicides, and homicides (U.S. Department of Health and Human Services, 1987).

The percentage of all alcoholics who are females was estimated to be about 10% to 14% in 1948 (Jacobsen, 1981). However, by 1985, 6 million women or about one-third of all alcoholics were female (Blume, 1991). The growing rate of alcohol misuse among females is even more alarming in view of the danger that drinking during pregnancy results in the birth of a child with fetal alcohol syndrome (FAS), fetal alcohol effects (FAE), or other developmental difficulties.

Drinking patterns and consequences among African Americans vary somewhat from drinking patterns among Whites. Although abstention is more common among African Americans than among Whites (Clark & Midanik, 1982), the occurrence of drinking related medical problems and social consequences (e.g., DWI, alcohol-related arrests) is especially high among African Americans (Calahan, 1970; U.S. Department of Health and Human Services, 1987). Moreover, although abstention is also more common among African American than White women (Herd, 1986), those African American women who drink are more likely than White women to drink heavily (U.S. Department of Health and Human Services, 1987).

According to Herd (1986), African Americans are somewhat overrepresented in treatment programs. Moreover, the fact that African Americans are likely to enter treatment later in the disease process than Whites (U.S. Department of Health and Human Services, 1987) suggests that the overrepresentation of African Americans in treatment programs is not due to any increased motivation among African Americans to pursue treatment. Rather, this overrepresentation may be an indication of the problems caused by alcohol among African Americans.

Beckman and Kocel (1982) argue that the theoretical notions used to explain other health seeking behaviors are useful in understanding participation in substance abuse treatment as well. Their model utilizes a model proposed by Aday and Anderson (1974) that emphasizes societal influences on the response to the health care system, consumer response, and Becker's Health Beliefs model, which focuses on cognitive influences on behavior. Beckman and Kocel integrate these two approaches by stressing how predisposing characteristics such as gender directly influence treatment participation via their effects on perceptions and beliefs about self, treatment norms associated with women's roles, and structural features of the treatment arrangements. This research examined gender differences on one health seeking behavior, that is, treatment participation rates among African Americans in alcoholism treatment programs.

Despite growing evidence that alcoholism treatment does work (Saxe, Dougherty, Esty, & Fine, 1983), and even though growing numbers of women might benefit from treatment, Herd (1986) found that males were about three times as likely to seek treatment for their drinking behavior as females. Moreover, African American women appear even less likely to seek treatment than White women. Herd (n.d.) found that although 13% of males who were current or former heavy drinkers indicated they had talked to someone about their drinking, less than half as many women had done so. Furthermore, about half as many African American women (3.3%) as White women (5.8%) had spoken to someone about their drinking. Moreover, attrition rates for females who do enter treatment are generally higher than attrition rates for males.

Beth Glover Reed (1981) argued that gender must be considered in planning intervention services because gender plays a fundamental role in individual identity, the structure of one's life cycle, and the opportunities and resources available to support behavior change. Furthermore, according to Reed, traditional programs do not consider that chemically dependent women differ from chemically dependent men in a number of fundamental ways that have treatment implications. Specifically, she pointed out that chemically dependent women compared to their male counterparts have lower incomes, are more dependent on social services, have less of a job history to promote future economic self-sufficiency, are more responsible for their children, lead more socially isolated lives, suffer with lower levels of self-esteem, and endorse more of a sense of helplessness. Moreover, women are more likely than men to attribute the onset of their abusive drinking to a stressful event, to report higher levels of psychological distress such as anxiety and depression, and to be motivated to enter treatment because of health or family concerns, whereas males are more likely to enter treatment to resolve job or legal problems (Blume, 1991). Lawson and Lawson (1989) add that women and even their families may cling to an even higher level of denial about their chemical dependency. This may be attributable to the perceived inconsistency between addiction and femininity.

Others argue that traditional substance abuse programs are more compatible with the treatment needs of males than females. Nalerman, Sarase, Haskins, Lear, and Chase (1979) suggest that the typical program is less available to women, does not offer the type of services women need, and does not provide adequate referral and follow-up services for women.

Group treatment has become widely accepted as an effective component of the treatment package for alcoholics. According to Vannicelli (1982), the group offers opportunities to (a) have contact and hold discussions with others with similar problems, (b) to examine and better understand one's attitudes and defenses about sobriety by confronting similar attitudes in others, and (c) to develop skills in communicating needs and feelings more directly.

However, gender (and race), again, may also be an important consideration in the planning of the group experience. One consideration is the reality that, because males outnumber women in treatment, they are likely to outnumber women in the group itself. In addition to the low number of women in treatment groups, others point out that inadequate attention is paid to issues that are pertinent to the lives of women in mixed or majority male groups.

Trotman and Gallagher (1984) argued that the sexual/racial composition of the group affects the effectiveness of the group experience for the African American woman. Specifically, the four group settings they discussed are (a) the integrated male/female group, (b) the integrated women's group, (c) the all African American, mixed sex group, and (d) the all African American women's group. Trotman and Gallagher asserted that the African American woman who participates in the first two types may feel peripheral and may be reluctant to address important issues such as family problems or relationships with men in the presence of White group members. For example, one study demonstrated that two-thirds of women entering treatment bring a history of childhood abuse to treatment (Miller & Downs, 1986). Obviously, such experiences may be more difficult to reveal in a mixed group. Moreover, African American compared to White women have been reported to enter treatment more suspicious, guarded, self-protective, and angry (Carroll, Malloy, Roscioli, Pindjak, & Clifford, 1982).

An all African American male/female group overcomes some of the problems of the two groups mentioned above because African American males and females live within the same subculture and, thus, share similar worldviews. However, Beth Glover Reed (1981) argued that males and females even within the same racial group may be described as living in two separate cultures because of some basic differences in societal expectations about appropriate roles and behaviors for males and females, fundamental differences in the socialization process, and differences in the interactional styles between males and females. Stuart and Brisbane (1982) suggested that African American males cannot relate to the condition of the African American female substance abuser and, thus, find it difficult to be supportive. Moreover, Trotman and Gallagher (1984) note a tendency for African American women to defer to African American men in such groups and, thereby, still be unable to devote a sufficient amount of group time to issues that are important to African American women.

For all the above reasons, Stuart and Brisbane (1982) argued that the rate of attrition among African American women in treatment centers may be attributed at least in part to the lack of fit between needs of African American women and the mixed treatment groups in which many women find themselves.

Jacobsen (1987) reported in summarizing his study of 17 alcoholism treatment units that the percentage of women who completed treatment rose from 35% to 59% when women were treated in all female groups. Others also argued that all female groups are the most effective (Beckman & Kocel, 1978; Doshan & Blursch, 1982). Thus far, although these findings appear generalizable to African American women, these assertions have only been subjected to limited empirical investigation within this population. This study began to address this question by examining gender as a factor in the treatment outcomes of African Americans in alcohol treatment programs.

The present study examines participation rates as one indicator of treatment effectiveness. Specifically, the participation rates of African American females and males in mixed treatment groups for African males and females were examined. Because the program included mixed-sex group sessions, it was predicted that the participation rates for males would exceed the rates for females. Two indices of participation were examined—completion rates and attendance rates.

## Methods

### SAMPLE

The sample included 148 individuals who participated in the program over a 4- to 6-month period. Only those individuals who had terminated from the program were included. However, every terminated case with available records was included. All participants were enrolled in a substance abuse treatment program for African Americans. The program offers culturally sensitive treatment. The treatment program included individual counseling as well as participation in a weekly sobriety group.

### MEASURES

Three outcome measures were included. The first measure was the type of termination. Participants were terminated before completion of the program primarily because of lack of attendance. These were considered negative terminations. Participants who terminated upon successful completion of the program were considered positive terminations. The second outcome measure was attendance at group sessions. Participants were expected to attend weekly mixed-sex group sessions led by a counselor. These sessions focused on issues related to maintaining sobriety as well as difficulties in everyday life that threatened sobriety. The typical format focused on group discussions although didactic presentations on the disease of alcoholism and drinking patterns with the Black community were included. The third outcome measure was attendance at individual sessions. Participants were expected to meet regularly with an individual counselor assigned to them. Client records were used to determine type of termination and attendance.

In addition to these measures, sociodemographic information was also gathered from the records of clients. These measures included gender, employment status, education, marital status, and drinking history.

## PROCEDURE

The present research was part of a larger study conducted at the same treatment facility to identify factors related to treatment outcomes. Trained research assistants reviewed existing records using a data gathering form developed for this research. The data were coded for computer analysis.

## Results

### CHARACTERISTICS OF THE SAMPLE

The median age for the sample was 38.5 years. However, the actual age range varied from 19 to 71. The unemployed represented 52.9% of the sample, while 40.0% worked full-time and 7.1% worked part-time. Fifty-three percent indicated they did not complete high school. Most of the others (41%) completed high school but did not continue their education beyond high school graduation. Only a minority (30%) were currently married. The others were mainly single (35%), or separated or divorced (39%). Most individuals reported that they had been involved in heavy drinking for a prolonged period. When asked during intake about the number of years of heavy drinking, the median number of years reported was 13. Despite the years of heavy drinking, 75% indicated that this was their first treatment experience. Most (71%) had been referred by the court primarily because of a DWI. The others were mainly self-referred (8.8%), or referred by a job (9.1%). No outstanding gender differences were apparent on these background variables.

Sixty-two percent of the participants completed the program. The median number of group and individual sessions attended was 15.5 and 6.0, respectively.

ANALYSIS PLAN

Chi-square statistics were used to determine whether the two groups (males and females) differed in the type of termination. Because individuals participating in different group sessions had the opportunity to attend a slightly different number of sessions due to holidays, cancellations, and so on, the percentage of sessions attended was used to measure the rate of attendance rather than the actual number of sessions attended. *T* tests were then used to examine whether the mean attendance rates for males and females were significantly different at individual and group sessions.

GENDER DIFFERENCES IN PARTICIPATION

Females were less likely than males to complete the program with a positive termination. Specifically, 67.3% of the males completed the program but only 45% of the females. This difference was statistically significant ($\chi^2$ (1, $N = 124$) = 3.61, $p < .05$).

The two groups also differed in their attendance rates at both group and individual sessions. Specifically, males (mean ($M$) = 88[1]) attended more group sessions than females ($M = 76$), ($t(88 = 2.45, p = .01$). Males ($M = 84$) also attended a higher rate of individual sessions than females ($M = 64$), ($t(79) = 3.1, p < .002$).

## Discussion

Generally, these findings support the prediction that gender is related to rates of participation in alcohol-related treatment programs among African Americans. Specifically, males were more likely to complete the program than females. Moreover, males attended more group and individual sessions than females. Together, these two findings argue that women are not as likely as men to participate in a program emphasizing a mixed-sex group format. It was not clear initially whether to expect differences in attendance rates at individual sessions. That is, the individual sessions with the therapist do not provide the same potential for group dynamics as the mixed group sessions. However, if a woman withdraws or is terminated from the program for whatever reasons, then the option to attend the individual sessions is no longer available. Obviously, that reality would lower the attendance rates at individual sessions.

These findings add support to the position of Trotman and Gallagher (1984) that mixed-sex groups may not be the ideal treatment setting for African American women. Rather these women may experience difficulties in using such a setting to work through their own issues.

For all the above reasons, Trotman and Gallagher (1984) argue in favor of African American women's groups as the best group setting for these women to work through some of the important issues in their lives. These authors argue that such groups provide a woman with "a safe environment in which she can speak expressively and directly about issues of vital importance to her mental health, while developing and modeling her unique style in the intimacy and love of her Black sisters." Our findings suggest that treatment programs ought to offer such groups as an alternative for those women who choose this treatment option. The particular treatment setting in which this research was conducted has since initiated a women's program for African American female alcoholics. The program provides an alternative for those women who prefer to participate in women's groups and other treatment activities that address their unique needs as Black women.

In the future, it will be necessary to study this issue more fully by comparing the participation rates of African American women in mixed groups to the participation rates seen among similar women in groups designed for African American women. It was not possible to do so in the present study because a similar program that involved only African-American women was unavailable. Nevertheless, the present study contributes to our understanding of the treatment needs of these women by documenting their low participation rates relative to males in mixed-sex group treatment.

In conclusion, the findings suggest that African American women relative to African American men are more likely to withdraw early or attend infrequently in mixed groups. Hence, program planners need to consider alternative treatment options, especially the option of an all African American women's group, to increase the participation of this group.

## Note

1. Mean percentage of sessions attended.

# References

Aday, L., & Anderson, R. (1974). A framework for the study of access to medical care. *Health Services Research, 9,* 208-220.

Becker, M. H. (1974). The health belief model and sick role behavior. *Journal of Social Issues, 38*(2), 139-151.

Beckman, L. J. (1978). Self-esteem of women alcoholics. *Journal of Studies on Alcohol, 39,* 491-498.

Beckman, J. L., & Kocel, K. M. (1982). The treatment delivery system and alcohol abuse in women: Social policy implications. *Journal of Social Issues, 38*(2), 139-151.

Blume, S. (1991). Women alcohol, and drugs. In N. Miller (Ed.), *Comprehensive handbook of drug and alcohol addiction.* New York: Dekker.

Calahan, D. (1970). *Problem drinkers.* San Francisco: Jossey-Bass.

Carroll, J. F. X., Malloy, T. E., Roscioli, D. L., Pindjak, G. M., & Clifford, S. J. (1982). Similarities and differences in self-concepts of women alcoholics and drug addicts. *Journal of Studies on Alcohol, 42,* 432-440.

Clark, B. & Midanik, L. (1982). Alcohol use and alcohol problems among U.S. adults: Results of the 1979 national survey. In *Alcohol consumption and related problems. Alcohol and Health Monograph 1* (DHHS Publication No. (ADM) 82-1190). Washington, DC: Government Printing Office.

Doshan, T., & Blursch, C. (1982). Woman and substance abuse: Critical issues in treatment design. *Journal of Drug Education, 12,* 229-239.

Herd, D. (1986). *A review of drinking patterns and alcohol problems among U.S. Blacks* (U.S. Department of Health and Human Services Report of the Secretary's Task Force on Black and Minority Health). Washington, DC: Government Printing Office.

Herd, D. (XXXX). *Family life-cycle variables and drinking patterns and problems: A comparison of Black and White Americans from a national study.* Unpublished manuscript.

Jacobsen, G. (1981). Alcohol and drug dependency problems in special population: Women. In R. Herring, G. Jacobsen, & D. Benser (Eds.), *Alcohol and drug handbook.* St. Louis, MO: Warren Green.

Lawson, G., & Lawson, A. (1989). *Alcoholism and substance abuse in special populations.* Rockville, MD: Aspen.

Miller, B. A., & Downs, W. R. (1986). *Conflict and violence among alcoholic women as compared to a random household sample.* Paper presented at the 38th annual meeting of the American Society of Criminology, Atlanta, GA.

Nalerman, N., Sarase, B., Haskins, B., Lear, J., & Chase, H. (1979). *An assessment of the extent of sex discrimination in the delivery of health and human development services. Phase II Report* (Report to the U.S. DHEW, Office for Civil Rights, Contract #HEW-100-78-0137). Cambridge, MA: Abt.

Reed, B. G. (1981). Intervention strategies for drug dependent women: An introduction. In G. Beschner, B. G. Reed, & J. Mandanaro (Eds.), *Treatment services for drug dependent women.* NIDA of U.S. Department of Health and Human Services, Public Health Service.

Saxe, L., Dougherty, D., Esty, K., & Fine, M. (1983). *The effectiveness and costs of alcoholism treatment.* Health Technology Case Study 22. Office of Technology Assessment, U.S. Congress. Washington, DC: Government Printing Office.

Stuart, B. C., & Brisbane, F. L. (1982). The Black female alcoholic: A perspective from history to 1982. *Bulletin of the New York Chapter of NBAC, 1*(2), 5-7.

Trotman, F., & Gallagher, A. (1984). Group therapy with Black women. In C. M. Brody (Ed.), *Women therapists working with women: New theory and process of feminist research.* New York: Springer.

U.S. Department of Health and Human Services. (1981). *Fourth Special Report to the U.S. Congress on Alcohol and Health* (DHHS Pub. No. ADM 81-1081). Washington, DC: DHHS.

U.S. Department of Health and Human Services. (1987). *Sixth Special Report to the U.S. Congress on Alcohol and Health, Public Health Service. Alcohol, Drug Abuse, and Mental Health Administration, NIAAA.*

Vannicelli, M. (1982). Group therapy with alcoholics: Special techniques. *Journal of Studies on Alcohol, 43*(1), 17-37.

# 26 Improving Health Outcomes of African Americans: A Challenge for African American Psychologists

## FAYE Z. BELGRAVE
*The George Washington University*

Seven causes of death account for more than 80% of the excess deaths[1] in the African American community and are the leading causes of mortality, morbidity, and disability in the African American community. These causes are (1) heart disease and stroke; (2) homicide and accidents; (3) cancer; (4) infant mortality; (5) cirrhosis; (6) diabetes; and (7) AIDS.

The common denominator of all of the above cases is that they are linked to modifiable behavioral and life-style factors. Every one of these causes could be eliminated or substantially reduced if behavioral changes were made. Smoking and cancer provide an excellent illustration of the link between modifiable at-risk behaviors and mortality and morbidity. According to the National Center for Health Services Research (1987), African Americans have the highest overall cancer rate of any U.S. population group. Lung cancer is 45% higher for African American males than for White males—and accounts for approximately 45% of all cancer cases in African American males. An examination of smoking patterns indicates that a large percentage of African American males 20 years or older smoke, 40.7% compared to 32.7% of White males. Other high risk factors that lead to increases in morbidity and mortality are diet and nutrition. Approximately 50% of African American females are overweight or obese—a high risk condition for diabetes and cardiovascular disease. The National Center for Health Services Research (1987) shows a much higher incidence of diabetes and cardio-

Correspondence regarding this article should be addressed to Faye Z. Belgrave, Assistant Professor, Department of Psychology, The George Washington University, Washington, DC 20052.

vascular disease among African American women than among White women. Lack of and insufficient prenatal care account for much of the large disparity in infant mortality of African Americans and Whites. Infant mortality in the African American community is twice that of the White community. These examples are only a few of many high risk behaviors that, if changed, could substantially reduce morbidity and mortality of African Americans.

When one reviews the health outcome statistics of African Americans, the high prevalence of morbidity, mortality, and disability are distressing. Yet, on the positive side, these statistics can be changed. African American psychologists can make a substantial contribution to changing them. How can we make a difference? First of all, we have access to the African American community. Second, we have the expertise to change behavior. Using our expertise in the areas of (1) community assessment, (2) behavioral intervention, and (3) research and evaluation we can develop, implement, and evaluate programs for reducing at-risk behaviors. These three areas are commented on briefly below:

*Community Assessment.* The development of a health promotion, primary prevention, and intervention program begins with an assessment of the community. The key questions here are: (1) Who is at risk? and (2) What are the factors leading to the adoption and the maintenance of at-risk behaviors? African American psychologists trained in assessment of minority communities can make a contribution in this area. Three points are worth mentioning here. First, the psychologist has to gain credibility in the community by demonstrating sincerity and commitment to the community. Second, when conducting an assessment, the norms, values, and beliefs of the community must be recognized and taken into consideration. Third, the needs and the problems of the community must be defined by the community with involvement from community leaders and residents.

*Primary Prevention and Intervention Programs.* Using information gathered from the community assessment, prevention and treatment programs designed to change behaviors can be developed. These programs must also be sensitive to the life-styles, norms, and values of the African American community. One important point to remember is that there are many resources in the African American community that can be used to develop and implement programs. Churches, recreational facilities, housing projects, and schools have been used with success in the African American community for health promotion, prevention, and treatment. Examples of such programs include programs for prenatal care, blood pressure screening for sickle cell disease, and diet and nutrition programs. Community youth programs that focus on social and recreational activities can also be viewed as preventive resources because these programs and activities teach youths acceptable ways to deal with stress, anger, and frustrations, ways that reduce the incidence of substance abuse and violence in the African American community.

*Research.* There is a need for more research to answer questions such as (1) Who in the African American community is at risk? (2) What are the determinants of at-risk behaviors? (3) What at-risk behaviors are most likely to lead to morbidity, mortality, and disability? (4) What is the perception of being at-risk? (5) What factors are associated with adherence to treatment regimen? (6) What interventions have worked? As with assessment and intervention, research questions and methods must be guided by the values and the norms of the community.

To summarize, statistics on health outcomes overwhelmingly show that health outcomes are very unfavorable for African Americans. Millions of us are dying early deaths, and the quality of our lives is poor because of disease and disability. African American psychologists can make a contribution. We have both the access and the expertise to do the job. This is an enormous challenge for African American psychologists—one which I hope will be met by more of us.

### Note

1. *Excess deaths* are defined as the number of deaths among minorities that would not have occurred had mortality rates for minorities equalled those of nonminorities.

### Reference

National Center for Health Services Research. (1987). *Health, United States* (Vol. 12). Washington, DC: Public Health Service, U.S. Department of Health and Human Services, Office of Health Research, Statistics, and Technology, National Center for Health Statistics.

# 27 The Relationship Among Type A Behavior, Styles Used in Coping With Racism, and Blood Pressure

**VERNESSA R. CLARK**\*
*Virginia State University*
**JULES P. HARRELL**
*Howard University*

The relationship between six cognitive styles used in coping with racism and blood pressure in 32 Black students was studied. It was hypothesized that an apathetic style would be associated with lower blood pressure readings. Also, the relationship between the Type A coronary-prone behavior pattern and blood pressure was examined. As expected, weight was shown to have a strong relationship with blood pressure. The Type A dimension was positively related to diastolic pressure at rest and during mental arithmetic (mild stress). A style associated with a proactive and flexible orientation to the problems of racism was positively correlated with resting systolic blood pressure and the recovery of a diastolic pressure after stress.

Hypertension is a particularly prevalent and troublesome disease among Blacks. Because of the stressful conditions to which many Blacks are subjected, psychological causes of the disorder in the Black community have not been ruled out (Saunders & Williams, 1975). As research to determine the role that stressful environments play in causing elevated pressure continues, studies of the relationship between personality variables and blood pressure levels in the Black population should not be neglected. Accordingly, this investigation focused on the relationship between the blood pressure of young Blacks and a number of personality dimensions.

Some of the findings reported in this paper were presented at the Third Annual Norfolk State College Undergraduate Psychology Conference, Norfolk, VA, April 1979. The assistance of Ms. Joyce Williams, Ms. Joyce Drummond, and Ms. Shelia Wooden in preparing the manuscript is gratefully acknowledged.
Vernessa R. Clark, Department of Psychology, Howard University, Washington, DC 20059.
Jules P. Harrell, Department of Psychology, Howard University, Washington, DC 20059.
\*EDITORS' NOTE: Currently at Morehouse College.

Two approaches to examining personality variables were taken. The first centered on assessing certain cognitive styles that Blacks have developed in response to racism, and on correlating these assessments with blood pressure readings. The second involved examining the relationship between the blood pressure of Blacks and a behavioral pattern that has been shown to be a risk factor for major coronary illnesses.

Harrell (1979) described the characteristics and assessment of six cognitive styles that Blacks utilize to cope with racism. These coping styles include (a) an apathetic style that is characterized by passivity, (b) a "piece of the action" style, (c) a style opting for countercultural solutions to racism that transcend the problems of life rather than address them directly, (d) a Black nationalistic style, (e) an authoritarian style, and finally, (f) a style characterized by cognitive flexibility, historical awareness, and open-mindedness.

One hypothesis advanced by Harrell (1979) was that the apathetic style would actually be associated with fewer psychosomatic symptoms. Apathetic individuals, in this system, are those who do not tend to engage in active coping responses. Active coping has been associated with psychosomatic disease in animals (Weiss, 1972) and psychophysiological reactivity in humans (P. A. Obrist, 1976). One aim of this study was to determine whether Black students had lower and less reactive blood pressures when the apathetic style was a dominant feature of their personalities.

The present study also focused on the relationship between blood pressure and a second personality dimension called "the Type A behavior pattern." This dimension is characterized primarily by excessive drive, aggressiveness, involvement in competitive activities, an enhanced sense of time urgency, and restless motor mannerisms. A number of reports have associated this behavior pattern with coronary heart disease (Rosenman, Friedman, Straus, Wurm, Jenkins, & Messinger, 1966). Though a structured interview is often used to measure Type A behavior, objective methods for measuring the dimension in various populations are available. For example, Krantz, Glass, and Snyder (1974) described a modification of the Jenkins Activity Scale (JAS), the scale used to assess Type A behavior patterns among working adults. They modified the scale for use with a student population.

Using the JAS to assess Type A behavior, Shekelle, Schoenberger, and Stamler (1976) determined that Type A women 45-64 years of age evidenced higher diastolic blood pressure than Type B women; that is, women who are much less competitive and aggressive. In contrast, a negative correlation between Type A behavior and blood pressure was reported in a separate study with women of the same age group (Waldron, 1978). Smyth, Call, Hansell, Sparacino, and Strodtbeck (1978) also found Type A females to be no more likely to have hypertension than non-Type A individuals. Other findings, however, indicated that resting blood pressure levels are higher in Type A individuals (Howard, Cunningham, & Rechnitzer, 1976; Scherwitz, Berton, & Leventhal, 1978). A series of recent studies has reported that Type A individuals show greater blood pressure reactivity under stress (Manuck, Craft, & Gold, 1978; Dembroski, MacDougall, Shields, Petitto, & Lushene, 1978; Scherwitz et al., 1978). But Black subjects participated only in the study of Smyth et al. (1978), which used the interview method, not the JAS, to assess Type A behavior. Clearly, the relationship between this dimension and the blood pressure has not been studied extensively in the Black population. A second aim of this research was to determine if the relationship between Type A behavior and blood pressure existed in a population of young Black adults.

As has been noted, personality variables may show a relationship not only to resting or casual blood pressure readings, but also the extent of blood pressure increases during stress (see also Harrell, 1980). Therefore, a difficult mental arithmetic task was used to elicit blood pressure increases in the present study. Though this procedure is, at best, mildly stressful, its effectiveness in producing blood pressure increases in the laboratory has been established (Brod, 1970). The effects of weight were also taken into consideration as the relationship between personality and blood pressure was examined. Since weight has been shown to have a strong positive correlation with blood pressure (see Saunders & Williams, 1975), the possibility of this variable's masking of existing relationships between personality and blood pressure was anticipated. Therefore, appropriate statistical procedures were used to examine the relationship between the blood pressure measures and personality, independent of the effects of weight.

In this study, then, it was hypothesized that blood pressure would be higher, and more reactive to a mild stressor, in Black students who evidenced the Type A behavior pattern. In addition, the coping style that these individuals used to deal with elements of racism that they encountered in their lives was posited to have an effect on their blood pressure readings. Specifically, it was hypothesized that those showing an apathetic cognitive style would have lower and less reactive blood pressure readings.

## Method

### SUBJECTS

Thirty-two Black students from an introductory psychology course at Virginia State University participated in this study in order to obtain course credit. Twenty-one females and 11 males between the ages of 18 and 24 years participated. The average age was 19.8 years. The participants were told that blood pressure measurements would be taken during the course of the study, but were given no additional information about the experiment.

### QUESTIONNAIRES

The JAS, in the form modified for students (Krantz et al., 1974), was used to measure the Type A behavior pattern. The cognitive styles for coping with racism were measured with the Coping Styles Scale (CSS) (Knight & Benn, Note 1). This is a sixty-item questionnaire, in which the degree of agreement or disagreement with the items is measured on a five-point scale. The CSS contains a subscale for each coping style. The scores on the scales have been shown to have no correlation, or in some cases low correlations, with each other. Hence, rather than consider the CSS as a measure of a pure coping strategy, the scores are viewed as a profile in which a particular scale may or may not be elevated. The test-retest reliability coefficient for the individual styles ranges from .58 to .74.

### PROCEDURE

A standard blood pressure cuff was used to obtain blood pressure readings at three intervals: after a two-minute initial rest period, following a mental arithmetic task, and after a two-minute final rest period. Upon arrival of the subjects at the experimental room, their weight and height were obtained. The subjects were then instructed to be seated in a high-backed, cushioned chair, and to relax for two minutes. At the end of this period, designated "the initial rest period," a blood pressure reading was taken. The subjects were then asked to perform a "simple but challenging task." A mental arithmetic task was administered in which they were given tape-recorded instructions to count backwards from a four-digit number by a two-digit number. They were instructed to count aloud, to attempt to keep the rhythm of a beat

**TABLE 27.1** Blood Pressure Readings for Three Periods

| Measure Period | X mm Hg. | Standard Deviation |
|---|---|---|
| Diastolic (Initial Rest) | 68 | 7.53 |
| Diastolic (Stress) | 71 | 6.60 |
| Diastolic (Final Rest) | 65 | 6.51 |
| Systolic (Initial Rest) | 116 | 5.16 |
| Systolic (Stress) | 121 | 7.29 |
| Systolic (Final Rest) | 115 | 5.90 |

provided on the tape, and to do their best. After thirty seconds of counting, the tape instructed them to stop, and the blood pressure reading for this, the stress period, was quickly obtained. Following a two-minute final rest period, in which the subjects were then asked to complete the JAS and the CSS in a separate room. A formal presentation explaining the nature of the experiment was given to the participants at the conclusion of the study. Questions were encouraged at that time.

## Results

Table 27.1 provides the means and standard deviations of the blood pressure readings obtained during the three periods. In this relatively young group, all of the individual pressure readings were in the normal range, using a criterion of 140/90 mm Hg. Also, the scores on the JAS (mean $(M) = 11.70$, $SD = 2.55$) were comparable with those reported in other work (Krantz et al., 1974).

Pearson correlation coefficients[1] were computed to determine the relationship between the blood pressure measurements and the scores from the JAS and the CSS. A significant correlation was found between the JAS and the diastolic blood pressure readings taken during the stress period ($r = .31$, $p < .05$) and the final rest period ($r = .30$, $p < .05$). Since the JAS is scored in such a way that Type A behavior is associated with the higher scores, these correlations indicated that Type A individuals were more likely to have higher diastolic blood pressures during these periods. Also, significant negative correlations resulted between the apathetic style measured by the CSS and the systolic blood pressure readings taken during the initial rest period ($r = -.32$, $p < .05$) and the final rest period ($r = -.30$, $p < .05$). Apparently, those subjects with the higher scores for the apathetic style evidenced lower systolic blood

**TABLE 27.2** Correlation Between Weight and Blood Pressure

| Measurement Period | r | p < |
|---|---|---|
| Diastolic (Initial Rest) | .33 | .05 |
| Diastolic (Stress) | .36 | .01 |
| Diastolic (Final Rest) | .30 | .05 |
| Systolic (Initial Rest) | .57 | .01 |
| Systolic (Stress) | .42 | .01 |
| Systolic (Final Rest) | .64 | .01 |

pressure readings during these periods. No other significant relationships between blood pressure and the personality measures were found. Although the purpose of this study was not to examine the relationship between the Type A behavior pattern and the six cognitive styles for dealing with racism, the correlational analyses indicated that there were no significant relationships between these dimensions.

As expected, weight proved to have a strong relationship with blood pressure according to the correlational analysis (see Table 27.2). Therefore, a partial correlation analysis was used in order to first adjust for the effects of weight on blood pressure and then to examine the relationship between the personality variables and the blood pressure measurements. The partial correlation analysis determined that Type A behavior, as measured by the JAS, was again associated with higher diastolic blood pressure readings during the stress period ($r = .36$, $p < .05$) and the final rest period ($r = .34$, $p < .05$), independent of the effects of weight. However, in this analysis, the scores for the apathetic style were no longer significantly related to systolic blood pressure. Instead, an unexpected relationship between the scores for the coping style associated with cognitive flexibility (hereafter called the flexibility style), as measured by the CSS and the systolic blood pressure measurements taken during the initial rest period ($r = .35$, $p < .05$) and the final rest period ($r = .48$, $p < .01$), was found. This partial correlational analysis then determined that when adjustments were made for the effects of weight on blood pressure, the high scores on the flexibility style were associated with higher resting systolic blood pressure.

Finally, multiple regression analyses were used to determine the efficacy of weight and the personality measures as predictors of the blood pressure readings in this population.[2] The scores from the personality scales that were entered into the multiple regression equations included the scores from the JAS and the CSS measure of apathy. Because of the strong relationship that was found in the partial correlation analysis between systolic blood pressure and the scores for flexibility style, these scores were also used as predictor variables. Criterion variables included both the systolic and the diastolic blood pressure readings that were obtained during the two rest periods and the stress period, and the differences in the blood pressure readings from the initial rest periods to the stress periods and from the stress periods to the final rest periods. As Table 27.3 illustrates, the results of these analyses generally supported the results obtained in the partial correlation analysis. Furthermore, these analyses showed that the four predictors accounted for approximately 50% of the variance in the systolic blood pressure readings obtained during the initial rest periods and stress periods, and accounted for more than 25% of the variance in the diastolic blood pressure readings obtained during the stress period.

## Discussion

Limited support for the two hypotheses advanced in this study was obtained. Type A individuals tended to have higher diastolic blood pressures at rest and during stress. Individuals with high scores for the apathetic coping style tended to have lower resting systolic blood pressures. However, the latter relationship was not found when a partial correlation analysis was used to adjust for the effects of weight on blood pressure. Surprisingly, when adjustments were made for the effects of weight, higher scores for the flexibility style were associated with higher resting systolic blood pressures, as well as with larger recoveries to baseline in diastolic blood pressures, from the stress period to the final rest period.

Although the apathetic coping style is specifically concerned with behaviors related to racism, conceptually there are similarities between this dimension and the Type A dimension. It would appear that both may focus on a tendency to actively engage the social environment and the tendency to exercise coping behaviors in response to environmental stress. However, these dimensions were not correlated in this study ($r = .009$). Furthermore, though the correlation analysis initially indicated that Type A was indeed positively related to blood pressure and that the apathetic style was negatively related to it, the apathetic style was not a useful predictor of blood pressure independent of the effects of weight. Hence, although these dimensions are conceptually similar,

**TABLE 27.3** Multiple Regression Findings for Weight, Personality, and Blood Pressure

| Predictor | Systolic Blood Pressure Initial Rest Period Beta | F | p |
|---|---|---|---|
| Flexibility | .30 | 3.75 | <.05 |
| Weight | .66 | 16.02 | <.01 |
| | $R^2 = .44$ | 5.40 | <.01 |

| Predictor | Systolic Blood Pressure Final Rest Period Beta | F | p |
|---|---|---|---|
| Flexibility | .38 | 8.18 | <.01 |
| Weight | .76 | 27.45 | <.01 |
| | $R^2 = .57$ | 8.94 | <.01 |

| Predictor | Diastolic Blood Pressure Stress Period Beta | F | p |
|---|---|---|---|
| Type A | .35 | 4.58 | <.01 |
| Weight | .48 | 6.71 | <.01 |
| | $R^2 = .28$ | 2.69 | <.05 |

| Predictor | Diastolic Blood Pressure Final Rest Period Beta | F | p |
|---|---|---|---|
| Type A | .32 | 3.65 | .05 |
| | $R^2 = .20$ | 1.77 | NS |

| Predictor | Difference in Diastolic Pressure From Stress to Final Rest Beta | F | p |
|---|---|---|---|
| Flexibility | .36 | 3.58 | .05 |
| | $R^2 = .13$ | 1.00 | NS |
| | degrees of freedom—4.27 | | |

they are not empirically related to each other, and only Type A is a useful predictor of blood pressure in this population.

What dimension of the Type A behavior pattern leads to higher levels of blood pressure? The findings of Dembroski, MacDougell, Shields, Petitto, and Lushene, (1978) suggested that when Type A is measured with the JAS, it is the competitive/hard-driving component that has the strongest association with autonomic arousal. Evidence is mounting in support of the notion that active coping behavior exacerbates cardiovascular responses to stress in the laboratory (Manuck, Harvey, Lechlieter, & Neal, 1978; Obrist, Gaebelein, Teller, Langer, Gringnolo, Light, & McCubbin, 1978). As noted earlier, there is evidence that Type A individuals show greater blood pressure reactivity during stress than Type B individuals (Dembroski et al., 1978; Manuck, Craft, & Gold, 1978; Scherwitz et al., 1978). In fact, the Type A pattern probably predisposes one to engage in coping during stress. To the subjects in this study, the laboratory situation was an uncertain, unfamiliar, and possibly mildly stressful setting. It may well be that the higher diastolic readings associated with the Type A dimensions were mediated by attempts to effect some measure of control over the anxiety experienced in this uncertain setting. It is reasonable to assume from available data that competitive, hard-driving attempts to effect physiological control during stress may actually result in larger cardiovascular responses.

The score for the flexibility style was as strong a predictor of resting systolic blood pressure as the Type A pattern was of diastolic blood pressure. This style was defined (see Harrell, 1979) as involving some awareness of the complex nature of the struggle for full equality in which Blacks are engaged and of an open posture to new solutions to the problems faced by Blacks. Since the CSS is still being refined, and the relationship of this style to blood pressure was not expected, no precise explanation for its predictive utility is possible, and the present finding is being used to guide further research efforts.

However, earlier work (Knight & Benn, 1978, Note 1) has established that the scores for the flexibility style are negatively related both to authoritarianism as defined by Sanford (1956) and to the apathetic style as measured by the CSS. It is likely that the flexibility style is related to the tendency for Blacks to approach the environment in an open-minded and proactive fashion. But until the current construct validational work with the CSS is completed, the reasons for the relationship of the flexibility style to systolic blood pressure, and to the recovery of diastolic pressure after stress, will remain unclear.

Though it may be that the measurement procedure used in this study was somewhat unreliable, for two reasons it is unlikely that experimenter bias resulted in the blood pressure readings being related to the personality dimensions. First, the personality scores were not obtained until after the blood pressure measurements were obtained. Second, the two best predictors, the Type A pattern and the flexibility score, were not related, and therefore, even if these dimensions could be assessed informally through personal contact, it would have been difficult to manipulate the blood pressure measurements in such a way as to be related to both. Still, studies replicating these findings using automated measurements of blood pressure are planned.

In the present study, then, significant predictions of casual blood pressure readings in young Blacks, using weight and two personality measures, were possible. Type A behavior was related to diastolic blood pressure in the same fashion as had been reported in earlier studies with White subjects. The assessment of the coping styles of Blacks, using the CSS, also seems to be useful in developing personality predictors of blood pressure. The scores for the flexibility style proved to have a significant positive relationship to systolic pressure and to the recovery of diastolic pressure after stress. These findings, then, encourage the inclusion of personality variables as predictors of elevated blood pressure in Blacks.

## Notes

1. Degrees of freedom for each reported correlation coefficient equal 31.
2. Multiple regression equations were computed separately for males and females also. Since the results of these parallel those found in the entire sample, only the latter are presented.

## References

Brod, J. (1970). Haemodynamics and emotional stress. In M. Koster, H. Mushaph, & P. Visser (Eds.), *Psychosomatics in essential hypertension*. New York: S. Karger.

Dembroski, T. M., MacDougall, J. S., Shields, J. L., Petitto, J., & Lushene, R. (1978). Components of the Type A coronary-prone behavior pattern and cardiovascular responses to psychomotor performance challenge. *Journal of Behavioral Medicine, 1*, 159-176.

Harrell, J. P. (1979). Analyzing Black coping styles: A supplemental diagnostic system. *The Journal of Black Psychology, 5*, 99-108.

Harrell, J. P. (1980). Psychological factors in hypertension: A status report. *Psychological Bulletin, 87*, 482-501.

Howard, J. H., Cunningham, D. A., & Rechnitzer, P. A. (1976). Health patterns associated with Type A behavior: A managerial population. *Journal of Human Stress, 2*, 24-31.

Krantz, D. S., Glass, D. C., & Snyder, M. L. (1974). Helplessness, stress level and the coronary-prone behavior pattern. *Journal of Experimental Social Psychology, 10*, 294-300.

Manuck, S. B., Craft, S., & Gold, K. J. (1978). Coronary-prone behavior pattern and cardiovascular response. *Psychophysiology, 15*, 403-411.

Manuck, S. B., Harvey, A. H., Lechlieter, S. L., & Neal, K. S. (1978). Effects of coping on blood pressure responses to threat of aversive stimulation. *Psychophysiology, 15*, 544-549.

Obrist, P. A. (1976). The cardiovascular-behavioral interaction—As it appears today. *Psychophysiology, 13*, 95-107.

Obrist, P. S., Gaebelein, C. J., Teller, E. S., Langer, A. W., Grignolo, A., Light, K. C., & McCubbin, J. A. (1978). The relationship among heart rate, carotid *dp/dt* and blood pressure in humans as a function of the type of stress. *Psychophysiology, 15*, 102-115.

Rosenman, R. H., Freidman, M., Straus, R., Wurm, M., Jenkins, C. D., & Messinger, H. B. (1966). Coronary heart disease in the Western collaborative group study: A follow-up experience of two years. *Journal of the American Medical Association, 195*, 130-136.

Rosenman, R. H., Friedman, M., Straus, R., Wurm, M., Kositchek, R., Hahn, R., & Werthessen, N. T. (1964). Predictive study of coronary heart disease: The Western collaborative group study. *Journal of the American Medical Association, 189*, 15-26.

Sanford, N. (1956). The approach of the authoritarian personality. In J. L. McCray (Ed.), *Psychology of personality*. New York: Grove.

Saunders, E., & Williams, R. A. (1975). Hypertension. In R. A. Williams (Ed.), *Textbook of Black-related diseases* (pp. 333-357). New York: McGraw-Hill.

Scherwitz, L., Berton, K., & Leventhal, H. (1978). Type A behavior, self-involvement and cardiovascular response. *Psychosomatic Medicine, 40*, 593-609.

Shekelle, R. B., Schoenberger, J. A., & Stamler, J. (1976). Correlates of the JAS Type A behavior pattern score. *Journal of Chronic Diseases, 29*, 102-122.

Smyth, K., Call, J., Hansell, S., Sparacino, J., & Strodtbeck, F. L. (1978). Type A behavior pattern and hypertension among inner-city Black women. *Nursing Research, 27*, 30-35.

Waldron, I. (1978). The coronary-prone behavior pattern, blood pressure, employment and socio-economic status in women. *Journal of Psychosomatic Research, 22*, 79-87.

Weiss, J. M. (1972). Psychological factors in stress and disease. *Scientific American, 226*(6), 104-113.

# 28 Life Stress, Health, and Blood Pressure in Black College Students

HECTOR F. MYERS
ROCHELLE T. BASTIEN*
*University of California, Los Angeles*
RALPH E. MILES
*Fanon Research and Development Center*

A multivariate stress and health risk model is proposed to test the contribution of stress on blood pressure in Black college students. Measures of stress reaction pattern, level of stress exposure, personal level of distress, the availability of social supports, personal and family health history, and health status were obtained from a sample of 191 Black university students. Multiple regression analyses predicting systolic and diastolic blood pressure overall and by gender supported the hypothesis that stress interacts with prior familial health history, personal health status, and level of subjective distress to predict blood pressure. Stress affected health and blood pressure differently for Black males and females.

Essential hypertension or high blood pressure is one of the more prevalent chronic diseases in the United States. Major epidemiologic and actuarial studies on the estimated more than 23 million Americans who suffer from this disease have demonstrated quite convincingly that high blood pressure is a major independent risk factor for coronary heart disease, cerebrovascular diseases, aortic aneurysms, and for peripheral

This study was partially supported by a grant from the Institute for American Culture and the Center for Afro-American Studies, UCLA, and by a grant from NIMH to the Fanon Research and Development Center.

Hector F. Myers, Department of Psychology, University of California, Los Angeles, 405 Hilgard Ave., Los Angeles, CA 90024, or Fanon Research & Development Center, 12714 S. Avalon Blvd., Suite 301, Los Angeles, CA 90061.

Rochelle T. Bastien, Office of Graduate Studies & Research, Mail Point Q-003, University of California at San Diego, La Jolla, CA 92093.

Ralph E. Miles, Fanon Research & Development Center, 12714 S. Avalon Blvd., Suite 301, Los Angeles, CA 90061.

*EDITORS' NOTE: Currently in private practice in San Diego.

vascular disease. Additionally, high blood pressure significantly reduces life expectancy (HDFP Report, 1979).

For Blacks, and especially those in the lower socioeconomic status groups, high blood pressure is considered by many as the major medical problem of today. It is estimated that between 22.2% and 28.2% of Black Americans are diagnosed as hypertensives compared to 15% to 17% of Whites (National Center for Health Statistics Report, 1976; National Black Health Providers Task Force Report, 1980). Extending this analysis to include gender, age, SES, and pattern of risk for cardiovascular-related diseases by ethnic group illustrates even more fully the extent of the racial differences in risk for high blood pressure. Recent vital and health statistics published by the National Center for Health Statistics (NCHS, 1974, 1976, 1978, 1981), and the recent report by NIH's National Black Health Providers Task Force (NBHPTF, 1980) on high blood pressure identify several important differences in the prevalence of high blood pressure between Blacks and Whites. For example, the prevalence of hypertension is greater for Blacks than Whites both overall and for all age groups 17 years and older. Blacks are also overrepresented at the higher blood pressure levels where the disease is more severe, end organ damage more likely, and the risk of death much greater (i.e., diastolic BP levels of 105mm Hg or greater). Blacks are also known to be at greater risk for cerebrovascular accidents, for hypertensive heart disease secondary to high blood pressure, and are significantly more likely than Whites to die from these disorders.

These reports also note that the highest prevalence of high blood pressure per 100 population aged 17 and older is found in Black females (28.6%), and the lowest in White females (17.7%). Black males (27.8%) and Whites males (18.5%) show intermediate prevalence rates. It is noteworthy, of course, that the prevalence rates for Black males is also significantly higher than those for both White males and females. Socioeconomic status was also found to be inversely related to prevalence of high blood pressure, such that highest prevalence is found among the lower SES groups regardless of race or gender (Keil, Tyroler, Sandifer, & Boyle, 1977; Saunders & Williams, 1975; Stamler, 1980.)

In sum, these data underscore the severity of the risks of high blood pressure for Blacks and the poor. These risks include biologic, socioenvironmental, and personal life-style factors that increase susceptibility to developing the pattern of sustained elevated blood pressures and related end organ damage associated with hypertensive disease.

Efforts to understand these disproportionate racial and SES trends, as well as to understand their implications for the etiology, pathophysiology, and treatment of hypertension have generated considerable research designed to identify the contributory factors in this disease. Weiner (1979) and Stamler (1980) recently reviewed the existing evidence on the etiology of high blood pressure and identified four general factors as implicated etiologically in hypertension; (a) genetic vulnerability reflected in a family history of the disease, and where disease risk increases proportionally with the degree of direct blood relatives affected (i.e., grandparents, parents, siblings, etc.); (b) cardiovascular system features, such as high normal resting blood pressure and high cardiovascular reactivity to stress; (c) a series of dietary-dependent traits, such as being overweight or gaining weight; consuming diets high in sodium, caffeine, alcohol, and animal fats; and (d) life-style factors such as smoking, inadequate exercise, and high life stress and tension.

Several studies have also offered some suggestive evidence of psychological and personality factors believed to discriminate between hypertensives and normotensives. Among these are high arousability, anxiety, and nervousness (Smith, 1972; Weyer & Hodapp, 1979), greater tendency to suppress anger in response to legitimate provocation (Gentry, Chesney, Gary, Hall, & Harburg, 1982), greater tendency to have an external locus of control and to experience higher levels of discontentment (Naditch, 1973), and a tendency to deny arousal and tension (Meyer, Derogatis, Miller, & Reading, 1978; Singer, 1967; Thomas, 1961).

Unfortunately, although there is general agreement on a multicausal etiological model of hypertension, there is little agreement about which factors should be included in the model, and what their causal linkages are to the disease. More specifically, the evidence consistently links biogenic, cardiophysiologic, and dietary factors to the pathogenesis of hypertension, but the evidence in support of the equally appealing role of psychosocial factors such as stress and personality characteristics is provocative at best (Harrell, 1980). The failure of the latter to live up to their heuristic appeal probably rests in several conceptual and methodological weaknesses in this research. Central among these is the tendency to define stress as a singular status variable, and to seek direct, dose-effect relationships between stress and disease (Cassel, 1974). As several investigators have recently suggested, a more productive approach to the study of psychosocial factors and diseases such as hypertension is to use a multidimensional approach in which known risk factors such as family history of the disease, cardiophysiologic characteristics, diet, and life-style are included in the design along with the more elusive psychosocial variables (Lazarus, 1978; Stahl, Grim, Donald, & Niekirk, 1975). Harrell (1980) and Schwartz, Shapiro, Redmond, Ferguson, Ragland, and Weiss (1979) go a step further and recommend that experimental stresses be used rather than self-reports of phenomenal life stresses. Regardless of the type of stressors studied, it is important that studies of the contribution of stress in disease take into account the interplay of the following four factors: (a) individual, ethnic, and social class differences in appraisal and responses to stress (Askenasy, Dohrenwend, & Dohrenwend, 1977; Goldstein, 1973); (b) interpersonal interaction factors such as personal stress-coping styles (Diamond, 1982; Lazarus, 1974), and the availability and use of social supports (Billings & Moos, 1981; Cobb, 1976; Dean & Lin, 1977); (c) physical-environmental variables such as socioecologic stress levels in the living environment (Harburg, Erfurt, Hauenstein, Chape, Schull, & Schork, 1973; Kosa, Antonovsky, & Zola, 1969); and (d) larger societal and sociopsychological variables, such as the status-related effects of ethnicity and social class on stress exposure and stress-related health risks (Dohrenwend, & Dohrenwend, 1970; Myers, 1982).

Consistent with the present state of knowledge of stress and its impact on health, we would conclude that psychosocial processes act as conditional stressors that increase susceptibility to illness generally, rather than causing any specific disease outcome. Furthermore, stress contributes to illness mainly as a cumulative process in predisposed individuals, with the extent of its detrimental impact mediated by the appraisal and meaning of the stresses (Lazarus, 1974), by the effectiveness of the coping efforts made (Ilfeld, 1980), by the availability and usefulness of social supports (Cassel, 1974; Liem & Liem, 1978; Nuckolls, Cassel, & Kaplan, 1972), and by present health status, health history, and health habits (Weiner, 1977).

Applying these concepts then to the question of how psychosocial factors contribute to risk of high blood pressure, we would conclude that the greatest risk for high blood pressure should be in Blacks, in the poor, in persons with a familial history of the disease, in those who were overweight, who use considerable amounts of salt and animal fats in their diets, those who habitually smoke, consume caffeine, and who lead a sedentary life. Additional risks should result from a high level of exposure to negative life stresses, from a tendency to appraise life crises as threatening, from difficulty expressing anger openly and without guilt, and from an unstable and sterotypically reactive cardiovascular system.

As a first step in testing this general conceptual framework of stress in hypertension, the present study was designed to assess the relative contribution of known and suspected stress and health risk factors in explaining observed differences in normal blood pressure levels in healthy, young, Black adults. This sample was selected because demographically they can be considered to be at low to moderate risk, yet have not developed the disease. Therefore, the possible confounding of hypothesized causes with the possible consequences of having a chronic disease are avoided.

The present study specifically hypothesized that observed blood pressure differences in an essentially normal sample of young Black adults would be best explained by a multivariate stress and health risk model that assessed: (a) level of trait anxiety, (b) level of stress exposure (i.e., episodic life events), (c) level of subjective distress, (d) family history of hypertension and related disorders, (e) personal health history, health status, and health habits, (f) availability of social supports, and (g) pattern of somatic reactions under stress.

## Method

### SUBJECTS

A nonrandom sample of 191 Black students at a major university volunteered to participate in a stress and health study in response to campuswide advertisements. All academic levels were represented, with slightly more freshmen and graduate students included in the sample. Thirty-six percent were male, 56% females, and 8% did not report their sex. The sample mean age was 22.1 years, and most of the participants were single (84%), were either unemployed (57% full-time students) or were employed part-time (41%). Seventy-six percent reported receiving some type of financial aid.

Using a multiple criteria of social class that included the income, education, and occupation of both parents, and a subjective rating of family and neighborhood social class (TenHouten, 1970), we found that roughly half of the subjects were from poor or working class, but upwardly mobile families (47%). There were no significant differences between parents' educational attainment, but fathers nevertheless tended to have higher status and better paying jobs than mothers. These demographic characteristics seem to be typical of Black college populations. Thus, our sample, at least in this respect, is reasonably comparable to other Black college samples.

MEASURES

Measures of blood pressure, the primary dependent variable, were taken under both resting and activity conditions. The latter consisted of activities not unlike the test and note-taking conditions common to life as a college student. Specifically, one blood pressure reading was taken after the participants entered the laboratory and following a 10-minute orientation period (i.e., resting BP). Three additional readings were then taken while the participants completed the written, self-administered questionnaire. A Marshall electronic sphygmomanometer (Astropulse 10, with standard Velcro cuff) was used for all readings, and standard blood pressure procedures were followed (Kirkendall, Burton, Epstein, & Fries, 1967). Mean systolic and diastolic blood pressures were used in all analyses as the best indicators of systemic blood pressures during the average day of these students.

The predictor variables of interest included: family history of hypertension and related disorders (8 variables), personal health history and health status (8 variables), level of trait anxiety (1 variable), objective level of life change stresses (6 variables), level of subjective distress (1 variable), pattern of stress-related somatic reactions (7 variables), and the availability of social supports (1 variable). A 33rd variable, stress-coping style, was also measured, but the results on this variable are reported elsewhere, and therefore will not be discussed here (see Myers & Tiggle, Note 1; Myers, Barthe, & Crespo, Note 2). These 32 health and psychosocial predictors are detailed below.

*Family Health History.* Participants were asked whether any of their blood relatives has suffered or died from any of a list of 8 diseases or conditions that have been implicated in hypertensive disease. These included high blood pressure, heart failure, coronary artery disease, stroke, diabetes, obesity, cerebral hemorrhage, or kidney disease. Scoring was based on the number of diseases or disorders reported, weighted by the degree of direct blood line of the affected relative (i.e., grandparents and parents = 2, brothers, sisters, and other relatives = 1). Scores were then summed for each disease, and included separately in the analyses.

*Personal Health History, Health Status, and Health Habits.* The revised Cornell Medical Index Questionnaire was used to identify mild symptoms related to the cardiovascular system (e.g., racing or thumping of the heart, pain in heart or chest), renal system (e.g., liver trouble, losing control of the bladder), and respiratory system (e.g., difficulty breathing, respiratory allergies, out of breath sitting still). Other symptoms or behaviors implicated in hypertension were also identified. These included: (a) health risk habits (e.g., smoking, drug and alcohol use, caffeine use, consumption of high levels of sodium and animal fats, being overweight, and having a sedentary life-style with minimal exercise), (b) disrupted thoughts and attention symptoms (e.g., thought disorganization, confusion, loss of memory), (c) anxiety and tension symptoms (e.g., feeling jittery, tending to push oneself, shaking or trembling), and (d) other symptoms (e.g., spells of dizziness or fainting, frequent numbness or tingling in the body). Symptom scores ranging from 0-40 were totaled for each subject and included as separate variables in the analyses.

*Level of Stress Exposure.* The widely used Holmes and Rahe Recent Life Change Questionnaire (RLCQ), which has been shown to be reasonably reliable and valid across ethnic groups, SES levels, and age groups (Holmes & Rahe, 1967; Ruch & Holmes, 1971), was revised for use with Black college students. Six scores were obtained from this measure taking into account three substantive dimensions of life change stress—(a) the number of events reported for the past year, (b) the subjective appraisal of these events as either positive or negative, and (c) the relative subjective rating of the impact of the events on the participants' lives. A fourth methodological concern, namely the problems of obtaining comparable life change scores despite differences in the number of events reported, was addressed by computing several ratio scores. Specifically, six life change stress scores were computed: (a) total number of events reported, (b) subjectively weighted sum life change score, (c) weighted ratio life change score (i.e., b/a), (d) algebraic sum life change score (i.e., sum positive − sum negative life events), (e) algebraic ratio change score (i.e., d/a), and (f) total number of negative life change events.

*Global Subjective Distress.* This variable is conceptualized as a global subjective appraisal of the relative stressfulness of one's life. It was measured using the Chapman, Reeder, and Bonin (1966) 4-item Subjective Stress Scale. This scale has been shown to correlate positively with personal and familial history of cardiovascular disease (Schar, Reeder, & Dirken, 1973), with elevated blood pressure levels, and with a wide variety of physical symptoms (Myers, 1981).

*Trait Anxiety.* An impressive body of research has been accumulating on the role that anxiety, both situational and characterological, plays in the experience of stress, and in physical and emotional disorders. Spielberger and his colleagues (1970, 1975) conceptually distinguish between short-term state anxiety and chronic, cross-situational or trait anxiety. They note that high trait anxiety has important implications for health and illness, and has been associated as a risk factor with coronary disease (Eden, Shirom, Kellumen, Aronson, & French, 1977), as interacting with life change stress to predict a variety of psychosomatic disorders (Pancheri et al., 1979), as related to job stress as a factor in hypertension (Weyer & Hodapp, 1979), and as related to overall health status (Myers, 1981).

In this study, the standard Spielberger, Gorsuch, and Lushene (1970), trait anxiety measures and 4-point scoring procedures were followed.

*Pattern of Somatic Reaction to Stress.* This variable is defined as the pattern of subjectively recognized somatic symptoms the individual reports as usually occurring when he or she is stressed. Guthrie, Verstrate, Deines, and Stern (1975), Lindy and Stern (1971), and Stern and Higgins (1969) note definable patterns of somatic reactions to stress that are consistent within individuals and across families and cultures. A recent study also reported significant associations between specific somatic response patterns, overall tendency to somatize stress, personal health status, and level of diastolic blood pressure (Myers, 1981).

This variable was measured using the 33-item Somatic Perception Questionnaire developed by Guthrie et al. (1975). The scoring of this variable consisted of the weighted sum of all items checked (i.e., never = 1, sometimes = 2, and usually = 3), such that the range of possible scores was 33 to 99. A principle components analysis with varimax rotations yielded a seven-factor solution, which accounted for 16% of the variance. The identified factors were:

  I. Disrupted thoughts (e.g., feeling confused, difficulty concentrating, feeling oppressed);
 II. Cardiorespiratory reactions (e.g., shortness of breath, awareness of heartbeat, quickening of heartbeat);
III. Gastrointestinal reactions (e.g., diarrhea, excess gas, acid stomach);
 IV. Sympathetic reactions (e.g., body sweat, sweaty palms);
  V. Loss of control reactions (e.g., trouble sleeping, muscle twitching);

VI. Skin and sleep disturbances (e.g., rashes & pimples, nightmares); and

VII. Attentional disturbances (e.g., sighing, feeling restless).

*Availability of Social Supports.* This final predictor was included consistent with the growing empirical evidence that social supports mediate the impact of stressful experiences, especially in terms of their health consequences (Dean and Lin, 1977; Gore, 1978; Liem and Liem, 1978; Nuckolls et al., 1972). A 15-item scale adapted from Nuckolls et al. (1972) was used to assess this variable. Scores ranged from 7 to 137, with a mean of 29.03.

PROCEDURES

Respondents to public recruitment efforts were contacted by one of three Black research assistants and scheduled in small groups of 2 to 4 for a two-hour interview. A comprehensive questionnaire was administered, and four blood pressure readings were taken at approximately 15 to 20 minute intervals. All participants received written statements of their average blood pressure readings, along with a token payment of $3.00 for their participation. Those participants with an elevated mean blood pressure were encouraged to see a physician for a medical examination.

Data analysis was conducted in four steps. First, means and standard deviations were computed for all variables, both for the entire sample and for males and females separately. Second, tests of association among the predictors and between the predictors and outcomes were computed. These tests served as an indicator of the strength of the simple linear association between each predictor and each outcome, as well as a test of concurrent validity of many of the scales used to assess theoretically related constructs (e.g., life events stress and global subjective stress, somatic stress reactions, and physical symptoms). Third, separate regressions were computed for stressful life events, family health history, and personal health history to determine which subsets of each of these three sets of highly intercorrelated variables were the best predictors of blood pressure, and therefore should be included in the final summary regressions. Finally, separate best subset regressions were computed for the entire sample for systolic and diastolic blood pressures, and then for males and females separately.

## Results

As a group, the participants were generally healthy, reported low to moderate levels of stress, and normal blood pressures (i.e., mean BP = 114.5/70.4). Males reported slightly, but not significantly higher average blood pressures than females, described themselves as under slightly more stress, and reported more negative life change stresses than females. However, females tended to view their life changes as more disrupting than did males.

As would be expected given such a young sample, the group reported very few physical symptoms or predominant somatic reaction patterns. However, there was a slightly greater prevalence of anxiety symptoms, health risk behaviors, and mild cardiovascular symptoms in their reports of present health status. The group was also low on trait anxiety, with males being slightly less trait anxious than females. The group also reported low to moderate availability of social supports, with males reporting slightly more social supports than females (see Table 28.1).

The results of the correlational analyses provided partial support for the measures as useful and valid indicators of the concepts studied. As expected, few of the predictors were found to be individually correlated with either systolic or diastolic blood pressure. However, we did find that mild cardiovascular symptoms ($r = .215$), and anxiety and tension symptoms ($r = .233$) were significantly, if weakly, related to mean diastolic blood pressure ($p < .01$ and $p < .005$, respectively), but not to systolic blood pressure (see Table 28.2).

These results suggest that of all of the predictors assessed, only the presence of cardiovascular symptoms (e.g., pain in heart or chest, bothered by thumping or racing heart, etc.), and reports of anxiety and tension symptoms (e.g., often shake or tremble, tend to push yourself, often feel anxious or jittery, etc.) are independently related to level of diastolic blood pressure. The findings somewhat contradict our expectations. Evidence to date suggests that systolic blood pressure is more variable and responsive to situational stresses and to anxiety. Yet, mean systolic blood pressure was singularly unrelated to stress level or to stress-related symptoms and reactions. Instead, the more stable and resistant diastolic blood pressure was found to be related to self-reported anxiety and tension. Several explanations could be offered to account for these counterintuitive results. These findings could signal early signs of meaningful structural changes in the cardiovascular systems of our participants that may indicate increased risk for hypertensive

**TABLE 28.1** Mean and Standard Deviations of Predictor and Outcome Variables for All Subjects and By Sex

| Predictor Variables | Total Group (N = 188) Mean | (SD) | Males (N = 75) Mean | (SD) | Females (N = 103) Mean | (SD) |
|---|---|---|---|---|---|---|
| Global Subjective | | | | | | |
| Stress (TSSS) | 8.316 | (3.11) | 8.280 | (3.18) | 8.175 | (3.03) |
| Life Change Stress (LE) | | | | | | |
| Total LE | 11.283 | (6.72) | 11.267 | (7.65) | 11.272 | (6.28) |
| Weighted LE | 330.449 | (228.92) | 309.827 | (231.96) | 345.369 | (232.30) |
| Ratio LE | 27.417 | (12.37) | 25.635 | (12.76) | 28.704 | (21.29) |
| Algebraic LE | −83.027 | (125.45) | −85.107 | (115.65) | −81.874 | (113.04) |
| Algebraic Ratio LE | −5.507 | (12.12) | −6.887 | (11.64) | −4.388 | (12.56) |
| Total Negative LE | 6.166 | (4.08) | 6.293 | (4.36) | 6.107 | (4.01) |
| Trait Anxiety | 38.112 | (10.21) | 36.387 | (8.38) | 39.049 | (10.98) |
| Level of Social Support | 29.032 | (5.17) | 29.793 | (5.12) | 28.476 | (5.26) |
| Pattern of Somatization | | | | | | |
| I. Disrupted Thoughts | 0.005 | (1.00) | −0.202 | (0.90) | 0.134 | (1.07) |
| II. Cardiorespiratory | | | | | | |
| Reactions | 0.007 | (1.00) | −0.050 | (0.98) | 0.062 | (1.03) |
| III. Gastrointestinal | | | | | | |
| Reactions | 0.005 | (1.00) | −0.093 | (0.85) | 0.051 | (1.04) |
| IV. Sympathetic | | | | | | |
| Reactions | 0.006 | (1.01) | 0.014 | (0.96) | −0.063 | (1.02) |
| V. Loss of Control | 0.002 | (1.00) | 0.131 | (1.00) | −0.076 | (1.00) |
| VI. Skin and Sleep | | | | | | |
| Disturbances | 0.003 | (1.01) | −0.303 | (0.78) | 0.234 | (1.11) |
| VII. Attentional | | | | | | |
| Disturbances | 0.007 | (1.01) | −0.016 | (0.85) | 0.026 | (1.11) |
| Family Health History | | | | | | |
| High Blood Pressure | 1.620 | (1.42) | 1.347 | (1.25) | 1.835 | (1.48) |
| Heart Failure | 0.551 | (0.91) | 0.533 | (0.88) | 0.537 | (0.95) |
| Coronary Heart Disease | 0.316 | (0.71) | 0.240 | (0.63) | 0.359 | (0.75) |
| Stroke | 0.706 | (1.00) | 0.667 | (1.00) | 0.738 | (1.01) |
| Diabetes | 0.727 | (1.09) | 0.693 | (0.96) | 0.757 | (1.16) |
| Obesity | 1.021 | (1.45) | 0.953 | (1.18) | 1.165 | (1.62) |
| Cerebral Hemorrhage | 0.053 | (0.32) | 0.027 | (0.23) | 0.078 | (0.39) |
| Kidney Disease | 0.353 | (0.76) | 0.253 | (0.66) | 0.456 | (0.84) |
| Personal Health History | | | | | | |
| Cardiovascular Symptoms | 0.786 | (1.25) | 0.600 | (1.09) | 0.893 | (1.30) |
| Renal Symptoms | 0.348 | (0.70) | 0.187 | (0.54) | 0.466 | (0.76) |
| Respiratory Symptoms | 0.396 | (0.58) | 0.360 | (0.51) | 0.447 | (0.76) |
| Disrupted Thoughts | | | | | | |
| and Attention | 1.283 | (0.61) | 0.133 | (0.45) | 0.369 | (0.67) |

*continued*

**TABLE 28.1** Continued

| Predictor Variables | Total Group (N = 188) | | Males (N = 75) | | Females (N = 103) | |
|---|---|---|---|---|---|---|
| | Mean | (SD) | Mean | (SD) | Mean | (SD) |
| Anxiety and Stress | | | | | | |
| Symptoms | 1.209 | (0.98) | 1.147 | (1.00) | 1.233 | (0.96) |
| Other Symptoms | 0.583 | (0.75) | 0.480 | (0.60) | 0.660 | (0.83) |
| Health Risk Behaviors | | | | | | |
| Health Habits | 0.920 | (1.09) | 0.773 | (0.92) | 0.971 | (1.12) |
| Total Symptoms | 7.455 | (3.57) | 6.600 | (3.05) | 7.990 | (3.44) |
| Outcome Variables | | | | | | |
| Systolic Blood Pressure | 114.501 | (12.84) | 121.117 | (12.86) | 4.999 | (−2.98) |
| Diastolic Blood Pressure | 70.406 | (10.43) | 72.637 | (8.67) | 68.078 | (10.52) |

disease. Another more parsimonious explanation for these findings is the often noted differences between blood pressure reactivity to overt experimentally induced stresses versus self-reported stress or anxiety states. The lack of association between stress and systolic blood pressure is consistent with this explanation. The unexpected direct association between anxiety and tension and diastolic blood pressure is more puzzling, however, and may be suggestive of early organicity.

FACTORS PREDICTING MEAN SYSTOLIC BLOOD PRESSURE

The results of the multiple regression analysis supported the principal hypothesis that psychosocial stress and health risk factors interact in a complex fashion to differentially account for variations in systolic and diastolic blood pressure. Variance on mean systolic blood pressure was best explained by a six-factor regression equation that included three personal health status factors (i.e., cardiovascular symptoms, which loaded positively; disrupted thoughts and attention, and renal symptoms, both of which loaded negatively), high global level of subjective stress, which loaded positively; and two somatic reaction patterns to stress (i.e., disrupted thoughts and cardiorespiratory reactions, both of which loaded negatively). This solution was significant ($F(6, 180) =$ 4.77, $p < .002$), and accounted for 13.7% of explained variance on systolic blood pressure (see Table 28.3).

**TABLE 28.2** Relationship Between Predictors and Systolic and Diastolic Blood
Pressures ($N = 187$)

| Predictors | Systolic Blood Pressure | Diastolic Blood Pressure |
|---|---|---|
| Global Subjective Stress | 0.115 | −0.008 |
| Total Life Events | −0.048 | −0.068 |
| Weighted Life Events | −0.064 | −0.054 |
| Ratio Life Events | −0.073 | −0.029 |
| Algebraic Life Events | 0.034 | 0.028 |
| Algebraic Ratio Life Events | −0.037 | −0.024 |
| Total Negative Life Events | −0.037 | −0.068 |
| Trait Anxiety | 0.001 | −0.028 |
| Social Support | −0.015 | −0.051 |
| Somatization I-Disrupted Thoughts | −0.139 | 0.015 |
| Somatization II-Cardiorespiratory Reactions | −0.107 | 0.008 |
| Somatization III-Gastrointestinal Reactions | 0.145 | 0.127 |
| Somatization IV-Sympathetic Reactions | −0.010 | 0.015 |
| Somatization V-Loss of Control | 0.038 | 0.008 |
| Somatization VI-Skin and Sleep Disturbances | −0.076 | −0.016 |
| Somatization VII-Attention Disturbances | 0.073 | 0.001 |
| Family Health History-High Blood Pressure | 0.054 | −0.074 |
| Family Health History-Heart Failure | 0.062 | −0.095 |
| Family Health History-Coronary Heart Disease | 0.093 | 0.088 |
| Family Health History-Stroke | 0.015 | 0.032 |
| Family Health History-Diabetes | −0.014 | 0.050 |
| Family Health History-Obesity | 0.001 | 0.087 |
| Family Health History-Cerebral Hemorrhage | 0.034 | 0.068 |
| Family Health History-Kidney Disease | −0.090 | 0.101 |
| Personal Health History of: | | |
|   Cardiovascular Symptoms | −0.188 | 0.215* |
|   Renal Symptoms | −0.135 | −0.093 |
|   Respiratory Symptoms | −0.002 | 0.018 |
|   Disrupted Thoughts and Attention | 0.128 | −0.044 |
|   Anxiety and Stress Symptoms | 0.046 | 0.233** |
|   Other Symptoms | 0.048 | 0.086 |
| Health Risk Behaviors | 0.096 | 0.125 |
| Total Symptoms | 0.097 | 0.181 |

*$p < .01$
**$p < .005$

## FACTORS PREDICTING MEAN DIASTOLIC BLOOD PRESSURE

Given the nature of the physiology of blood pressure, diastolic blood
pressure is typically less reactive to episodic stresses and more directly

**TABLE 28.3**  Best Subset Regression Predicting Average Systolic Blood Pressure
($N = 187$)

| Variable | Regression Coefficient | Standard Error | Standard Coefficient | T | p | Tolerance | Contribution to $R^2$ |
|---|---|---|---|---|---|---|---|
| Cardiovascular Symptoms | 2.32 | 0.78 | 0.23 | 2.99 | .003 | 0.836 | 0.043 |
| Disrupted Thoughts and Attention | −3.63 | 1.54 | −0.17 | −2.35 | .02 | 0.879 | 0.026 |
| Renal Symptoms | −2.96 | 1.33 | −0.16 | −2.23 | .03 | 0.900 | 0.024 |
| Global Subjective Stress | 0.686 | 0.320 | 0.17 | 2.15 | .03 | 0.789 | 0.022 |
| Somatization I-Disrupted Thoughts | −1.797 | 0.905 | −0.14 | −1.99 | .05 | 0.961 | 0.019 |
| Somatization II-Cardio-respiratory Reactions | −1.425 | 0.915 | −0.11 | −1.56 | .12 | 0.933 | 0.012 |

$R^2 = 0.137$
Adjusted $R^2 = 0.108$
$F(6, 180) = 4.77, p < .0002$

affected by structural changes in blood vessels and to biochemical
processes (Weiner, 1979). Therefore, it is reasonable to expect that
factors more indicative of the cumulative effect of tension and anxiety
such as trait anxiety, family history of hypertension, and present physical symptoms would account for more variance in diastolic blood
pressure than would episodic or subjective stress experiences. The
results of the regression analysis identified a six-factor equation somewhat consistent with these expectations. The two primary predictors
were anxiety and tension symptoms, and cardiovascular symptoms,
both of which loaded positively; and next were some disrupted thoughts
and attention, family history of high blood pressure, and renal symptoms, all of which contributed negatively to the equation. Finally,
global subjective stress made a small, but nonsignificant negative
contribution to the overall predictive equation. The overall equation
was significant ($F(6, 152) = 4.63, p < .0002$), and accounted for 15.5%
of the explained variation in diastolic blood pressure (see Table 28.4).

## GENDER DIFFERENCES IN SYSTOLIC
## AND DIASTOLIC BLOOD PRESSURE

When the data were partitioned by gender and analyses were conducted to assess whether the same factors were identified as contributing to explained variation on systolic and diastolic blood pressures,
important differences were obtained.

**TABLE 28.4**  Best Subset Regression Predicting Average Diastolic Blood Pressure
              (N = 187)

| Variable | Regression Coefficient | Standard Error | Standard Coefficient | T | p | Tolerance | Contribution to $R^2$ |
|---|---|---|---|---|---|---|---|
| Anxiety and Stress | | | | | | | |
| Symptoms | 3.317 | 0.968 | 0.31 | 3.43 | .001 | 0.704 | 0.065 |
| Cardiovascular Symptoms | 1.942 | 0.663 | 0.25 | 2.93 | .004 | 0.776 | 0.048 |
| Disrupted Thoughts | | | | | | | |
| and Attention | -2.440 | 1.365 | -0.14 | -1.79 | .076 | 0.870 | 0.018 |
| Family History of | | | | | | | |
| High Blood Pressure | -0.967 | 0.549 | -0.14 | -1.76 | .080 | 0.929 | 0.017 |
| Renal Symptoms | -2.163 | 1.236 | -0.14 | -1.75 | .082 | 0.877 | 0.017 |
| Global Subjective Stress | -0.458 | 0.289 | -0.14 | -1.58 | .115 | 0.698 | 0.014 |

$R^2 = 0.155$
Adjusted $R^2 = 0.121$
$F(6, 152) = 4.63, p < .0002$

For Black males, variance on mean systolic and diastolic blood pressure appear to be most parsimoniously explained by a balanced combination of physical symptoms (i.e., health status factors), life events stresses experienced, and somatic reaction patterns, and less significantly so by family history of relevant diseases.

Mean systolic blood pressure in Black males was best accounted for by a significant ($F(5, 69) = 3.63, p < .0056$) regression equation that included total number of physical symptoms, ratio life events stresses, renal symptoms, and two somatic reaction patterns to stress (i.e., cardiorespiratory reactions, and disrupted thoughts). Total physical symptoms contributed positively to the equation, and life stress, renal symptoms, and somatic reactions contributed negatively. The overall equation accounted for 20.8% of explained variance on systolic blood pressure (see Table 28.5).

Mean diastolic blood pressure for Black males, on the other hand, was best explained a significant six-factor equation ($F(6, 55)$ 3.23, $p <$ .009) that included respiratory symptoms, anxiety and tension symptoms, ratio life events, global subjective stress, family history of cerebral hemorrhages, and a somatic reaction pattern characterized by attentional disturbance. The physical symptoms, life events stress, global subjective stress, and family history variables all contributed negatively to the equation, and anxiety and tension symptoms and the disturbed attention somatic reaction pattern contributed positively. As

**TABLE 28.5**  Best Subset Regression Predicting Average Systolic and Diastolic Blood Pressures—Males ($N = 75$)

*Systolic Blood Pressure*

| Variable | Regression Coefficient | Standard Error | Standard Coefficient | T | p | Contribution to $R^2$ |
|---|---|---|---|---|---|---|
| Total Physical Symptoms | 2.143 | 0.592 | 0.51 | 3.62 | .001 | 0.150 |
| Ratio Life Events | −0.258 | 0.114 | −0.26 | −2.27 | .03 | 0.059 |
| Renal Symptoms | −6.484 | 3.119 | −0.27 | −2.08 | .04 | 0.050 |
| Somatization II-Cardio-respiratory Reactions | −2.846 | 1.535 | −0.22 | −1.85 | .07 | 0.039 |
| Somatization I-Disrupted Thoughts | −2.641 | 1.626 | −0.19 | −1.62 | .11 | 0.030 |

$R^2 = 0.208$
Adjusted $R^2 = 0.151$
$F(5, 69) = 3.63, p < .0056$

*Diastolic Blood Pressure*

| Variable | Regression Coefficient | Standard Error | Standard Coefficient | T | p | Contribution to $R^2$ |
|---|---|---|---|---|---|---|
| Respiratory Symptoms | −4.872 | 1.974 | −0.29 | −2.47 | .017 | 0.082 |
| Anxiety and Stress Symptoms | 3.244 | 1.435 | 0.36 | 2.26 | .03 | 0.069 |
| Ratio Life Events | −0.185 | 0.085 | −0.27 | −2.17 | .03 | 0.063 |
| Global Subjective Stress | −0.841 | 0.414 | −0.32 | −2.03 | .047 | 0.055 |
| Family History of Cerebral Hemmorhage | −8.237 | 4.151 | −0.24 | −1.98 | .05 | 0.053 |
| Somatization VII-Attentional Disturbances | 2.468 | 1.255 | 0.24 | 1.97 | .05 | 0.051 |

$R^2 = 0.261$
Adjusted $R^2 = 0.180$
$F(6, 55) = 3.23, p < .009$

a whole, the regression equation accounted for 26.1% of explained variance on diastolic blood pressure in Black males.

For Black females, variance on mean systolic and diastolic blood pressures were more significantly affected by their family histories of cardiovascularly related disorders, and less significantly so by their stress, somatic reaction patterns, and personal health status than were Black males.

Regression analysis on mean systolic blood pressure in the female sample yielded a significant ($F(6, 96) = 5.56$, $p < .001$) six-variable equation that included: family history of high blood pressure, heart failure and coronary heart disease, personal history of other symptoms, a gastrointestinal somatic reaction pattern to stress, and a family history

**TABLE 28.6** Best Subset Regression Predicting Average Systolic and Diastolic Blood Pressure—Females ($N = 103$)

*Systolic Blood Pressure*

| Variable | Regression Coefficient | Standard Error | Standard Coefficient | T | p | Contribution to $R^2$ |
|---|---|---|---|---|---|---|
| Family History of High Blood Pressure | 1.939 | 0.624 | 0.28 | 3.11 | .002 | 0.075 |
| Family History of Heart Failure | −2.945 | 1.037 | −0.28 | −2.84 | .006 | 0.062 |
| Family History of Coronary Heart | 2.978 | 1.272 | 0.22 | 2.34 | .02 | 0.042 |
| Other Personal Symptoms | 2.378 | 1.080 | 0.20 | 2.20 | .03 | 0.037 |
| Somatization Factor III- Gastrointestinal Reaction | 1.880 | 0.868 | 0.19 | 2.17 | .03 | 0.036 |
| Family History of Diabetes | −1.385 | 0.798 | −0.16 | −1.73 | .09 | 0.023 |

$R^2 = 0.258$
Adjusted $R^2 = 0.212$
$F(6, 96) = 5.56, p < .0001$

*Diastolic Blood Pressure*

| Variable | Regression Coefficient | Standard Error | Standard Coefficient | T | p | Contribution to $R^2$ |
|---|---|---|---|---|---|---|
| Cardiovascular Symptoms | 2.999 | 0.809 | 0.39 | 3.71 | .000 | 0.114 |
| Global Subjective Stress | −0.998 | 0.342 | −0.30 | −2.91 | .005 | 0.071 |
| Anxiety and Stress Symptoms | 2.815 | 1.205 | 0.24 | 2.34 | .022 | 0.045 |
| Family History of Obesity | 1.358 | 0.597 | 0.22 | 2.27 | .026 | 0.043 |
| Disrupted Thoughts and Attention | −3.436 | 1.550 | −0.21 | −2.22 | .029 | 0.041 |
| Family History of Heart Failure | −1.714 | 1.035 | −0.16 | −1.66 | .10 | 0.023 |

$R^2 = 0.335$
Adjusted $R^2 = 0.285$
$F(6, 80) = 6.72, p < .000$

of diabetes. Four of the six variables contributed positively to the equation, with family history of heart failure and of diabetes contributing negatively. The equation accounted for 25.8% of explained variance in systolic blood pressure (see Table 28.6).

The regression analysis on mean diastolic blood pressure, on the other hand, identified a greater balance of factors including personal symptoms of cardiovascular disorder, and anxiety and tension, and disrupted thoughts and attention, global subjective stress level, and family history of obesity and of heart failure. This equation was significant ($F(6, 80) = 6.72, p < .0000$), and accounted for 33.5% of explained variance in mean diastolic blood pressure in Black females.

## Discussion

This study was designed to test a multivariate approach to the study of the contribution of psychosocial stress on blood pressure in which multiple indicators of stress were compared against known risk factors of high blood pressure. Specifically, episodic life stresses, subjective level of stress, trait anxiety, and somatic reactions to stress were the measured psychosocial variables. These were compared with family history of cardiovascularly relevant disorders, personal health status, and health habits to determine the relative contribution these variables would make in accounting for variance in mean systolic and diastolic blood pressure. Given the greater risk Blacks face for developing essential hypertension, and their hypothesized greater exposure to socio-environmental stresses, a sample of Black adults was selected as the initial sample on which to test this approach.

The results obtained generally supported the two major premises of this study, namely, (a) that self-reported experiences of stress should be treated as a multifaceted factor whose impact on blood pressure, and on health and illness generally, is mainly indirect and cumulative; and (b) that a better understanding of the role of psychosocial factors in blood pressure is obtained when these factors are contrasted against other known and suspected risk factors in hypertensive disease in the same analysis.

In addition, the results suggest that experienced stress, characteristic patterns of reacting to those stresses, present health status, and family history combine in complex ways to account for differences in systolic and diastolic blood pressure, and that the variables combine differently in Black men and women. Therefore, it is perhaps the pattern of combined effect of these stress and health variables that is of clinical significance in the development of hypertensive disease.

Meaningful variations in normal blood pressure appear to be related to feelings of being under pressure and experiencing considerable distress, especially when these feelings occur concurrent with or result from facing personally significant life change stresses. This general sense of being stressed is more injurious to one's health, especially for

Black males, when distinct cardiovascular, renal, anxiety, and tension symptoms are also present. These findings are consistent with general knowledge in the field that a heavy stress load is more pathogenic for those who are in less than good health (Levi, 1971). However, the fact that this supportive evidence is obtained even in a relatively healthy and physically active sample of young Black adults is especially noteworthy.

The differences in the relative importance of the stress and family history variables in explaining blood pressure variability in Black men and women is also worthy of some discussion. Somewhat unexpectedly, given the absence of previous evidence, is the apparently greater pathogenic impact of life stresses on blood pressure for Black males compared to females is somewhat unexpected. This raises the possibility that this greater vulnerability to socioecological stresses might account in part for the trends in the epidemiological data that show that Black males tend to develop a more severe form of hypertensive disease and to die earlier from its consequences. Blood pressure in the Black women studied, on the other hand, appeared to be more affected by their familial history of cardiovascularly relevant disorders, and less to episodic stresses. This is consistent with the hypothesis of greater risk for hypertensive disease due to familial-related organic vulnerability. We cannot assume on the basis of these results, however, that family history of disease is only an important risk factor for Black women. Rather, these data suggest the need to explore the hypothesis that some gender differences may exist in the degree of risk associated with familial history.

In sum, the results of this preliminary investigation support a complex, multivariate conceptualization of the impact of stress on blood pressure. They underscore the prevailing view in the field that psychosocial stress factors play an important, but not a primary role in the etiology of essential hypertension. The rather small percentage of blood pressure variance explained by the stress and health indices measured (i.e., 13.7% to 33.5%) suggest that although important, other factors such as hereditary predisposition, actual biochemical and neurological functioning, and direct measurement of arousal and reactivity patterns may be better predictors of blood pressure level. Future studies in this area, therefore, will need to replicate the present approach and measures, as well as to include other important psychosocial factors such as stress coping style and measures of biochemical and psychophysiological functioning to obtain a more complete etiologic picture. An important next step will also be to replicate this multivariate model with borderline and mild hypertensives to test the utility of this approach with clinically meaningful levels of blood pressure.

## Notes

1. Myers, H. F., & Tiggle, R. B. (1981). *A path analysis model of stress and health in blacks*. Paper presented at the 6th Empirical Conference on Black Psychology, Oakland University, Rochester, MI.
2. Myers, H. F., Barthe, D., & Crespo, A. (n.d.). *Analysis of stress-coping disposition and affective reactions as a function of stressful situations*. Manuscript in preparation.
3. Smith, R. A. (1972). *State-trait anxiety inventory and the assessment of stress in private-pilot training*. Paper presented at the meeting of the American Psychological Association, Detroit, MI.

## References

*Advanced data: Hypertension, U.S., 1974.* (1976, November). Vital and Health Statistics Report, HEW Publication, November, 1976.

Askenasy, A. R., Dohrenwend, B. P., & Dohrenwend, B. S. (1977). Some effects of social class and ethic group membership on judgments of the magnitude of stressful life events: A research note. *Journal of Health and Social Behavior, 18,* 432-439.

Billings, A. G., & Moos, R. H. (1981). The role of coping responses and social resources in attenuating the stress of life events. *Journal of Behavioral Medicine, 4*(2), 139-157.

Brodman, K., Erdmann, A., Lorge, I., & Wolff, H. G. (1949). The Cornell Medical Index, an adjunct to the medical interview. *Journal of the American Medical Association, 140,* 530-534.

Cassel, J. (1974). Psychological processes and "stress": Theoretical formulation, epidemiology and methods. *International Journal of Health Services, 4*(3), 471-482.

Chapman, J. M., Reeder, L. G., & Bonin, E. R. (1966). Relationship of stress, tranquilizers and serum cholesterol levels in a sample population under study for coronary heart disease. *American Journal of Epidemiology, 83*(3), 537-547.

Cobb, S. (1976). Social support as a moderator of life stress. *Psychosomatic Medicine, 38*(5), 300-314.

Dean, A., & Lin, N. (1977). The stress-buffering role of social support. *Journal of Nervous and Mental Diseases, 165*(6), 403-417.

Diamond, E. L. (1982). The role of anger and hostility in essential hypertension and coronary heart disease. *Psychological Bulletin, 92*(2), 410-433.

Dohrenwend, B. S., & Dohrenwend, B. P. (1970). Class and race as status-related sources of stress. In S. Levine & N. A. Scotch (Eds.), *Social stress* (pp. 111-140). Chicago: Aldine.

Eden, D., Shirom, A., Kellumen, J. J., Aronson, J., & French, J. R. P. (1977). Stress, anxiety and coronary risk in a supportive society. In C. D. Speilberger & I. G. Sarason (Eds.), *Stress and anxiety* (Vol. 4, pp. 251-267). Washington, DC: Hemisphere.

Five year findings of the hypertension detection and follow-up program: I. Reduction in mortality of persons with high blood pressure, including mild hypertension. (1979). *Journal of the American Medical Association, 242*(23), 2562-2571.

Gentry, W. D., Chesney, A. P., Gary, H. E., Hall, R. P., & Harburg, E. (1982). Habitual anger coping styles: I. Effect on mean blood pressure and risk for essential hypertension. *Psychosomatic Medicine, 44*(2), 195-202.

Goldstein, M. J. (1973). Individual differences in responses to stress. *American Journal of Community Psychology, 1*(2), 113-137.

Gore, S. (1978). The effect of social support in moderating the health consequences of unemployment. *Journal of Health and Social Behavior, 19,* 157-165.

Guthrie, G. M., Verstrate, A., Deines, M. M., & Stern, R. M. (1975). Symptoms of stress in four societies. *Journal of Social Psychology, 95,* 165-172.

Harburg, E., Erfurt, J. C., Hauenstein, L. S., Chape, C., Schull, W. J., & Schork, M. A. (1973). Socio-ecological stress, suppressed hostility, skin color, and Black-White male blood pressure: Detroit. *Psychosomatic Medicine, 35,* 276-296.

Harrell, J. P. (1980). Psychological factors and hypertension: A status report. *Psychological Bulletin, 87,* 482-501.

Holmes, T. H., & Rahe, R. H. (1967). The Social Readjustment Rating Scale. *Journal of Psychosomatic Research, 11*(2), 213-218.

Hypertension detection and follow-up program cooperative group: Race, education, and prevalence of hypertension. (1977). *American Journal of Epidemiology, 106,* 351-361.

Ilfeld, F. W. (1980). Understanding marital stress: The importance of coping styles. *Journal of Nervous and Mental Diseases, 168,* 34-40.

Keil, J. E., Tyroler, H. A., Sandifer, S. H., & Boyle, E. (1977). Hypertension: Effects of social class and racial admixture: The results of a cohort study in the Black population of Charleston, South Carolina. *American Journal of Public Health, 67*(7), 634-639.

Kirkendall, W. M., Burton, A. C., Epstein, F. H., & Freis, E. D. (1967). Recommendations for human blood pressure determination by sphygmomanometer. *American Heart Association.*

Kosa, J., Antonovsky, A., & Zola, I. K. (1969). *Poverty and health: A sociological analysis.* Cambridge, MA: Harvard University Press.

Lazarus, R. S. (1974). Psychological stress and coping in adaptation and illness. *International Journal of Psychiatry in Medicine, 5*(4), 321-333.

Lazarus, R. S. (1978). A strategy for research on psychological and social factors in hypertension. *Journal of Human Stress, 4*(3), 34-40.

Levi, L. (Ed.). (1971). *Society, stress and disease: Vol. 1. The psychosocial environment and psychosomatic disease.* New York: Oxford University Press.

Liem, R. T., & Liem, J. (1978). Social class and mental illness reconsidered: The role of economic stress and social support. *Journal of Health and Social Behavior, 19,* 139-156.

Lindy, F. J., & Stern, R. M. (1971). Factor analysis of a somatic perception questionnaire. *Journal of Psychosomatic Research, 15,* 179-181.

Meyer, J., Derogatis, L. R., Miller, M., & Reading, A. (1978). Hypertension and psychological distress. *Psychosomatics, 19*(3), 160-168.

Myers, H. F. (1981). *Life events stress, subjective appraisal, somatization and blood pressure in Black college students* (Tech. Rep.). Los Angeles: University of California, Institute for American Cultures, Center for Afro-American Studies.

Myers, H. F. (1982). Stress, ethnicity and social class: A model for research with Black populations. In E. E. Jones & S. J. Korchin (Eds.), *Minority mental health.* New York: Holt, Rinehart & Winston.

Naditch, M. P. (1973). *Locus of control, relative discontent and hypertension.* Paper presented at the 81st Annual Convention, APA, Montreal.

National Black Health Providers Task Force on High Blood Pressure Education and Control. (1980, October). U.S. Dept. of Health & Human Services, NIH. (Publication No. 80-K474). Washington, DC: Government Printing Office.

National Center for Health Statistics Report. (1978, April). *Cardiovascular conditions of children 6-11 years, and youths 12-17 years, U.S., 1963-1965, and 1966-1970.* (Series 11, No. 166).

National Center for Health Statistics Report. (1981). *Vital statistics of the U.S., 1978, Vol. II: Mortality, Part B., Section 7. Deaths from 69 selected causes by age, color and sex: U.S., 1978.* (7-140-7-141).

Nuckolls, C. B., Cassel, J., & Kaplan, B. H. (1972). Psycho-social assets, life crisis and the prognosis of pregnancy. *American Journal of Epidemiology, 95,* 431-441.

Pancheri, P., DeMartino, V., Spionbi, G., Bundi, M., & Mosticoni, S. (1979). Life stress events and state-trait anxiety in psychiatric and psychosomatic patients. In I. G. Sarason & C. D. Spielberger (Eds.), *Stress and anxiety* (Vol. 6, pp. 169-197). Washington, DC: Hemisphere.

Ruch, L. O., & Holmes, T. H. (1971). Scaling of life change: Comparison of direct and indirect methods. *Journal of Psychosomatic Research, 15,* 221-227.

Saunders, E., & Williams, R. A. (1975). Hypertension. In R. A. Williams (Ed.), *Textbook of Black related diseases* (pp. 333-357). New York: McGraw-Hill.

Schar, M., Reeder, L. G., & Dirken, J. M. (1973). Stress and cardiovascular health: An international cooperative study, II. The male population at a factory in Zurich. *Social Science and Medicine, 1,* 585-603.

Schwartz, G. E., Shapiro, A. P., Redmond, P., Ferguson, D. C. E., Ragland, D. R., & Weiss, S. M. (1979). Behavioral medicine approaches to hypertension: An integral analysis of theory and research. *Journal of Behavioral Medicine, 2,* 311-363.

Singer, M. T. (1967). Enduring personality styles and responses to stress. *Association of Life Insurance Medical Directors of America, 51,* 150-173.

Speilberger, C. D. (1975). Anxiety: State-trait process. In C. D. Speilberger & I. G. Sarason (Eds.), *Stress and anxiety, Vol. 1.* Washington, DC: Hemisphere.

Speilberger, C. D., Gorsuch, R. L., & Lushene, R. E. (1970). *The State-Trait Anxiety Inventory.* Palo Alto, CA: Consulting Psychologists Press.

Stahl, S. M., Grim, C. E., Donald, C., & Niekirk, H. J. (1975). A model for the social sciences and medicine: The case of hypertension. *Social Science and Medicine, 9,* 31-38.

Stamler, J. (1980). Hypertension: Aspects of risk. In *Hypertension update: Mechanisms, epidemiology, evaluation and management* (pp. 22-37). Bloomfield, NJ: Health Learning Systems.

Stern, R. M., & Higgins, J. D. (1969). Perceived somatic reactions to stress: Sex, age and familiar occurrence. *Journal of Psychosomatic Research, 13,* 77-82.

TenHouten, W. D. (1970). The Black family: Myth and reality. *Psychiatry, 33,* 145-173.

Thomas, C. B. (1961). The precursors of hypertension. *The Medical Clinics of America, 45*(2), 3-13.

Weiner, H. (1977). *Psychobiology and human disease.* New York: Elsevier North Holland.

Weiner, H. (1979). *Psychobiology and essential hypertension.* New York: Elsevier North Holland.

Weyer, G., & Hodapp, V. (1979). Job stress and essential hypertension. In I. G. Sarason & C. D. Speilberger (Eds.), *Stress and anxiety* (Vol. 6, pp. 337-350). Washington, DC: Hemisphere.

# Author Index

# Subject Index

Abstract problems, 243, 244, 245, 246, 247, 249, 250, 251
Abstract rules, 241, 242, 248, 250
Accidents:
  as cause of death in Blacks, 356
Achievement tests, 231, 233
Adequatio principle, 16
Affect:
  as part of African belief system, 263
African American children, 155-189
  literature and interventions concerning learning styles of, 260-275
  racial group concept and self esteem in, 159-170
  racial identification in preschool, 190-193
  racial preference in preschool, 190-193
African American families, 59-151
  awareness of racial oppression in, 83
  closeness in, 146-148, 149
  colonial conceptual model of, 84
  cultural memories and, 82
  discrimination and, 60, 77
  diversity of, 73, 84
  educational aspirations in, 81-82
  extended family and, 60, 71-72, 88
  impact of economic stress on, 59
  interpersonal trust and, 60
  pan-African model of, 84
  parenting behavior of grandmothers in, 60
  overprotectiveness of children in, 71, 84
  self-esteem and, 60
  self-sufficiency of, 59
  three-generational, 87-101
  upward mobility and parenting in middle-income, 63-84
African American psychology, 296
  practice in, 1-57
  research in, 1-57
  theory in, 1-57

African belief system, 263
African cognitive structure, 24
African cognitive style, 24
African cosmology, 55
African Cultural Ideology Scale, 286
Africanity, 284, 285, 315
African people:
  scientific inferiorization of, 2
African personality disorders, 312
African personality research, 316
African personality theory, 316
African philosophy, 6
African psychology, 301-304, 317, 318
  community, 317
  key concepts in, 54-55
African self-consciousness, 55, 283, 284, 289, 293, 295, 296, 297, 298, 317
  as key concept in African psychology, 54
  assessment of among black college students, 283-298
  behavior, 294
  Black personality and, 288
  Black psychologists and, 54-57
  construct of, 283, 284, 303
  research, 286-287
African Self-Consciousness Scale, 280, 283, 287, 289, 290, 291, 292, 293, 294, 295, 296, 297
African self-extension orientation, 284, 285
African worldview based psychology, 2
Africentric cultural activities, 288
Africentric customs, 289
Africentric institutions, 289
Africentric nosology, 314
Africentric personality theory, 287, 296, 302
Africentric psychology, 56, 280
Africentric psychotherapies, 317
Africentric reinforcements, 285
Africentric social reality, 55

# About the Editors

**Daudi Ajani ya Azibo** is a noted personality and social psychologist who specializes in African/Black Psychology. He served from 1987 to 1992 as an Assistant Professor of African American Studies/Psychology at Temple University in Philadelphia. He received the Ph.D. in social psychology from Washington University in St. Louis, Missouri, studying under the renowned Dr. Robert L. Williams. He is a prolific writer and a psychological theorist and researcher. His work represents some of the seminal contributions that have been made in the areas of African American personality, personality assessment, cultural oppression, and mental health. He is the author of one of the few Africentric diagnostic systems of African American mental disorders, and of a book entitled *Liberation Psychology* (Africa World Press). He is also the editor of a special monograph on African Psychology to be published by Africa World Press later this year. His most recent works appear in *The Journal of Black Psychology* and *The Western Journal of Black Studies.* Forthcoming publications (Spring 1992) appear in *The Afrocentric Scholar* and *Word: A Black Culture Journal,* and (Summer 1992) in the *Journal of Negro Education.* Dr. Azibo is the recipient of The Association of Black Psychologists Outstanding Scholarship Award (1989), and serves on the editorial board of two prominent national periodicals, *The Journal of Black Psychology* and *Imhotep: An Afrocentric Review.*

**W. Curtis Banks,** Ph.D., is Professor of Psychology at Howard University. He served for nine years as the Editor of *The Journal of Black Psychology.* He also edited the *Publication Manual of the Association of Black Psychologists,* and established the *Black Psychology Monographs.* Dr. Banks received his M.A. and his Ph.D. from Stanford University. He served as Assistant and later Associate Professor and Class of 1939 Bicentennial Preceptor in Psychology at Princeton University. He was Senior Research Scientist and Director of the Social Learning Laboratory at Educational Testing Service. He has conducted research in the areas of self-concept, achievement motivation, locus of control, delayed gratification, and reinforcement processes in performance of Black populations. He has received awards from the Association of

413

Black Psychologists, the American Educational Research Association, and the Society for the Psychological Study of Social Issues, among many others. In addition to his research and teaching, Dr. Banks has provided expert consultation on innovative research methodologies in the development of personnel evaluation and selection instruments to such clients as the City of Chicago, the City of Philadelphia, the City of Baltimore, and the Minneapolis Civil Rights Commission.

**A. Kathleen Hoard Burlew,** Ph.D., is an Associate Professor of Psychology at the University of Cincinnati. She received her doctorate in social psychology from the University of Michigan and later completed postdoctoral training in clinical psychology. She is Editor-in-Chief of *The Journal of Black Psychology* and coauthor of two other books— *Reflections on Black Psychology* and *Minority Issues in Mental Health.* Her numerous publications include articles on psychosocial aspects of sickle cell disease, women in nontraditional careers, and attrition among women in substance-abuse treatment. She currently has two research grants. One federal grant was awarded to extend her work on how the presence of a child with sickle cell influences family dynamics. The other grant was awarded by the Ohio Department of Mental Health to examine alternative methods of diagnosing schizophrenia among African American patients. Dr. Burlew also has completed several program evaluations of substance-abuse programs and employment training programs, an area survey of Black Cincinnatians, and a recent survey of disadvantaged youth in a large subsidized housing project.

**Harriette Pipes McAdoo,** Ph.D., is a Professor in the Department of Family and Child Ecology in the College of Human Ecology at Michigan State University. She formerly was a professor and Acting Dean at the Howard University School of Social Work. She received her B.A. and M.A. from Michigan State University and her Ph.D. from the University of Michigan, where she was a Postdoctoral Fellow in the Institute of Social Research. She has also done postdoctoral work at Harvard University. She is Director of the Groves Conference on Marriage and the Family and a member of the Governing Council of the Society for Research in Child Development. She has been a Director and is the President-Elect of the National Council on Family Relations. She received the Outstanding Researcher of the Year Award from the Association of Black Psychologists and the Marie Peters Award from NCFR. She has edited *Black Families* (2nd edition) and *Family Ethnicity:*

*Strength in Diversity.* She is a co-author of *Women and Children, Alone and in Poverty.* She co-edited *Services to Young Families, Program Review and Policy Recommendations* and *Black Children: Social, Educational, and Parental Environments.*

# About the Contributors

**Jenise Ross Anthony,** Ph.D., received her Doctorate in Social Psychology from Princeton University in 1983. During graduate school, she conducted research on self-reinforcement and delay of gratification behavior in Black adolescent populations. She currently serves as director of a social service program, which provides substance abuse outpatient treatment, mental health counseling, and transitional housing. Prior to assuming her current position, Dr. Anthony worked as a personnel specialist and was responsible for the administration of an employee assistance program for Prince George's County Government, Maryland.

**Irene Atwell,** M.Ed., received her Master's degree in Counseling Psychology at Temple University in Philadelphia. She has practiced as a psychotherapist for the past 15 years with individuals, families, and groups.

**Joseph A. Baldwin** is a Professor of Psychology and the Chair of the Department of Psychology at Florida A&M University in Tallahassee. He received a B.A. in Psychology from DePaul University in Chicago in 1969 and his Ph.D. in Personality and Social Psychology at the University of Colorado at Boulder in 1975.

**Rochelle T. Bastien,** Ph.D., is a clinical psychologist in private practice in San Diego and a Trustee elected to govern the Grossmont-Cuyamaca Community College District. While working on her doctorate at UCLA, she conducted research and created a minor—Sociocultural Influences on Personality Development. Her work for several years on the psychological services staff at UCSD and in her practice has focused on recovery for victims of abuse, including bigotry as emotional assault. She is active in the People to People delegation of community college representatives, assisting the South African government in restructuring the system of public higher education.

**Faye Z. Belgrave,** Ph.D., is an Associate Professor in the Department of Psychology at The George Washington University. Her current research is in the areas of health promotion and disease prevention and psychosocial aspects of chronic illness and disability in ethnic minority populations. She has authored several publications in this area. In addition, she has done work in the areas of self-esteem and cultural identity among African Americans.

**Yvonne R. Bell** is an Associate Professor of Psychology at Florida A&M University.

**Phillip J. Bowman,** Ph.D., is currently Associate Professor with the Graduate Programs in Counseling Psychology as well as Human Development and Social Policy at Northwestern University. Trained in Social Psychology at the University of Michigan, he has held joint appointments in Psychology and Afro-American Studies at both Michigan and the University of Illinois. After directing a postdoctoral training program in survey research and Black mental health at Michigan's Institute for Social Research, he conducted a series of national survey studies as a Rockefeller and Senior Ford/National Research Council Postdoctoral Fellow. His publications focus on the social psychology of chronic role strain with emphasis on mechanisms associated with adaptive coping in family, work, and student roles. He is also active in related consultation on culturally relevant interventions at the individual, organizational, and urban policy levels.

**Jacqueline Butler,** L.I.S.W., M.S.W., C.A.C., C.D.C.C, is an Associate Professor of Clinical Psychiatry and the Director of the Alcoholism Division of Central Psychiatric Clinic, College of Medicine, University of Cincinnati. She received her B.A. from Holy Family College and a Master of Social Work from Smith College, School of Social Work. She has been working in the field of substance abuse as an educator, planner, and advocate for 33 years. She is currently serving on a number of local, state, and national boards, including National Black Alcoholism and Addictions Council, Ohio Department of Alcohol and Drug Addiction Services Advisory Board, Hamilton County Alcohol and Drug Addiction Services Board, American Red Cross Board of Southwestern Ohio, the Urban Minority Outreach Alcoholism and Drug Board, and the Ohio Black Coalition. Ms. Butler has published in the areas of substance abuse treatment and Africentric treatment services. She also serves on the Minority Health Commission of the State of Ohio.

**Maxine L. Clark,** Ph.D., is Associate Professor of Psychology and Director of the African American Research Institute in the Center for Public Service at Virginia Commonwealth University. She received her Ph.D. from the University of Illinois and is currently studying the friendships and social networks of African American children and adolescents. She has published articles on racial stereotypes, ethnic identity, self-esteem, and the friendships and social relationships of African American children and adolescents. Recent publications appear in the *Journal of Youth and Adolescence* (1992) and *Education and Urban Society* (1991).

**Vernessa R. Clark,** Ph.D., is an Associate Professor at Morehouse College in Atlanta, Georgia. Her research has focused on factors that affect cardiovascular responses to psychological stressors. Specifically she is interested in the way an individual's personality may affect the way she/he responds to stressful situations. Most recently, Dr. Clark has been studying the relationship between certain personality variables and physiological responses to stress caused by racism.

**Harold Dent** is currently the Coordinator of Collaborative Outreach at the National Center for Minority Special Education Research and Outreach at Hampton University, Hampton, Virginia. Until recently, Dr. Dent was Vice President/Secretary of Psychological and Human Resources Consultants, Inc. He served as consultant and expert witness in the landmark case *Larry P. v. Riles,* which resulted in the ban on the use of culturally biased IQ tests on African American students in California for special education placement.

**Saundra T. Drumming,** C.P.A., Ph.D., is an Associate Professor in Accounting at Florida A&M University. She received a M.A.S. from the University of Illinois and a doctorate from the University of Wisconsin. She has published articles in the areas of behavioral accounting and cognitive psychology.

**James A. Duncan** is a doctoral student in Personality Psychology at Howard University in Washington, D.C. He earned a B.S. in Psychology in 1985 at Baptist College in Charleston, South Carolina and his M.S. degree in Community/Counseling Psychology at Florida A&M University in Tallahassee.

**Sharon-ann Gopaul-Mc.Nicol,** Ph.D, is the founder and Executive Director of Multicultural Educational and Psychological Services (MEPS). She is an Adjunct Assistant Professor at St. John's University, Graduate Department of Psychology. Dr. Gopaul-Mc.Nicol received national attention in 1987 and 1988 for her cross-cultural study on racial preference and racial identity among pre-school children. She is also a licensed psychologist in private practice, and a bilingual consulting psychologist for Long Island and New York City Board of Education and for mental health clinics. In addition, she supervises psychologists on issues related to multicultural assessment, multicultural counseling, and cross-cultural research. Moreover, she conducts workshops for mental health workers, teachers, and parents in the areas of assessment, counseling and cultural assimilation issues with West Indians and Latinos. Dr. Gopaul-Mc.Nicol is the author of two books: *A Handbook for Immigrants: Some Basic Education and Social Issues in USA* and *Working With West Indian Families.*

**Henry Jefferson Grubb,** Ph.D., is owner and clinical director of Behavioral Consultants, an outpatient full-service psychological service center in Johnson City, Tennessee. He is a clinical psychologist specializing in the diagnosis and treatment of childhood/adolescent disorders. Dr. Grubb has also taught at the university level and published numerous articles on minority intellectual assessment and cross-cultural psychology. His research has been honored with awards by the National Council for the Social Sciences, American Mensa Education and Research Foundation, American Psychological Association, and Psychological Service Center of New York City.

**Jules P. Harrell,** Ph.D., is a Professor of Psychology at Howard University. His primary area of research is the study of individual differences in physiological and subjective responses to various forms of psychological stressors. Currently he is examining the extent to which Afrocentric orientation and several African cultural variables mediate responses to stressful racist events. At Howard he teaches courses in psychophysiology, race and racism, as well as personality assessment.

**Asa G. Hilliard III** is the Fuller E. Callaway Professor of Urban Education at Georgia State University. He earned an Ed.D. in Educational Psychology from the University of Denver. He has participated in the development of several national assessment systems, such as proficiency assessment for professional educators and developmental assessments of young children and infants. He has been active in forensic psychology, serving as an expert witness in several landmark federal cases on test validity, including the lead expert witness in the landmark *Larry P. v. Wilson Riles* IQ test case in the 9th Federal District, California.

**Derek S. Hopson** is a licensed clinical psychologist currently in private practice at the Hopson Center for Psychological and Educational Services in Middlefield. He is also coauthor with Dr. Darlene Powell-Hopson of a book titled *Different and Wonderful: Raising Black Children in a Race Conscious Society*. Dr. Hopson received his Bachelor of Arts degree in Psychology at Rutgers University in 1975. He completed his Master's degree in 1978 and his Doctorate in 1982 in Clinical Psychology at Southern Illinois University.

**Anna Mitchell Jackson** is a Professor and the Assistant Dean for Student Affairs in the School of Dentistry at Meharry Medical College.

**Reginald S. Johnson** is an Assistant Professor in the Department of Psychology at Howard University.

**Nina Lewis** is employed at the Alcoholism Clinic in the Department of Psychiatry at the University of Cincinnati.

**Gregory V. McQuater,** Ph.D., is the Manager of Management Development at the PepsiCo Corporate Division, where he has been responsible for its management development and training function since 1990. Prior to joining PepsiCo, he was a member of the faculty and administration at Cornell University for seven years. Trained as a social psychologist, Dr. McQuater has coauthored numerous publications in the areas of achievement motivation, delay of gratification, and locus of control. One of his current areas of interest is managing diversity in the work place.

**Ralph E. Miles,** M.P.H., is a doctoral student in Education at the University of San Francisco. Prior to returning to graduate school, he worked for 13 years at the Fanon Research & Development Center at Drew University. While at Drew University, his principal research effort was developing robust indicators of stress. He is currently Associate Chief of Biostatistics for the Air Force Medical Service Agency, a health system comprised of more than 120 health and ambulatory care centers. His research has focused on using dynamic graphics as an analytical tool for predicting occurrence of coronary artery disease and the development of episode of care database by linking inpatient episodes to ambulatory visits.

**Fayneese S. Miller,** Ph.D., is currently an Associate Professor of Education and Child Study at Brown University. Trained as a social psychologist, Dr. Miller's research has focused on the ways in which minority adolescents and youth perceive and reason about themselves, other people, and society in general. She has authored a number of papers on social adaptation and reasoning processes for adolescents and is currently developing a research model on notions of hope among minority populations. She is the author of two forthcoming books: *Adolescents, Schooling and Social Policy* and *Dilemmas of Ethnic Adolescents: Alienation vs. Social Integration.*

**Hector F. Myers,** Ph.D., is an Associate Professor of Psychology and Director of Minority Mental Health Training at UCLA, and Director of the Biobehavioral Laboratory at the Charles R. Drew University of Medicine and Science. His research has focused on illucidating the relationships between stress and other psychosocial and biobehavioral factors in health and illness in African American adults, children, and families. He has authored numerous papers testing models of stress as a contributor in racial differences in hypertension and coronary disease, biobehavioral processes in depression in African American adults, stress and functional outcomes in African American families, psychosocial predictors and mediators of child behavior outcomes in African American children, and psychosocial contributors to African American student adjustment to college. His current work includes psychosocial factors in HIV and AIDS in African American men.

**Linda J. Myers** is a professor at The Ohio State University with appointments in the Department of Black Studies, Psychology, and Psychiatry. She holds a Ph.D. in the area of Clinical Psychology from The Ohio State University. Known primarily for her work in the development of optimal psychology, an Afrocentric theory for human behavior, Dr. Myers has published numerous articles and two books, one titled *Understanding an Afrocentric World View: Introduction to Optimal Psychology.* Her psychotherapeutic approach called Belief Systems

Analysis has been expanded and used widely in psychoeducational programming in areas ranging from behavioral medicine to business ethics.

**Melvin R. Novick** was Professor of Educational Measurement and Statistics at the University of Iowa at the time of his death in 1986. Prior to joining the faculty at Iowa, he had held research positions at Educational Testing Service and American College Testing Program and visiting lectureships at University College of Wales and University College, London. He is widely recognized for his contributions to mental test theory and Bayesian statistical methods. He was the author of two texts: *Theories of Mental Test Scores* (1967) with Frederic Lord, and *Statistical Methods for Educational and Psychological Research* (1974) with Paul H. Jackson. He is also widely known for his work as chair of the committee that produced the fifth edition of the influential monograph *Standards for Educational and Psychological Testing*.

**Darlene Powell-Hopson** is a licensed clinical psychologist and a certified school psychologist in private practice at the Hopson Center and a consultant to various schools and family services agencies. Dr. Powell-Hopson conducted research on children's racial attitudes and doll preferences that received national recognition. Dr. Powell-Hopson received a Master's degree in Research Psychology from Adelphi University in 1980 and a second Master's in Clinical-School Psychology from Hofstra University.

**Barbara J. Shade** is a Professor of Teacher Education. Her doctorate in Educational Psychology was obtained from the University of Wisconsin-Madison in 1973. Throughout her career, she has concentrated on identifying the personality traits of educationally successful African Americans with a particular emphasis on their cognitive style profiles. Her current work focuses on the identification of gifted and talented youth using cognitive style as a variable.

**Wilbur I. Smith,** Ph.D., is Associate Professor of Business at Florida A&M University. His research has focused on identifying individual and group differences in people's use of heuristics in learning, logical reasoning, and inference. He is currently investigating the intuitive rules people use to recognize and classify patterns in cues.

**Jerome Taylor** is an Associate Professor in the Department of Black Community Education Research and Development, Faculty of Arts and

Sciences, and Psychology in Education, School of Education at the University of Pittsburgh. He also is Director of the Institute for the Black Family and Right Start Programs.

**Wanda E. Ward** is a Program Director of the Career Access Program in the Division of Human Resource Development at the National Science Foundation. She has served as founding Director of the Center for Research on Multi-Ethnic Education (1986-present) and Associate Professor of Psychology at the University of Oklahoma, Norman. She received her B.A. in Psychology and the Afro-American Studies certificate from Princeton University in 1976 and her Ph.D. in Personality Psychology from Stanford University in 1981. She has held research and teaching positions at the University of Illinois at Urbana-Champaign (1984-1985). She was a Fellow of the Ford Foundation's National Fellowships Fund from 1976 to 1981. She has published basic research articles concerning racial group differences on various psychological constructs, including locus of control, time orientation, self-concept, and delay of gratification, as well as research on social influences on self-evaluation processes. In addition, she coedited the book, *Key Issues in Minority Education: Research Directions and Practical Implications.* She has served on various grant review panels, including the National Science Foundation and the U.S. Department of Education. She is a member of the American Psychological Association, the Association of Black Psychologists, and the Western Psychological Association.

**Kenneth Washington,** M.A., is a doctoral candidate in Clinical Psychology at the University of Cincinnati and is currently employed as the Coordinator of the Crossroads Program at the University of Cincinnati Medical Center, Department of Psychiatry. The Crossroads Program is a culturally sensitive program developed to treat minorities who are chemically addicted. He has worked in the area of substance abuse for several years and has received training from such institutions as New York University-Bellevue Hospital Medical Center and from the University of Cincinnati Medical Center, Alcoholism Clinic.

**Madge Gill Willis,** M.S., is a doctoral student in Educational Psychology at Georgia State University. She has been a school psychologist for nine years, consulting with teachers, conducting in-service training, developing educational and support programs for students, as well as doing assessments of students. Prior to that, she was a classroom teacher and school counselor. Her research interests emphasize qualitative research approaches to studying the roles of culture and language in African American children's cognitive development and learning.

**Melvin N. Wilson,** Ph.D., is an Associate Professor of Psychology at the University of Virginia, Charlottesville. His research has focused on various aspects of family process and functioning in diverse African American families. He has authored numerous papers on the extended-family structure of many African American families. He is the principal investigator on the project titled "Social Interaction in Two- and Three-Generational Black Families."

**Carl O. Word** received his B.A. in Psychology from Lincoln University in Pennsylvania in 1969. He was awarded the Woodrow Wilson National Fellowship in 1969 to attend Princeton, where he received his Ph.D. in Social Psychology in 1972. He has served on the faculties of Baruch College, City University of New York, Wright Institute in Berkeley, California School of Professional Psychology in Berkeley/Alameda, and the University of California Medical School in San Francisco. He is currently Senior Research Scientist at Bayview Hunter's Point Foundation, where he is principal investigator for a health promotion study, and co-investigator for two studies examining HIV risk behavior among urban adults. His research interests include cross-cultural personality and attitude measurement, non-biased assessment, and health promotions among African Americans.